TO THE DISTANT OBSERVER

*To the distant observer*
*They are chatting of the blossoms*
*Yet in spite of appearances*
*Deep in their hearts*
*They are thinking very different thoughts*

    KI NO TSURAYAKI

Noël Burch

# To the Distant Observer

Form and Meaning in the Japanese Cinema

Revised and edited by Annette Michelson

Scolar Press   London

First published 1979 by Scolar Press
39 Great Russell Street London WC1B 3PH

Copyright © Noël Burch 1979

Filmset in 10/12 point Times
Printed and bound in Great Britain
by W & J Mackay Limited, Chatham

ISBN 0 85967 490 8 (cloth)
ISBN 0 85967 491 6 (paper)

# Contents

Foreword and Acknowledgements 7
Preface 11
Some Terminological Indications 18

### Part 1. Grounds, Premises
1. A System of Contradictions 25
2. A System of Signs 35
3. A Boundless Text 42

### Part 2. A Frozen Stream?
4. A Machine Appears 57
5. A Parenthesis on Film History 61
6. A Rule and its Ubiquity 67
7. Bulwarks of Tradition 75

### Part 3. Cross-Currents
8. Transformational Modules 89
9. Lines and Spaces 93
10. The Fate of Alien Modes 100
11. Displacements and Condensations 110
12. Surface and Depth 117
13. Kinugasa Teinosuke 123

### Part 4. Iron Trees, Golden Flowers
14. The Weight of History and Technology 141
15. Some Remarks on the Genre Syndrome 151
16. Ozu Yasujiro 154
17. Naruse Mikio and Yamanaka Sadao 186
18. On Architecture 198
19. Ishida Tamizo 202
20. Mizoguchi Kenji 217
21. Shimizu Hiroshi and Some Others 247
22. Epilogue to a Golden Age 262

### Part 5. A Chain is Broken
23. Film and 'Democracy' 271
24. Kurosawa Akira 291

**Part 6. Post-Scriptum**
25  Oshima Nagisa  325
26  Independence: its Rewards and Penalties  345

List of Works Consulted  365

Appendix 1: Check-list of films by Ozu, Mizoguchi, Kurosawa and Oshima  368

Appendix 2: Archive holdings in Japan: Japanese films produced before 1946  372

Publisher's Acknowledgements  377

Index of Films  378

Index of Names  385

NOTE

Illustrations are numbered Figs. 1–66. Some figures consist of sequences of shot analyses taken from the frame; the individual shots are numbered Pl. 1, 2, 3, etc. Frames from the same shot are numbered e.g. Pl. 1a, 1b, 1c.

# Foreword and Acknowledgements

All the Japanese names are written in the standard Japanese form: family name before given name. The single exception is that of the Americanized actor, Sessue Hayakawa.

Titles of Japanese films are given in English with the Japanese title and the production date at the head of the main entry. I have tried to render them faithfully. My translation does not always correspond to those given by other sources particularly in the case of films unreleased in English-speaking countries. Whenever films have one or more English release titles, these are given in a footnote to the main entry. Thus, a well-known film may often be found in the index under three or more titles.

Unless otherwise indicated all translations from French are mine.

This book could never have been written without the help of many friends in Japan and elsewhere. First of all, I must thank Shibata Hayao, Kawakita Kasuko and the entire staff of the Shibata Organization for having made possible my first trip to Japan and for having done so much to facilitate what is inevitably a difficult acclimatization. On my second trip, it was my dear friends Kuraoka Akiko and Philippe Ferrand who helped to make bearable the gruelling rhythm of Tokyo life.

Special thanks are due to Ohba Masatoshi of the Tokyo Museum of Modern Art Film Centre whose devoted assistance made it possible for me to make shot-by-shot transcriptions of dozens of films and to examine scores of others. I am also greatly indebted to Kawakita Kashiko and Shimizu Akira of the Japan Film Library Council, who arranged for me to study many films from their collection and who helped me in so many other ways. Credit in particular is due to the Council for all the separate film stills illustrating this volume, as well as the sequence from *A Tale of Late Chrysanthemums*. And I especially wish to thank Ema Michio of the Kyoto Film Library for entrusting me with

**FOREWORD AND ACKNOWLEDGEMENTS**

some twenty 16mm prints and a projector. I was thus able to screen those rare films in my hotel room when I unwittingly arrived in Kyoto on the eve of a holiday. Matsuda Shunji graciously made available to me even rarer films from his collection, while Hiroko Govaers gave me invaluable practical and linguistic help in both Tokyo and Paris.

My talks with Donald Richie and Yoshida Tieo were extremely helpful in clearing up certain points of film-history. The critics Kawarabata Nei and especially Sato Tadao gave me much valuable guidance. I also wish to thank Iwamoto Kenji for his stimulating theoretical insights and James Leahy, Dr Barry Salt, Jorge Dana and P. Adams Sitney for their suggestions and criticisms.

However, my greatest debt is to Annette Michelson. As the title page suggests, without her severe editing and criticism, as well as her helpful suggestions, this book, my first in my native language, could never have been made readable or, indeed, comprehensible.

N.B.

FOR MARTINE

The point is not to seek truth or salvation in the pre-scientific or the philosophically pre-conscious, nor to transfer whole segments of mythology into our philosophy; in dealing with these variants of mankind who are so different from us, our aim should be to gain further insight into the theoretical and practical problems which confront our own institutions, to gain new awareness of the plane of existence in which they originated and which the long record of their achievements has made us forget. The 'puerility' of the East has something to teach us, if only the narrowness of our adult ideas.

Maurice Merleau-Ponty: *Signes*, p. 175

# Preface

Let it be clear from the outset that this book lays no claim to being yet another 'history of the Japanese cinema'. In the native language there already exists Tanaka Junichiro's four-volume factual compendium;[1] in English, it is hoped that the reader will be familiar with the several writings of Donald Richie and in particular *The Japanese Film*, written in collaboration with Joseph Anderson and drawing much data from Tanaka; in French, a forthcoming volume by Max Tessier will display, I understand, similarly comprehensive ambitions.

Mine are at once more modest and, considering the limited tools at my command and the material at my disposal, considerably more ambitious, not to say presumptuous. My approach is, of course, historical in every sense. In fact Japanese cinema from the period 1917–45, to which the bulk of this essay is devoted, is likely to seem quite remote to both Western and Japanese readers. My reading of the films is conducted, moreover, with constant reference to the history of 'Japanese culture' as a whole. For it is beyond doubt that Japan's singular history, informed by a unique combination of forces and circumstances, has produced a cinema which is *in essence* unlike that of any other nation.

This essential difference between the dominant modes of Western and Japanese cinema is the main concern of this study. It is intended, furthermore, as a step in the direction of a critical analysis of the ideologically and culturally determined system of representation from which the film industries of Hollywood and elsewhere derive their power and profit. It consequently may be understood as part of a much broader movement, that of the modern search for a Marxist approach to art, initiated by Brecht and Eisenstein, and which involves a *detour through the East*.

Paradoxically, it is in France that the scrutiny of *le texte de l'Orient* has been most productive. Paradoxically, because oriental scholarship *per se* in post-war France

1. *Nihon eiga hotatsu*, Chuo Koran-sha, Tokyo, 1957.

has been scant and on the whole mediocre. The writers associated with the review *Tel Quel*,[2] who have been at the centre of this new concern with the East, have had to rely almost exclusively on the pioneer work of Marcel Granet, *La Pensée chinoise* (1934), or on more recent writings in English (in particular those of Joseph Needham and his team). Understandably, the writings of Philippe Sollers, Julia Kristeva and their colleagues have tended, in so far as they have touched on the Orient, to stress the implications for contemporary developments in the theory of dialectical materialism of the thought-systems of ancient China. They have emphasized, in particular, the importance of non-phonetic writing in the development of modes of thought and social practice antithetical to those characteristic of the West within the structure of capitalism and its Aristotelian and Christian heritage. Comparatively little attention has been paid to Japan by these authors, partly no doubt because modern Japanese history would seem to indicate, on the contrary, remarkable compatibility between 'Japanese thought patterns' and the ideological superstructures of capitalism. Japanese artistic and social practice have, moreover, produced almost no theoretical practice comparable to the logic and linguistics of ancient India or the cosmology and science of China.

The fate of Buddhist logic, subsequent to its importation into Japan as part of the body of Buddhist teachings, typifies the Japanese disdain of theoretical practice. This highly refined discipline of Indian origin rapidly became a form of ritualized debate which

> continues to be held at Mt Kōya, even to this day. In this ritual, the answerers (*rissha*), the questioners (*monja*), the judge (*tandai*), the stenographer (*chūki*), and the manager (*gyōji*) sit in pious attitude around the statue of the Buddha according to fixed rule. Buddhist hymns are sung and sūtras are read. Thus, in Japan, logical debate was reduced to a mere Buddhist meeting, a decorum of the most pious form. *Further, the form of the ritual was extended without change to the poetic debate or* utaawase.[3]

The specific traits of Japanese 'theory' must be sought, not in any body of theoretical writings, ancient or modern, of Japanese origin, but in the practice of her arts and letters. It is significant in this respect that the only rudimentary attempts at aesthetic theory, indeed theory of any sort, are to be found in the incidental writings of such figures as Tsurayaki, the Heian poet and anthologist, Zeami, actor/author and codifier of the *nō* play, Chikamatsu, the eighteenth-century dramatist, etc.[4] The larger theoretical implications of Japanese practices are to be derived

---

2. Advanced literary review which in the late 1960s and early 1970s played an important role in the development of a seminal but often debatably metaphorical theorization of literary history and practice grounded in structural linguistics, psychoanalysis and historical-dialectical materialism.

3. Nakamura Hajime, *The Ways of Thinking of Eastern Peoples*, p. 545. (N.B. The italics are mine.)

through a reading conducted from outside the culture which has produced them, for the very notion of theory is alien to Japan; it is considered a property of Europe and the West.

One of the principal assumptions of this study is that the critical framework developed in France over the past decade (partly through an investigation of Eastern thought) provides elements towards an understanding of the far-reaching theoretical implications of *le texte japonais*. For, just as it is possible to *read* a written text as complex *system*, both self-contained and historically determined, so too with a culture – and Japanese culture perhaps more relevantly than any other. I like to think that it was this clarifying vocation of French thinking in general which a Japanese scholar, Toki Zemmaro, had in view when he remarked to the French Japanologist René Sieffert that 'French was the only language precise enough to render with precision the full imprecision of the *nō* play'.[5] Of course, this 'imprecision' of the language and 'thought-patterns' of Japan is another cliché, belaboured by Western-centred scholars but also by many Japanese, impressed by the marvellous compatibility which they observe between the highly 'rational' linguistic and theoretical practices of the West and the technological tasks involved in the construction of a 'modern' (i.e. industrial) society. This cliché is one of many to be disposed of in this study. Still, this statement does point to the possibility of an immensely productive relationship which could and should be developed between contemporary European theory and Japanese practice. And Marxism has always regarded such mutually informative relationships between theory and practice as essential to its growth.

One French author loosely associated with the *Tel Quel* group, Roland Barthes, has in fact turned his attention to Japan, and the essay which he produced following a brief stay in that country, though a minor, circumstantial piece in the context of his writings as a whole, is nonetheless a pioneer text.[6] It is the first attempt by any Western writer to *read* the Japanese 'text' in the light of contemporary semiotics, a reading informed by a rejection of ethnocentrism – and indeed of all the 'centrisms' which have anchored ideology in the West since the industrial revolution and the rise of capitalism. I shall have occasion to refer again to this essay, which has stimulated my own thought and research. The following, concluding passage of Barthes' book, which contains the key to its title, points to the common ground of our concerns:

Empire of Signs? Indeed, if we imply that the signs are empty and the ritual is a godless one. Just look at *the study of signs*

4. See Ueda Makoto, *Literary and Art Theories in Japan*.

5. Sieffert, René, *La Tradition secrète du Nō*, p. 56.

6. Barthes, Roland, *L'Empire des signes*.

(Mallarmé's dwelling place), in other words, out there, any view, be it urban, domestic or rural. And so that we may see how it is put together, let it be illustrated by the Shikidai corridor: papered with openings, framed by empty space and framing nothing, decorated, it is true, but in such a way that the figuration (flowers, trees, birds, animals) is swept away, sublimated, shifted far from the forefront of vision ... in this corridor, as in the ideal Japanese house, devoid or nearly so, of furniture, there is no place which in any way designates property; no seat, no bed, no table provides a point from which the body may constitute itself as subject (or master) of a space. The very concept of centre is rejected (a burning frustration for Western Man, everywhere provided with his arm-chair and his bed, the owner of a domestic *position*). Non-centred, this space is also reversible: you can turn the Shikidai corridor upside down and nothing will happen other than an inconsequential inversion of high and low, right and left. Content has been irrevocably dismissed: whether we pass through, or sit on the floor (or ceiling, if you turn the picture around) there is nothing to *grasp*.[7]

All of the themes suggested in this dense text have their place in my examination of Japanese film-making: the essentially 'irreligious' character of the Japanese, their rejection of anthropocentrism and of all the 'centrisms' that derive from it in the West (the role which, in this respect, their architecture has played in their films is absolutely crucial, as Barthes indirectly suggests) and, of course, the all-important 'irrevocable dismissal of content', i.e. of the form-content hierarchies which are ours.

I have called my undertaking presumptuous, and some explanations are in order. I do not read Japanese, and my knowledge of the spoken language is elementary to say the least. I was forced to rely upon interpreters in viewing the vast majority of the films referred to here. I was, however, able to study most of them at my leisure on an editing table. As the reader will quickly perceive, my main concern is with the *modes of representation* common to, and distinctive of, most Japanese films within given periods, and with the highly refined styles generated by these modes in the work of a handful of *auteurs* (a concept here applicable only with major reservations, as we shall see). The language handicap is therefore not as serious as it might have been to my 'content-oriented' predecessors in this field. More constricting certainly are the objective conditions under which the corpus of Japanese cinema is accessible to the scholar today, and particularly, of course, to the visiting scholar. I have spent altogether five months in Japan. I have had free access to the four main collections of Japanese films: the National Film Centre of the Tokyo Museum of Modern

---

7. Barthes, op. cit., pp. 148–50.

Art, the Japan Film Council Library, the Kyoto Film Library and the private library of Matsuda Shunji. However, it must be understood that less than three hundred complete films made between 1897 and 1945 are preserved and readily accessible in one of the above-mentioned archives. Several hundred fragments collected by Matsuda Shunji are also available for study; but that is all.

This does not mean, I hasten to add, that all of the remaining tens of thousands of films produced by the Japanese industry (from the outset, one of the world's most prolific) are irremediably 'lost', despite the fact that there was certainly a greater readiness in Japan to destroy commercially obsolete films than in the West.[8] Since 1970, for example, several early Ozu films, including the remarkable *Inn in Tokyo*, all of which had been considered 'lost', were unearthed in the warehouses of one of the major production companies. To date, only about half of the forty-one or forty-two films (see Appendix 2) directed by Ozu between 1927 and 1945 are known to be preserved. I am confident, however, that more will be found as the number of Japanese scholars and professional or amateur collectors gradually increases.[9] At present, their number is pitifully small, considering the immensity of the task. It is, moreover, no accident that the films brought to light in recent years have been the work of acknowledged masters (such as Ozu and Mizoguchi); in Japan as elsewhere, the rule of film conservation dictates that discovery is determined by demand. Ishida Tamizo, whose film *Fallen Blossoms* is analysed here in some detail, is known to have directed scores of films; at the time of my last visit to Japan, only two were known to be preserved. The unanimous opinion of the small community of Japanese film scholars at that time was that, apart from those two films, Ishida produced only 'pot-boilers'. This had clearly deterred attempts to ferret out any other films of his that might have survived and continued to confirm, as well, his reputation as the maker of a single 'good' film. Or rather more accurately gave him no reputation at all, since even *Fallen Blossoms*, in my view one of the masterpieces of Japanese cinema, is known only to a few specialists – precisely because Ishida's name is not attached to a body of work.

These cases are not exceptional; every pre-war director constitutes a 'case', the most tragic being that of Mizoguchi, whose mature work (1934–47) survives in only about half of twenty films! Chance and *arbitrariness* necessarily, therefore, inform these pages. I discovered Ishida quite by accident. None of the scholars consulted strongly recommended his films to me. Most of them were unfamiliar with his work. And while I have tried to see at least one film by

PREFACE

8. For reasons which will become clear as we go on to examine the Japanese approach to the conceptions of originality and authorship.

9. In illustration of this and in correction of all the 1975 figures cited here regarding the conservation of films, see Appendix 2.

PREFACE

as many directors as possible from that golden age of the Japanese cinema, the 1930s, I have had to follow, in large part, a hit-or-miss approach. It is true that my more or less random soundings did tend to confirm the existence of a number of permanent traits which define a specifically 'Japanese approach', recognizable at every level of cultural ambition. They also reinforced my view that Japan has had only a few authentic 'masters'. Their work stands out in a decisive way from the bulk of the national production, either through the 'de-construction' of the Western codes which, at certain periods in history, have tended to gain prevalence there, or else through a supreme refinement and systematization of those traits which are most specifically Japanese.[10] Of course, the random approach is always in danger of neglecting a master or two; I might conceivably have overlooked Ishida or, had I seen the wrong film first, Shimizu Hiroshi. This arbitrariness should be underscored here, if only because previous authors, whose work was similarly conditioned, have failed to do so. It is not, however, incompatible with the purpose of a study which is, as I have suggested, not a history of the Japanese cinema, but rather a reading of a body of Japanese film in the light of Japanese history.

If I wish to imagine a fictional people, I can make up a name for them, treat them declaratively like an entity in a novel, found a second Garabagne[11] to avoid compromising any real country in my fantasy (but then it is the fantasy that will be compromised by the signs of literature). I can also, without claiming to represent or analyse any reality whatsoever (such being the major endeavours of Western discourse) gather, somewhere in the world (*out there*), a number of features (in both the pictorial and linguistic sense) and with these features deliberately form a system. It is this system which I shall call Japan.[12]

Although the specialized nature of my present project precludes this radically theoretical stance, I do share the basic premises of this opening statement of *L'Empire des signes*.

The reader may be struck by my reference to the 1930s and early 1940s as the 'golden age' of Japanese cinema, whereas most Japanese and Western specialists (the former explicitly, the latter implicitly) situate it in the immediately post-war period, the period of 'democratization'. The reasons for this reversal will be analysed in their proper place. This period of Japanese cinema is *terra incognita*, not only to virtually all Western film-students but to most Japanese under fifty. It is my contention that the emphasis placed, in Europe, in America and, to a large extent, in Japan, on, for example, the later films of Ozu and Mizoguchi, is due to the relative compatibility of those films with

10. Kinugasa in the 1920s, Kurosawa in the 1950s are outstanding examples of the first approach, while Ozu and Mizoguchi in the 1930s and early 1940s perfectly embody the second.

11. A reference to Henri Michaux's mytho-poetic 'travelogue' *Voyage en Grande Garabagne*.

12. Barthes, op. cit., p. 6.

the ideology of representation and signification which informs the dominant culture (and of course the dominant cinema) of the West. The physical inaccessibility of earlier but mature work by these directors can be seen, at least in part, as a correlative of a fundamental *in*compatibility. For if the films of that earlier period are unknown in the West – Mizoguchi's *Tale of Late Chrysanthemums* and *Tale of Loyal Retainers in the Genroku Era* are significant examples – it is largely because Western distribution, criticism and cultural policy, as well as Japan's own scruples over cultural commerce with the West, express the intuition that such films are profoundly antithetical to canons of Western cinema.

Needless to say, it is my hope, offered without undue optimism, that the present study will stimulate interest in the authentic golden age of Japanese cinema so that hitherto unavailable films by masters, whether unknown, like Ishida and Shimizu, or, like Ozu and Mizoguchi, celebrated within the Western cultural establishment as assimilable to its own self-perpetuating values, can be seen at last by viewers who no longer accept those values. As Bertolt Brecht trenchantly put it: 'The only people who can profitably study a piece of technique like Chinese acting's A[lienation]-effect are those who need such a technique for quite definite social purposes.'[13] The people who most need to study this cinema in its most 'radically Japanese' form are those committed to constructing a thorough-going critique of the dominant modes of Western cinema. This critique, inscribed within seventy-five years of film practice in Japan, remains unread. It is this reading which I hope to initiate here.

13. Willett, John (trans.), *Brecht on Theatre*, p. 93.

# Some Terminological Indications

The spatio-temporal audio-visual continuum which we call a motion picture (or a video presentation or a slide-show . . .) may be regarded as a flux/field of signs. In the view of Ferdinand Saussure – which has served to constitute a semiology of the **dominant cinema** (that body of films subordinated essentially to the interests of the dominant class and hence informed at every level by its ideology) – the sign has two aspects, **signifier** and **signified** (Saussure compared them with the two sides of a sheet of paper, indissociable yet in binomial opposition). The signifier is the sign in its materiality: it may be a pictorial element or set of elements, or writing *per se*, a sound or set of sounds, or speech *per se*. While this enumeration covers the **substance of expression** peculiar to the 'audio-visual media', it by no means accounts for all such substances. Setting aside the codes of taste, touch and smell, rudimentary in our cultures, we may say that all substances of expression are ultimately visual or auditory, they may be transposed to film in either pictorial or auditory representation (i.e. codes of clothing) or in terms of 'form' – the codes of social distance translated into shot sizes. This possibility of transposition provides one foundation for the 'illusion of reality'.

The signified is the concept (and only the concept) which, denotatively or connotatively, is . . . signified. The signified is not the referent. Even a word as 'abstract' as *philosophy*, while it may signify a concept answerable to some such definition as 'search for the underlying causes and principles of reality',[1] also refers to an aspect of human history, to an actual body of texts and practices. A **referent** is 'that which refers a linguistic sign to extra-linguistic reality as it has been articulated by a human group . . . We speak of a referential function when the message is centred on the context.'[2] It is this concept of referential function which points to a provisionally useful, though incomplete definition of the **diegesis**, helpful above all because it designates it as one dimension of film among others, not as its very substance. The diegesis may be said to be the imagi-

1. *Webster's Third New International Dictionary*.

2. *Dictionnaire de Linguistique Larousse*, pp. 414-15.

nary referent or sum of referents. The density of the diegesis, its presence, its powers of absorption, depend upon the status of the referential function. Most simply, the diegesis is for instance the 'world of Balzac' which his readers 'enter', those imagined drawing-rooms and cobbled streets, those imagined people, their 'characters', their *souls*. (It should be clear that diegesis and narrative are in no sense equivalent, since there is much more to diegesis than narrative; the process of narration, which is part of the narrative, is extra-diegetic.) In the cinema, of course, the sign/referent relationship is clearly very different from what it is in a written text, since we are dealing with an audio-visual facsimile of the referent. Hence,.in film, the referential function is always more heavily emphasized than in literature.

SOME TERMINOLOGICAL INDICATIONS

The diegesis must not, however, be treated as a fixed, simple object. It must be studied under two complementary and *dynamic* aspects. For the constitution of the diegesis is a process, and a more proper term would indeed be **diegetic process**. It combines a mental process (the development of the spectator's 'absorption'), and a process of 'writing': the implementation on the screen of the 'codes' which catalyse that absorption. Both processes are, to varying degrees, implicated moreover in an ideological process. The resultant is a **diegetic effect**, whereby spectators experience the diegetic world as environment. Closely related and indeed constituent effects have been designated in theatre as identification (Brecht) and in painting as illusionism. However, it is also essential to consider the place of the audio-visual diegesis in the historical process. The stages of formation and the on-going elaboration of the basic mode of representation in the cinema of the West point to an all but universal tendency within the dominant cinema (as well as theatre and literature) to *maximize* and *generalize* the diegetic effect. And this tendency, in turn, must be understood as entering into a dialectical relationship with cultural and ideological conditioning.

This maximization of the diegetic effect implies the effacing of the sign and of the process of signification as consciously perceived, and is only incidentally related to ideological categories such as 'realism' or 'naturalism'. The diegetic effect is truly as 'strong', as unadulterated in *Hellzapoppin*, *The Five Thousand Fingers of Doctor T* or late Fellini as it is in *Ladri di Biciclette*. Conversely, it is still intermittently operative for many spectators of Michael Snow's *Wavelength* or Jean-Luc Godard's *Deux ou trois choses que je sais d'elle*. Here, it is true, the status of the diegesis changes, qualitatively and quantitatively, from one moment to the next. These films designate the diegetic

SOME TERMINOLOGICAL
INDICATIONS

effect as such, making it difficult or impossible for the reader-spectator to enter 'permanently' into the imaginary space-time constituted through the diegetic process. Films of this sort function as critical texts.

As indicated in Chapter 5 the development of the 'language' of the dominant cinema was principally determined by the need to improve the effectiveness of diegetic production, to intensify the presence of characters and 'their' world. The so-called Griffith codes of editing, and concomitantly of framing, constitute one of the three main supports of that production. To it were added the norms of 'three-dimensional' lighting/composition, developed chiefly during the 1920s, and, of course, lip-synch sound. To what extent are we justified in calling these basic systems, which obviously correspond to such different orders of semiosis, **codes**? A code may be defined as 'a system of signals – or signs or symbols, which by pre-established convention, is intended to represent or to transmit information between the origin or transmitter of the signals and the destination or receiver.'[3] The notion of pre-established convention has been so generally extended by the science of semiotics to cultural and ideological determinations of an 'unconscious' nature (e.g. the codes of clothing) that it is reasonable to postulate the existence of codes of expectation with regard to the established procedures of editing, for example. True, the information transmitted by the dominant 'codes' of editing is elementary and most often negative (e.g. 'no time has elapsed between this shot and the last'). It is also true, however, that their structural functioning is in accordance with the considerably more complex codes of, say, any given *genre*, which will combine certain specialized and sophisticated codifications of the 'ground-rules' (for example, shot-size codes) with signifying patterns of a 'purely diegetic' character (dialogue, set design, etc.).[4] The 'editing codes' are in fact part of the foundation supporting the more complex codes of the dominant system. When this is understood, the semantically elementary principles of dominant editing (together with the norms of frame-composition and lighting, and the technology of synch-sound) are seen to constitute a **mode of representation** which is primary with respect to the codes of genre, among others. Western film has known, prior to around 1912, a period dominated by a different mode of representation, the 'primitive mode', which has had a significant counterpart in Japan ever since the introduction of the Western invention. This claim, essential to our investigation, will be substantiated by comparative analysis.

The concept of **matching** is crucial to the dominant system of editing/camera placement. Practice has come to

3. ibid, p. 92.

4. When these 'diegetic' codes depend solely upon visual representation of socially pre-existent systems, they are called **iconographic codes**.

define the **match** as any element which guarantees, from one shot to the next, the illusion of diegetic, spatio-temporal continuity – an 'illusion' distinct from the diegetic effect *per se*, though constitutive of it. Thus, the fact that a character is holding the same high-ball glass filled with what appears to be the same amount of liquor from one shot to the next constitutes a **correct match**. If, on the contrary, the character appears, in the second shot, to have lost the glass with an abruptness defying verisimilitude or to be nursing noticeably more or less whisky than before, without having drunk or been served – or been hidden from view long enough for one or the other to have occurred – we are dealing with a **mismatch**, a **bad** or **incorrect match**. More fundamental, however, is the set of **orientation match-cuts** whose development between 1900 and 1930 may be said to provide the framework of the history of the dominant cinema during the silent and early sound eras. This development appears, in part at least, to have been the material consequence of the growing awareness among film-makers that perceptual left-right screen-orientation had to be given priority over actual orientations to **pro-filmic space**, the space of the 'studio'. Two characters looking at each other in pro-filmic space may or may not appear to the average Western spectator to be looking at each other in two shots appearing successively on the screen, accordingly as the respective placings of the camera did or did not comply with certain conditions. As was generally agreed, although only after some twenty years of film-history, what matters is that the **eyelines**, the orientation of gaze with respect to lens/screen-centre, must appear to 'meet', to cross in an imaginary space formed by the placing side by side (and not 'face to face') of the two successive shots. Similarly, a character walking in a straight line along a road through pro-filmic space who exits screen-left in one shot and re-enters screen-left in the following shot (because he has, for example, been filmed from the opposite side of the road) may well appear, in contradiction with all other data supplied, to have abruptly retraced his steps. This anomaly is termed an incorrect (screen-) **direction match**. Similarly, reversals of the respective positions of people or objects on the screen can, under certain conditions, be equally disruptive of diegetic verisimilitude. As evidenced in the example of the apparent reversal of walking, the **180° match** (not to be confused with the reverse-field) often brings about reversals of all three types, which are in fact merely different manifestations of the self-same phenomenon.

The eyeline match and to some extent the direction match ensure temporal continuity and spatial communica-

SOME TERMINOLOGICAL INDICATIONS

**SOME TERMINOLOGICAL INDICATIONS**

tion between shots designated as contiguous in diegetic space. The most common device used to establish and to exploit an impression of contiguity/continuity is a series of eyeline exchanges which I have chosen to call **reverse-field** set-up or succession of **reverse-angle** shots.[5] A reverse-field series may occasionally involve 180° reversals; usually, however, these will produce 'bad' matches.

A **contiguity cut** is one which implies spatial contiguity and temporal continuity. The reverse field is only one, albeit the most important form of the contiguity cut.[6] In terms of spatial (as opposed to temporal) relationship, there are two other basic modes of shot-change: the **direct cut** or **direct match**, in which two successive shots contain common visual elements, present two successive aspects of a single fragment of diegetic space; and the **alterity cut**, a shot-change which involves neither spatial nor temporal continuity at all in the ordinary sense, but may present a considerable range of temporal or other semantic variations on the alterity mode. Historically, it was the first type of shot-change, the purely disjunctive equivalent of the curtain between scenes on the theatrical stage, which derived spatio-temporal signification only from the appropriate indications in the text of the play (or the programme). The alterity cut was also the first shot-change to be clearly and massively encoded: as **ellipsis** ('time has elapsed between the end of the last shot and the beginning of this one'), and as (unsituated) **cutaway** ('this shot is taking place "elsewhere" with respect to the previous one').[7] The dialectical development of these two functions produced the simultaneous mode of **cross-cutting** ('the separate actions shown in these alternating shots are taking place at the same time'). The era-to-era cross-cutting at the end of *Intolerance*, the rhetorical associations of *Strike, October, The Man with a Movie Camera*, etc. are advanced developments of the alterity cut. They create far more complex problems of definition, which the classical distinction between *parallel montage* and *alternate montage* is quite inadequate to resolve.

The earliest form of direct cut (*c*. 1905) was the **concertina**, i.e. a 'cut-in' or 'cut-back' to or from a given subject which remains the centre of each successive shot composition.[8] This was to be one of the chief *centering* strategies of the cinema after Griffith. The 90° match and, ultimately, the 180° reversal were introduced gradually over the next decade and a half, and the development of the contiguity match and reverse field, initiated somewhat later, took a comparable period of time (1910–25). *Matching on movement* developed somewhat more slowly (1905–25), in reaction to the disconcerting discovery that the direct cut was

---

5. The procedure is sometimes called 'shot-counter-shot' in excessive fidelity to the very common French term *champ-contre-champ*. However, the word 'reverse' does figure in a number of related expressions employed among British and American professionals.

6. The cutaway may also operate on the contiguous mode, which may in fact be shown to have derived historically from that of alterity.

7. See my *Theory of Film Practice*, ch. 1.

8. The term *concertina* seems no longer in current usage in the British film industry where it originated. However, I find it the most satisfactory equivalent for the common French term *raccord dans l'axe* provided by actual practice in English.

not necessarily the least disruptive of the three modes once the other two had been properly mastered. The direct cut proved in fact to be more of a 'jolt' than the other forms unless the kinetic effect of the cut were absorbed by a shot-to-shot chain of *perceptually continuous* diegetic movement.

Finally, though I refer often to these 'rules' and practices, and to the principles that subtend them, as 'editing codes', they are of course, strictly speaking, the codes of **découpage** (i.e. of the editing/camera set-up relationship). The success of orientational matching is ultimately contingent upon the 'correct' placing of the camera, while the very possibility of matching on movement depends upon the placing of camera and actor(s).

SOME TERMINOLOGICAL INDICATIONS

# Part 1 Grounds, Premises

# 1. A System of Contradictions

A great deal has been written about 'Japanese culture' since the opening of the country to foreign exchange, much of it uninformed nonsense from the pens of well-meaning globe-trotters, sensitive indeed to the *otherness* of the East but able to comprehend it only as the last refuge of 'universal human values' – those of middle-class idealism. One feels, therefore, reluctant to enter into general discussion of Japanese modes of representation, of Japanese aesthetics, of the 'Japanese mind', reluctant to add, perhaps, to that century-old slag-heap. It is nevertheless impossible to deal with Japanese film, indeed with any aspect of Japanese society, without constant reference to almost every one of its other aspects. That this should be especially true of Japanese society is an assertion which in itself requires some historical substantiation.

The pertinent traits of Japanese aesthetics were defined almost entirely between the ninth and twelfth centuries, known as the Heian period. It was, however, under the rule of the Tokugawa Shōguns (1633–1867), the first of whom, Ieyasu, is celebrated as the consolidator of national unity and the initiator of three hundred years of peace, that Japan became the most *integrated* large-scale society in the world, East or West.

Although the Shogunate thought to preserve its power by maintaining carefully drawn class distinctions, and although the end of the Tokugawa period was a time of social ferment, the long isolation of the country created a uniformity of habits, beliefs, and tastes among all classes. The farmer, the townsman, and the samurai moved in different hierarchical spheres but they shared a mundane world in which their differences were not of kind but of degree. The diet of all, except in times of famine, was essentially the same, consisting principally of rice with a few vegetables and a little fish, prepared according to a very few standard recipes. . . . The house of a townsman was more elegant than that of the peasant, but the architectural arrangement, the household articles, the system of heating, the furniture – all had the same basic form, size, shape and function. The wealthy townsman could warm his hands in winter over a charcoal brazier made of bronze while the peasant had to be content with one of clay and with somewhat less charcoal . . . Wealth could provide greater abundance of food and better quality materials; it could purchase nothing essentially different in form or function. The code of morality and social behavior, based largely upon the Japanese interpretations of the commentaries of Chu Hsi on the works of the Chinese sages, at last permeated into all social groups, so that finally the Edo fireman shared an ethical climate not immediately distinguishable from that of the samurai.

Similarly, tastes in art were built up out of commonly shared artistic experiences. . . . Identical tastes in music and in the graphic arts were so widespread that, until modern times, the body of artistic canon did not differ significantly according to social stratification. A maid serving tea moved in a style similar to that used at court ceremonies; shop clerks were taught to sit, move, and stand in patterns used in the *Nō* and were intensively drilled to speak in a manner closely resembling that of the Kabuki actor.[1]

Even the Japan of the 1970s, after a hundred years of capitalism and a thirty-year inoculation of American individualist ideology, still bears the unmistakable stamp of three centuries of standardization (e.g. the *ken* or module upon which *tatami* matting, and all other household furnishings, as well as all traditional dwellings, are patterned). And in the first forty years of this century, the period during which Japan's principal modes of filmic representation developed, the above description of Tokugawa society was still remarkably relevant. Small wonder, then, that so many of the specific traits of Japanese society are explicable and comprehensible, not as 'borrowings' from the older arts but rather as specific manifestations of that vast circulation of *modules* – of 'empty' signs, as Barthes might say – which is the very substance of Japanese society.

Before attempting to define some of the principles governing this circulation, it may be useful to respond to one question which arises at the inception of any historically-oriented investigation of Japanese cinema: how is it that while several of the non-Western nations – China, of course, but even more prolifically, Egypt and India – have long produced motion pictures, only Japan has developed modes of filmic representation that are wholly and specifically her own, only Japan has produced a body of 'masterpieces'.[2] Indeed, an observation made by Jay Leyda about the transition from silence to sound, in his very informative history of the Chinese cinema, seems to characterize the entire history of cinema as it unfolded, not only in China

---

1. Earle, *The Kabuki Theatre*, pp. 67–8.

2. The inverted commas here call attention to a dubious but for the moment unavoidable reference to the occidental concept of the unique, irreplaceable work, a concept irrelevant in the traditional Japanese context.

but in India and Egypt as well: 'The limitations of the American sound film were taken over wholesale by Chinese producers when they finally achieved sound productions of their own, and it cannot be said that Chinese films have yet escaped from their entangling admiration of the efficient American film.'[3] Leyda shows how the entire Chinese industry depended throughout its formative years (basically, up to 1930) on American and English capital and, most important, perhaps, on American and English cameramen. Yet China was not even a 'full-fledged' colony (though much actual production does seem to have been concentrated in Shanghai and Hong Kong, both dominated by European interests). To what lengths, one wonders, was the reliance on 'Western know-how' carried in 'protectorates' or colonies of such long-standing as Egypt and India during the formative period? In the absence of any comparably authoritative histories of the Egyptian or Indian cinemas in French or English, I am reduced to conjecture. Both nations remained under British rule until after the Second World War. Since the British cinema has from its very inception been totally enthralled by what were to become the 'Hollywood modes and codes', it is not difficult to understand why the modes of spatio-temporal representation found in the films of those countries appear to be so utterly divorced from the representational systems at work in their traditional arts.

Even a cursory examination of Asian history immediately provides the answer we are looking for: in two thousand years of recorded history, no part of Japanese territory had ever been occupied until the 1945 defeat. Japan was never subjected to the semi-colonial status which was China's for over a century, or to complete enslavement as were Egypt or India. She is the *only* major non-Western country to have escaped the colonial yoke. Her cinema, of course, is but a minor consequence of this crucial fact, which in turn is one of a series of historical features by which Japan may be identified as belonging simultaneously to several apparently incompatible types and stages of historical development. The definition of these primary traits, essential for the understanding of the secondary traits as evinced by Japanese films, is our next task.

The fact that Japan was able to avoid colonial rule in the nineteenth century (by 'accepting Western influence', i.e. using Western technology to build a bulwark against Western imperialism) contributed directly to the originality of the Japanese film, since it made possible the technical and economic autonomy of her film industry. From a very early date, Japan trained her own technicians, developed and

A SYSTEM OF CONTRADICTIONS

3. Leyda, Jay, *Dianying*, p. 64.

printed her films in laboratories owned and operated by Japanese; she even manufactured her own raw film-stock.[4] And, of course, this self-sufficiency of the infrastructure was a *sine qua non* for a 'free' interaction between the cinematograph and the cultural milieu.

Historically speaking, Japan's avoidance of the 'colonial stage', the corollary of the construction of a modern capitalist state, carried out at twice the pace of advanced Western nations, was determined in part by a prior condition, another unique feature of Japanese history. Although Japan's 'Asiatic-ness' is undeniable (geographical situation; agrarian, rice-dominated economy), she is also the only major Asian nation never to have known what Marx defined as the Asiatic Mode of Production, characterized from earliest times in China, India, Persia, Egypt, etc., by vast hydraulic enterprises entailing the mobilization of thousands of labourers and consequently the early establishment of a powerful central government with a large civil service in its employ, and a drastic curtailment of city autonomy. This form of government, analysed by K. A. Wittfogel in his classic study of the hydraulic society,[5] has been termed 'oriental despotism'. Marx had observed, however, that 'Japan, with its purely feudal organization of landed property and its developed *petite culture*, gives a much truer picture of the European middle ages than all our history books, dictated as these are by bourgeois prejudices.'[6] Wittfogel sheds further light on this anomaly:

Why did Japan's rice economy not depend on large and government-directed waterworks? Any competent economic geographer can answer this question. The peculiarities of the country's water supply neither necessitated nor favored substantial government-directed works. Innumerable mountain ranges compartmentalized the great Far Eastern islands; and their broken relief encouraged a fragmented (hydroagricultural) rather than a coordinated (hydraulic) pattern of irrigation farming and flood control . . .

The rulers of the dominant political center effected a loose political unification at a rather early date, but they were not faced with hydraulic tasks that required the coordinated operation of large corvée teams. Nor were they conquered by the forces of an orientally despotic state. They therefore failed to establish a comprehensive managerial and acquisitive bureaucracy capable of controlling the non-governmental forces of society as did the men of the apparatus on the Chinese mainland . . . Many elements of Chinese culture notwithstanding, the decentralized and property-based society of the Japanese Middle Ages resembled much more closely the feudal order of the remote European world than the hydraulic patterns of nearby China.

---

4. This was in keeping with the general policy of early Japanese capitalism: 'Foreign instructors, advisers and engineers were brought in to run a number of the new factories and train the technicians who were to run them in the future, as many as 130 being employed by the Department of Public Works alone by 1879. Official policy, however, was to replace them as soon as possible by Japanese whose salaries were smaller, an attitude which led one British resident to observe that "the Japanese only look upon foreigners as school-masters. As long as they cannot help themselves they make use of them; and then they send them about their business." It was precisely this, of course, that eventually made Japan's industrial technology self-sustaining, *in contrast to that of other Asian countries, which remained for the most part dependent on foreign help*'. (Beasley, W. G., *The Modern History of Japan*, p. 144. The interpolated quote is from O. R. Black's *Young Japan, 1880–1*; the italics are mine.)

5. Wittfogel, Karl A., *Oriental Despotism*.

6. Marx, Karl, *Capital*, p. 718.

However, Wittfogel goes on to add significantly:

## A SYSTEM OF CONTRADICTIONS

We must be careful not to oversimplify the picture. The Oriental quality of many Japanese institutions and ideas is beyond doubt. On the lower and local level, Japanese irrigation agriculture required quasi-hydraulic coordination and subordination; and feudal lords' insistence upon absolute obedience may, at least in part, reflect such quasi-hydraulic relations. Rudiments of a postal system seem to have existed prior to the Tokugawa period; ... The members of the ruling group, although strongly imbued with a military spirit, continued to think in terms of somewhat adjusted Confucianism; and although they invented simplified phonetic symbols, they employed with genuine pride the Chinese script, which, like Confucius' conception of the gentleman-bureaucrat, was better suited to a civil and learned officialdom than to a war-minded knighthood.[7]

(We shall explore later and at some length the crucial matter of the Japanese writing system, an essential emblem of the multiform *bivalence* implicit in this description.)

Japan was related 'in a submarginal way' as Wittfogel puts it, 'to the institutional patterns of the Asiatic world' and this undeniably made the islands a privileged terrain for the extra-mural development of important aspects of Chinese culture. Nevertheless, the remarkable parallels between Japanese and European feudalism undoubtedly made possible the rapid conversion during the Meiji period (1867–1912) to a unique variety of state capitalism, involving an immediate priority to heavy industry, a conversion paradoxically contingent upon the *perpetuation of feudal social structures*.[8] For Japan is also the only major capitalist nation in the world today which has never known a true bourgeois revolution in any guise whatsoever.[9]

The Meiji Restoration of 1867 in no sense constituted a sudden shift of power from the feudal classes to the bourgeoisie. Insofar as this shift took place at all, it did so over a period of almost a century and hence so gradually that the two classes in many ways may be said to have interpenetrated (as to some extent they already had under the Tokugawas); which of course goes a long way towards explaining the longevity of ancient customs and modes of thinking. This fact is essential to any attempt to understand twentieth-century 'bourgeois ideology' in Japan, where the term is perhaps not even adequate. As for the events of 1867, the Meiji Restoration was simply the linchpin of Japan's uniquely concatenated transition to capitalism. As Sir George Sansom points out:

The driving force at the Restoration and in political life for the best part of a generation thereafter was provided by leaders who

7. Wittfogel, Karl A., *Oriental Despotism*, pp. 197–200.

8. See Norman, E. Herbert, *Japan's Emergence as a Modern State*.

9. Bismarck's construction of German industrial capitalism 'from the top down' bears some relation to the similar stage in Japan, and it is no accident that those who drafted the Meiji constitution (1889) took as their model the constitution of Germany. However, fundamental differences subsist between the histories of the two countries, as witness in particular the fact that while Nazism was the solution to the crisis of capitalism adopted by a German middle-class which, after the failure of the proletarian revolution, indisputably held the reality of power, the Japanese middle class was still an opposition, 'liberal' force during the period of exacerbated militarism which preceded the Second World War and which constituted the neo-feudal aristocracy's final attempt to perpetuate its absolutist rule.

had been brought up in a feudal, or at any rate feudalistic, atmosphere. They were for the most part dissatisfied and ambitious samurai, and their outlook was coloured by their antecedents. It was these men, and not the bourgeoisie, who laid the foundations of a capitalist structure and at the same time developed a political system that bore little resemblance to those which came into force in the advanced industrial countries of Western Europe under the influence of a powerful moneyed class.[10]

As for the agrarian aspects of the Restoration, Takahashi Kohachiro sums up thus the conclusions of Japanese Marxist scholars:

> The agrarian reform of the Meiji Restoration made the *jinushis* the actual owners of the land, but they had nothing in common with the English landlords who let their land to farmers who, in keeping with the capitalist mode of production, were in turn agricultural entrepreneurs employing wage-earners. Nor do the *jinushi* have anything in common with the squireens of Eastern Europe who farmed their own land directly with serf-labour... The *jinushi* divided his land into small lots and had it worked by small farmers (*kosakus*) who paid as rent nearly half of their harvest, like the poverty-stricken *métayers* under the old régime in France... Thus historical comparison and perspective provide proof that the Meiji Restoration was not, properly speaking, a bourgeois revolution of the 'classical' type.[11]

A prosperous non-European nation which was never colonized, an Asian nation with only a 'submarginal' experience of the Asiatic Mode of Production, a nation which moved from feudalism to full-fledged capitalism without the hiatus of revolution: there are anomalies here and it is interesting to consider what role they have played in determining the constitution of a specifically and uniquely Japanese 'outlook', and what their bearing is on that 'Empire of (empty) signs' described by Roland Barthes. A comprehensive answer to such a far-reaching question is not only beyond the scope of this book but beyond the capacities of the avowedly amateur Japanologist that I am. I can only point to the direction in which I feel the answer(s) may lie, and occasionally, with more special reference to 'film history', contribute observations which I feel relevant to the problem.

Now it is at this point in our undertaking that we unavoidably encounter another pair of 'contradictory' traits, exhausted by specialists of 'things Japanese'. They are described, depending upon the writer's inclinations, either as 'faculty for assimilation' and 'sense of tradition' or, alternatively, as 'lack of originality' and 'stagnant conservatism'. In either case, they are seen as sure symptoms of

---

10. Sansom, George B., *The Western World and Japan*, p. 327. W. G. Beasley (op. cit., pp. 224-5) demonstrates that the domination by the oligarchy issued from this class remained complete until the end of the Pacific War. The organs of expression of the new middle class as such – the Parties and Diet – had no more real power than the Tiers Etat under Louis XVI.

11. Takahashi Kohachiro, 'La Restauration de Meiji au Japon et la Révolution Française', in *Recherches Internationales*, no. 62, 1970, pp. 84-5.

**A SYSTEM OF CONTRADICTIONS**

the 'irreconcilable dichotomy' of the 'unfathomable' Japanese character. We must of course move beyond these stereotypes, but we cannot bypass them: an analysis of the ideologies which they conceal is crucial to the present undertaking. Nothing has better served detractors of 'Japanese culture', nor more keenly embarrassed the bulk of its Western admirers, than the ease, indeed the eagerness, with which the Japanese, at certain periods in their history, have adopted techniques and concepts of foreign origin – among which the cinema and the modes of representation attached to it in the Western context are not the least insignificant. In drawing the inevitable comparisons between Japan and China, those who recently saw China as an ally in the struggle against fascism, those who see her today as the vanguard of socialism, were/are quick to compare the 'originality' of China's 'age-old wisdom' with Japan's 'habit of copying'. Were not Japan's writing and much of her vocabulary, broad sectors of her arts and her most 'sophisticated' religion 'lifted' wholesale from China? The ease with which she has adopted Western techniques in modern times is merely additional proof that her only 'aptitude' is a mimetic one. The champions of Japanese culture – whose number has multiplied rapidly, especially in the United States, since Japan has become 'a bulwark against Communism' – are quick to counter, but they too invoke the value of *originality*: the Japanese do not copy, they *adapt*; whatever has been borrowed has been profoundly and *creatively* transformed, and besides, many aspects of Japanese culture are entirely indigenous (and the list adduced in evidence is a long one, from *kabuki* theatre to a dish like *sushi* and from the *Tale of Genji* to *origami* paper-folding. Of course, there is a good deal more 'truth' in the second type of statement than in the first; what interests us here, however, is that both arguments have an ideological base since both call upon the virtues of originality. And this is where Japan has the greatest power to *perturb*, for in Japan, as I will abundantly illustrate, and notably in her cinema, originality has never been a dominant value. In particular, the specifically bourgeois notion that the artist is the *creator* and *proprietor* of his work is utterly meaningless within the framework of the traditional arts of Japan, and of the East in general. Plagiarism seems to have been a meaningless concept until the opening of the country. Here, then, is a fundamental point of conflict with the modern West, where the notion of the artist as demiurge, creator of works which are his inalienable property, has been an essential article of faith since the end of the eighteenth century.[12] The Japanese social system denies the very concept of originality, acknowledges and

12. That this notion is intimately linked with the growth of capitalism is amply demonstrated by the *acknowledged* intertextual practices that continued right up to the French Revolution (Chaucer's and Shakespeare's extensive borrowing of forms and material are celebrated; Michel Corrette's choral adaptation of a Vivaldi concerto is an exemplary illustration).

indeed deliberately emphasizes the material reality of the circulation of signs. This system erodes the very foundations of our ideology of the Creator as the Supremely Free Human Being, of the Artist-God, of the Book and the Word.

The Japanese attitude here described is bound up with modes of thinking that go back to very ancient times (we shall see some of its earliest manifestations in Heian literary practice), and this preservation is the other term of our hackneyed dichotomy, traditionalism. It is true, of course, that the Japanese as a nation have always tended to 'keep things': once it's in the house, once it's proved its usefulness, you never throw it away. Trivial as this formulation is, I believe it adequately describes a phenomenon epitomized by the Imperial House with its 'two thousand years' of unbroken continuity, and perhaps even more vividly by the Shōsōin at Nara, 'a warehouse of all the useful objects of the court given by the Emperor Shomu in AD 756 and almost completely preserved to the present day in its original log storage building'.[13] The survival of such massive fragments of 'tradition' is largely explained by the above-mentioned lack of any revolutionary disruption in Japanese history, by the gradualness of the elimination of feudal institutions, and by Japan's long period of isolation. This 'sense of tradition' is most remarkable in the permanence of its forms. Once these achieve stability, they tend to remain 'as is' for centuries. Of this complex and strange phenomenon, even the casual visitor to Japan is immediately aware.

In the Meiji period, Japanese with modern tastes built into their homes a Western Room, furnished in the late nineteenth–century style of interior decoration, and such rooms, although they have largely ceased to exist in the West except in museums, remain a necessary adjunct of the well-appointed Japanese home. Some of these rooms are today decorated in a style that can be described loosely as Swedish Modern, but the majority repeat the doily, the antimacassar, the fringed table cover, the elaborate gilt picture frame, the floral carpeting and the busy design of chair and table which characterized the Victorian parlor.[14]

Many Western ideas have also been poured into a similarly permanent mould: by and large, contemporary 'liberal' and even 'socialist' thinking in Japan bears a remarkable resemblance to the ideas gleaned from the writings of Spencer, Mill and Rousseau as they were propagated in the 1880s by Tokutomi Sohō, the intellectual leader of the reformist opposition to the Meiji government.[15]

Why is Japanese society the most 'conservative' in the

13. Lee, Sherman E., *A History of Far Eastern Art*, p. 272.

14. Ernst, Earle, op. cit., p. 272.

15. See Pyle, Kenneth B., *The New Generation in Meiji Japan*. However, this thesis is entirely my own.

modern industrial world? It is true, of course, that for three hundred years the Tokugawa Shogunate went to extremes to preserve the *status quo*, encouraging infanticide in order to maintain the population level, allowing bridges and roads to fall into disrepair so as to discourage trade, etc.; conservatism and its 'fixative effect' can, however, be traced back another thousand years, to Japan's earliest history. It is no doubt related to the extremely difficult natural conditions under which the Japanese nation was built, in a tiny archipelago of which only 16 per cent of the land is arable, ravaged by typhoons, torrential rains, landslides, earthquakes, tidal waves and volcanic eruptions. In such precarious circumstances – and protection against the elements remained problematic until well into the twentieth century – a predominantly agrarian population will quickly seize upon any new tool which may seem useful, at the same time refusing to discard the old, as it is associated with so many tragic struggles, and may well serve again if the new tool fails. Whatever its origins – and they are certainly more complex than I can suggest here – the 'fixative effect' has played an absolutely vital role in the history of Japanese culture and particularly in the development of the arts including, as we shall see, the cinema. Its historical patterns are aptly described by the critic, Kato Shūichi:

A SYSTEM OF CONTRADICTIONS

... different types of art, generated in different periods, did not supplant each other, but co-existed and remained more or less creative from the time of their first appearance up to our time. Buddhist statues, a major genre of artistic expression in the period from the sixth to the ninth century, continued to evolve in style during the following eras, even when the picture scroll opened new possibilities for the visual representation of the world in the Heian period. Brush works with india ink flourished during the Muromachi period [1336–1573], but one school of artists remained faithful to the techniques and style of the picture scroll. Under the Tokugawa regime, a new style of painting and decorative art was established by Sōtatsu and Kōrin; the technique of the woodcut print was elaborated to perfection. Yet artists never ceased to carve Buddhist statues or engage with great passion in brush-work painting. Practically no style ever died. In other words, the history of Japanese art is not one of succession but one of superposition.[16]

The contrast, we might add, with Western art, is absolute. We encounter once again the question of originality, for the birth and death of forms and styles in the West have long been regulated by the law of supersession (and of self-consciously neo-classical revivals) and this can be observed as easily on the walls of a museum as in the pages of a history of fashion. Conversely, the principle of superposition

16. Kato Shūichi, *Form, Style and Tradition*, p. 4.

GROUNDS, PREMISES   described by Kato may be readily observed in the streets of any Japanese city today, where Western-style business suits and blue jeans co-exist unostentatiously with clothes that have not changed in any significant detail for over three hundred years, which still occupy an entire floor of any popular department store. And, as we shall see, the cinema of Japan has borne at almost every stage the stamp of this superposition, even up to the present day.

# 2. A System of Signs

It is in the period of the Fujiwara Regents[1] that there were formed among upper-class men and women in privileged situations certain standards of personal behaviour and certain canons of aesthetic judgement which are the source, or it might be better to say the foundation of Japanese social life as it developed in later centuries.[2]

It follows from this judgement by the West's most eminent historian of Japan that a detour through the social and literary practices of the Heian court is indispensable if we are to bring to light the theoretical implications of Japanese aesthetic practice as a whole. And our first task will be a cursory consideration of the writing system which made Heian literature materially possible and which in itself contained some of the seeds from which the forms and styles of that period, its *writing* in the strongest sense, may be seen to grow.

We know that it was long before the Heian period, probably in AD 552, that Chinese writing was first introduced to Japan by way of Korea, in several volumes of Buddhist scriptures, which were also to initiate the spread of the great continental religion to the island empire. Almost from the outset it seems that while the learned clergy strove to master the Chinese language as a written (and occasionally spoken) whole, efforts were also made to adapt the Chinese characters to the forms of spoken Japanese, a polysyllabic, inflected language, quite in contrast on these two fundamental counts to Chinese.

The methods used were several and complex, but in summary we may say that a partial phoneticization of the essentially non-phonetic Chinese writing was undertaken: the sounds of spoken Japanese were assigned to characters whose pronunciation in Chinese was thought to approximate those sounds, while at the same time these same characters – and many more whose original sound may have been irrelevant to the native language – were also used to represent 'ideographically' Japanese words of equivalent meaning.[3]

[1]. The reign of the Fujiwara family as the power behind the throne is associated with the first of several periods during which the imperial capital, Heian-Kyō (later Kyoto), was the seat of actual political power (794–1191).

[2]. Sansom, George, *A History of Japan*, Vol. 2, p. 73.

[3]. The main source here is Sansom, George, *An Historical Grammar of Japanese*.

This method of writing (*kana majiri*, i.e. mixed phonetic writing) made possible the first written poetry, recorded in the early chronicles and in the first of the great imperial anthologies, the *Manyoshu* (759). However, this phonetic use of the Chinese characters was cumbersome at best: the ambiguities involved in the double function of certain signs made reading an arduous task, while the inflexions of Japanese verbs and adjectives often required as many as five or six complex characters to express phonetically what in pure Chinese would have been a single sign/concept. Gradually, however, during the course of the Heian period, by a process of stylization and codification, a specifically Japanese syllabary (*hiragana*) was developed, partly in relation to a general reaction to the overwhelming Chinese influence of the previous three centuries, partly in response to the growing needs of both the administration and court society. Not only did the new script 'liberate' the Chinese characters (*kanji*) from the burden of phonetic expression but it promoted the emergence of one of the world's great literatures. For a long time, *kana majiri* in its many forms continued to be assiduously practised by statesmen and clergy in their non-literary writing, while the great novels and poetry of the Heian period were written in a script largely dominated by the phonetic system. The ultimate result of this co-existence of two fundamentally different types of writing, the one phonetic and the other primarily non-phonetic, was the creation of a unique system which incorporates both.[4]

The walls of a Tokyo subway station today bear signs on which the name of the station can be read in three different scripts: *kanji*, since every Japanese proper name possesses a Chinese character or set of characters which has become attached to the phonetic signifier through a process of historical selection; *hiragana*, since of course the syllabary may at least theoretically be used to transcribe any word used in the Japanese language, even if it is not normally so written (or to render, in terms of Japanese pronunciation, any words of foreign origin that need to be incorporated into the language); and finally *romāji* or Roman characters. This last adjunct, needless to say, is intended for foreign visitors or residents, just as *hiragana* assists out-of-towners or anyone else who may know the name of the station they want, but do not necessarily know how it is written in *kanji*, a fact which often causes arduous problems in the use of the telephone directory, for example. The individual Japanese maintains throughout his or her lifetime a continually growing relationship with the written language, one which moves constantly towards a greater mastery of the non-phonetic[5] but which can never entirely abandon the phone-

[4]. The Korean writing system has, for three hundred years, been similarly dual. I do not know if this is related to the Japanese invasion of Korea at the end of the fifteenth century.

[5]. In the sense that Chinese writing itself can be said to be non-phonetic. Actually Chinese characters contain quasi-phonetic 'operators', but the Chinese language contains no purely phonetic characters, as any text written in Japanese invariably does (there are no *kanji* for such particles as *no*, *wa*, *to*, for Western loan words or verb inflexions).

tic, which involves indeed continually turning back to the phonetic, whenever it is necessary to distinguish between the several possible meanings (and pronunciations) of a given *kanji*. Japanese school-children learn successively four different scripts: *hiragana*, *rōmaji*, *katakana* (equivalent to our block printing and derived from the Chinese characters of *kana majiri* by a process of subtraction and geometricalization as opposed to the cursive stylization which produced *hiragana*) and *kanji*. Of course, very few Japanese ever learn all of the thousands of Chinese characters which constitute the supposed baggage of a highly educated Japanese. The minimum number of characters required of the high-school graduate is 1,850, but every Japanese, to some extent, goes on learning new characters all his life (and needless to say, the literary sophistication of an individual is judged by his or her repertoire of *kanji*, of a text by the ratio of *kanji* to *kana* or phonetic signs).

This rather long historical résumé was necessary to demonstrate one basic point of great theoretical importance: the Japanese are the only people in the world who, for over a thousand years, have practised simultaneously and in close symbiosis a phonetic and a non-phonetic writing without taking either as the privileged centre of language.[6] This is in marked contrast with the experience of the Vietnamese, for example, upon whom a phonetic alphabet was bestowed by French priests early in their colonial history and who soon lost touch completely with the Chinese script which they too had adopted from their northern neighbours. (This effect of European colonialism is of considerable significance, as we shall see.)

What is the relevance to our investigation of this unparalleled cohabitation? The answer to this question is facilitated by a consideration of one of the basic premises of the work of the French philosopher Jacques Derrida.[7]

Derrida's fundamental critique may be said to proceed from this simple observation: throughout the modern history of the Western world, writing has been regarded as the passive member of the family of language, a mere transcription of speech, of the *logos*, regarded as the repository of ultimate truth, whilst writing was merely the contingent temporal 'form' given to the essential and ultimately divine *content*.

As it has been more or less implicitly defined, the essence of the *phonè* is regarded as immediately next to that which in 'thought' is related as logos to 'meaning', producing, receiving, articulating and resembling meaning. If Aristotle, for example, holds that 'the sounds uttered by the voice . . . are the symbols of the moods of the soul . . . and written words the symbols of the words uttered by

A SYSTEM OF SIGNS

6. The earliest Chinese translations of Buddhist scriptures from sanskrit involved a phonetic use of Chinese characters in the transcription of both untranslatable Indian names and semantically meaningless incantations (see Sansom, *An Historical Grammar*). The fact that this practice never developed into a full-fledged syllabary but died out rapidly points to a fundamental distinction between Chinese and Japanese 'cultures'.

7. I am fully aware of the schematic and incomplete character of the following account, but it is impossible to explore this subtle body of thought in depth here. Readers already familiar with Derrida's writings will, I hope, grant me their indulgence, while others who find special interest in these problems will refer to the original text (Derrida, Jacques, *De la Grammatologie*).

the voice' (*On Interpretation*, 1, 16 3) it is because the voice, as producer of the *primary symbols*, is in a relationship of essential and immediate proximity to the soul. As producer of the primary signifier, the voice is not just one signifier among many. It signifies the 'mood of the soul' which in turn reflects back, or is a reflection of, things in terms of resemblance. Between Being and Soul, between things and affections, there is assumed to be a relationship of natural translation or signification; between the Soul and the Logos, a conventionally symbolic relation. And the *prime* convention, regarded as immediately related to the order of natural and universal signification, is presumably produced as spoken language. The written language in this view merely fixes conventions linking other conventions.[8]

This Aristotelian doctrine has been refined and developed by nine centuries of Christianity and two centuries of bourgeois rule. It has, however, never ceased to determine that Western attitude towards language which Derrida terms *logocentrism*, demonstrating its decisive complicity with metaphysics and philosophical idealism – often through the metaphorical conceit by which the Word significantly becomes Book, Scripture. This outlook Derrida illustrates by a quotation from Rousseau:

'It was as if Nature spread out before our eyes all Her Magnificence as text for our conversations . . . And so I closed all books, for there is one that is open for all eyes, the Book of Nature. And it is through that great and sublime Book that I learn to serve and worship its author' (*Emile, Profession de foi*). Thus good writing has always been that which is precisely meant to be *understood*: within a Nature or a Natural Law, created or not, but originally conceived as an eternal presence. Understood and contained, then, within a totality and wrapped in a tome. The idea of a book is that of a totalization, finite or infinite, of the signifier; that constituted totality of signifiers is pre-existent to the book, watches over its inscription and its signs, ideally it is independent from it. It is the encyclopaedic protection of theology and logocentrism against the disruption of writing . . .[9]

(We shall begin to see the importance of this opposition closed book/open text in relation to Heian poetry.)

At the same time, *phonetic* writing – which Derrida takes care to distinguish, as we shall see, from the 'generalized' notion of writing (*the sense of writing*) – has been intimately linked with the growth of science which empowered Western capitalism to exercise an undisputed world hegemony, for 'the very notion of science was born at a certain stage of writing . . . it was conceived and formulated as task, idea, project in a language implying a certain type of specific

8. ibid., pp. 21–2. This theme is also dealt with at length in Derrida's *Speech and Phenomena*.

9. ibid, pp. 30–1.

relationships – structural and axiological – between speech and writing'.[10] Another quotation from Rousseau, placed as epigraph to the first part of Derrida's essay, points to the essentially *ethnocentric* character of logocentrism: 'These three manners of writing correspond fairly accurately to the three various states under which we may say that men come together as a Nation. Depicting objects is suited to savages; signs and words and propositions to barbarians; and the alphabet to civilised peoples' (*Essai sur l'origine des langues*). The Japanese, of course, unbeknownst to Rousseau, were already a 'civilized people' and it is not perhaps entirely absurd to think that there is some real correlation between the instrumental requirements of a feudal warrior class whose objective ambition for some nine hundred years was national unity organized in a strictly policed hierarchy around a strong central government, and the social 'practicality' of a phonetic script. Many war-lords of the pre-Tokugawa era who contributed to Japan's unification could write only *kana*; it is more than probable that the time-consuming mastery of the Chinese characters would have been incompatible with their political and military activities. And it may even be argued that the secular practice of phonetic writing contributed substantially to the preparation that enabled the Japanese to cope with Western science and technology far sooner and better than peoples whose writing has remained entirely non-phonetic to the present day.

However, we must avoid the all too familiar temptation of placing Japan 'on our side'. For the purposes of this study, the most important single consequence of this unique double practice is that the Japanese, during most of their 'civilized' history, had a continual, day-to-day experience of an absolutely critical linguistic *difference* which the peoples of Europe *and China* could grasp only 'theoretically' through the study of foreign systems. This difference is inscribed within their language, where it may not be too far-fetched to see it as a 'functioning emblem' of that difference which Derrida, developing an idea of Saussure's, has taught us to be the *intangible principle of language*:

If the conceptual part of value is constituted solely by relationships and with regard to the other terms of the language, the same may be said of its material part; what counts in a word is not the sound itself but the phonic differences which enable us to distinguish this word from all others, for it is they that convey meaning... A fragment of language could never be founded on anything but its non-coincidence with the rest.

Derrida argues from this passage in Saussure's *Cours de linguistique générale* (p. 163) that

10. ibid, p. 42.

before being or not being 'noted', 'represented', 'figured'... the linguistic sign implies originating writing.

Whence the generalization in his work of the notion of writing in order to demonstrate that logocentrism and a hypothetical 'grapho-centrism' are equal and opposite ideologies; both speech and writing derive from 'difference as the source of all linguistic value.'[11]

Whatever the metaphysical perils of this originating postulate, Derrida's analysis does point up the fact that the Japanese writing system occupies a privileged middle ground, nearer perhaps than either the Chinese or the Indo-European systems to a dialectically constituted level of reference of languages. It may thereby afford access to both a *linear mode* of linguistic representation, such as that of the West, and to an 'oriental' mode which it is legitimate to regard, in a theoretical perspective, as a 'practical' critique of linearity. The linearization of writing and the linear conception of speech are rooted in the Western sense of time based on movement in space. Saussure's whole theory of 'the linearity of the signifier' can, according to Derrida, be interpreted from this point of view.[12] That Chinese writing (and hieroglyphic writing in general) is distinguishable from phonetic writing by its (semantic) non-linearity is a truism. That this difference should correspond to that between ancient Chinese thought and the main-stream of the Greco-Christian tradition is not quite so obvious. A glimpse of this fundamental hiatus is offered by Joseph Needham:

The implication was that the universe itself is a vast organism, with now one now another component taking the lead – spontaneous and uncreated it is, with all the parts co-operating in a mutual service which is perfect freedom, the larger and the smaller playing their parts according to their degree 'neither afore nor after.'

... The conviction that the universe and each of the wholes composing it have a cyclical nature, undergoing alternations, so dominated [Chinese] thought that the idea of succession was always subordinated to that of interdependence. Thus retrospective explanations were not felt to involve any difficulty. 'Such and such a lord, in his lifetime, was not able to obtain the hegemony because, after his death, human victims were sacrificed to him.' Both facts were simply part of one timeless pattern.[13]

Our examination of certain aspects of Japanese literary practice will demonstrate that Japan has always resembled China in this 'indifference' to linear causality: 'Chinese cosmology when it became known to the Japanese undoubtedly impressed them by its range and its coherence. It had great influence upon their minds, an influence which still

---

11. ibid., p. 77.

12. Derrida adduces in support of this statement the following quotation from Saussure: 'The acoustical signifiers have only the line of time at their disposal; their elements appear one after another; they form a chain. This characteristic is apparent as soon as they are represented in writing... The signifier, as it is auditory by nature, unfolds only in time and possesses the characteristics which it borrows from time (a) it represents an extension and (b) that extension is measurable in only one dimension: it is a line.' (*Cours de linguistique générale*, p. 103.)

13. Needham, Joseph, *Science and Civilization in China*, Vol. 2, pp. 288–9.

endures. Far Eastern people are apt to hark back to this ancient theory and think in terms of its catalogue for the guidance of their lives.'[14] In conclusion, I would further claim that in those areas in which the Japanese mind has been most productive (not in philosophy or science, but in the arts and letters), this double experience of linear and non-linear writing modes may have helped them to radicalize Chinese thought in their aesthetic practice.

14. Sansom, George, *A History of Japan to 1334*, p. 73.

# 3. A Boundless Text

The earliest examples of Japanese writing convey the prime social importance which this activity was to assume, even at its most literary, throughout the formative years of her history. The *Kojiki* (712) and the *Nihon Shoki* (720) were both chronicles designed to legitimize the reign and power of the imperial house by *instituting, through writing*, Japanese mytho-history and in particular, the divine ancestry of the imperial house. Not only did writing remain for centuries the privileged instrument of the dominant political class – a characteristic of the early stages of all societies – but within that class writing was to occupy a place in the social order such that it may practically be said to have been *the social equal of speech*.

However, it was not until after the seat of imperial rule had moved from Nara to Heian-Kyō in 794 that textual practice became in fact a way of life for court and clergy (i.e. virtually all of literate Japan). It is indicative of the social concern with language in general that characterizes this age (and which can certainly be traced to China) that the very name of Heian-Kyō should be *polysemous*. Read as such, the words mean the City of Peace and Tranquillity, but 'apart from having an auspicious ring (the latter part of the eighth century had witnessed a great deal of political strife and bloodshed), the name combined the first and last syllables of *Heijō*, Japan's earliest real city, and Ch'ang an, the great T'ang metropolis on which Heian, like the former capitals, was modelled.'[1] As we shall see, this polysemy will be an essential feature of Heian literature.

I have already pointed out that Japanese literature began to flourish about the time of the codification of the native syllabary, which soon became so dominant in the novels and poetry of the next few centuries, while the Chinese script continued to hold sway with comparable exclusiveness in documents of state, commerce, etc. This division of labour, so to speak, was related to the radical discrimination between the sexes in the upper classes,

---

[1] Morris, Ivan, *The World of the Shining Prince*, p. 18. This remarkable portrait of Heian society was the source of much of the material set forth here.

who considered it unseemly for women to read or write *kanji*. China and her language were still regarded as the repositories of all true learning (much as were Greece, Rome and their languages in the West), and of course too much learning was 'not good' for women. It was among the idle and often, in fact, highly educated women of the court that there arose the world's earliest corpus of novels, as we understand the term today. Foremost among these was Murasaki Shikibu's monumental *Tale of Genji* (*Genji Monogatari*). Despite this sexual segregation, male courtiers also employed the syllabary in the writing of poems, partly because many were in fact epistles addressed to women who, in theory at least, could not read *kanji*. Another reason was the fact that this poetry presumably derived from specifically oral tradition and was, as we shall see, associated with specifically oral practices. Still another reason was that, considering the amount of versification required by even the most trifling social occasion, the syllabary was much more convenient.

The composition, exchange, and quotation of poems was central to the daily life of the Heian aristocracy, and it is doubtful whether any other society in the world has ever attached such importance to the poetic versatility of its members. . . . Upper-class Heian life was punctuated with poetry from beginning to end, and no important event was complete without it. Birth was attended by an avalanche of congratulatory verse; poetry exchanges were a central part of the formal courting ceremonies; and, when death approached, the Heian gentleman would round out his existence with a parting poem.[2]

And, of course, poetry-writing was essential to the countless love-affairs which were among the chief occupations of that society: upon first glimpsing (or even simply hearing about) a prospective partner, a man would send her a poem, and she would reply with another. This preliminary exchange might continue for days or even weeks; if the gentleman's suit were ultimately successful, a meeting would be arranged at which the moment of consummation was preceded by graceful allusions to the themes and phraseology of the poetry that had led up to it, including perhaps oral improvisations of new poems. Next came the obligatory 'morning after poems,' and then for days, weeks or months messengers were kept busy scurrying back and forth between the two lovers, often at intervals of only a few hours, until at length the inevitable poems of parting were exchanged. And the beauty of the writing itself was as important as the text: it was quite customary for a man or a woman to fall in love with a person of

2. ibid., pp. 190–92.

whom he or she had glimpsed only a sample of his or her calligraphy. 'Handwriting, it was the general belief, revealed (or rather expressed) character, breeding, distinction, and other qualities more clearly than speech, and it ranked high among the fine arts.'[3] For it must be pointed out that this 'reading' of calligraphy had nothing in common with Western handwriting analysis; it was the purely aesthetic quality of the writing, its plastic rather than its personal or 'psychological' qualities which were being weighed thus, as *signs* of personal virtues: for good and evil in this society were equated with beauty and ugliness.

One significant feature of Heian poetry is that an overwhelming share of it was written in a single, strictly codified and remarkably brief form, the *tanka*: five periods consisting of five, seven, five, seven and seven syllables respectively. It is remarkable – and this is but one instance of that 'boundless' textuality with which we are concerned – that this alternation of five- and seven-syllable periods, already present in pre-Heian poetry, continued to determine the morphology of nearly all Japanese verse (in both its literary and theatrical forms), even after *tanka* had 'given way'[4] to *renga*, *renga* to *haikai* and *haikai* to the late Tokugawa lampoons called *senru*. And the same will be found to be true of the decisive characteristics of Heian literature as a whole, namely *polysemy* and *intertextuality*.

One of the earliest masterpieces of Japanese poetry, and which pre-dates the installation of the imperial capital at Heian-Kyō by nearly a century, already constitutes one of the most staggeringly sophisticated uses of polysemy to be found in the literature of any language. It is 'On Seeing the Body of a Man Lying Among the Stones on the Island of Samine in Sanuku Province' by the greatest master of the period, Kakinomoto Hitomaro (*c*. 680–700).[5]

---

3. Sansom, George, *A History of Japan to 1334* p. 186.

4. Given way only in the sense that it ceased to be the *dominant* verse form. *Tanka*, like *renga* and *haikai*, continue to be practised to this day by millions of Japanese.

5. The relatively rare (to the *tanka*) form of this poem is called *chōka* in this early period, *nagauta* when it became, in the seventeenth century, the foundation of the *kabuki* text.

| | |
|---|---|
| Tamamo yoshi | O the precious land of Sanuki |
| Sanuki no kuni wa | Resting where the seaweed glows like polished gems! |
| Kunikara ka | Perhaps for its precious nature |
| Miredo mo akanu | I never tire in my gazing on it, |
| Kamakura ka | Perhaps for its holy name |
| Kokoda tōtoki | It is the most divine of sights. |
| Ametsuchi | It will flourish and endure |
| Hitsuki to tomo ni | Together with the heavens and earth, |
| Tariyuka | With the shining sun and moon, |
| Kami no miomi to | For through successive ages it has come down |
| Tsugite kuru | That the landface is the face of a god. |
| | |
| Naka no minato yu | Having rushed our ship upon the breakers |
| Fune ukete | From the busy port of Naka |
| Wa ga kogikureba | We came rowing steadily till the wind |
| Toki tsu kaze | That rises with the tides |
| Kumoi ni fuku ni | Stormed down from the dwelling of the clouds – |
| Oki mireba | Looking back upon the open sea, |
| Toinami tachi | I saw waves gathering in their mounting surges, |
| He mireba | And looking off beyond the prow |
| Shiranami sawaku | I saw the white waves dashing on the surf. |
| | |
| Isanatori | In awe of the terrible sea, |
| Umi o kashikomi | Where whales are hunted down as prey, |
| Yuku fune no | We clutched the steering oar, |
| Kaji hikiorite | Straining the plunging ship upon its course; |
| Ochikochi no | And though here and there |
| Shima wa ōkedo | We saw the scattered island coasts |
| Nakuwashi | To dash upon for safety, |
| | |
| Samine no shima no | We sought haven on rugged Samine |
| Arisomo ni | The isle so beautiful in name. |
| Torite mireba | Erecting a little shelter we looked about, |
| Nami no to no | And then we saw you: |
| Shigeki hamabe o | Pillowed upon your shaking beach, |
| Shikitae no | Using those wave-beaten rocks |
| Makura ni nashite | As if the coast were spread out for your bedding: |
| Aradoko ni | On such a rugged place |
| Korofusu kimi ga | You have laid yourself to rest. |
| | |
| Ie shiraba | If I but knew your home |
| Yukite no tsugen | I would go tell them where you sleep; |
| Tsuma shiraba | If your wife but knew this home, |
| Ki mo towamashi o | She would come here searching for you, |
| Tamahoko no | But knowing nothing of the way – |
| Michi dani shirazu | The way straight as a warrior's spear – |
| Oboboshiku | How must she be waiting, |
| Machi ka kou ran | How anxiously longing for you, |
| Hashiki tsumara wa. | She the dear one you called wife. |

## GROUNDS, PREMISES

| | ENVOYS |
|---|---|
| Tsuma no araba | If your wife were here, |
| Tsumite tagemashi | She would be out gathering your food, |
| Sami no yama | She would pick the greens |
| No no e no uhagi | From the hillslopes of Samine – |
| Suginikerazu ya. | But is their season not now past? |
| Oki tsu nami | So you rest your head, |
| Kiyoru ariso o | Pillowed on the rocky spread-out bedding |
| Shikitae no | Of this rugged shore, |
| Makura to makite | While the furious, wind-driven surf |
| Naseru kimi ka mo. | Pounds ever in from off the sea.[6] |

In order to give some small idea of the *essentially* polysemous nature of this text, I shall quote two fragments of the extensive analysis given by Brower and Miner.

The most remarkable thing about this syntax is the way in which it plays upon certain inflectional endings of verbs and adjectives in an ambiguous fashion. In eleven instances there are constructions that may be taken as finite and so conclusive, but at the same time as attributives to what follows ... In short, what Hitomaro has really done is to present us with a poem that consists of a single sentence in which every successive syntactic element is governed by what precedes, all the way back to the beginning of the poem. More than this, the last word and the particle *tsumara wa* (topic: 'as for [your] wife', with the suggestion in the endearment plural *ra* of family, homeland, and all associated with her), are not only governed by everything that precedes but also are the beginning of the 'main' sentence of the poem, a sentence that stops with no more than this topic. Such syntax is unimaginable in English, but something of its effect can be gained by beginning with the last word of the Japanese and working back in translation, without a break, to the initial line of the poem. ... Primarily what interests [Hitomaro] is not so much the actors as the actions, not so much the issue of responsibility as the integrated nature of the process of a complex experience. Consequently, there are verbs in abundance and noun images to create the scene vividly. And the syntax is so organized that in spite of the numerous semi-stops, the stops are transformed into attributives for the noun-clauses that follow. The skill involved is prodigious, as one can see from the transition between the first and second section. The first section ends with the verbs *tsugite kuru* forming an idiom something like 'transmitted'. The effect is to say that it has been transmitted that the land of Sanuki is divine. But *kuru* is also used separately, apart from the idiom and attributively, for the next clause. Here *kuru* achieves more of its usual sense as an active verb in a clause something like 'coming to the harbor of Naka', as if one could take in English the '-mit' from 'transmit' and use it in its root Latin sense of 'send' as part of the relative clause. There are, as we have

---

6. Brower, Robert H. and Miner, Earl, *Japanese Court Poetry*, pp. 97–8. If I have quoted this beautiful poem in full, it is only partly as an illustration of the sophisticated constructions of ancient Japanese poetry. For here also is one of the earliest recorded manifestations of an *approach to narrative* which is a constant of Japanese literature and which was to reach its final and by no means least significant *avatar* in the cinema of the 1930s, which also 'revived' some of the structural strategies of that early poetry.

46

said, eleven such double-functioning verbs and adjectives in the poem, and the result is that by such hypotaxis, Hitomaro manages to integrate all the elements of the poem into one continuous poetic and linguistic process, into one experience.[7]

This procedure became standard practice throughout Heian poetry under the generic name of *kakekotoba*, or pivot-word, 'a rhetorical scheme of word-play in which a series of sounds is so employed as to mean two or more things at once by different parsings. For example, *nagame* used to mean reverie (*nagame*) and long rains (*naga ame*).'[8] Like the alternation of five- and seven-syllable periods, it has remained a constant component of Japanese verse-forms. This feature of Japanese poetry shows the extent to which the 'Japanese mind' rejects linearity and the 'transparency of the signifier' which has dominated both Western thought and art since the eighteenth century. The language process is constantly at work on the very surface of these poems.

In the West it was in the eighteenth century, which witnessed the rise of the bourgeoisie and the reassertion of logocentrism and the emergence of an ideology of representation suited to the needs of the bourgeoisie, that the masking of the process of the production of meaning became as important, on its own level, as that of the process of production of *goods*. This ideology continues to dominate our notions of representation to this very day. As we shall see in the next chapter, it is this ideology of the transparency of the sign which dominated the emergence of the Western film from its 'primitive' stage. Conversely, no Japanese artistic practice, from the earliest known poetry under discussion up through the theatre and literature of the Edo (i.e. the Tokugawa) period, ever subscribed to such a notion. This observation may be regarded as central to my thesis. The poem by Hitomaro reproduced above is 'about language', it is about *the process by which we make meaning* and in the original Japanese can scarcely be called representational at all, so compressed is the syntax. It is this inscription of the signifying process in the 'text' which is such an essential characteristic of the traditional Japanese arts and which was to influence the development of Japanese cinema in this century.

Another important feature of Heian poetry for the purposes of this study is that to which we have already referred as *intertextuality*, a practice which, in various ways, totally contests the myth of the closed text and the concomitant notion of originality.

This concept of intertextuality has broad implications for, as we shall see, it ultimately includes the 'text' of the

7. ibid., pp. 143–6.

8. ibid., p. 507.

society in which it was operative. The practice of relating one poem to another by allusive variation (*honkadori*)[9] quite naturally led to the composition of *poetic sequences*, first in connection with the contests (*utaawase*) in which poems were composed upon common themes in order to establish grounds for comparative judgement, and in the imperial anthologies, of which twenty-one were composed between 905 and 1433. These anthologies are unique in world literature, for they are not merely collections of what the compiler considered to be the 'best verse of the reign'. The poems are arranged (and in many instances, one supposes, *chosen*) to fit into successive and/or *overlapping* patterns of various sorts. The supreme sophistication reached by this technique is generally regarded to be found in the *Shinkokinshū*, commissioned by the ex-emperor Go-Toba in 1201.

A close reading of the *Shinkokinshū* would give us almost innumerable examples to illustrate the techniques. A sequence of travel poems (x:896–907) shows that the arrangement for progression alone is based in part on what might be called a plot (since there is a concatenation of situations), which takes us on a voyage from a forest, to the coast, to the sea, to China, back to Japan and so on and on. But, incredible as it seems, this book is at the same time also ordered as a kind of history of Japanese poetry. It opens with poems from the early literary period and moves down to the poets of Go-Toba's own time. Or, to take another example, the first four poems on love in Book XI (990–993) show the techniques of associational development: the unity of the age of the poets who wrote the poems, in the distant past; a succession from mountains to hills to uplands to plains; an even subtler sequence of images from snow to waterfalls to grain; and all of these contained within a progression of geographical distance and further unified by the point of view of the speaker of the poems.[10]

The organization of these anthologies, which is both intertextual and polysemous, manifests the fundamental need for refined patterning in all human activity – from religious sculpture and architecture to the arrangement of flowers and food – which has informed Japanese culture for centuries. This impulse may be said to have received its definitive impetus in the mid-Heian period under the Fujiwara regents.

The anthologies were marked by another feature which is also of interest to us here: with increasing frequency, the poems were prefaced[11] by explanatory headnotes (*kotobagaki*),[12] which generally amounted to a few lines about the situation in which the poem was composed. It is said that this practice was often due to certain 'obscurities' in the text, deriving from the private nature of certain

---

9. '... an echoing of an older poem or poems, not just to borrow material or phrasing, but to raise the atmosphere – something of the situation, the tone, the meaning – of the original.' Brower and Miner, op. cit., p. 14.

10. ibid., p. 324.

11. They were consequently *separated* from each other, which appears to be one of the reasons why the very existence of these sequences was not re-discovered until this century.

12. Etymologically: 'framed words'.

allusions. From our viewpoint, however, it primarily embodied the fact that poetry was an activity within a *context*, either private or public. This awareness is in sharp contrast with traditional Western attitudes which tend to close off the text, not only from other texts but, above all, from the social 'text' in which it is nonetheless inevitably inscribed. This *presence of the context* is a permanent feature of the Japanese *difference*, in both Heian literature and modern film practice.

After the first anthologies, a new literary form, clearly derived from this poem-headnote relationship, began to emerge: these were collections of 'poem-tales' (*uta-monogatari*) each illustrating or recounting the production of one or several poems. The most famous example of this transitional but important form was the *Tales of Ise*, (*Ise Monogatari*) ascribed to the poet Ariwara Harihira (825–80) and purportedly describing his life and loves. The following episode is representative.

Once a man and a woman lived in a remote district. The man, saying that he had to go in order to serve in the Palace and regretting to part from his wife, went away. Thereafter, three years elapsed and he did not come back, so that his wife had grown tired of waiting, but, just when she had promised to another man who had made advances to her in a very kind way: 'Let us meet to-night', that man came back. He knocked on the door, calling: 'Please open this door,' but without opening it, she just composed a poem and had it brought to him:
  Tired of waiting
  Three of these years
  Which always renew themselves
  I am to try a new pillow
  This very night.
As she had just sent word to him, the man returned the following poem:
  Just like I have been to you
  Through the years
  As different as different kinds of bows
  You should be affectionate to him
When he was about to go after these words, the woman recited:
  No matter whether others draw my sleeves or not
  – Minding of the drawing of a bow of Catalpa wood
  Always
  Has my heart
  Been drawn to you . . .
But the man had gone back to the capital. Although the woman, feeling very sad, started after him and pursued him, she could not overtake him, and at last she had fallen down at a place where there was a spring. On a rock which was there she wrote with the

blood of a finger the following poem:
> Unable to hold back
> The man who was departing
> Without answering my love,
> Now my body
> Seems to have faded away to nothing.

Having written these lines, she passed away.[13]

Here the notion of narrative is consubstantial with a presentation of the process of literary production. The text as a whole is also a reductive dramatized *model* of the life-pattern of the Heian court in so far as it hinged upon textual practice and sexual relations.

The next stage in this amazingly integrated development was the fictional tale (*tsukiri monogatari*), of which the six-volume *Genji Monogatari* is the most famous example, although the term does also designate very brief texts, often little longer than that quoted from the *Ise Monogatari*. Again, in these tales and in the diaries which no courtier of the day failed to keep, poetry is constantly present *in its social function*; present, as well, are all the modes of inter-textuality and of polysemy with which we are already familiar.

One example, which combines the two, is taken from an anonymous text, *Ochikubo Monogatari*, a title which is sometimes rendered inadequately into English as *The Tale of the Room Below*. A court official, the Shōshō, is secretly courting the Lady Ochikubo, who is subject to constant persecution by the Kita no Kata, the wife of another court official, in whose house the Lady lives in Cinderella-like humiliation and exploitation.

> Hardly knowing what she was doing, the Lady began to pleat the folds of the *hakama* but the Shōshō caught hold of her skirt and urged her to go back to bed. Smiling, she went back to bed, for there was nothing else to do.

> 'How hateful she is! [referring to the Kita no Kata]. Do not do any more sewing. Let her become more angry still. What horrible language she uses towards you! Has she been as abusive as this all these years? How have you been able to endure it?' he exclaimed. 'I am a flower of the wild-pear-tree,' the Lady quoted in answer.[14]

The translators, who are constantly obliged to explain allusions, indicate, somewhat enigmatically, that this is a quotation from the following poem:

> Although in this house
> I am able to find nought
> But care and sorrow;

---

13. Vos, Frits, *A Study of the Ise-Monogatari*, p. 191.

14. Whitehouse, Wilfrid, and Yanagisawa Eizo (trans), *Ochikubo Monogatari*, p. 61.

> Yet it seems that nowhere else
> Can I find a hiding place.

Though the aptness of the poem is clear, the translation contains no mention of 'a wild pear tree.' As the translators explain, 'the reference to the "pear-flower" disappears when the *meaning* of the poem is considered.'[15] Or rather, *one* of its meanings, since clearly we are dealing with an oblique instance of polysemy.

In connection with *Ochikubo Monogatari*, it is interesting to point out that in the novels of that period, almost none of the characters are ever designated by their names but rather by their titles or other terms which situate them in their social functions. '*Kita no Kata*' and '*Shōshō*' are official court titles, while 'Ochikubo no kimi' (translated as Lady Ochikubo) means the 'Lady of the Lower Room', a mock-title with a slightly pejorative nuance to 'lady'. This is a highly significant practice, to be compared with the long-standing Japanese custom (maintained even today among professional practitioners of the traditional arts) of changing a person's name according to his or her social situation. The Shōguns of the Kamakura period (1185–1333), for example, were often called by as many as four names during their lifetimes: as a child, then perhaps as Shōgun-to-be, as Shōgun proper and then, in the event that they retired before death or were removed from office by the regent, as monk, priest or whatever. This is a significant instance of the Japanese attitude towards the notion of the person or *subject*: in the West, the *name* is co-extensive with the *self*, it is the mark of the *soul*. For a man to change his name is a serious sacrifice of identity, to be consented to only for very serious reasons (to escape police detection or racist persecution, for example) while for a woman that 'sacrifice' has always been the symbol of her subordination to man, in other words her voluntary abandonment of a vital part of her identity. In Japanese history, there was no such attitude; a name, it was felt, was more properly attached to a function than to a physical person, and when the function changed, it was normal that the name should change too.

It must not be imagined that the advent of a more 'realistic' form of literature, the *tsukuri monogatari*, meant a slackening of the 'structural vigilance' which characterized the other forms of the period. Ivan Morris points out several recurring formal devices worthy of Flaubert which give the huge text of *Genji* a structural coherence which did not appear in the Western novel until the late nineteenth century. Repetitions of situational patterns, 'sustained imagery', (the repetition of a single central image in both the

15. My italics.

narrative passages and the frequent poems), are two of the most representative, and most clearly related to *the work of the signifier* in poems and anthologies.[16]

Any account of the intertextuality typical of Heian literature must include its ties to nearly all Japanese literature for the seven centuries that followed the political and cultural decline of the imperial capital. As the *tanka* began to lose its vitality in the thirteenth and fourteenth centuries, there arose a new form, linked verse (*renga*). This was an obvious derivation from the poetry contests and anthologies: several poets would gather for the purpose of composing a collective poem according to very strict rules.[17] Here we are dealing with perhaps the most radical effacing of the 'creator' to be found in any post-primitive practice, for indeed the avowed aim of these poets, as expounded by Yoshimoto Nijō (1320–88) and as paraphrased by the contemporary Japanese scholar Ueda Makoto, was the effacing of the creator-subject and the *identification of the processes of reading and writing*.

The poet and the reader are nowhere more closely related than in linked verse, because here the reader of one stanza may become the poet of the stanza immediately following. To compose a stanza for linked verse the poet must first try to become a perfect reader of all the stanzas preceding his; he has to put himself in the positions of all his fellow poets sitting around him. One obvious consequence of this is a demand for the poet to suppress his individuality: the poet must work within the framework set by other poets as well as by the contemporary rules of poetic composition. In this respect, the theory of linked verse stands directly opposite from that of lyric poetry; instead of speaking out his personal emotion, the poet must dissolve it for the sake of the team of which he is a member.[18]

This demonstration of the profound equivalence of reading and writing speaks directly to modern artistic practice and theory. Eisenstein's materialist conception of film-making, as described in the following statement, can be seen as related to this attitude: 'It draws the spectator into a creative act in which his own personality is not dominated by that of the author, but fully develops in harmony with the author's conception, just as the personality of a great actor fuses with that of a great playwright in the process of creating a classical image on the stage.'[19] We will further consider this attitude at a later time.

In connection with *renga* it is also worth noting here that besides its multiple affiliations with Heian literary techniques, it is intimately related to a three-fold module which gives the *nō* theatre its characteristic form. Traditionally a *nō* performance lasts a full day and involves a complete set

16. See Morris, op. cit., pp. 277ff.

17. Some of these bear remarkable similarities to the privative rules governing orthodox serial music, in particular the prohibition to use certain words more than once or certain others more than twice.

18. Ueda Makoto, *Literary and Art Theories in Japan*, p. 38.

19. Eisenstein, Sergei, *Notes of a Film-Director*, p. 78.

of plays. Each play, each section of the play and each sequence of plays is divided into three sections called *jō* (introduction, 'quiet in mood and tempo'), *ha* (central section, 'with a lighter mood and leisurely changes of pace') and *kyū* (finale, 'with heightened rhythm and forceful impact').[20] This module, like so many others to be found in the 'text' of Japan, is remarkably ubiquitous, for not only does it condition the progression of *renga*, of certain forms of classical music and of the *nō*, but it was also observed in a non-competitive form of football! And of course the *nō* play itself, despite its 'humble' origins in the early medieval popular theatre known as *sarugaku*,[21] is also directly related to the textual practices of Heian court poetry (e.g. the five/seven pattern, the allusive variation, the pivot word) and to a fund of traditional lore on which all Japanese narrative arts (including the cinema) draw so extensively.

The 'novels' of Ihara Saikaku (1642–93) (and particularly *The Japanese Family Storehouse*) provide a further extension of the Heian module. They consist of apparently aimless, 'uncentred' short-stories, whose sections are ordered according to techniques derived from a later development of linked verse (which also produced the *haikai*, of which Saikaku was a master). Saikaku's work will enter into the examination of narrative structures employed in certain films of the 1930s.

With this admittedly skeletal account, I hope to have set forth four basic contentions which are closely related and which will recur in one form or another throughout this study. Firstly, tradition inclines the Japanese to read any given text (and this may also be a film, as we shall see) in relation to a body of texts. Secondly, the sacrosanct value placed on originality, the taboo placed on 'borrowing', on 'copying' in the West are as utterly foreign to Japan as are Western 'individualism' and the primacy of the person or subject. Thirdly, the linear approach to representation is not a privileged one. Finally, the precedence given 'content' over 'form', or rather the hypostasis of meaning to the detriment of its *production*, is a specifically Western attitude. It has informed all Western methods of analysis, explanation, reading or interpretation; it has also been imported into Japan to fill an undeniable theoretical and instrumental void. It has, however, no place in any artistic or other practice that can be identified as specifically Japanese.

This preliminary exposition is confined to Heian literature and its descent. Other, more recent artistic practices have made distinct and specific contributions which have informed, directly or indirectly, film-making in Japan.

20. Ueda Makoto, op. cit., p. 45.

21. Literally 'monkey music', possibly referring to the acrobatic and comic mimicry of *sarugaku* actors.

GROUNDS, PREMISES

Heian writing is linked with these other practices (scroll painting and 'picture-poems' are especially striking instances). Many of these – especially in painting, theatre, architecture and garden design – will be referred to in connection with the films of specific periods or directors. The 'boundless text' *generated* by Heian society contains, explicitly or implicitly, all the basic theoretical challenges that Japan offers Western thought and practice. As such, it constitutes a proper introduction to the problems implicit in any coherent study of Japanese cinema. Although many of the modern theoretical concepts touched upon here have not yet been sufficiently delineated, especially for readers unfamiliar with their Western European context, it is my hope that through repeated illustration in the pages to follow, remaining obscurities may be progressively clarified.

# Part 2  A Frozen Stream?

# 4. A Machine Appears

Motion picture production began in Japan in 1898, just thirty-one years after the Meiji Restoration. The urban population had been swept by a mass emotional response to the ruling oligarchy's proclaimed recognition that the country's future independence was contingent upon her achieving the status of an industrial power on a footing with the great nations of the West, and to their concomitant policies of accelerated assimilation of Western techniques. This had taken the form of a craze for Westernalia which led even reflective men to advocate such radical abandonments of national identity as the wholesale adoption of the English language in lieu of the native tongue and script, or the promotion, on a nationwide scale, of mixed marriages between Japanese men and Western women to 'fortify the race'. The peak of this craze had already begun to pass, especially after Japan's easy victory over China in the war of 1894–5, which greatly strengthened the position of the advocates of the 'preservation of the national heritage'. The very real enthusiasm which nonetheless greeted this latest novelty from overseas may still be considered as part of that first great élan towards things Western which did not completely subside until the beginning of the second war with China early in the 1930s. At the same time, as I hope to show, the cinematograph struck a number of fundamental chords in what is termed the Japanese sensibility.

Japanese film-production developed so swiftly that by 1909 four companies were in operation and, between 1909 and 1911, Makino Shozo, 'the first man to deserve the name of director in the Western sense of the word',[1] together with his phenomenally popular star, Onoue Matsunosuke, turned out no less than 168 films (mostly one-reelers); their annual average for the next decade was nearly one hundred, with the length of the films gradually increasing as well. With respect to quantity and length, then, Japan kept pace with the West; when one remembers that Louis Feuillade, a very prolific French

1. Richie, Donald, and Anderson, Joseph L., *The Japanese Film*, p. 31. Unless otherwise stated, all factual information on early Japanese cinema is drawn from that source.

director of the same period, made 'only' some 700 films between 1906 and 1923, it becomes fairly probable that eventual comparisons between early Western and Japanese cinema are grounded in comparable bodies of film production. We are not dealing with an industry of marginal status such as that of all other non-Western cinemas during what I shall refer to as the Primitive (1894–1908) and Formative (1909–19) periods of Western film history. Japanese film-making strove, and in some respects successfully, to 'stay abreast' of the West. This was a goal which the country had set herself in all fields of industry, but here, for the first time, it was immediately feasible, since her entry into the field coincided almost exactly with the birth of cinema in the West.

In 1909, the Nippon Katsudo Shashin (Japan Cinematograph Company) was formed by the merger of the four production companies which had developed since the turn of the century. In this they were taking their cue from the Pathé-Biograph-Edison . . . cartel in the West, but also from the general pattern of concentration established from the very outset by the architects of Japanese capitalism. By 1912, this Japanese trust was operating four studios and seventy permanent theatres throughout the country. The majority of film-showings, however, were still being organized in non-permanent settings, as they were in the West.

A programme of films by Louis Lumière, including the pioneer *Entrée d'un train en gare de La Ciotat* (1895), constituted the first public film-showing in Japan in 1897 (though the Edison Kinetoscope had been imported three years before). More important for our purposes, perhaps, is the fact that these screenings, and those of Edison's Vitascope a few days later, constituted the first presentation in Japan of a Western 'performing art' *in its original form*, just as the West had produced it and as Western audiences, at that very moment, were viewing it.

The Meiji period had witnessed an influx (or rather a burgeoning) of 'Western styles' in theatre, the novel and painting. The visual arts of the West were becoming directly available, in reproduction, to those Japanese who were in a position either to appreciate them as connoisseurs or to draw upon them as practising artists. The earliest 'Westernization' of the novel in Japan was based on a far more limited familiarity with Western practices. Understandably, only a few texts were selected for translation according to criteria determined by the peculiar needs of Japanese society in a period of vertiginous change. And these texts were translated into a language so radically different from those of the West that the

Japanese versions are hardly translations at all, but rather very free adaptations.² The late 1880s, however, brought a completely new approach to written prose, more suited in particular to Western literature in that it involved the introduction into the written language of the constructions and vocabulary of spoken Japanese. This was certainly one of the most far-reaching effects of this period of Western influence, and it is significant of the impact of Western modes of representation on those of Japan.

A new form of theatre, known as *shimpa*, arose after 1888; it soon came to rival, and briefly to eclipse, the popularity of *kabuki*. *Shimpa* purported to be a 'Western' form, which no doubt explains its having played a direct role in the constitution of the repertory and the modes of representation in early Japanese cinema. However, it is important to understand that it was developed mostly by non-professionals who had practically no first-hand knowledge of the Western theatre. *Shimpa* was a fantasy creation, comparable in many ways to Kafka's portrait of *Amerika*; understandably, it bore little if any resemblance to its Western model.

These men conceived the Western drama to be couched in colloquial language, as opposed to the stylized language of the *kabuki* plays, to be concerned largely with the contemporary scene, and to be acted not in the strictly designed movement of the *kabuki* but with an imitation of the movement of life. During the nineties, *shimpa* enjoyed such a wide vogue that even the foremost *kabuki* actors of the day felt impelled to play *shimpa* roles, and Morita Kanya, of an old *kabuki* family, established a *shimpa* theatre. With this, the *kabuki* began to influence the amateur *shimpa* performers, and their acting techniques came more and more to resemble those of *kabuki*. Soon *shimpa* showed little difference, either in mode of production or in subject matter, from the plays of the traditional *kabuki* performance. The roles of women in these 'realistic' *shimpa* pieces were played on the same stage during the same play by both men and women.³

One of the typical and most picturesque originators of *shimpa* was Kawakami Otojirō, former policeman turned 'revolutionary', who came to the theatre through comic story-telling (*rakugo*). He began in 1888 to produce and act in the new genre but it was not until 1899 that he went abroad to glean some first-hand knowledge of the Western theatre.

Upon his return, he staged a production of *Hamlet* in which he played the leading role. The legend exists that in one scene of

A MACHINE APPEARS

2. *See* Sansom, George, *The Western World and Japan*, pp. 403-4; and Ernst, Earle, op. cit., p. 251. As for the works selected for translation, these were generally either chosen for their compatibility with the traditional forms of Japanese literature (*The Bride of Lammermoor, Les Aventures de Télémaque*) or for what was conceived as their usefulness in understanding the problems of the day, as raised by the accelerated process of 'Westernization' (the non-fiction best-seller of the period was *Self-Help* by one Samuel Smiles, a primer for coping with 'modernity') while the literary successes included the novels of Jules Verne, Michel Robida's fancifully illustrated vision of *Le Vingtième siècle*, and for reasons no doubt related to the success of both *Self-Help* and *Les Aventures de Télémaque*, two successive translations of *Robinson Crusoe*.

3. Ernst, Earle, op. cit., p. 249.

the play, Kawakami, as Hamlet, made his entrance to the stage riding a bicycle. Legend or fact, the story embodies a good deal of truth about Japanese conceptions of Western drama at that time.... Hamlet on a bicycle was not incongruous to the audience of that period, for both Hamlet and the bicycle were new and foreign and therefore logically belonged together.... In short, *shimpa* was based primarily upon what men of such dubious knowledge as Kawakami conceived Western drama to be, expressed throughout in terms of Japanese life and attitudes.[4]

It is a very particular type of transformation which produces Hamlet on a bicycle, a process typical of Japan's habitual reading of Western artefacts and techniques: one may question the judgement that the 'dubious knowledge' of men such as Kawakami was responsible for this failure to reproduce the Western modes of theatrical representation (a failure which, as Ernst points out and as today's visitor to Japan may easily observe, remains, in many respects, a reality). This matter might be clarified by comparison with the evolution of the cinema in Japan since, as we have seen, for the first time the Western model was present in its authentic, original form for *all* to see, spectators ('readers') and film-makers ('translators') alike.

Before analysing the gradual but ineluctable and far-reaching divergence between the dominant practices in Western and Japanese film industries, we must open another parenthesis, a rather lengthy one, in order to establish the salient features of the 'evolution of film language' in the West during the period 1894–1919. Fundamental differences between the cinemas of Japan and the West are, by the latter date, clearly visible, albeit in embryonic form. However, unless we understand, if only in broad outline, the process by which nineteenth-century ideologies of representation came to determine the representational modes of Western film, we shall not understand the origins and development of these differences.

4. ibid, pp. 250–1.

# 5. A Parenthesis on Film History

The earliest motion picture ventures of Edison and his associates in the United States and of the Lumière brothers in France objectively introduced the antithetical directions in which Western and Japanese films were to move, predominantly, during the next fifty years.[1] They also prefigured the basic conflicts which were ultimately to develop in the cinema of both Japan and the West, considered separately.

The history of cinema has generally been interpreted as a development of the alternatives proposed by the pioneer work of Lumière and Méliès. These two alternatives are thought to form the basis for the distinction between documentary and fiction film. I regard the work of Méliès and Lumière, however, as two aspects of the same phenomenon. Conversely, the contradiction between the films shot by the Lumières and their cameramen, and some of those produced for the Edison company during the first few years by Dickson and Raff and Gammon is I believe absolutely fundamental.

The first relatively successful attempt to develop the technology of *talking motion pictures* came out of the Edison laboratory. It took the form of the kinetophonograph of 1895. It was 'total reproduction of life' that interested Edison.[2] It was no accident that the first close-ups came out of that black-walled structure in Edison's garden. And his talking pictures were in advance by some twenty-five years.

Edison sought the reproduction of perceptual reality as a whole, of 'life'. The silent reproduction of perceptual movement seems to have interested him rather little. The orientation of his research perfectly reflects an essential aspiration of the bourgeoisie with regard to representation. Auguste and Louis Lumière, on the other hand, were still the direct heirs of the pioneers Muybridge and Marey, whose work was motivated by an essentially scientific aspiration to analyse movement. This in part explains why, in their earliest period, they approached

1. Friese-Greene in England and a host of others are not discussed here. Considering, however, the importance which the films of France and the United States were to assume during the Primitive and Formative periods, it seems reasonable to pay special attention to the implications of the implicit attitudes of these two pioneer figures.

2. I am fully aware that Edison's personal responsibility for the film work that took place under his name has been shown to be slight indeed. What is at stake here, however, is not a personality at all but the characteristic attitude of a class, incidentally – and contradictorily – reflected in this or that individual, manifest attitude, but above all *inscribed in the films themselves*.

A FROZEN STREAM?

their invention as though it were a scientific toy – which was to some extent how the cinema was viewed on the fairgrounds of Europe for over a decade to come. Edison, on the other hand, from the very start, clearly saw his Kinetophonograph as a fulfilment of 'the age-old dream of man', the perfectly illusionistic reproduction of the human likeness *and voice*, i.e. the bodily envelope *and its soul*.[3] This apparatus, with the viewer's isolation (via headphones and eye-piece) and his submersion thereby in diegetic space-time, is an astounding prefiguration of the achieved illusionist rapture of the 1930s. Edison's personal conviction that the ultimate cinematic goal was the filming of opera, is a significant extension of the *Gesamtkunstwerk* ideology.

The neologisms coined by Edison (Vitascope) and the Lumière brothers (Cinématographe) are also emblematic of their antithetical positions: a 'vision of life' as opposed to 'an inscription of movement'. Nothing better illustrates, however, the objective ideological difference between their earliest ventures than the actual conditions in which they were carried out: Edison and Dickson barricading themselves in their black-walled, sound-proofed Black Maria, which prefigures the sound-stage of the 1930s and after; the Lumières setting up their camera in front of their own factory gates a few minutes before the end of the working day. It is not simply because they were filming 'things as they are' that the Lumières' method implied a world-view crucially opposed to that inscribed in the films of Dickson, Raff and Gammon *et al*. After all, the bar and barber-shop scenes reconstituted against the black background of Edison's tank are in their way strongly 'realistic'. The 'greenhouse' constructed by Méliès in Montreuil, on the other hand, was also designed to exclude the world of contingency (as was Edison's 'studio'), but it was in order to construct a world as radically and avowedly artificial as possible; his aim was not to exclude elements which might impinge on the 'vision of life', but simply to prevent any intrusion on a perfectly ordered world of artifice. In short, the opposition studio/location is not in itself fundamental.

It is true that the Lumière brothers, in their earliest period, regarded the motion-picture camera/projector/printer which they had designed as particularly well-suited to recording images of the real (and especially the distant) world. For some months they treated their invention as a scientific development, a valuable instrument for research. It clearly seemed most natural for them at that time to set up their apparatus in some well-chosen place and then 'leave it on its own', so to speak. In that sense, each of those early 'documentary shootings' – and there were several

3. The development of the work of Demenÿ, Marey's assistant, who began by prolonging his master's analysis of movement, is emblematic of the contradictory forces at work in this period, for he later became the staunch promoter of the *talking portrait*, destined in his mind to supplant the photographic portrait in both family and public archive. The drive for a greater 'totalization' of the signs of reality was very strong during the first ten years, as witness Gaumont's steadfast attempts to impose synch sound and the English experiments in colour cinematography. The various efforts to create a 'total', *enclosing* cinema, to produce the moving image as *environment* were especially significant of those contradictions: totally non-linear in effect (spectators could see no more than one portion at a time of the panorama surrounding them, and were free to look wherever they pleased), these were nonetheless naïve attempts to achieve what Griffith and others ultimately achieved through editing.

hundred of the sort – may be likened to a scientific experiment, in which the organisms or substances under study are allowed to interact with complete freedom within the specific confines of set conditions. Of course, the Lumières were not engaged in any actual programme of research, except insofar as they developed details of their technology and filming techniques as they went along. They, and the cameramen who followed their 'reporting' techniques, were first demonstrating their 'toy', and later exploiting an *attraction* (far more profitably than Edison did for a while). The Lumières as individuals were not, in any sense, above or outside the ideology of their class (Georges Sadoul has shown how strong was the class *content* of their first films).[4] Yet one may postulate that their socially and historically determined 'scientific reflexes' neutralized for a time certain aspects of that ideology, so that they inaugurated 'spontaneously' the representational model which dominated the budding industry for the next ten or fifteen years.

At this point, it is enlightening to observe the extent to which the work of the Lumières and others who best characterize the Primitive mode of representation, resembles some of the most advanced of contemporary film-making, that which is most radically and explicitly in conflict with the cinema typified by Hollywood and prefigured in part in the Black Maria.

For example, Warhol's famous quip 'I want to be a machine' objectively echoes the Lumières' attitude towards the process of recording movement on film, just as their earliest practice is, in miniature, that of Warhol's pioneering period.

When Peter Kubelka, Kurt Kren and others arrange to show two or more times the self-same images, their practice recalls that of the Lumières' (and also Edison's) projectionists screening several times over those first reels of film to the same unflaggingly attentive audiences, whose 'naïve eye' told them that they did not 'see everything the first time', that the second time around the film would still be new, who did not have a 'linear response' to the film experience, did not as yet demand (or had not yet been trained to expect) a chain of signifiers on the Saussurian model, in which each new link would necessarily devour the previous one.

Finally, the Lumières' spatially *non-centred* street scenes elicit a free-floating *scan* as opposed to the increasingly ordered and guided gaze that Griffith and others were to introduce. Their work was temporally non-centred as well, devoid as it so often was of beginning or end. Here, the modernist ramifications are evident.

While D. W. Griffith certainly played a crucial role in the

A PARENTHESIS ON FILM HISTORY

4. *Histoire générale du Cinéma*, Vol. 1, p. 284.

A FROZEN STREAM?

5. The term *codes*, insofar as it implies the existence of a totalizing semiological system at work, will henceforth be used with inverted commas implied throughout. For although it is my firm conviction that such a system – or set of systems – has certainly been at work in Western cinema at least since Griffith and his contemporaries undertook what was, at least in part, a codification in the strictest sense, the actual nature of these codes, the hierarchical relations that organize them, the differing degrees of permanence that distinguish them, the threshold beyond which they give way to a *mode of representation* irreducible to the language model, in short the analysis of these codes and their genesis has not, despite the pioneering prospecting of Christian Metz and others, been formulated to my satisfaction. Jorge Dana and myself are at present preparing a book on this matter. In the meantime, I continue to regard the 'codes' as a convenient bit of shorthand.

6. Repeated screenings of the same film or group of films at a single sitting as already noted, but also spectators seated on both sides of a translucent screen, films run backwards for comic or 'magical' effect, mixtures of live and screen performance, etc.

7. At one point in the subsequent archival history of *The Life of an American Fireman* (exactly when and under what circumstances, I have not yet been able to ascertain, but this version has been distributed by the Museum of Modern Art) these two shots were divided up and intercut so as to 'reconstitute' temporal linearity (i.e. 'continuity').

systematization of the rules of 'illusionist' editing, to which his name remains understandably attached, he was preceded by others, in particular the English pioneers (Smith, Williamson, Hepworth, *et al*.) and in a sense by the ambivalent Porter. He was, moreover, quickly outdistanced by Ince, De Mille and Barker. The Janus-like figure of William S. Porter is especially illuminating since although he is in every essential respect a Primitive director, he is also one of the 'inventors' of many of the modes of shot-change, including the reverse field, cross-cutting and ellipsis, which were to constitute the basis of the 'Hollywood codes.'[5] His work very explicitly embodies the 'Lumière-Edison contradiction' which is at the heart of the dialectical development of film during the first twenty-five years.

For example, Porter introduced a medium close-up into *The Great Train Robbery* (1903) in a pioneer attempt to alleviate the 'impersonality' of those long shots in which the characters never occupy full screen height and in which the outlaws are distinguishable from the posse only in so far as they wear the traditional bandana over their faces. However, he had this shot delivered to theatres in a separate roll, so that the now celebrated image of a cowboy shooting into the camera (and what better way to acknowledge the implications of the spectators' forced involvement in the screen image) *could be spliced on to either the beginning or the end of the film proper*, a practice related both to the 'open screening' practices of Primitive cinema[6] and to such modern experiments in the 'film-mobile' as *Chelsea Girls*. Porter also introduced, in the final sequence of *The Life of an American Fireman* (1902), the 180° reverse-angle set-up on a grand scale. His camera filmed a fireman saving a mother and her child from the second-storey bedroom of a flaming house, first from the street and then from inside a studio reconstruction of the room. Fearing, no doubt, that his audience would be confused if the shots were inter-cut in the manner that was to become common some years later, he then proceeded to juxtapose the two complete versions of the action, which was thus seen to *unfold twice on the screen*, in complete contradiction with the linear concept of narrative time which otherwise prevails throughout the film, as it had throughout eighteenth- and nineteenth-century drama and literature and would continue to do in American and most European cinema for decades to come.[7]

The gravest 'deficiency' of the films made between the time of the Lumières' first productions and those of Griffith, judged by the criteria derived from the nineteenth-century novel and drama, was the lack of individualization of character, the absence of the *persona*. The 'people' on the screen were mere silhouettes; not only did they lack the voices and the colour of the theatre to give them individualized presence and 'human' three-dimensionality, but the face, the only visual sign that could both distinguish between them severally and provide some insight into the 'interior' self, into the *soul*, was to all intents and purposes absent from the screen, since characters were generally so 'far' and so 'small'.

The reasons for this were the same that prevented Porter, in his historical experiment, from actually incorporating his medium close-up into the 'continuity' of his film, and impelled him to let it wander about the perimeter, so to speak. For it was still tacitly assumed, and perhaps actually experienced, by all those who made film, that any violation, not only of the single, frontal theatrical view-point, but of theatrical distance, would lead to the breakdown of the illusion of reality achieved in the single-shot 'full-frame' scene, inadequate though that illusion may have been. The audience was judged unable to relate, for example, subsequently projected details of a given *tableau* to the total space defined by an earlier glimpse of that *tableau* as a whole. Whether or not this conviction was based on actual experience is irrelevant to this discussion. The first decade of European and American film-making shows that this was the basic assumption, just as the film-making of the following ten years showed how 'correct' it had been; for it took at least that long to establish the 'rules' of match-cutting which were ultimately to overcome completely the sense of hiatus, of disorientation which did at times result from the first attempts by Griffith and others to juxtapose several successive 'prosceniums'.[8] Contiguity matching was introduced through the use of exits and entrances with matching directions from shot to shot. As this procedure developed it was ultimately established that two opposite segments of pro-filmic space could be presented successively in the same screen rectangle (reverse-field cut). And finally, through the use of eyeline matching, the spectator was made the mediator between two interlocutors (the mediator of their gazes *and* their imagined speech).

This eyeline match, the veritable keystone of the 'Hollywood system', was the last piece to fall into place (towards the end of the First World War), the last device to become staple practice, several years after cross-cutting and even the ellipsis had become established figures. The general adoption of the reverse field and of the 'correct' eyeline match were part of the last, most crucial and most difficult stage in the process of breaking down the barrier of 'alienation' which, despite the ducking heads that purportedly greeted the arrival of the Lumières' train, informed

A PARENTHESIS ON
FILM HISTORY

8. Exactly for whom it resulted is of course difficult to determine today. We know that from our vantage point, such an impression seems inevitable, but it is quite probable that audiences were less 'critical' then. What is certain is that some film-makers and, above all, the first trade-paper critics (see Kauffmann, Stanley, *History of American Film-Criticism*) were preoccupied by these imperfections (in this, the latter were the vanguard of ideology, spokesmen for their class *and not for an essentially proletarian public*), and this contributes much to an understanding of the relatively rapid 'progress' of cinema, i.e. the progression of the dominant system of representation in Europe and North America. In Japan, as we shall see, with an audience and film-makers *less* disturbed by such 'faults' of continuity, etc., this 'progress' was considerably delayed.

A FROZEN STREAM?

the relationship between the Primitive film and its essentially working-class audience. That process lasted twenty years, from the first economic recession affecting the film industry (*c*. 1907) and impelling the first search for a 'better class' audience, intimately related to the first naturalization in cinema of the middle-class norms of representation (Films d'Art) and the second recession which led to the introduction of synch sound, completing the project inaugurated by Smith, Porter, Griffith *et al*. – and imagined in the early 1890s by Thomas Alva Edison.

Needless to say, this is an extremely simplified over-view of a complex and contradictory historical movement.

I wish to claim, however, that the phenomenon which virtually all specialists of the Japanese cinema, Occidental and Eastern, regard as the 'lag' between Japan and the West prior to 1920[9] and even 1930, was actually the manifestation of a fundamental incompatibility between the West's developing 'codes of illusionism' and Japanese indifference to 'illusionism' in the Western sense. This incompatibility determined, even through the 1920s when Western influence was relatively strong, the preservation within the Japanese cinema of traits common to the Primitive cinema of the 1890s, and even to some of the most radical Western films of the 1960s and 1970s (as, for instance, those by Warhol and Godard). They are triumphantly affirmed in the fully developed structures which underlie the masterpieces of Ozu and Mizoguchi, Naruse and Shimizu made during the 1930s and 1940s. And we find them in the films of many other minor but 'uniquely Japanese' directors. Before attempting to trace the development of this implicitly critical separation, we must locate its origin.

9. Anderson and Richie assert that in 1913 Japanese cinema 'had not even left the cradle'. Op. cit. p. 29.

# 6. A Rule and its Ubiquity

We have already observed that it was in 1910 or 1911 that the merger of the four existing production firms resulted in the first Japanese major company. In 1912 it adopted the name under which it is known today, Nikkatsu. This move coincided almost exactly with a similar concentration of the means of production and distribution in the United States after which it was patterned, and with the world-wide emergence of cinema as an economically profitable industry. One now observes, as I have pointed out, a shift within the dominant Western modes of filmic representation. The so-called 'theatrical' period[1] is succeeded by that of codification, to which Griffith (who began directing just one year before the constitution of the first American film trust) contributed so decisively. It is said that until that time (1909-12) the Japanese adhered quite closely to the pattern of development of Western film, submissive to what is generally and categorically described as 'the influence of the theatre'. This synchronism is confirmed by my experience, but is still open to question, as less than half a dozen films of that early period of Japanese cinema (1897-1912) have survived. This presumption of 'theatricality' also tallies with the undeniable tastes of what was indeed a mass audience. For although the Japanese cinema may have been, during its first few years, an object of curiosity for the upper classes,[2] it soon acquired a predominantly proletarian public, a situation which prevailed the world over for the next three decades.[3] In Japan, tastes in the matter of performing arts had been formed by the popular theatre: *kabuki* until the mid-nineteenth century, its derivative *shimpa* during the period that immediately preceded and followed the introduction of cinema. The tastes of plebeian Western audiences had similarly been formed by vaudeville, circus, magic lantern and other popular arts, but these were viewed by the dominant bourgeois taste as archaic forms, suitable at best for children and their nannies, for they were in complete contradiction with the fully developed 'illusionism' of the dominant theatre of the

1. Not in the narrow sense that the *Films d'Art* and Famous-Players films were 'stagey' but in the sense that the whole of Primitive Cinema is regarded as subordinated to theatrical forms (which is of course neither simply nor completely true).

2. Richie and Anderson, op. cit., p. 22.

3. In the West, the audience came to include a fringe of the intelligentsia. This seems to have been true as well in Japan, but I have no actual data.

period: Shaw and Ibsen, but also Feydeau and Sardou. The integration of taste achieved in Tokugawa Japan and perpetuated during the Meiji era and after, has never been achieved in the West since the rise of capitalism, largely because of the forms and intensity of class struggle. And it is to the extent that these 'pre-bourgeois' forms contributed to the constitution of popular taste at the turn of the century that it may be legitimate to characterize certain aspects of Primitive Western cinema as traces of an authentically proletarian art. Conversely, its gradual contamination by naturalism may be seen in part as a class strategy.

In *kabuki* and the related doll theatre, we are dealing, it is true, with a typically bourgeois theatre: both matured during the rise of the merchant class in the Edo period. In them we see the manner and the extent to which the aesthetics of the Heian period, which remained alive and dominant well into the nineteenth century (despite a long coexistence with Chinese canons of poetry and painting) were 'revised' to meet the needs of the emerging class. A cursory examination of this development and of the nature of the theatrical practices which issued from it is unavoidable here.

*Kabuki* had origins as humble as those of the aristocratic *nō* – a prostitute-priestess dancing in a dry riverbed. Due to the historical circumstances of its growth,[4] it remained a truly popular art throughout the eighteenth and early nineteenth centuries:

> The rise of the *kabuki* theatre, as well as that of the coeval doll theatre, was linked with the rise of the townsman, for it was the *chōnin* who principally attended the *kabuki*, and the *kabuki* became the expression of the townsman's artistic tastes and ethical beliefs. The *nō* theatre was familiar to the commoner, but the *kabuki* was lustier stuff, more suited to the tastes of a newly important economic class than the esoteric *nō*.[5]

The severe restrictions – theatres were often closed down, plays banned, actors banished – placed upon *kabuki* by the Tokugawa *bakufu* ('headquarters') were associated with the fear which a ruling class (in this case the landed samurai) entertains with regard to a rising class which objectively threatens its power. Indeed, the economic influence of the wealthiest *chōnin* (townsmen) was already very real by the mid-eighteenth century. The pattern is, in this instance and in almost the same period, very close to that of Europe. The ban on Beaumarchais' *Mariage de Figaro* was a symptom of the contradictions that led to the French Revolution.

The history of the modes of representation attached to the rise of the bourgeoisie throughout the West, as well as

---

4. See Ernst, Earle, op. cit., pp. 1–23.

5. ibid, p. 9.

those later developed in connection with the rise of the proletariat, amply demonstrate that an ascending class requires more directly 'realistic' representations than the dominant class. Japan was no exception to this rule. *Kabuki* and even the doll theatre moved away, in several significant respects, from the purely presentational theatre of the *nō*, towards (but only towards) a representational theatre. *Shimpa*, which catered to the newly urbanized peasants of the Meiji period, and *shin-geki* ('modern theatre'), directly an expression of the struggle of the liberal bourgeoisie, indirectly of the embryonic working-class movement, were further steps. The *nō*, we must remember, had been an almost purely lyrical form, in which the narrative was reduced to a commentary on some theme or conflict drawn from a fund of folklore and old chronicles. The text itself displayed the same polysemous and intertextual complexity as Heian poetry, and was also intricately woven into a sophisticated fabric of music and dance. *Kabuki* and the doll theatre, on the other hand, had strong, amply developed plot-lines, and though some of the material was drawn from the semi-legendary past (often via the *nō* texts), many plays – and of course those of the great Chikamatsu Monzaemon come immediately to mind – had contemporary settings, drew upon actual incident and constituted, to a remarkable extent, 'portraits' of the life-styles of the *chōnin*. They accurately described the economic and social pressures of modern life and seemed, in general, to follow the pattern of emerging bourgeois art in the West. They were not, however, political in content, partly because of the extreme vigilance of the censors. It quickly became expedient, for example, when writing plays about the celebrated incident of the forty-seven *rōnin* (masterless samurai) who avenged their lord's forced suicide by killing his rival, a protégé of the Shōgun, to set it in the remote Kamakura period, even though it had actually been a contemporary event. Moreover, as I have already pointed out, there was in fact no revolution brewing, nor any middle-class political activity whatsoever; the only manifest social discontent came from the peasants, who rose up periodically to claim tax reductions and other limited reforms.

Despite this tendency towards bourgeois realism, both the 'live' *kabuki* and the doll theatre nevertheless remained essentially *presentational* arts and were still significantly closer to the *nō* than to any Western theatrical practice between that of the Elizabethans and the modernist renewal of our century.

The terms presentational theatre and representational theatre have been used to describe antithetical forms which the theatre may take. The *kabuki*, because of the nature of its means of expression and the quality of its rapport with the audience, can be called presentational. This is an abstract term, not referring to a specific historical theatre, but useful in outlining a general form, such as that which the theatre took in Greek civilization of the fifth century, in the Elizabethan public playhouse, in the contemporary theatre of Meyerhold, or in vaudeville. In the presentational theatre, the actor does not lose his identity as an actor. The audience does not regard him as a 'real' person but as an actor acting. His make-up, costume, movement, and speech emphasize the difference between the actor and the concept of a 'real' person that exists in the mind of the audience.... The stage is distinguished from the rest of the theatre building, but it is not conceived to be spatially discontinuous from it. The actor, the audience, and the performance exist within the same psychologically undifferentiated world....

At the opposite pole from the presentational theatre is the representational. This generalized form appeared in the Greek theatre of the fourth and third centuries, in the European medieval mystery plays, but it probably reached its ultimate statement in the theatres of Antoine and Belasco at the turn of the century. In the representational theatre every effort is made to convince the audience that the stage is not a stage and that the actor is not an actor. To this end, the stage is disguised by the use of settings, properties, and lighting so that it will appear to be a specific and 'real' place. Various technical means are employed to create in the audience a sense of spatial discontinuity between the auditorium in which they sit and the stage on which the play is being performed. In essence, the stage becomes an area of illusion, while the auditorium remains a part of actuality. The actor, although he may have to resort to highly 'unreal' methods to do so, seeks to convince the audience by his make-up, costume, movement and speech that he is a 'real' person, not an actor acting.[6]

In contrast, *kabuki*'s 'rapport with the audience' is of special importance to us here; it exemplifies the Japanese concept of *reading* incorporated in artistic/social practice. The *kabuki* audience of the eighteenth and nineteenth centuries generally expressed their appreciation by calling out to the actors at the moment of their entrance along the *hanamichi* (a ramp running through the auditorium to the stage and which of course is an essential element of that 'presentational' quality described by Ernst) or while they were performing on the stage proper. This tradition is preserved today by small groups of connoisseurs who occupy the front seats at every performance. These calls may be simply the (nick-) names of

6. ibid., pp. 18–19. It should also be pointed out that Ernst's excellent description parallels Brecht's distinction between epic and bourgeois theatre. The fact that Brecht's name is never once cited by the author of this otherwise very useful study is indicative of its ideological limitations.

the actors or else conventional exclamations, such as *'Matte imashita!'* ('That's what we've been waiting for!'), uttered just before or after a particularly well-known and important passage in the play. These cries have nothing in common with the bravos or outbursts of applause with which connoisseurs of Western presentational arts, the classical ballet and opera, momentarily blotting out the musical text, express their delight at the execution of a set piece which they have learned to admire for its difficulty of execution. The reactions of the Japanese, uttered in a vocal style which is both distinctive and *closely related to that of the performers themselves*, are carefully placed by those who utter them, either individually or in close-packed clusters, in such a way as to become part of the 'text' of the play, part of its musical rhythm and timbre and its dramatic structure. The 'shouters' (in Edo days, most of the audience) have an extremely intimate relationship with that text, somewhere between that of the audience for flamenco music and the music-student with his nose in a pocket-score. Such is the 'completeness' of the total effect, that one wonders to what extent the codifiers of *kabuki* may have taken this factor into account in conceiving the texture of the musical accompaniment, the pace and length of certain scenes: today it is impossible to imagine the auditory space of *kabuki* without these Webern-like flashes which actually seem to organize the movement of certain episodes.[7] Audience participation of this sort may be regarded as the acme of presentationalism.

*Kabuki*, in rejecting representationalism, evolved a type of performance which further bore *the inscription of its own production* in the stylized 'femininity' of the *oyama* (female impersonator; see Chapter 7) and in the visible stage assistants dressed in black who remove accessories when they are no longer needed, help with on-stage costume changes, etc. Other strategies include: the completely free contraction and dilation of narrative time; the polysemy and intertextuality of the actual 'libretto' (less intricate, perhaps, than in the *tanka* or *haiku*, but still present); the rejection of illusionist depth in set design and in blocking (both related to what remained the fundamental attitudes of Japanese graphic art).

The popular wood-prints of the period, *ukiyo-e*, were, it is true, a step in the direction of 'representationalism', since through them linear perspective was first popularized in Japanese art. However, pictorial art of the eighteenth century continued to differ profoundly from Western illusionist painting in the acknowledgement of surface and of the frame-line as disruptive edge. It

A RULE AND ITS UBIQUITY

7. Curiously enough, no Western commentator, including the perspicacious Ernst, seems to mention this aspect of the 'calling' practice. I am therefore unable to verify my hypotheses about the musical codification of these cries or their influence on the 'writing' of *kabuki*.

continued, as well, to ignore 'centering' and its underlying anthropocentrism.[8]

Ihara Saikaku, who wrote novels and collections of tales dealing specifically with the economic realities of his day, at the same time remained faithful to a concept of the *signifier at work* derived, as I have said, from Heian poetry, via the *haiku*. Perhaps the most significant example, however, of the resistance offered by Heian values to representationalism appeared in the doll theatre. At the time (1727) when a supreme degree of realism had been achieved involving articulated fingers and eyeballs, as well as texts which recounted the most recent *faits divers*, a step was taken which made this theatre a paradigm of the distancing effect and of the inscription of the process of production. The three manipulators, as well as the musicians, began to operate in full view of the audience, *which they had not done before!*[9]

It is important to consider the doll theatre,[10] especially as its development hinged upon its association with one of the musical forms of Japanese narrative art called *gidayu bushi* (also incorporated into *kabuki*, especially in association with the performance by live actors of plays written for the dolls – an extraordinary instance of 'intertextuality' in its own right) and which had as its direct descendant the art of the *benshi*, the live 'narrator' of all silent films in Japan, who was to play such a vital role in the preservation of the *presentational character* of Japanese cinema.

Here is the descriptive analysis of Roland Barthes, by far the most perceptive observer of the doll theatre.

The *Bunraku* dolls are from three to six feet tall, little men or women whose limbs, hands and mouths can move; each doll is manipulated by three men in full view who surround, support and accompany it. The master holds the upper part of the doll with his right arm; his face is bare,[11] smooth, pale, impassive, cold as 'a freshly washed white onion' (Bashō); the two assistants wear black and their faces are hidden behind cloth. One man, wearing thumbless gloves, holds a large pair of stringed scissors with which he operates the left arm and hand; the other, moving close to the floor, supports the body and walking feet. These men move about in a shallow pit which leaves their bodies visible. The set is behind them, as in a theatre. On one side, there is a platform for musicians and narrators; their role is to *express* the text (as one squeezes juice from a piece of fruit). This text is half-spoken, half-sung; punctuated with great sweeps of the plectrum by the *shamisen* player, it is both measured out and hurled forth, with violence and artifice. Sweating and motionless, these voice-carriers[12] are seated behind little music stands on which is placed the 'master text',

---

8. 'The earliest designers of this type of print... from the first showed no compunction in handling the human figure as they would any other element of composition. Quite often this meant that a figure would be cut in half vertically by one side or the other of the print with a resultant asymmetry which is a marked trait of Japanese pattern.' Hillier, J., *The Japanese Print*, p. 92.

9. Donald Keene sees this as the final manifestation of a 'law' governing the entire development of the doll-theatre and which called for an 'even balance' between 'the real and the unreal' (Keene, Donald, *Bunraku*, pp. 13–14). This somewhat mechanistic presentation of the phenomenon – supported by a declaration made by Chikamatsu himself – is quite applicable, as far as it goes, to all the arts of Edo.

10. Generally, though incorrectly, called *Bunraku*, which is simply the name of the one Osaka troupe which preserved the art-form through the period of its decline in the nineteenth and twentieth centuries.

11. Actually, this is true only of certain plays, in particular those derived from the *nō*; the master is usually dressed like the assistants.

12. *Porte-voix*: megaphone, but used here in its literal sense.

whose vertical characters may be glimpsed from afar as the pages are turned; a triangle of stiff cloth, clinging to the shoulders like a kite, frames a face suffering all the tortures of the voice . . .

The *Bunraku* thus practices three separate modes of writing, and produces them to be read simultaneously on three different planes: those of the marionette, the manipulator and the vociferator. The effective gesture, the effecting gesture, the vocal gesture. It is the voice that is basically at stake in modernity, that particular substance of language striving to triumph in every domain. The *Bunraku*, on the contrary, has a limited concept of the voice, it does not do away with it but assigns it to a definite, essentially trivial function. Indeed, the narrator's voice combines extravagant declamation, tremolo, a feminine high-pitched tone, broken intonations, sobs, bursts of rage, of plaintiveness, of supplication and surprise, indecent pathos and indeed all the stock recipes of emotion, openly developed on the level of that inner, visceral body of which the larynx is the mediating muscle. . . .Thus, without being eliminated (this would be a mode of censure and would designate it as important), the voice is put to one side (in the actual theatre the narrators occupy a side-platform). The *Bunraku* gives it a counter-weight or rather a counter-march in the form of gesture.

Gesture here has two faces: that of emotive gesture on the level of the marionette (people cry over the doll-lover's suicide), that of the transitive act at the level of the manipulators. In our theatre, the actor pretends to act transitively, but his actions are never more than gesture; on the stage there is nothing but theatre and yet it is ashamed of its theatricality. The *Bunraku*, on the other hand (and this is its defining quality), separates the act from the gesture; it shows the gesture, reveals the act, sets forth both art and work, reserves a mode of writing to each. The voice (which can now be allowed with impunity into its most excessive reaches) is flanked by a huge volume of silence in which other traits, other modes of writing may be inscribed with all the more subtlety. . . .

All this, of course, is linked to the distance effect recommended by Brecht. That distance is reputed impossible, useless or trivial in our culture and hastily abandoned, even though Brecht very precisely situated it at the centre of a revolutionary dramaturgy (and the one no doubt explains the other). The *Bunraku* enables us to understand how this distance functions: it functions by the discontinuity of the codes, by this caesura imposed upon the different traits of representation, so that the copy made on stage should be, not destroyed but broken, so to speak, spared the metonymical contagion of voice and gesture, of voice and soul in which our actors are mired.[13]

**The unusual length of this quotation is justified by its dense and multi-faceted relevance to all the principal themes under consideration: the relationship of Japanese systems**

13. Barthes, Roland, op. cit., pp. 68–75.

A FROZEN STREAM?

14. They are, in fact, no more 'naturally' fused than the Chinese characters with the native syllabary, which 'communicate' with one another only through an extremely sophisticated *correlational reading*, no matter how 'instantaneously' it may in practice often take place.

of representation with regard to logocentrism, the irrelevance of the concept of originality in this culture, the division of the representational process into distinctly separate texts, relatable only through an act of *reading*,[14] and the relevance of the whole to Western revolutionary thought and artistic practice.

This radical disjunction between signifiers in the doll theatre is present in the *nō* and, to a lesser extent, in *kabuki*. It made a profound, *direct* impact on the Japanese silent cinema and has indirectly affected the sound film as well.

# 7. Bulwarks of Tradition

Very shortly after films first began to be shown in Japan, it became general practice to have a *benshi*, a live commentator in the theatre to accompany the film with vocal explanations. There is every reason to believe that this was not based on a simple calculation that 'people aren't going to understand'; it was a natural, i.e. culturally and historically determined, development. It did not come about because 'the Japanese like to have things explained to them.'[1] The assertion that 'the Japanese like to have the signifier disjoined' may be scarcely more convincing; it does nevertheless point to the existence within Japan of a concept, a 'module' present in all human activity.

The *benshi* is not a bastard outgrowth of a specifically Japanese defect or 'convention'[2] as it is likely to be called when it appears in the doll theatre and other approved cultural products. Neither is there anything intrinsically 'low' about the *kabuki*-derived genre called *chambera* or sword-play films[3] which, during the latter part of the silent era (1920–36), practically monopolized the screen. This ideological repression of *intertextual ramifications* of two traditional arts and of the popular forms by which the early cinema is rooted in them, is doubly significant. It reflects the onus traditionally attached to the Western cinema owing to its plebeian ('theatrical') beginnings, the sense of shame, not unrelated to the notion of Original Sin, which those beginnings continue to inspire. We know that these theatrical beginnings are, in fact, the instrumentality of the camera *stripped bare*. Its essential transformational powers (its production of meaning) are thereby *acknowledged*, since even filming the theatre stage as such (i.e. filming the entire proscenium) destroys the representational effect, *causes the image to appear as that of a stage*. The Lumières' attempts to give their production a certain entertainment status, as in *La Mort de Marat* (1897), were framed in such a way that (an imaginary) proscenium-arch and frame-lines coincide: the de-personalization becomes more radical than ever, since the characters are tiny puppets, overwhelmed

1 During the very first decade or so of film-making in France, England, America and elsewhere, when screenings were held mainly in a (presentational) amusement-park context, this practice also held sway. The outside barker would often step inside to continue his spiel during the screening as *lecturer*. In England and especially the U.S.A., another important source for this practice was the 'lantern lecture'. As the mores of the bourgeois theatre took over, however, the practice gradually disappeared; in Japan it lasted until 1937, is still an appurtenance of archive screenings. If ever there was needed conclusive proof of the profound *otherness* of the Western Primitive cinema by comparison with the standard post-Griffith product, this extraordinary brief encounter with the cinema of Japan provides it.

2. This word is often used to mask our ethnocentric repugnance for non-transparent representation: it implies that in the culture which produced the *sign*, it is read as fully transparent, 'their representations are just like ours', basically everyone is like us, all have their conventions and all take them for 'the real thing'. It is just possible, however, that the audience at the *Buroraku* aren't crying over *characters* at all but over dolls, over the 'convention' itself.

3. 'Chambera' is an onomatopoeia suggesting the clash of swords (see Ch. 11).

by empty height. A scant decade later, when the need for gentility began to assert itself in the vogue for 'serious' theatrical subjects, such films as *L'Assassinat du Duc de Guise* (1907) which were slightly behind their time in terms of editing, nevertheless ignored the proscenium. However, it was not until the system of narrative editing, with its close-ups, matching devices, etc., was fully developed that it became possible to recover the theatre's power of characterization, personalization, etc. Paradoxically, it is for the development of this system that Griffith is celebrated as the man who brought cinema out of the theatrical stage! The so-called theatricality of the earliest cinema is in many instances a rudimentary and fugitive transmutation of the *popular* theatre of that period into an objective prefiguration of modernist theatre and cinema. It is not surprising that this period of cinema should be, in Japan as in the West, the object of systematic repression.

More generally, analysis of prevailing attitudes towards the relations between the cinema and the popular theatre of Japan reveal a phenomenon that I shall term 'repression of the Japanese text'. Our presupposition is that Cinema is One, just as Man is One, that the Hollywood codes are those of Cinema, East and West, the Codes of Man! As a consequence of this we also admit that an individual artist who *plays* on them, disrupts or subverts them, may be a genius – or a charlatan. Anyone who simply ignores them, however, who pretends they do not exist and wishes to preserve the cinema in the state which it knew before the coming of the Codes, who keeps on 'doing his thing', is either a fool or slightly backward. Yet this is exactly what Méliès and, to a large extent, Feuillade were doing between 1910 and 1915, until the former had to abandon the cinema forever and the latter was condemned to making futile efforts to 'catch up'. It is what the whole of Japanese cinema did for some ten years after the start of the 'Griffith revolution' but also, to a surprising extent, throughout the 1920s.

By Western standards, and in contrast with the situation in Europe, the 1920s do not seem to have been a very 'rich' period in Japanese cinema. It was this stubborn refusal to 'grow up' which nevertheless provided the conditions for the remarkable preservation through the 1920s of several of the basic elements of the 'primitive' attitude, and which ultimately made possible the remarkable developments of the 1930s. It is my contention that the *benshi* played an historically positive role in this period of tacit resistance.

The function, perhaps the need, of the *benshi* derived from the theatre of Edo and from the many solo narrative genres which abound in Japan. In contrast with these by then respectable origins of their practice, the first generation of *benshi* seem to have been composed predominantly of politically ambitious men intent on improving their oratory and ex-street vendors seeking to rise in life.[4] Indeed, the *benshi* soon became a public figure of considerable importance; in the decade from about 1915, people went to the pictures to hear their favourite *benshi* rather than to see a particular movie star, and would call out his nickname at the beginning of the performance in the manner of a *kabuki* audience.[5] These men, who are generally felt to have been of singularly modest intellectual capacities (at least until around 1919), seem to have acquired a considerable say in the actual *production* of films. If the finished work seemed in some way unsuitable to their talents, they demanded cuts, the shooting of new scenes; they wanted existing scenes lengthened to allow for development of their discourse (e.g. touching farewells). Above all, they fought bitterly against the introduction of new narrative structures such as the flashback. We will examine the consequences of this attitude in the next section. It may already be evident, however, that the conservatism with which the *benshi* is commonly taxed primarily reflects his efforts to save not only his means of livelihood but also a certain *mode of presentation* which was the central artistic ideology of his class and nation. We can, on the evidence of this limited data, concur with those who see the influence of the *benshi* as profound and diverse, without accepting the all but unanimous opinion that his role was harmful, that he 'retarded' the growth of the Japanese cinema.[6]

Needless to say, the films of this earliest period had absolutely no inter-titles (or 'spoken titles', as they were to be called in Japan when they were first introduced in the early 1920s), except for an occasional indication of the setting to follow or a title given to a section of the film.[7] In the early days (roughly, until about 1912), the *benshi* not only supplied a voice for all the characters but provided a running commentary on every detail of the image and action, often repeating himself in chanting patterns if he ran out of anything new to say. The style of many *benshi* was fairly straightforward, but variously shaded by the techniques of other narrative arts. And of course there was a musical accompaniment, consisting generally of a mixture of native Japanese instruments (*shamisen, taiko*, etc.) and such convenient European instruments as the violin.[8] It seems quite certain that the overall acoustical effect had little of the plasticity of *gidayu bushi*. At the same time, and though admirers of the traditional theatre may only scoff at this degraded version of a sophisticated art, the effect

BULWARKS OF TRADITION

4 This and other information in this section, I owe to private conversations with the Japanese film scholar Yoshida Tieo, who has published in Japanese a history of the *benshi* ('Katsuban no rekishi' in *Eigashi Kenkyun*, nos. 1 & 2, 1973). The rest of the information is from Richie and Anderson unless otherwise stated.

5. There is no evidence as to whether this was also done *during the film*; nor do we know how, if at all, it was related to the *benshi*'s delivery or to the music that accompanied him.

6. The title of Chapter 2 of a recent, rather sketchy history of Japanese cinema expresses this attitude: 'Exit Benshi, Enter Beauty'.

7. Deslandes and Richard assert (*Histoire comparée du cinéma*, Vol. 2, p. 201) that 'titles do not seem to have come into general use until around 1901.' This would be another link between the earliest primitive cinema in the West and the Japanese films of the first twenty-five years.

8. Eventually the musicians were supplied with 'repertoires', as in the West: scraps of music corresponding to this or that mood.

A FROZEN STREAM?

described by Barthes as a fragmentation of the representational gesture *could not help but be produced.*

It would be naïvely ethnocentric of us to consider the institution of the *benshi* as simply 'a crude dubbing effect', a puerile attempt to make the picture talk before the advent of sound. The time did come (in the 1920s) when for Japanese (as opposed to foreign) films, several such speakers divided up the various roles. Even then, however, the desire for ever greater realism can scarcely be regarded as a primary cause. Such a desire was infinitely less strong among the Japanese of the first quarter of the century than in the Western middle class – for of course it was *they* who shunned the silent cinema and came in droves to the talkies, thereby determining the second and final stage of the process by which Western cinema was at last fully subordinated to a middle-class ideology of representation.

The key to these 'film performances'[9] is the fact that through the *benshi* the image was purged of speech and relieved to an almost equal degree of the narrative burden. In a sense, the Japanese silent film was the most silent of all, if by silence we mean, as most people do when they talk about that film era, the absence of speech. Speech was indeed explicitly absent, since it was *removed*, put to one side; the voice was there, but detached from the images themselves, images in which the actors were thereby all the more mute and were confined, moreover, in many instances, to remarkably static visual renderings of the scenes unfolding through the *voice*, much like the dolls or, to a lesser extent, the *kabuki* actors of the Edo stage.[10] And the 'transference' of the written word from its Western position between the pictures to a 'libretto' on the *benshi*'s lectern is as significant here as the analogous phenomenon in the doll theatre. In the dominant cinema of the West, the dialogue titles always made it clear that Speech, the Word, was an intangible, ineradicable presence *inside* the diegesis, that printing was merely its passive *outward* vehicle: this was implicit in the way in which the title demanded a momentary *suspension* of the images. It was isolated in a decorative frame, and against a timeless black background, signifying the parenthetic suspension (not the acknowledgement) of representation. Except in very rare experiments, such as L'Herbier's *L'Homme du large*, it was never super-inscribed on the picture, as it so often was in the Japanese films of the 1920s, a phenomenon we shall examine in the next section.

To return for a second to the 'libretto' just mentioned, it should be explained that it actually came to exist though for foreign films only, since they, contrary to the Japanese product, did have inter-titles . . . *in their native language.*[11]

9. Of course, they weren't really *film* performances at all, since often the *benshi* was felt to be the *centre of interest* (though in practice it is probable that there was an oscillation of that centre between *benshi* and screen as happens in the doll theatre). It is this 'de-centering' of the performance that most outrages the 'serious' filmgoer today, with his quasi-religious attitude towards the screen (exemplified by the pew-like seating architecture of the first Anthology Film Archive Theatre in New York).

10. A film made in 1922, at the height of the *benshi*'s popularity, by one Oboro Gengo, *Two People Named Shizuka (Ninin Shizuka)*, consists largely of static conversations between seated figures and contains absolutely no inter-titles other than 'chapter-headings'.

11. Contrary to the practice among Western nations of supplying untitled prints and letting distributors title them in the local tongue, Japan was supplied with *exhibition prints* prepared for the domestic use of the exporting country.

The *benshi* was nominally expected to translate those titles in addition to giving his usual comments on the heroine's dress, the weather, etc., but in actuality he often made up the lines entirely, and significantly enough, even *changed the narrative meaning of the images* at his pleasure – or rather in accordance with a cultural outlook shared with his audience. It is also said that the characters in foreign films were nearly always given the same names: Mary for the heroine, Jim for the hero and Robert for the villain.[12] This practice may be seen as a de-construction of the Hollywood film, read in terms of its stereotypical structures by a culture which *values* the stereotype. We may, in fact, consider the *benshi*'s entire discourse as a *reading* of the diegesis which was thereby designated as such and which thereby ceased to function as diegesis and became what it had in fact never ceased to be, *a field of signs*. The most 'transparently' representational film, whether Western or Japanese, could not be read as transparent by Japanese spectators, because it was already being read as such *before* them, and had irrevocably lost its pristine transparency.

The *benshi* removed the narrative burden from the images and eradicated even the possibility of the images producing a univalent, homogeneous diegetic effect. In the West, on the other hand, the need for such unity was so strongly felt that it gradually resulted, towards the end of the silent period, in a tendency to do away with titles altogether or nearly so, and 'let the pictures tell the story'. Films like *Der Letzte Mann, Ménilmontant, Ueberfall* attempted to refine existing codes of *découpage* to a point where it became possible to dispense with the disrupting titles and yet maintain *the control of the flow of signification*, the linearity of the narrative, the 'naturalness' of the diegesis. Perhaps the most systematic and sophisticated of these attempts was that by Kirsanoff in *Ménilmontant*. However, the fundamental semantic ambiguity of the uncaptioned photographic image confers upon this film an obscurity which may be responsible for the interest it has aroused on the apparent assumption that failed prose is poetry.[13] This tendency towards the 'all-picture movie' had a curious development in the early 1930s, especially in the United States. Many prominent directors, out of an instinctive distrust of canned theatre, felt that 'the picture should still tell the story', as they might have put it, and often went to extravagant lengths (at times with preciously witty results) to develop a point of narrative without relying on titles or dialogue, using sound only as a 'counterpoint' (an elaborate dolly-shot linking two hotel balconies in order to *co-locate* two key sets, a series of clock-face close-ups and snatches of off-screen dialogue to indicate the passing of an

12. Richie and Anderson, op. cit., p. 25.

13. See, in particular, Michel, Walter S., 'In Memoriam of Dimitri Kirsanov, a Neglected Master', in Sitney, P. Adams (ed.), *Film Culture Reader*, Praeger, New York, 1970; Secker & Warburg, London, 1971.

A FROZEN STREAM?

evening are two typical examples from Lubitsch's *Trouble in Paradise* of 1932). Interestingly enough, these developments were not unrelated to Eisenstein's aspiration to an 'intellectual montage' – the expression of a relatively complex theoretical discourse through images alone, whose degraded equivalent is the 'montage sequence' of dominant cinema – which crystallized at about the same time (1927–30). It is very significant that Iwamoto Kenji,[14] asserting that the institution of the *benshi* amounted to a rejection of the narrative codes of editing, cites not Griffith first and foremost, but Eisenstein. And indeed for a cinema *indifferent* to the organization of images in accordance with the language model, the 'Griffith' codes and Eisenstein's montage of attractions and intellectual montage can be considered equivalent. This matter will be developed in connection with the cinema of the 1920s.

In conjunction with the semantic dissociation effected by the *benshi*, it is necessary to mention a material dissociation which, although less extensively practised, is nonetheless highly symptomatic. It appears that in the earliest years of film-showing, at least one exhibitor set up rows of seats allowing spectators who wished to do so *to watch the projection rather than the film.*[15] Together with the early, quite general practice of commencing every performance by a demonstration of the workings of the projector, this would seem to provide evidence that the cinema made its debut in Japan under the auspices of what we may well call, again taking our cue from Barthes, the co-presentation of the effective and effected gestures.

By 1915, practices of this kind were anomalous in the cinema of the West. In the earliest period they were not. As we know, the projector was in the hall, shop or tent for several years, and we have already mentioned the early absence of titles and the ephemeral Western equivalent of the *benshi*, the lecturer. It is also interesting to note that the pronounced flicker effect, whose final eradication in 1909 (through the invention of a new type of projector shutter) significantly coincided with the beginning of a veritable mutation in the modes of representation of Western cinema, was presumably present to a far more 'irritating' extent in all of Japanese cinema until around 1912 and in much of it well into the 1920s. For it was the practice in Japan to shoot at twelves frames per second,[16] rather than the sixteen to twenty frame average which was customary in the West. In Japan, as in the West, the projector, like the camera, was hand operated; it is probable that projectionists varied the speed of the film as they did in the West, according to the nature of the action. Needless to say, the flicker produced at such low speeds was one which had

14. Unpublished essay in Japanese. See note 8, page 98.

15. Richie and Anderson allude to this (op. cit., p. 24) and I owe some complementary data to a private conversation with Mr Richie. The original source is Tanaka Junichiro, op. cit.

16. According to Sato Tadao, some (oral) sources speak of eight frames per second, but this practice was unlikely to have been very common.

rapidly become intolerable in the West, impinging as it did upon the illusionist force of the filmic image, if only through the eye-strain induced by the viewing of films that were increasingly long.

The 'look' of the Japanese film during the period of the Western Primitive cinema was very close to that of the European film. It is with the beginning of the Formative period that differences begin to appear,[17] since the Japanese continued along the same path. Japanese film-makers were quite aware of new developments in the Western cinema; Western films were, after all, shown in Japan with increasing frequency and, according to Richie and Anderson,[18] Griffith's pioneering short films had already been seen there by 1913. The common assumption is that the Japanese directors paid no attention to these innovations from abroad and did not, in consequence, know how to use them. We have evidence that this was not the case. In this matter, too, we encounter the ethnocentrism of Western scholars, and we must reckon, as well, with the unfortunate tendency among all but the youngest Japanese scholars to accept unquestioningly Western and 'Western-type' ideas and criteria regarding the cinema. They are unconsciously inclined, one feels, to consider films as the 'natural property' of the West.

If we examine what may or may not be Makino's first full-length version of *Chūshingura* (*A Tale of Loyal Retainers*, commonly called 'The Forty-seven Rōnin' – 1913 or 1917)[19] we find that he 'kept his camera running without interruption through an entire sequence and never moved it from its front-on angle of a spectator at a stage-play', (see Fig. 1) and 'completely ignored Griffith's editing concepts.'[20] Except that he did not ignore them *completely*. There are, in fact, several match-cuts in this film (concertinas) which show that Makino had mastered the technique of cutting on movement far better than Louis Feuillade ever did, far better, indeed, than *most* Western directors did until about 1915. In any case, we need hardly dwell on the well-known rapidity with which the Japanese grasp new *techniques*. There are also lateral re-framing pans which show that his cameraman was skilled in manipulating tripods that were every bit as manoeuvrable as those of Hollywood (they might even have been American or French).[21]

Most significant of all is the brief but dramatically capital sequence in which Lord Asano attacks Kira, an act for which he will be sentenced to commit ritual suicide. This *tableau*, the starting point of the whole saga of the Forty-seven, is immediately followed, during the moment of 'shocked reaction', by a pair of medium close-ups in

17. The differences could be observed in Japan, not in the West. The first Japanese film to be shown in the West (to non-Japanese audiences, at least) was Kinugasa's *Crossways* (1928).

18. Op. cit., p. 32.

19. There is a serious conflict as to the date of this film: Richie and Anderson give it as 1913, the catalogue of the Matsuda Film Library, where it is preserved, as 1917. I find the later date better substantiated by internal evidence, but in the event that the earlier were proven correct it would certainly give even greater weight to the claim made here.

20. Richie and Anderson, op. cit., p. 32.

21. The earliest 'theatrical' production that I have seen, *Chronicle of Taiko* (c. 1908, director unknown), also contains several perfectly smooth lateral and vertical pans serving to enlarge the fragment of a *kabuki* set used as background.

Fig. 1. Makino Shozo, *A Tale of Loyal Retainers* (1913 or 1917)

22. I use the term reverse field in this historical context to designate its most general form: a contiguity cut involving eyeline matching. It was not until the early 1920s in the West that the actual camera reversal, with eyelines close to lens-centre, was added to the illusionist edifice, ultimately to become a keystone of that edifice.

23. Even if the film is a compilation, such as were often made and shown just after the Second World War, at one point in his early career, Makino did film this long sequence consisting of two typically 'primitive' shots, interrupted by this brief 'flurry' of editing. The perfection of the matching (movement, costumes, lighting, make-up, sets, emulsion quality) excludes the possibility that the close shots were added after the fact.

reverse-field construction,[22] bracketed by a pair of concertinas. This passage occurs very near the beginning of the film, and with the exception of a few more deftly executed concertinas, such editing never recurs.[23]

As later developments amply demonstrate, the Western codes had impinged upon Japanese perception, but Japan was on the whole not interested in them *as a system*; they were merely used on occasion to produce special dramatic effects. The implications of this are clear enough. By 1913, certainly by 1917, the reverse field and concertina, the medium close-up, even the cut on movement, were in the United States and most of Europe, *banal devices*. When successfully executed, as they increasingly were, they were not perceived as the signifiers of anything more strictly defineable than 'continuity', 'contiguity' and other basic semes of linear representation. Makino, in contrast, uses them as privileged dramatic signifiers, comparable to the *signs* used in Japanese theatre to displace the gestures of emotion (the *oyama* tugging with her teeth at the sleeve of her kimono to signify weeping). This reading of the Makino film would scarcely be conclusive were it not for the fact that throughout the 1920s and particularly during the late years, for reasons which I shall attempt to make clear, the Western mode of *découpage* was to be greeted in Japan with three distinct attitudes. The first of these was utter unconcern, underlined by the rare but 'technically correct' introduction of Western editing devices either as privileged signifiers, as in the early instance just cited, or in a way which can only be described as *random*. The second response was the adaptation of devices as signifiers of a completely different and more 'open' code; the signifiers thus adopted were secondary, specialized signifiers in their Western context, such as the swish-pan or dissolve. The rarest response was mastery and constant utilization of the codes according to the norms of Western practice; this seems to have been true of Ozu and Mizoguchi, whose earliest films are, however, presumably lost. It was, as well, the case of one Futagawa Montabe, some of whose films have come down to us and who, by 1928, had nothing left to learn from Hollywood. We will explore the interplay of these conflicting currents in the next section.

The overwhelming majority of films from this early period, then, drew their substance from the *kabuki* repertoire, or from the repertoires of its derivatives, *shimpa* and *shin-kabuki* (modernized kabuki). Scholars dispute the importance of *kabuki*'s 'influence' on the Japanese cinema.[24] This is due to a misunderstanding about the very nature of influences. I shall attempt to clarify this matter in the next section, in attempting to reconstruct the historical role of the *benshi* during the twenties and in defining the most general relationships of the whole of Japanese theatre to the cinema. In this early period, however, there can be absolutely no doubt that the pertinent *visual* traits of *kabuki* appear constantly on the screen as a surrogate of that presentational character defined by Earle Ernst as common to all Japanese theatre.[25] They helped to preserve the Japanese cinema against the ideology of 'realism' which rapidly took over the cinema of the West. The stylized fighting sequences in which no actual blows are exchanged, the use of the backward somersault signifying the death of a fighter, the translation into Méliès-like 'special effects' of the transformational machinery of *kabuki* and, above all, the action-stopping *mie*, or *tableau vivant* (which terminates most of the scenes of Makino's early *Chūshingura*),[26] are clear 'distancing devices' which need no special elucidation. Less self-evident, perhaps, is the even greater importance of the use in film of traditional theatrical make-up and its corollary, the *oyama*, or female impersonator.

It is not surprising that one of the great 'battles' fought just after the First World War, at the beginning of the movement to import the Hollywood codes, was over the elimination of the *oyama* from films. Her presence was absolutely inimical to those codes whose goal is to be

24. D. Richie feels that it was insignificant, while Iwamoto Kenji holds the opposite view. This is a corollary of the degree of importance which they attach respectively to the popular cinema of the 1920s and before.

25. Until the advent, that is, in 1906 of *shin-geki*, the first 'reasonable facsimile' in Japan of Western theatre, and which was to play its role in the cinema when the Western codes were introduced in the twenties (see Chapter 10).

26. It is interesting to compare this *kabuki*-derived practice with a similar device used by Griffith in *A Corner in Wheat* (1909). The characters are shown in a frozen *tableau vivant* between two black-outs, a device clearly derived from the vaudeville and melodrama stages where it had, as in this film, a function diametrically opposed to that of the *mie*: it introduced into a 'life-like' context a 'symbolic', 'allegorical' gesture designed to generalize the *meaning* of the play/film. It is true enough that on the stage as in the film, such suspensions were at odds with the dominant need for continuity and homogeneity, and were soon eliminated from the theatre and cinema of the bourgeoisie. Ambiguous as they are, however, they are far removed from the *mie*, which functions as the quintessence of the presentational attitude and has no 'expressive' dimension whatsoever.

schematically summarized in terms of the 'psychological depth' of the image and the fusion of the diegesis with a 'real world' in which women are women and men are men. As for the theatrical make-up which remained customary in *chambera* until the mid-1920s, it was of course in complete contrast with that of the West. Although still often visible as such until about the same period, make-up in Western film was designed to *heighten the expressiveness of the face*, felt to be diminished by the absence of words, of three-dimensionality and of colour. *Kabuki* make-up, on the other hand, is purely graphic; it reduces, on the contrary, both the expressiveness and the singularity of the face.

One of the traits that strikes the modern viewer as most significant in Makino's early *Chūshingura*, is the fact that the super-star, Matsunosuke, plays at least three different roles. He is first seen as Lord Asano. After the latter's forced suicide, he acts Ōishi, the Lord's principal retainer and organizer of the *rōnins*' vendetta against Kira. Finally, during the vendetta he plays Kira's principal bodyguard. This practice also derives from *kabuki*, in which certain plays call explicitly for double roles, and spectacular stage-business is derived from the possibilities thus created.[27] Its preservation in films, especially *without any change of make-up* (as was the case, not only in Makino's early *Chūshingura* but, I am told, in many films up through the mid-1920s), implied, of course, the audience's perfect familiarity with a story like *Chūshingura*. It also required the presence of the *benshi* in the theatre to identify the successive characters for any members of the audience whose memory might be deficient. The *benshi*'s task was not to 'restore' to the image some virtual reality, garbled by an unfortunate effect of the star system, but simply to *name the roles* which were, quite unmistakably, avowedly being played by one and the same actor, by Matsunosuke. Once again the *benshi* was part of a *fragmentation of the signifier*.[28]

We find the most remarkable instance of disjunction in early Japanese film in a genre known as *rensa-geki* (chain theatre) which presented *shimpa* pieces whose interior scenes were performed by live actors on stage whilst exterior scenes were performed by the same actors on a motion-picture screen. Though the filmed sections of one or two of these pieces have survived (in the Matsuda collection) we have only scant accounts of the actual nature of the full performances. The most remarkable quality of *rensa-geki*, however, was its long life (1904–22). Similar attempts at *mixed media performances* were made in the West, within the period we call Primitive (here again the encounter with the contemporary avant-garde is striking). An acrobat from Jean Durand's troupe, the Pouittes,

27. The heroine and one of the male principals in *Tokaido Yotsuya Kaidan (Ghost Story of Yotsuya)* (1825) are played by the same actor, which allows for the presentation in rapid succession of their dead bodies on opposite sides of a door floating down a river in one of the play's most famous scenes. (It is seen in Mizoguchi's masterpiece, *Tale of Late Chrysanthemums*).

28. Of course, the hypothesis that this is a composite film might modify the reading of this practice here. However, I have been assured (by Sato Tadao) that this was indeed a general practice at the time. Moreover, audiences did at one time or another see and presumably 'accept' the feature-length film which I have seen. And the relationship between the images and the discourse of the *benshi* (or *naniwa bushi*, a form of narration added to silent films for early post-war revivals of such films) was inevitably as I describe it.

opened a roof trap-door (on film) and clambered down a ladder on to the actual stage of the Gaumont Palace. In Australia, one of the world's earliest feature-length audio-visual productions (staged, c. 1906, by the Salvation Army) was a mixture of film, lantern-slide and scenic *tableau*. All such Western experiments were, however, extremely short-lived.[29] Their discontinuous use of different media was incompatible with the unity of the 'illusionist' system.

In this connection, one should also cite the juxtaposition, in the early version of *Chūshingura* already discussed and in many other films up to the late 1920s, of *tableaux* representing out-of-door scenes by ostentatiously painted backdrops, with other scenes actually shot on location. These latter, moreover, would often involve the papier-mâché props of the theatre. Examples of a related practice are to be seen in the remarkable semi-documentaries produced by Pathé around 1906 – *Le Mineur, Sauvetage en mer*, etc; by the end of the war, however, such a practice had been banished from the Western cinema, since it had quickly become a hindrance to *credibility*.

It is but one step from this evocation of the use of back-drops in the early films to the vital problem of the *representation of space* as practised in *Chūshingura* and in most other films of the period. This is a matter of far-reaching implications; it raises the problem of illusionist depth, in both a literal and a figurative sense of the word. For the moment, it will suffice to observe that the flatness derived from the *kabuki* and doll theatre stages seems to have been the general rule in the early films;[30] it is a trait which lasted late into the 1920s, and left an indelible mark on the films of some of the masters of the 1930s. The same is true of the most striking compositional feature of these early films, also related to the flattening of the image: there is frequently an inordinate amount of empty space over the actors' heads, owing to the simple fact that most of the time they are sitting on the floor. No effort is made to compensate for this, whereas it would have automatically been made in 'advanced' Western films from about 1914 on. This de-centering, which was one of the principal traits of Primitive cinema in the West – where it also contributed to a flattening of the image, since the background appears to be above rather than behind the figures – was preserved in the Japanese cinema for decades to come and may still be perceived to this day. In fact, there are grounds for maintaining that just as Japan has acted as the custodian of much ancient Chinese culture that has been lost in the vicissitudes of her great neighbour's history, she is also the 'storehouse' of what were universally the Primitive modes of filmic representation.

BULWARKS OF TRADITION

29. Earle Ernst's erroneous description of *rensa-geki* as a 'nine-day wonder' (op. cit., p. 252) indicates our difficulty in conceiving a 'bastard' form such as this as achieving real mass popularity within the context of cinema as our society has shown us it 'must' be.

30. A Makino film entitled *Thunder Boy (Jirai-ya)*, a good example of the Méliès-like trick films which were a speciality of his, involves a considerable amount of axial movement in location shots, which shows that he, at least, was not insensitive to this lesson of Western cinema. However, the date of 1914 assigned to this film in the Matsuda catalogue seems very unlikely (in many other ways, the film seems more Westernized than the early *Chūshingura*) so that it is difficult to know how meaningful this example was. In any case, axial movement did not become common in Japanese films, so far as I have been able to ascertain, until the late 1920s, one of the earliest examples I know being Makino's last version of *Chūshingura* (1928).

It is also possible to detect, during this early period, signs of the problem elicited by the 'realist vocation' of the camera, i.e. its faculty for recording facsimile representations of perceptual reality. The pressure exerted by the 'Western-ness' of the machine is implicit of course in the use made of the camera in *rensa-geki*. It is perhaps more significantly to be observed in the subtle changes brought about in the techniques of *kabuki* as they were transferred to the screen. One such example is to be seen in the very early film *Chronicle of Taiko* (*Taiko junanme*, c. 1908): it is part of *kabuki* practice that whenever an important property has ceased to serve an active purpose on stage it is removed by one of the black-clad stage assistants (*kurombo*). In *Chronicle of Taiko*, the hero at one point lays his bowl-shaped straw hat on the ground. In a live performance, it would have been deftly carried off by an 'invisible' stage assistant; here, however, it is whisked out of shot at the end of an invisible thread. I have, in fact, never seen a silent film in which the stage assistants appear, however close the film may have seemed to theatrical practice otherwise. Considering the degrees of stage artifice which became 'naturalized' in the Japanese cinema for so long, it is difficult to understand why this particular practice seems to have been systematically excluded, unless it can be seen as one of the first effects of Western attitudes defining the cinema as more 'realistic' than the stage, and thereby as the first sign of a conflict which was to persist throughout the next two decades and which was to determine the entire course of Japanese cinema. It is to the development of this conflict that we must now turn.

# Part 3 Cross-Currents

# 8. Transformational Modules

There is an awkward problem which the observer of things Japanese must confront. It is one to which we have already alluded in its ideological formulation: the uniquely Japanese faculty for assimilating and transforming elements 'borrowed' from foreign cultures. To my knowledge, no substantial effort has yet been made in the West to define or analyse this phenomenon, though it has often been commented upon.

We are dealing with Japan's use of a foreign machine, with a medium which has been largely dominated by Western capitalism. These two circumstances could not fail to have some specific impact on the cinema of a nation whose goal has been, for over a century, that of taking her place among the 'Powers'.

This historical pattern, this 'borrowing', was not, of course, limited to Japan's relations with her Western 'mentors'. Long before Europe and the United States came to be viewed in this role, she was China-oriented.

It has been suggested that an inventory of the pertinent traits of Japanese social and artistic practices would seem to designate them as *radicalizations* of traits characteristic of one or more of the great mainland cultures (China, India, Tibet). This assertion must be understood in terms of the political and ideological co-ordinates within which it is made. For not only does Japan offer traits which seem even more remote from our own, Western ways of thinking and doing, more remote than comparable traits of other Far-Eastern societies; these traits also lend themselves to *a Marxist critique of modern Western history in many of its aspects*. The claim for the radicalism of Japanese practice is therefore not to be taken as the assertion of some metaphysical absolute, but as an attempt to describe the situation which Japanese 'culture' effectively occupies today with regard both to the dominant ideological profile of Western Europe and the Americas, and to those practices, scientific, literary and artistic, which instantiate the Marxist critique of that dominance.

CROSS-CURRENTS

The key to an understanding of this process of radicalization in Japan might be suggested by an inventory of the *transformational modules* that can be observed during the periods of Chinese influence and of subsequent Westernization. These modules bear directly upon the ways in which the codes developing in the cinema of the West between 1900 and 1920 were transformed, displaced, truncated in Japan during the 1920s and 1930s.

To begin with, we may say that the Japanese have reacted to foreign importations – ideas, techniques and artefacts – by wholesale acceptance, global rejection or transformation/adaptation. Obvious as they may seem, their unparalleled importance in Japanese history suggests that the singular circulation of these modes of reaction, the remarkable constancy of their social integration, is of special interest to us. These reactions, moreover, often co-existed in overtly contradictory forms, a factor of importance for our discussion of cinema proper.

Foreign methods and, more often, techniques have been adopted in whole insofar as they proved compatible with the geo-political context of Japanese reality, and, in particular, with the goals of the ruling class; hence the rejection of the administrative structures engendered by the Asiatic Mode of Production and imported for a time from China but which proved totally unsuited to Japan.

In areas of artistic practice, the principle of wholesale adoption is often applied in an apparently contradictory manner. Foreign procedures which are fundamentally at odds with native methods are nonetheless adopted *in toto* and thrive *alongside* their contraries, as in Chinese Buddhist architecture and its emphasis on ornate detail and emphatic contours, antithetical to the geometrical simplicity of native architecture. The busy, furniture-crowded room of Meiji times occupies something of the same position with regard to Japan's Westernization as the neo-Chinese pagoda to her sinicization; both are emblems of cultural interaction at the level of practical social procedures. So were the emulation of Western science and industry, the temporary adoption of Chinese administrative procedures, the permanent adoption of Chinese writing and Confucianism. It should be added that sudden, wholesale adoption has always been linked with the need of a ruling or a rising class to reject 'traditional values' in order to increase or perpetuate its power. For indeed, the disavowal of such values may *alternatively* favour, according to circumstances, either the perpetuation of power under a new guise (the imperial family in pre-feudal times, the feudal oligarchy in the middle of the nineteenth century) or the rise of classes excluded from it (the liberal middle-classes after the First and Second World Wars).

It is, of course, the median category, the process of adaptation and transformation, which has been most profusely illustrated throughout Japanese history. I shall cite only three symptomatic instances: the ritualization of Indo-Chinese Buddhist logic, already described, the introduction of linear perspective during the period of Western influence which immediately preceded the opening of the country in 1852, and the adaptations of Western clothing which were so prevalent during the Meiji era.

Nakamura Hajime[1] regards the rejection of 'logic' ('illogicality') as a basic trait of the 'Japanese way of thinking'. Schooled in Occidental logic, this eminent philosopher understandably regards this trait as a fundamental *deficiency*. However, it is also clear that in his view the cultural filter which brought about the final ritualization of Indian logic is closely related to the Japanese rejection of metaphysics, to their emphasis on the material world, on the 'here and now', on the 'limited social nexus'. And that all of these factors bear upon the ultimately 'non-transcendental' character of all religious practice in Japan.[2]

Specifically Japanese modes of pictorial representation (which may be traced from the early hand-scrolls of the Heian period, through the screens of the Muromachi and early Edo periods down to the *ukiyo-e* prints of middle Edo) exclude the concept of depth representation more radically than Chinese painting, which made very precocious and systematic use of aerial perspective and sophisticated compositional techniques suggestive, albeit ambiguously, of illusionist depth. Traditional Japanese graphic art, one of the most advanced the world has known, never departed from a resolute acknowledgement of surface, despite the schools of Chinese painting that continually thrived at its side.

It was not until the eighteenth and especially the nineteenth centuries that the print-makers of Edo (notably Hiroshige and Hokusai) introduced linear perspective, no doubt as part of the movement toward greater 'realism' linked with the rise of the merchant classes. However, even a cursory examination of, for example, *The Fifty-three Stages of the Tokaido* by Hiroshige shows that the function of linear perspective within the framework of *ukiyo-e* was never predominantly illusionistic in the Western sense. It was primarily a procedure for the articulation of the surface, only secondarily a rendering of the eye's perceptual production. This impression of

TRANSFORMATIONAL MODULES

1. In *Ways of Thinking of Eastern Peoples*.

2. Including, I would add, Christianity, which clearly attracted the Japanese because of its ritualized emotionalism and its erotic content. The Portuguese Jesuits were deeply perturbed by their fifteenth-century converts' enthusiasm for the sado-masochistic aspects of Christian self-denial.

reversal of emphasis appears to be historically confirmed by the excitement which these works were soon to cause in Europe among painters who were precisely trying to move away from the illusionist tradition in painting. A similar reversal can be detected in the Japanese adaptation of certain codes or fragments of codes of Western filmic 'illusionism'. And the Japanese attitude towards the 'perspectival production' of the motion-picture camera lens is one of the most interesting examples of the transformational system at work within our field of interest.

The Meiji overcoat, with its kimono-sleeves and Western-style skirt, still to be purchased every winter in Japanese department stores, may seem a frivolous example, but constitutes a practical, comfortable and handsome combination of Japanese and Western styles[3] and demonstrates the manner in which these transformations have affected every aspect of Japanese life.

These three attitudes – acceptance, rejection, adaptation – co-existed, then, during the 1920s and 1930s in Japan – and in particular with regard to the representational system of Western narrative cinema, as they did throughout the country's history, whenever she was open to foreign exchange. As we examine these two decades, we shall come to see how these attitudes functioned, thus gaining a better understanding of contemporary developments in the Japanese cinema and of the remarkably intense contradictions which characterized Japanese society during those two crucial decades.

3. As did urban Meiji dress in general, combining Western trousers and short 'hapi' coat, bowler and fan, watch-fob and wooden clogs (*geta*).

# 9. Lines and Spaces

By the end of the First World War, the predominance of the American film in the world market was complete. It was, of course, the war itself which had enabled Hollywood to triumph over France, her principal competitor. The American studios had continued to work at full capacity, while those of France and her European allies were obliged to curtail their production drastically.

Japan's commercial and political ties with the Western Powers grew stronger through her token participation in the Allied war effort (occupation of the German concessions in Shanghai), her presence at Versailles and her action on the counter-revolutionary front in the Soviet Union. Before the war had ended, she was seeing a far greater number of American films than previously, since Hollywood was able to fill the gaps left by the French, Italians and English on the Asian market as well.

As I have already indicated, it was during the war, too, that Hollywood, through the efforts of such men as Barker, De Mille and the Ince brothers, had brought the silent narrative codes to what may be regarded as their peak of perfection. American products had commercial success in Japan, and *Intolerance*, shown in 1919, seems to have made a particularly strong impression. The success of films which clearly illustrated Hollywood's abandoning of the primitive mode of representation seems to have been the main drive behind a short-lived but intensive emulation of American production methods and narrative techniques. It was around this time that the Shochiku Company, which for some years had dominated live theatrical production – *kabuki* and *shimpa* – turned to the cinema. Bringing home several Japanese technicians from Sessue Hayakawa's Hollywood entourage, the firm launched into the production of films which were resolutely 'progressive' in spirit and designed to compete with the American product. Actresses were hired to replace the still universally employed *oyama*, location settings were used as much as possible, 'spoken titles' were introduced for the first time and there were even hopes of eliminating the *benshi*. Above all, of course, the 'Griffith codes' of editing were used in accordance with what were felt to be the Western norms.[1] However, even in this period of keen attentiveness to the Western model, the Japanese reading of the Hollywood codes brought about, as we shall see, transformations similar to those which had characterized *shimpa vis-à-vis* its (imaginary) Western model in the 1890s. Similarly, the attention paid to the West by the new film-makers was comparable and indeed related to the Westward-looking attitude of the Meiji advocates of liberal reform.

The 1920s saw the rapid development of class struggle on several fronts. Immediately after the war came the country's first major outbreak of industrial strikes, compounded by a recrudescence of peasant agitation, as Japan was hit by the world-wide wave of inflation. At the same time, big business was fighting to wrest power from the post-feudal oligarchy and democratize Japan. Its chief allies in this struggle, despite secondary contradictions, were the new liberal middle class (particularly the intelligentsia) and a fast-growing proletariat. The attempt to 'Americanize' Japanese films was in fact a direct consequence of this situation, just as the first attempts to Westernize the theatre had been linked with the political struggles of the 1880s.

The earliest manifestations of *shimpa* were known as *soshi shibai* (political theatre). Its ideology and even its leading personalities issued directly from the largest bourgeois political party, *Jiyu dantai* (Liberal Party). Significantly, the first of the new plays celebrated the man who drafted the first Japanese Constitution, whose promulgation was a victory for the liberal bourgeoisie. *Shimpa* plays proper generally contain some mild social protest, and the *shin-geki* movement was in large part the expression of a Left that was just beginning to organize itself around the turn of the century.[2]

Of course, all of Japanese literature had had a social content, in the sense of dealing with class relationships. And many if not most of the new style films of the early 1920s advocate in fact a very traditional fraternity: the feudal allegiances of the Edo stage were perpetuated in portrayals of class collaboration. Such films were no more revolutionary than the social melodramas of Griffith. However, as we shall see, some more truly radical films were produced later in the decade as the strength of the working-class movement continued to grow.

In its earliest manifestation, then, the Americanized film was short-lived.[3] Not unexpectedly, the Japanese

---

1. The movement was also characterized by some remarkably picturesque excesses: scripts written in roman characters, a Japano-American director, Henry Kotani, who insisted on using English to direct uncomprehending actors (see Anderson and Richie, p. 42). Clearly this was a phase of *wholesale adoption*.

2. Although only a few of the first new-style films, made around 1920, were ideologically related to the *shin-geki* movement, it seems that the acting techniques of that theatre are preserved in the few surviving examples.

3. Curiously enough, it died at about the same time as the last performances of *rensa-geki* were being given in remote provincial towns, and this double demise is typical of that period of cross-currents. I should perhaps add that an important factor in the rather abrupt cessation of this first 'Western school' was the destruction of the Shochiku studios by the terrible Kantō earthquake of 1923, together with most of the studios of Tokyo, where this brand of film-making was concentrated.

audience was unwilling to accept alien modes of representation, which they had hitherto applauded only as *exotica*, a category which the Japanese tend more than other peoples to isolate (as, for example, the 'Western room'). Explicit pressures were also brought to bear. These were no doubt political, to the extent that the films reflected the aspirations of the liberal middle classes. However, they were primarily corporate pressures, since important professional groups such as the *oyama* and the *benshi* were directly threatened by all the Western innovations.

We have seen that the objectively progressive forces in Japan at this time identified their struggle with the introduction of the Hollywood codes and the elimination of the *benshi, oyama* and other elements inherited from the traditional arts and culture. It may therefore appear surprising that the partial failure of this movement should be regarded in the framework of this study as a positive factor. However, it is a mistake, as Western history has taught us, to establish mechanistic equivalences between historical and artistic progress. The development at that time of a specifically Japanese cinema, whatever its failings, was an essential condition for the emergence of what was to be, objectively, *a materialist approach to film art*. This is a contradiction one repeatedly encounters at every subsequent stage of development of Japanese films until the 1960s.

Of course, the non-concordance of historical and artistic progress is a universal phenomenon. However, Japan must be viewed as an extreme instance. For the struggle between dominant and ascending classes has, since the opening of the country and until only very recently, always corresponded to a conflict between the objectively materialist artistic practices of the native culture and idealist dominant practices of the capitalist West. There is, consequently, on both the theoretical and practical levels, an irreducible contradiction between the reading of their own culture's accomplishments by the most enlightened and progressive Japanese (especially the Marxists) and a Western reading which takes into account one of the major theoretical acquisitions of contemporary Marxist thought, i.e. the non-equivalence of art and history. The full implications of this issue, central to the present essay, will be realized when we examine the cinema of the 1930s.

The active hostility of the *benshi* was certainly a major factor in the failure of the abortive movement to 'Americanize' the Japanese film. As already pointed out, they were hostile to complicated narrative forms, and a profusion of flashbacks and cross-cutting were essential ingredients of the new style. The *benshi* were, moreover, the mainstay of a mode of representation which the Japanese audience overwhelmingly preferred.[4] The *benshi* reached the height of their popularity just about this time, a fact which is at least as significant of the social status of certain modes of representation in this period as of the supposed universality of the star system.

The *benshi* as an institution was, however, by no means immutable from its inception at the turn of the century to its demise in the late 1930s. The earliest *benshi* worked, of course, mostly with the first American and European films, many of which were documents, authentic or fabricated.[5] They simply held forth as steadily as possible explaining the obvious and the obscure with the same unfailing verve, often repeating themselves imperturbably. By the end of the Meiji era (1912), however, the spread of fiction films and the development of a native industry had led the *benshi* to concentrate almost exclusively on rendering the supposed dialogue. Stylized sound-effects were also used (as in the West during the hey-day of the 'lecturer', only to be quickly abandoned when the cinema moved away from the side-show and into the theatre). In the years that followed, as the technique of dialogue was mastered, the *benshi* began increasingly to interlard comments 'of their own', and to describe, in particular, 'wordless' scenes. In short *they would read the images aloud*. Thus by the end of the war, there had developed in the cinema a procedure closely related indeed to that of the doll theatre, whose texts similarly mingle description with dialogue, often in rapid succession.[6]

As I have indicated, the peak of the *benshi*'s popularity (c. 1918–25) corresponded with the post-war period of inflation and social unrest. Interestingly enough, it was in 1918 that a form of censorship came to affect the twenty-year-old institution.[7] It seems to have been requested by the most respected and high-minded *benshi* themselves, who felt that the good name of their profession was being besmirched by unscrupulous *parvenus* who interspersed their commentaries with smutty and, one suspects, topical remarks which purportedly disturbed members of the audience. In any case, the police instituted a licensing examination; henceforth a certain level of 'culture' and, presumably, of social standing, was required of a would-be *benshi*. One of the results, by no means fortuitous, was that the number of *benshi* practising at any one time was limited. Since it was the established *benshi* who instigated this regulation of their profession, it would seem to be

---

4. Richie and Anderson (op. cit., p. 39) point out that 'the Japanese audience was not yet trained to expect perfect illusionism in films' and that, consequently, a convincingly feminine *oyama* wearing heavy workers' boots was a 'fault' which did not disturb them, even in the context of these 'naturalistic' films (which also continued to employ the same actor in more than one role).

5. I am indebted for this information also to Yoshida Tieo.

6. See Keene, Donald (trans.), *The Major Plays of Chikamatsu*.

7. The films themselves had of course been the object of censorship from the very beginning. This was to be expected in a country where censorship had existed in some form or other for centuries and where it still applied to every form of entertainment and expression including, of course, the press.

linked with the practice of dividing the roles of Japanese films among several *benshi*. This practice did not exist in the doll theatre, but it had far more to do with the *benshi*'s employment problems than with any concern for greater realism, at least at this stage.

Although the *benshi*, and the modes of representation which he helped to preserve, constituted the major hindrance to the implantation of the Hollywood codes, he must not be simplistically viewed as an obstacle in the path of progress. In Japan, the successful introduction of the Hollywood codes, in association, for example, with a very different development of the political and ideological struggle – in other words, with an impossible rewriting of history – would have been artistically far less productive than in the West. The hegemony of bourgeois ideology over the modes of filmic representation did at least make possible the reiteration/translation of the great forms of our literary and theatrical past and hence the creation of such undeniable masterpieces as *Mabuse der Spieler*, *Nana* or *Foolish Wives*. No hypothetical *tabula rasa* of culture could ever have produced the equivalent in Japan (we have only to look at the fate of painting and music there). And while it was to take another decade for the specificity of the Japanese cinema to assert itself fully, that development was determined in large part by this resistance to the Hollywood codes offered by the *benshi* and his allies – such as the *oyama* and *chambera* – and their audience.

The Hollywood codes can, as I have suggested, be described with a fair degree of accuracy as narrative codes, not because they function only on the narrative level as such, but because they have been so intimately associated with *a mode of representation dominated by a certain type of narrative attitude*. Their most characteristic function has been to give linear organization to the signifiers, to the objects of audience perception within a given pro-filmic space, in other words to line them up in those ordered chains which began, after the 'Griffith revolution', to constitute narrative in cinema. This narrative was consubstantial with the literal sequence of images and titles. Its mode of apprehension was preordained. The spectator 'went in' at one end and 'came out' at the other, having followed a path determined with maximum precision, as univocal as the procedures of editing, the organization of angles, shot sizes and camera movements, could make it. Each of these *infrastructural signifiers* had one and only one corresponding meaning. Each was concatenated in a one-to-one relationship with its immediate neighbours in the chain and, through these, with the totality of the chain as it stretched into the 'past' and 'future' of the narrative.

The new-style producers and directors shortly before and after 1920 failed, as we have said, to gain acceptance for their ideas among the Japanese movie-going public, failed to transform the Japanese cinema according to the canons of Hollywood and its European emulators. This failure is imputable to the fact that this need for a linearization, a re-ordering of the 'primitive' image in terms of a pseudo-linguistic montage, was meaningless to the Japanese. It was antithetical to Japanese art, literature and language.[8]

Narrative as such is not foreign to Japanese tradition; it is, on the contrary, omnipresent, but its modes are radically different from ours. As we have already seen, in *kabuki* and the doll theatre the primary narrative dimension is isolated, set apart from the rest of the theatrical substance, *designated as one function among others*. In the West on the other hand, since the eighteenth century, our major narrative arts – the novel, the theatre and more recently the cinema – have tended towards a kind of *narrative saturation*; every element is aimed at conveying, at expressing, a narrative essence. Even in much of nineteenth-century opera, the musical text was regarded as an exteriorization of inner states (feelings, unstated conflicts, memories, etc.) implicit in the libretto.

There exists a large and ancient body of Japanese solo narrative arts, sung and/or spoken, to which both the doll theatre's *gidayu bushi* and the silent cinema's *benshi* are closely related. The complete list, which also includes the already mentioned *naniwa bushi* and *rakugo* (comic monologues), is far too long and specialized to be set down here, but one of the oldest and most seminal instances is the *heikyoku*. Drawing upon a vast body of verse which describes the struggle for power at the end of the twelfth century between the Taira and Minamoto clans, these lyrical narrations employ a set number of typed melodic phrases. The *heikyoku* singer, who accompanies him- or herself on a stringed instrument called the *biwa*, almost always sings and plays *successively*.[9] The singing itself is strictly divided into two types. The narrative singing *per se* calls for the use of a 'white voice', one which is 'transparent' to the factual narrative; the lyrical passages which constitute commentaries, involve the use of a codified set of 'colours', i.e. elaborate vocal techniques. One of these three modes of discourse (chant as against song or instrument alone) has been set aside for the narrative function, the other two have clearly non-narrative functions. Here is a horizontal prefiguration of the type of disjunction which was to achieve such radical perfection in the doll theatre.

Of all the pre-Edo arts, however, the hand-scrolls of the Fujiwara (Heian) and Kamakura periods offer the most

---

8. I wish once again to pay tribute to the work of Iwamoto Kenji, who arrived independently at conclusions essentially identical to my own in this matter. They have been set forth in his unpublished lecture, *The Benshi and Montage in the Japanese Cinema*.

9. See Ueda Makoto, op. cit., pp. 114–27.

remarkable examples of an art in which the narrative dimension is thus circumscribed and isolated. Each scroll is related to some pre-existing text, of oral or literary origin. It was the Heian period which saw the introduction of this genre from China and the birth of a pictorial system of representation which uniquely characterizes Japanese art. These early scrolls consisted of separately framed images alternating with text relating the corresponding narrative. The effect is something like a strip cartoon with written panels in place of balloons. The best-known example of this form is the *Tale of Genji* (*Genji Monogatari*) scrolls, probably dating from the mid-twelfth century. In the Kamakura period, these texts disappear and the scroll becomes one long, continuous 'narrative surface', divided into episodes by various representational or quasi-representational procedures. In neither form, however, can one say that the narrative is 'contained' by the imagery. These scrolls were intended to be 'read' in conjunction with the texts and, at the time of their making, they were. On the other hand, their rhythmic articulation of the painted surface is supremely sophisticated, offering an autonomous plastic statement. The scrolls in no way seek to 'clarify' the text, or to give greater 'presence' to the action or 'depth' to the characters, in the manner of the great Western illustrators. In the *Tale of Genji* series and in the other Heian scrolls, it is impossible to distinguish between faces; they are drawn according to a system of dots and dashes which precludes personalization. The scrolls are both autonomous and redundant with respect to a narrative text; they depend upon their audience's supposed familiarity with the literature and oral tradition of the culture. It was the custom to read aloud in small groups the texts of the Heian scrolls while looking at the images, but this type of *combined performance* does not seem to have survived the disappearance of the inserted texts. I nevertheless maintain that the relationship between the scroll and narrative material is essentially analogous to that established between the *gidayu bushi* and the stage-craft of the doll theatre. Both provide, to quote Barthes, 'a total but divided show' – the doll theatre within the space of the theatre, the scrolls within a vaster socio-cultural space.

It is the heritage exemplified by these practices that determined the rapid rejection of the linear narrative codes of the West by the Japanese film-going public.

# 10. The Fate of Alien Modes

The films made in the new pseudo-American style were predominantly films with a 'social content'; resolutely contemporary, moreover, in setting, they generally reveal efforts to emphasize the aspects of Japan which were visually Western. They depicted milieux in which people predominantly if not exclusively wore Western clothes and lived in Western houses.[1] The actors' make-up, bearing and gesticulation were often modelled on those of American movie stars. And of course, as we have seen, these films adopted wholeheartedly the codes of *découpage* of Hollywood and Europe.

Each of the above-mentioned 'borrowings' involves without a doubt a specific transformation deserving special analysis. In examining these films, however, I shall confine myself almost exclusively to a consideration of the ways in which the codes of *découpage* were displaced, condensed, etc. This choice may appear arbitrary. But our understanding of the manner in which iconographic codes – which convey messages through photographic reproduction, through the perceptual simulation of the real – is, in my view, still embryonic. Moreover, this study is primarily designed to trace the development of Japanese cinema *in terms of its specific modes of representation*. Those modes do not exist independently of the iconographic codes. These, however, will concern us only insofar as they are involved in specific transformations of the basic representational system of Western cinema. This system may be analysed as functioning along three fundamental axes: surface/depth; centering/decentering; continuity/discontinuity. These issues had been 'resolved' within Western cinema in a direction already indicated in Chapter 5. Our task now is to see how they were dealt with during a similar period in Japan.

Among the handful of films which have survived from this brief period, the best known is *Souls on the Road* (*Rojō no reikon*, 1921) directed by Murata Minoru and Osanai Kaoru. Since *Intolerance*, shown in Japan two

---

1. How 'faithfully' these were depicted I have no way of knowing with any certainty. The scant evidence I have seems to point to the existence of such thoroughly Westernized milieux.

Fig. 2. Murata Minoru and Osanai Kaoru, *Souls on the Road*

years earlier, had made a very strong impression there, we may suppose that it provided the chief impetus for what appears to have been a veritable infatuation with cross-cutting procedures among the directors of the new persuasion.

Based in part upon an episode in Gorki's *The Lower Depths*, the scenario of *Souls on the Road* consists of two interwoven stories; to combine them its intricate uses of flashback and cross-cutting have few if any equivalents in the Western cinema of that period. Four groups of characters are involved: an ageing, well-to-do country squire, his devil-may-care daughter (Fig. 2) and his household; a neighbouring farmer in less fortunate circumstances, his family and household; the prodigal son of the latter returning home on foot with his wife and child, after years of estrangement from his father; a pair of workers just released from prison and making their way to their homes, also on foot, and who ultimately find temporary lodging and work at the home of the wealthy squire ... at exactly the same moment as the prodigal son reaches his father's house. To complete this sketch of the character relationships, we must know that the farmer's younger son is involved in a rather desultory romance with the squire's daughter.

During the period (about one third of the film) when the 'souls' are on the road, the narrative editing is particularly complex, moving back and forth along parallel and/or intersecting 'time-lines' of several of the main characters. We see, often in rapid succession, the present and then, in mental flashback, the past of the son and his wife on the road and of his father and mother in the old homestead. The son's flashbacks, and those of his wife and parents, tend to centre around the same events (in particular the circumstances in which the son quarrelled with his father and left home), so that we see the same scenes from different 'viewpoints'. Furthermore, during this part of the film, the present-tense scenes, laid in the two houses – those of the squire and the poor farmer – compose in a sense the 'future' of the two travelling groups. There are consequently four present times, four pasts and two 'futures' in this film; they are strung out over the 'time-lines' of seven adult individuals and one couple, the ex-cons, who never separate, either mentally or physically. We are thus given ten different *stations* in the space/time of the diegesis.[2] If this film is in any way typical it is understandable that the *benshi* were befuddled by the new narrative approach and that the new directors, partly hoping to pre-empt the *benshi's* function, should have introduced a profusion of sequence-prefacing explanatory titles as well as many spoken titles.

This first section of the film, remarkably symmetrical in its organization of the elements described above, caps that regularity with a chance meeting, at a crossroad, of the two travelling groups. In the next section, which almost totally excludes flashbacks (these return at the end of the film), the cross-cutting is accelerated and the suggestion of simultaneity is consequently more emphatic: the prodigal son returns causing heavy emotional turmoil in the old homestead *while at the very same moment* (but see below) the two ex-cons bungle an attempt to burgle the squire's house, are punished by the squire but then, at his daughter's charitable behest, are taken on as gardeners and handymen. In these sequences, the cross-cutting, of an intensity comparable to that of the final section of *Intolerance*, achieves a degree of spatio-temporal intricacy far more complex than that of any Griffith film. Let us consider the opening of this section in some detail:

– the prodigal son's mother sees her son and his wife in the distance, although still off-screen, presumably still struggling across the fields

2. I would consider the sequences which open the film and in which the squire's daughter flirts with the poor farmer's younger son, as a further (eleventh) station, for while it is indeed an association of the two future/presents (the two homes), it is also a sub-plot, a pure present in its own right, though at the same time implying another future, since it is ultimately clear that this affair will have a 'happy ending'.

– the ex-cons are preparing to steal food from the squire's house
– the prodigal son is now with his wife and mother inside the house;[3] they hear the father arriving outside (cross-cut with shots of father)
– the ex-cons stealthily open a window (cross-cut with interior scenes showing preparation of the food which they covet) (striking symmetry with the preceding sequence)
– the squire drives up in a cart and starts to unload it, a direct echo of the very similar arrival of the other father
– in the poor farmer's house, father and returning son are locked in tense confrontation (this scene is fairly long, much longer than the implied time-lapse 'on the other side')
– the squire, shotgun at the ready, captures the ex-cons; a close-up of the squire cuts to . . .
– a close-up of his counterpart, deep in a violent quarrel with his son, inter-cut with shots of the younger son, the mother and the servants listening in the next room (this sequence is very long and we tend to forget the other story)
– the devil-may-care squire's daughter is prancing about in her devil-may-care way; suddenly she overhears . . .
– the ex-cons and her father, who is still holding them at bay with his shot-gun (there is no real sense of time-lapse at all here). They lunge at the older man, and the action is suspended on a close-up of the squire preparing to defend himself
– poor farmer/prodigal son confrontation continues
– returning to the other action, we find one ex-con thrashing the other under the threat of the squire's gun; when the old man feels the punishment is sufficient, he orders the two vagrants to change roles
– poor farmer/prodigal son confrontation continues
– continuation of whipping scene: the injured and unwilling castigator is hardly able to hold the switch (all these punishment scenes are inter-cut with shots of the daughter watching from a nearby hiding-place)
– the prodigal son sits down to table with his father (scene inter-cut with extra-narrative shots of animals feeding – again an effect of symmetry)
– the ex-cons now plead with the squire, invoking the bad treatment received at farms along their way (illustrated flashback) to justify their act of desperation[4]

From this point onward, the frequency of scene changes is somewhat abated: the girl intervenes, pleads with her father; the prodigal son and his father argue over the

THE FATE OF ALIEN MODES

3. As it went without saying that the mother's welcome would be one of warm devotion, this meeting is played down to the point of obliteration.

4. I wish to stress that this transcription is scene-by-scene, not shot-by-shot, which would be non-pertinent here. Nor have I taken into account the numerous dialogue titles. All the characters, of course, have Japanese names; the stereotypes used here are an attempt to convey the remarkable resemblance, on the diegetic level, to the products, grounded in nineteenth-century melodrama, of Western cinema of the same period.

103

dinner table; the ex-cons are (symmetrically) fed by squire and daughter. The squire then goes to an inn to invite other 'poor souls' to the Christmas party, complete with tree, which we had seen his daughter preparing in the first section of the film; in the meantime, the prodigal son's intractable father has sent him out into the snow to sleep in a shabby barn.

This bare account should make clear the manner in which this film differs from its Western models. Its truly hypertrophied cross-cutting is developed beyond Griffith's wildest dreams. For the bulk of Western audiences and film-makers, cross-cutting was still what the young Griffith understood it to be – a means of showing alternate aspects of a *diegetically homogeneous* action.

Constantly wavering between the cross-diegetic cutting of *Intolerance* and the homogeneous system of *Birth of a Nation, Souls on the Road,* through a varied and quite subtly graded use of rhymes and other correspondencies, sets up a system whose sophistication remotely anticipates that of *Strike* or *October. Souls on the Road* is, moreover, an excellent illustration of the inadequacy of the classical distinction between 'alternate montage' and 'parallel montage', since it partakes of both: at one level, the film is composed of two 'separate' diegeses. Yet these nonetheless communicate with each other through peripheral characters and two chance meetings on the road, one near the beginning of the film, the other near the end.[5]

Western audiences were not yet equipped to deal with such complexities and would not be for at least two decades, notwithstanding the various European avant-gardes. Whether or not Japanese audiences of that time were any better equipped is open to question The highly intricate plot structures of so many *chambera* and their modern derivatives indicate, however, that on this level too the topological habits of thinking we have previously alluded to had their role to play.

In *Souls on the Road*, we also have a markedly symmetrical patterning of both pro-filmic events and narrative articulations. This manifest formalization of what in Griffith was a purely signifying figure also 'anticipates' the structured alternative to transparency at its most coded which was soon to be offered by Lang and Dreyer. The organization of the cross-cutting and other elements in this film, though determined culturally and ideologically on a totally different plane, is not unrelated to that of *M* or *La Passion de Jeanne d'Arc*.[6] It too contains objective radicalizations of the Western narrative codes, *a geometrization of certain signifiers which is beyond the requirements of the codes* as defined by the corpus which they underpin.[7]

---

[5]. Christian Metz's category of the 'alternate syntagma' encompasses all such figures, including presumably the extra-diegetic, metaphorical parallels developed by Eisenstein (final sequence of *Strike*) and others. This is a far more useful concept than the alternate/parallel opposition (*Film Language*, pp. 102–5).

[6]. See my articles on Lang and Dreyer in Roud, R. (ed.), *A Dictionary of the Cinema* (forthcoming).

[7]. The exaggerated dilation/contraction of the two narrative time-streams and the very strange use, in scenes I have not described, of overlaid images implying the mental presence of a distant character (the 'real' character speaks to this visualization of his or her thoughts as to a 'ghost') are also examples of a significant licence.

The attitude manifest in this film does not seem to have been a matter of individual style, particularly if we consider the probability that, although this film was related to the anti-*benshi* movement, the spatio-temporal shifts suggested above[8] would have been too great a risk to take at that time in Japan without the presence of the *benshi*. For no matter how 'topological' the Japanese mind, we must not forget that the codes were brand new in the decisive context of the native film. Yet the Japanese director of silent films never had to fear that the public might not understand the story. Even when he felt, as Murata and Osanai did, that the *benshi* should go, he instinctively relied on his presence. It is true that given the massive introduction of plot articulations of this kind (flashback, cross-cut), he might have to cope with the obtuseness of the *benshi*. However, while it was perhaps *benshi* resistance that nipped this new style in the bud, Kinugasa was, after all, able to find at least one *benshi* for his 'surrealistic' *Page of Madness* and Mizoguchi to construct a silent narrative as extravagantly intricate as *O-Sen of the Paper Cranes* – indications that this obtuseness was not unanimous. What is essential here is that throughout the 1920s and well into the 1930s, the problem of the elimination of spatio-temporal ambiguities at every level of articulation, from eyeline match to time lapse, though central to the very existence of illusionist codes in the West, never seems to have bothered the film-makers of Japan, almost undoubtedly because of the *benshi*, whose task it was to *spell out* the diegesis. On the strength of the picture alone, scene changes (spatial and/or spatio-temporal breaks) are often indistinguishable from simple shot changes within the scene. The lack of any clearly intended ambiguity (such as one detects on occasion in *Souls on the Road*) suggests that elementary information of certain kinds was not considered necessary to be conveyed by the picture. 'This is still the same set' or 'now we are elsewhere', were statements that explicitly or implicitly formed part of the *benshi*'s discourse.[9]

Knowing that the new-style directors universally scorned the *benshi* as a basic impediment of the old style, we may assume, as I have already suggested, that the plethora of inter-titles, both descriptive and 'spoken', also represented an attempt to set limits on the *benshi*'s activity, to *channel* his reading in accordance with the notions of unity and linearity which were inevitably a part of the process of Westernization. It appears, however, that the *benshi* countered this move by departing as far as possible from the text on the screen even while it was being projected, and this was often very far. Thus, throughout the period of inter-titled Japanese films, three *texts* were produced during a

THE FATE OF ALIEN MODES

8. At times so intimate that the 'seams' between two parallel actions are not always immediately apparent, even to the present-day viewer. Of course, iconographic elements may have facilitated this distinction for the Japanese viewer of the period. However, the rigorous adoption of the codes of *découpage* by film-makers such as Gosho during the period when sound was gradually eliminating the *benshi* does indicate that these are indeed *universally valid* if the objective goal is transparent representation as the West has defined it. At the same time, according to Iwasaki Akira, *Souls on the Road* was a commercial failure (in *Japan Film Yearbook*, 1936). Is this to be related to the general resistance of Japanese audiences to the naturalization of the Western codes or to the film's 'over-use' of them? Probably to both.

9. Inagaki Hiroshi is once said to have remarked that the Japanese directors took to sound without any difficulties at all since they already had it in the *benshi*. As we shall see, it is possible to take this to mean that Japanese directors already knew that sound and image were two separate parameters as are stage-craft and chant in the doll theatre.

performance: that of the image itself, that of the *written reading of the pictures* provided by those who had filmed and edited them, and of course by the *benshi*'s own oral reading, with its musical accompaniment.

*Souls on the Road*, then, was not a 'straightforward' adoption of the Hollywood system. This was inconceivable only fifty years after the Meiji Restoration, although it has, particularly since the Second World War, been achieved in Japan with far greater fidelity. It was not, on the other hand, the simple illustration of one of the typical transformation processes as I have tried to define them. The film is dominated by a contradiction between the intent to illustrate the foreign modes and their involuntary radicalization. The Hollywood codes are used with an extravagance that subverts to a degree their illusionist function; they are visibly inscribed in the text of the film. The superabundance of titles, presumably aimed, as in the West, at rendering the film as unequivocal as possible, at pre-empting the *benshi*'s discourse,[10] controlling and 'conscripting' it, actually resulted in an increased fragmentation of the signifying tissue, the substance of expression, thereby strengthening its ultimate similarity to the traditional theatre.[11]

It appears, however, that in this early period, and even among the films of the new style, such an intensive use of spoken and descriptive titles was exceptional. While the popular cinema (primarily *chambera*, but also *shimpa*-inspired modern dramas) was still totally without them, other 'advanced' films struck what might be regarded as a compromise between these two positions. However, as is always the case in these specifically Japanese transpositions, the result of the 'compromise' was more radical, from our point of view, than either of the extremes.

I have had access to only one example of this type of film, but several Japanese historians assure me that it is known, through eye-witness accounts and surviving fragments, to represent an aspect of the period. *Winter Camellia(s)* (*Kantsubaki*, 1921) was directed by Inoue Masao, 'a shin-geki actor recently returned from America', according to Anderson and Richie, for whom, in unfavourable contrast to *Souls on the Road*, 'it smelled too strongly of the stage' and 'was quite artificial'.[12] Setting aside the pejorative overtones, these assertions are perfectly correct and corroborate the exemplary ambivalence of this film, participating as it does of both *shimpa* and *shin-geki* – and yet which owed its commercial success to the presence on the screen of one of Japan's first movie actresses. Not surprisingly, this 'theatrical artificiality' went hand in hand with a greater regard for the *benshi* and his role, so that *Winter Camellia* – whose narrative need not concern us in detail

---

10. It is hard to say whether the elimination of the American and European lecturer was a strategy consciously adopted by directors and producers. Whatever the case, it was quickly achieved, whereas in Japan a fifteen-year anti-*benshi* campaign did not succeed in removing him, and it was not until the definitive implantation of the technological infrastructure necessary for the generalization of sound made his presence redundant and, in a time of economic depression, onerous, that he finally did disappear.

11. We shall soon see how Kinugasa, also wishing to dispense with the *benshi*, took the opposite course, completely eliminating titles, and he too ended by radicalizing the new modes rather than simply reproducing them.

12. Anderson and Richie, op. cit., p. 44.

here – employs very few inter-titles, several dozen at most.[13]

Titles in the film are of two sorts. There are laconic commentaries, no doubt related to the type of remark which the *benshi* would be making (for example: 'A strange guest', preceding the first visit of the miller's shy daughter to the house of the well-to-do family).[14] There are also 'spoken titles' which fulfil much the same purpose as in the West. However, many of these are *superfluous as titles*, since the words projected on the screen are redundant. They are what is known in linguistics as *phatic speech*, messages which, in cinema, are easily transmissible through pantomime. Conversely, long scenes of dialogue, where only the general sense is decipherable from the image, are totally untitled; here, clearly, the *benshi* was on his own. One of the most remarkable instances of this apparent reversal is provided by the two final scenes, in which the homicidal father is first prevented from committing suicide by a police inspector, and then, as he trudges down the road under arrest, is overtaken by his grief-stricken daughter. Neither the long farewell dialogue between father and daughter, nor the slightly shorter one with the policeman at the moment of the arrest, involves a single title; only the daughter's cry of 'Father!' as she runs down the road after him is honoured by a perfectly useless title, *useless according to the Western manner of titling*. Various explanations have been offered for this phenomenon. Film stars are said to have demanded titles to highlight their roles (a habit also prevalent in Hollywood). In this film, however, the few titles seem to be distributed quite evenly among the cast, although the woman, Mizutani Yaeko, is (and apparently was) regarded as the top star. It is also said that the *benshi* had considerable say in the use of titles; they may have thought titles deserved only trivial expressions beneath a *benshi*'s dignity. There is probably some truth in both these 'explanations'.[15] In any case, the *benshi* almost certainly tended to ignore these titles, either by silence while they were on the screen or by improvising a different, perhaps even contradictory, text.

These titles, then, were completely redundant; they institute, in fact, a new substance of expression, writing *in and for itself*, as graphic element, as opaque signifier, as a gesture of pure signification, which takes its place between the discourse of the *benshi*, pre-empting the other titles of their narrative function, and the image, pre-empting these titles of their phatic function. This mutual pre-empting of narrative functions could only heighten the divorce between screen and voice. Here we have a configuration doubly homologous with that of the doll theatre. For,

THE FATE OF ALIEN MODES

13. This film also deals with a situation based on class relationships, with the rich playboy compromising the only daughter of an ageing miller, who ultimately murders him. There is a faint echo here of the exactly contemporary *Foolish Wives* which attests, rather than to any less than hypothetical 'influence', to these film-makers' attentiveness to the thematic arsenal of Western naturalism. It is also interesting to note that the 'realistic' murder (of a superior by his inferior) was, judging by the present state of an otherwise impeccable negative, censored (in a way which would have made the sequence quite bewildering without the *benshi*'s helpful presence). This of course confirms that whatever their ultimate historical role as regards the development of film-art in Japan, *benshi*, *oyama*, etc. were objective allies of the political establishment in so far as they were hindering the rise of a cinema which it sought to repress.

14. Of course, such titles had also become common in the West, where they may be regarded as the surviving traces of the lecturer.

15. Richie and Anderson's only comment on titling at this period is a reference to distribution contracts by which producers were 'reimbursed on a direct per-foot basis.' This encouraged them to 'introduce long and meaningless titles, so much cheaper to shoot than live action' (op. cit., p. 61). This may explain *in part* the profusion of written text in a film like *Souls on the Road*. It certainly doesn't account for the rare and 'useless' titles in *Winter Camellia*.

extending Barthes' analysis, one may equate the *effective gesture* of the puppeteers' hands with that of the calligrapher's.

*Winter Camellia* complies in every other important respect with the codes of representation that were by then totally dominant in the West.[16] In particular, and in contrast with the then still prevalent character of most Japanese films, considerable pains were taken to film location and even some interior settings *at oblique angles*, a procedure[17] which has been a strategy basic to the system guaranteeing the visual illusion of depth (as opposed to its mental illusion, which hinges rather on the reverse field). The oblique angle had been the rule in the West ever since the film-makers of Griffith's day had succeeded in proscribing the frontal viewpoint, immediately inherited from the theatrical side of cinema's ancestry.

It should be emphasized that in *chambera*, the dominant genre of the period, oblique angles remained exceptional, despite the fact that when visual depth-effects were introduced, it was in connection with the sword-fighting scenes precisely typical of such films. Makino's *Jitsuroku Chūshingura* (*The True Story of the Loyal Retainers*, 1928) is certainly no *chambera*, but a long series of hieratic dialogues, filmed for the most part in a two-dimensional spirit (see Fig. 3). It ends nonetheless at the moment of Kira's punishment, with a bravura sequence in which foreground and background actions are skilfully opposed. The fact that the film was clearly a more elaborate, costly production than the period average may have stimulated this development. In any case, that last sequence is possibly one of the earliest in which the aptitude of Japanese architecture to produce a certain type of depth-effect is systematically exploited. More generally this dichotomy was characteristic of the average *chambera*, in which dialogue scenes were uniformly shot frontally[18] while the fights usually took place on location and by the mid-1920s were frequently filmed from all angles.

Between 1920 and 1926–7 the wide-angle, frontal shot remained the rule for both interiors and exteriors, though the concertina and reverse field did begin, very slowly, to spread, so that medium close-ups and close-ups became more frequent. However, it was not until Makino's maturity as represented by this late *Chūshingura* that the Western codes made real inroads on the serious period drama which was growing out of *chambera* largely due to the impetus of Makino. Previously to that, I feel that on the whole the use to which *chambera* put the concertina is, again, closer to the 'stage-economy' of *kabuki* than to the typically Western project of characterization/singulariza-

---

16. An interesting, though indeed incidental exception is the use of protracted long shots of a revolving water-wheel as a mode of punctuation closer to the 'pillow shots' of Ozu (see Chapter 16) than to the cutaway 'bridges' of Hollywood and Europe.

17. One might well call it a rule: whether trained in a school or a studio, our budding director or cameraman always learns never to set the camera up at right angles to a flat background.

18. This flatness derived quite directly from the conception of the *kabuki* 'interior': an open-front box of scarcely any perceptual depth set up here or there inside the proscenium frame.

Fig. 3. Makino Shozo, *The True Story of the Loyal Retainers* (1928)

tion prophesied by Dickson in *Fred Ott's Sneeze* and carried out by the generation of Griffith. It recalls rather the mechanical elimination of what is no longer part of the action, the removing of properties by stage assistants when they have served their purpose, the conventional closing of an 'interior' when the character(s) in it are no longer active in the scene.

Despite, then, this reluctant and somewhat 'unorthodox' introduction of the coded editing figures of the West, frontality in dialogue scenes (as against the increasing freedom of action scenes) remained a rule allowing for few exceptions until the late 1920s. This is important because, as we shall see, frontality long remained an important part of the vocabulary of even the most routine Japanese film-maker. In the West, apart from its renewal in advanced work such as Dreyer's *Gertrud*, the films of Godard, Warhol or Snow, it has been eliminated for over a half-century. In Japan, its role in, for example, the singular systemics of Ozu, was to be absolutely determinant.

# 11. Displacements and Condensations

The best-known director of *chambera* during this period was Ito Daisuke who was still making films until well after the Pacific War (as the Japanese call their part in World War Two). Though it would be wrong to say he was the inventor of this genre, he was certainly one of its major codifiers. *Chambera* grew out of a classical encounter between Japanese presentationalism and a demand for realism, stimulated by the impact of Western ideologies and modes of representation, but produced by the objective development of Japanese society. The chief difference between the earliest *chambera* and the transposed *kabuki* and *shimpa* plays of the previous two decades was the greater realism of the sword-fights. When a character died, he no longer performed a backward somersault but collapsed in bloody agony; above all, the actor's body struck the tense poses of actual combat as opposed to the stylized, *relaxed* gestures of the *kabuki* encounter. The word *chambera*, onomatopoeia representing the clash of swords, very precisely designates this difference, since on the *kabuki* stage swords never touch.[1]

Aside from this important change and the gradually increasing but still *perfunctory* use of the narrative editing of the West, the bulk of these films, as I have said, remained very similar to those of the previous period, with a predominance of head-on long shots and with the narrative burden still devolving on the *benshi*.

Ito seems to have made several interesting innovations, whether or not he did so thinking to emulate Western procedures directly. He seems to have been the first to introduce 'dynamic' editing into his combat scenes. He initiated, reportedly at the behest of his skilful cameraman, Karasawa Hiromitsu, that extravagant use of the hand-held camera which was to characterize a whole school of *chambera*, from the mid-1920s until at least the implantation of sound. An examination of these traits of the 'Ito style' will provide us with some insights into the

---

1. At the same time, it seems significant of the place assigned to realism by Japanese culture, that a verbal stylization of a *sound* should give its name to a *silent* film genre, in which the sound itself was never heard but was replaced ... precisely by the onomatopoeia of the *benshi* and by written (sometimes animated) onomatopoeia in the titles.

problem of the transformation of the Western codes during this period of Japanese assimilation.

At present, the only known surviving samples of Ito Daisuke's own art are a large number of fragments collected by Matsuda Shunji.[2] However, a film preserved in the Film Centre of the Tokyo Museum of Modern Art, *The Red Bat* (*Beni Kōmori*, 1931) by one Tanaka Tsuruhiko, clearly belongs to the Ito tradition. Since it is one of the few intact examples of the mature period of the silent *chambera*, comparisons are difficult. It is certainly related to the Ito fragments I have seen, and I have been assured by Sato Tadao[3] that it is typical of this important variety of *chambera*.[4]

This film retains few of the pertinent traits of the Japanese Primitive and what I would call the Neo-Primitive periods, apart from that typical Japanese predilection for the long shot and the frontal view. However, within a system of representation close to the Western model, it introduces a number of 'displacements and condensations'[5] which may be said to undermine decisively the basic purpose of those codes not only as articulated in the West but as faithfully adopted by those Japanese directors who were impressed by their commercial success, and/or experienced an artistic and ideological need for them.

I will not attempt to set forth the rambling plot of *The Red Bat*, which relates the swashbuckling adventures of an impetuous do-gooder named Chotaro who tries to repair the injustice done a jilted maiden. Our concern is with the strategies which Tanaka, closely following Ito's lead, borrows from the Western representational system, wherein they already played extremely circumscribed and/or exceptional roles; our concern is with the way he converts them into polyvalent signifiers, *as general as the cut itself*, insofar as it can acquire any of the different possible spatio-temporal significations according to the diegetic context.[6] These three strategies, in order of importance, are, the swish-pan, the lap-dissolve and 'dynamic editing', which I will pragmatically and provisionally define as a succession of unusually brief shots.

The swish-pan (and more generally the free-wheeling camera movements characteristic of the Ito school) presumably came to Japanese films when the first small cameras of American and French manufacture reached Japan in the mid-1920s. Now in the West, until the spread of hand-held techniques in television news-coverage and *cinéma-vérité*, the swish-pan was an exception and was always used connotatively, with what may be called an *exclamatory function*, while its denotative

DISPLACEMENTS AND CONDENSATIONS

2. The survival of so many fragments from that period and so few complete films is something of a mystery to me. Presumably it is related to the practice of compiling excerpts to make up for the scarcity of films just after the war. This practice was facilitated of course by the visual similarity of so many films from that period.

3. He has written, in collaboration with Yoshida Tieo, a history of the genre, *Chambera eigashi*.

4. There is some internal evidence that the film is, in part, meant as a parody of the Ito style, and this aspect of the project may be responsible for some of the paroxysms described. Responsible in degree, perhaps, but not, I am convinced on the evidence of surviving Ito fragments, in kind.

5. At present I am unable to provide theoretical justification for the use of a metaphor borrowed from Freud's analysis of the dream-work. I do feel, nevertheless, in dealing with the relations between such radically *other* cultures that the *Interpretation of Dreams* provides keys to some of the strange visions they will have of each other.

6. Spatial and/or temporal continuity, spatial contiguity, temporal simultaneity, spatial alterity, definite or indefinite time-lapse, ultimately flashback or temporal overlap. See Some Terminological Indications; also my *Theory of Film Practice*, Chapter 1.

value was almost always that of temporal continuity and spatial contiguity.[7] This sporadic, specialized role is still attached to the swish-pan in most narrative film.

In *The Red Bat*, the swish-pan occurs on the contrary with extraordinary frequency, and is used to fill, *alternatively but not invariably*, three different signifying functions which in the Western codes had long since devolved upon the cut, black-out or dissolve: reverse-field match, cross-cut (cutaway) and flashback. As I say, this practice is not invariable, for while many reverse-field series are articulated by swish-pans, these often alternate within the same series or from one series to another, with lap-dissolves – another anomaly with respect to what was by then standard Western practice – or plain cuts. Similarly, while most parallel action sequences are linked through swish-pans, simple scene-changes, often involving a mode of spatio-temporal shift semantically equivalent to the cross-cut, are only occasionally subject to this procedure.[8]

*The Red Bat*, like, apparently, many films of the same school, extended the denotative polyvalence characteristic of the cut alone within the Western codes to other types of shot articulations which, in the West, were pruned, as it were, of their polysemous potential and assigned a single, undisputed denotation/connotation set.[9] The connotative functions are effaced entirely; the swish-pan loses its exclamatory value and the lap-dissolve its poetic implication. And while the intended meaning of any given dissolve, swish-pan or cut in *The Red Bat* is ultimately specified by the diegetic context, as in the Western film, the process of specification is no longer the same.

This free polyvalence of the three articulative signifiers most frequently used in this film is directly at odds with what was already the irreversible tendency of the dominant Western cinema: an increasing specialization of all 'special effects' and an increasing polyvalence of the plain cut alone, in conjunction with a sophisticated refinement of the specifying powers of the diegetic organization. In contrast with the historical tendency towards economy in the Western codes, there is a kind of non-signifying residue in the swish-pans and dissolves of *The Red Bat*. A cut and a swish-pan may have the same semantic value; moreover, their choice as signifiers of, say, spatial alterity, is clearly *arbitrary* with respect to the narrative and precludes any 'expressive' codification. Thus, these particular forms of shot-change carry a *surplus mark* which is extraneous to the process of producing meaning at the primary, spatio-temporal level of the narrative.

---

7. Frequently today, exceptionally during the 'classical' period of Western cinema, the swish-pan has been assigned an *unexpected* denotative value (flashback, time-lapse and/or spatial alterity). Of course, the connotative/denotative opposition is an over-simplification, since we are actually dealing here with a set of *specifiers* which have meaning only insofar as they refer to the complex of codes which constitute the diegesis: a cut, a swish-pan have no semantic value whatsoever in themselves, as does a word which, even out of syntagmatic context, has a lexical meaning that has no equivalent here. However, on the level of this 'meta-code', it does seem legitimate to employ this terminology, since the difference between the two functions at stake can be shown to be homologous with that which separates linguistic connotation from denotation.

8. In such instances, the common practice is a variant on the 'cross-cutting' procedure of *lateral* swish-pans: the camera streaks upward to the sky; this shot is followed by a similar pan down from the sky to an action distant in diegetic time or space.

9. It was during the period of conversion to sound in the West that the dissolve became equated with time-lapse and/or spatial alterity. This development responded to a need for *specification* which had until then been satisfied by the newly proscribed inter-title, in conjunction or not with the iris or black-out. The Japanese extension of the lap-dissolve was, in Western terms, a 'restoration', since this procedure had originally been far more polyvalent than it was to become in the late 1920s and early 1930s.

**DISPLACEMENTS AND CONDENSATIONS**

Dominant ideology, in its relevant manifestations, qualifies such non-signifying differences either as signs of 'stylistic coherence' or as 'formalism', according to the social prestige attached to their contexts. These value judgements have no pertinence here. *The Red Bat* would be dismissed as 'trash' by most critics, with the possible exception of those who habitually make a fetish of popular culture. These films are indeed part of popular culture, but in a sense inapplicable perhaps in the West, since they derived their partly presentational approach from conceptions shared by an entire society for centuries. In the West, it was a dominant class which, in the course of its struggle to subdue a rising class, imposed upon that class (and ultimately upon most of society) a synoptic version of what were uniquely its own modes of representation. Most important of all, these were watered down to an impoverished functionalism in support of archetypal fantasies and an ideologically weighted illusionism. The silent films of Cecil B. De Mille are worlds removed from the novels of Dickens. *The Red Bat* was still very close to the Edo stage.

There are many types of articulations that can be used to join shots in a film. It is, of course, no accident that the briefest and the least perceptible assumed the basic function in the Western system of a highly developed diegetic continuum. Aside from its greater technological simplicity, the cut proved from the outset to be the *ideally transparent signifier*; its invisibility – through editing procedures such as eyeline matching or cutting on movement – was such that the 'meaning', the message, seemed to issue forth naturally from the context as a whole, from the flow of images itself. In other words, the *signification* of this articulation receded to a pre-conscious level. On the other hand, such articulations as the iris, one of the earliest to be coded, no doubt because of an evident analogy with the spotlight iris of the stage, or the dissolve, uncoded until the 1930s, were both experienced as disruptive, and continue to be so today. They were perceived as signs, whereas the cut was very quickly seen as 'change' or 'shift' or 'passage of time' *as such*. This very material event came to be the transparent, 'immaterial' representation of certain narrative dimensions, a representation as 'natural' as language. It was only after much trial and error, that an adequate code of 'punctuation' succeeded in locking the other shot-change procedures into a comparably 'natural' system. This system remained very fragile, always threatening to break down, precisely because of the duration and the positive, perceptual materiality of the signifiers involved: iris, fade, dissolve, wipe. This frailty explains in part the frequent redistribution of functions over the years among these signifiers, as one device becomes 'old-fashioned' (i.e. it is perceived as material signifier) and is superseded by another. Thus we may explain the gradual disappearance of the wipe during and after the Second World War, the more recent tendency to reserve the dissolve for special, expressive effects and to convey ellipsis through a combination of the plain cut with diegetic strategies. There are, however, no grounds for what is commonly regarded as the 'natural' distinction between the cut and, say, the dissolve. A space between words is a sign as much as a hyphen or a period.

In contrast to the cut, procedures such as swish-pans and dissolves, particularly when first introduced and still uncoded, were visible as such precisely because they impinged upon the representational integrity of the photographic image – of the iconographic codes. They were an impediment to the conviction that what we see on a motion picture screen is 'natural', a recreation of the conditions of actual viewing. For this reason, by the time the introduction of synch sound had completed the equipment of dominant cinema, it became urgent to assign these procedures, narrowly limited denotative and/or connotative functions, to create automatic reflexes which would efface them. They had, in other words, to conform to the linear model which ordered both the reading of the iconographic elements within the frame and the succession of the montage-pieces as such. It was essential that there be no superfluous, 'gratuitous' marks which could call into question the economy of this system: the bourgeois codes are *thrifty*.[10]

As we have seen, this approach to representation was completely foreign to the Japanese performing, literary and visual arts. Yet at the same time, the editing system of *The Red Bat* (and of the Ito scraps available to us) *contains* the Western system, which very often functions quite normally within it. The approach here is, in fact, non-committal. It refuses to constitute a system of its own. It is the ever-present possibility of emergence/submergence of the Western system which makes these films appear so 'deconstructive' of the codes that dominate our cinema. The articulative strategies are often presented as such, but very often they are not. The discourse shifts unpredictably, arbitrarily from a 'hieroglyphic' to a 'phonetic' system – which, of course, is one of the faculties of the Japanese language.

One can easily imagine a film made entirely according to Western norms in which, however, the cut would be systematically replaced by the swish-pan, and the dissolve by two feet of red leader. We would still be dealing with a perfectly linear code of discontinuities and once the code

---

10. For further remarks on this concept of bourgeois thrift, see Chapter 19.

had been learned, it would become perfectly 'transparent' for users. It is the fact that in *The Red Bat* a given set of meanings are associated with three *interchangeable and 'arbitrarily' chosen signifiers* which allows us to claim that this film does not simply substitute one code for another but constitutes, on this narrow but significant level, a challenge to the very notion of the code. It is true enough that this same challenge was set forth far more coherently in Europe the very next year (1932) by Dreyer's *Vampyr*. Dreyer, however, as we know, had already entered the forty-year purgatory when he would be allowed to make an average of one film every five years, seen only by an élite audience. Directors like Tanaka and Ito annually made dozens that were seen by the entire Japanese film-going public. *What was a mass cultural attitude in Japan was a deeply subversive vanguard practice in the Occident.*

The third Western strategy to be adopted and transformed by this school of *chambera* was that which I have schematically termed 'dynamic editing'. It is characteristic of the silent period of Soviet cinema and of Eisenstein's films in particular. It also characterizes some early films of the first French avant-garde or 'Impressionist School' (Gance, L'Herbier, Epstein). Together with the 'Paris Russians' (Volkoff, Mosjoukine and Kirsanoff) – who took most of their ideas from the experiments of Soviet and French pioneers – it seems it was the latter who were directly instrumental in acquainting Japanese directors with the European movement's reaction against the imposition of the system of representation that had been perfected in the United States.

The *découpage* of certain sections of *Potemkin* (I, II, IV) illustrates a critique of dominant cinema on the part of advanced film-makers in Eastern and Western Europe at that time. Simultaneously, other film-makers in the Soviet Union and elsewhere, from Pudovkin to Volkoff, wholeheartedly committed to the ethos of representation, illusion, expression, identification, etc., were employing 'fast cutting' to express 'violence', 'passion', 'music', 'dance',[11] or otherwise endowing it with *meaning*, reducing it, in fact, to a monovalent signifier. This is the form in which 'fast cutting' was eventually assimilated into the codes of dominant cinema throughout the West: a *specialized*, connotative element, much like the swish-pan.

This coded approach to 'dynamic editing' soon found its way into the Japanese film, where it often appeared side by side, however, with the polyvalent approach to other procedures as already described. In Makino's 1928 *Chūshingura*, swish-pan and dissolve often have that nominally 'neutral' function, equivalent to that of the coded cut,

DISPLACEMENTS AND CONDENSATIONS

11. Of course, such non-verbal signifiers cannot be reduced to verbal ones. The signifying process in film is *homologous* to, but not identical with, the linguistic process proper. I might also add that Eisenstein strayed into the paths of this 'expressivism' as well, not merely in the writings of the 1930s, but in the films of the 1920s (the final section of *Potemkin*, the Tartars' dance in *October*).

tending only intermittently towards a 'Western' connotative function (exclamatory, 'poetic'). At the same time, all the moments of greatest tension during the various meetings of the *rōnin* (to discuss the ethical problems involved in the pre-vendetta situation) are systematically underscored by an acceleration in the succession of medium close-ups which predominate in these scenes.

The *chambera* of the Ito approach also follows, *to some extent*, the dominant Western model. Scenes representing physical violence are similarly intensified by fast cutting and free-wheeling (hand-held) camera movements. A sequence near the beginning of *The Red Bat* in which Chotaro demonstrates his prodigious strength by hurling cart-wheels and various farming implements high into the air and on to his numerous assailants, is an excellent instance of a type of scene which seems to have abounded in Ito's own films as well as those which he influenced. However, this scene also reveals a contradiction which typifies the Japanese attitude at that period. For as it unfolds, it also results in a playful but nonetheless radical *decentering* of the imagery with respect to the narrative situation, a weakening rather than a strengthening of the diegetic effect. The introduction of vertical, lyrical developments of plastic and kinetic motifs brings the diegetic flow to a standstill (as in Eisenstein's *The General Line*, for example). At one point during Chotaro's exhibition – which in itself has the 'presentational' quality of an *aragoto* ('rough stuff') dance in *kabuki* – we abandon the earth-bound protagonists and onlookers completely for nearly a minute, to observe a pyrotechnical display of flying cart-wheels, harrows, etc., seen as black, abstracted silhouettes against a white sky. The effect is one of vertical accumulation of empty signs, a momentary negation of the diegetic plenitude from which they are nonetheless excerpted. And one may say that, starting from an attitude implying wholesale adoption of a Western code, a typical Japanese process of transformation and *radicalization* (traceable, through *benshi, kabuki*, etc. to the historical modules) issues, spontaneously, as it were, in the critical modes through which advanced Western film-makers challenged the domination of bourgeois illusionism.

# 12. Surface and Depth

We know that the modes of representation of volume and depth as developed in the visual arts between the thirteenth and fifteenth centuries constituted a fresh point of departure for figurative technique. This development was also an important moment in the intellectual history of the West. One of the main obligations incumbent upon those who later undertook to codify the modes of filmic representation in accordance with the values of the dominant class was to implement a filmic response to the need for the rendering of depth.[1] Conversely, the general lack of concern with visual depth in the arts of the East and particularly those of Japan (*e-makimono*, or picture scrolls, Muromachi screens, the prints of *ukiyo-e*; *nō*, *kabuki*, doll theatre) were preserved in cinema long after the 'laws'[2] of depth-representation by the camera were established in the West.

The acknowledgement of the pictorial surface in Japanese painting and the tendency of Japanese poetry to focus the reader's awareness on the *graphic and textual surface* may be seen as perfectly antithetical to the two-fold matrix, visual and dramaturgical, which was imposed on the cinema in the West during the Formative period. As we have already noted, some of the major efforts to set the Hollywood system at a critical distance (Godard, Dreyer's *Gertrud*, Warhol, Snow) have been directed against its modes of depth representation. The very first film to undertake systematically such a task, *The Cabinet of Doctor Caligari*, returns to the flat frontality of the Primitive cinema in conjunction with a very sophisticated exploration of the depth/surface and 'opacity'/'transparency' dichotomies. In *Caligari*, strategies of relief (oblique trajectories, perspective convergency) are introduced within a pictorial system whose painterly flatness contradicts and in fact *explodes* the conventions which had by 1919 developed to an unprecedented degree of efficiency in the West. For setting aside the complex, though ultimately trivial, problems of 3D, it may be said that by

1. It is not true that the machine itself, the camera, 'produced' from its very inception, a linear perspective in happy conformity with the needs of that bourgeoisie whose science had produced the machine. The notion of a bourgeois science is no more valid in our field than in genetics. We need only compare what was so often the patent flatness of 'Primitive space' with the developments which gave the depth-producing strategies the status of a system.

2. I have already referred to the hard-and-fast 'film-school' ban on filming at right angles to a wall. One might add the equally stringent rule against 'zooming' in such a position. These laws also include the complex codes manipulated by the lighting cameraman and set-designer, directly derived from the principles of post-Renaissance perspective.

the time the dominant mode had been completed on the visual level, thanks to the establishment of the 'enveloping reverse field', the cinema had succeeded in acquiring the illusionist strategies of painting, sculpture, theatre and literature as perfected during the nineteenth century. All that was missing was synchronous sound.

The flattening of the image in the work of, say, Ozu after 1933 may legitimately be regarded as a deliberate 'throwback', comparable to the strategy of *Caligari*. The persistence of *primitive flatness* in so many Japanese films during the 1920s is, on the other hand, 'accidental': it was a collective phenomenon and came about through the interaction of certain Western editing methods with certain characteristics of traditional Japanese architecture. Yet, insofar as it was determined by the general 'surface orientation' of the arts of Japan, especially of her architecture,[3] it was, of course, no accident at all. Nor was Ozu's strategy a purely personal invention.

When the traditional-minded Japanese director of the 1920s began moving his camera in for increasingly frequent medium and close shots, he felt no need whatsoever to modify the 90° angle of camera to background. (I am referring, of course, primarily to interior sequences or to exteriors involving architectural planes.) Nor did this sparing introduction of editing into most films diminish in any way the dominion of the frontal view and the long-shot (in marked contrast, by the mid-1920s, with the *découpage* of the average Western film). And, of course, these wide-angle shots allowed the native architecture to assert itself fully. The significant absence of furniture in the Japanese interior, the comprehensive articulation of every surface in terms of asymmetrically disposed *rectangles* (the purest expression of the concept of two-dimensionality) inevitably went a long way towards precluding from the master shot the issue of illusionistic depth. This being the case, the Japanese presumably felt that the introduction of depth-producing oblique angles in the close-ups, even though this was the rule in the Western context, would destroy what was for them an important factor of unity.

This resistance to a key element of the Western system suggests something other than a passive traditionalism; it corresponds to an essential, *active* component of the Japanese attitude towards representation. Compare it, for example, with those uniquely Japanese *picture gardens*, laid out in such a way as to be visible only from one vantage point and *to create the illusion of pictorial flatness in a three-dimensional field.*

A wall of plaster or board generally enclosed three sides of the

3. See Chapter 18.

plot: within this frame, the gardener 'painted' a picture, using stones for brushstrokes ... To compensate for the distortion brought about by having the 'picture plane' stretch away from the observer along the ground, predominantly vertical shapes were grouped at the rear and the ground itself was often pitched downward imperceptibly toward the veranda, from which the garden is seen. At Daitokuji temple, in the garden of *Diasen-in* ... there is a white plaster wall, now half-hidden, that once carried the tone of the sand-strewn ground up behind all the clipped shrubs, thus flattening on to an imaginary picture plane objects in reality some distance from each other.[4]

At the same time, as a supreme sophistication, the graphic techniques of (Chinese) perspective were re-introduced, as it were, into the 'picture plane' to indicate a scale many times that of the actual garden.

At *Diasen-in* too ... because the waterfall is supposed to be at a great distance away, the trees behind it are smoothly clipped: the stone bridge which indicates the middle distance is much larger in scale, and trees in the foreground, also larger in scale, are left untrimmed so they may have the detail one expects near at hand.[5]

This dialectical commingling of Japanese and Chinese modes of representation is an example of what so often results from such 'borrowings', a further refinement and radicalization of the dominant element in this union: the Japanese *system* which we have already seen at work in so many areas, that 'system of surfaces' which pervades all of Japanese thought and life.

As previously mentioned, aspects of Japanese architecture that might have contributed to a 'Westernization' of the Japanese approach to pro-filmic space, seem to have been almost systematically neglected by most film-makers until the very late 1920s. One notes, in particular, the neglect of those successions of communicating rooms, which in the future were to play such an important role in the development of sophisticatedly ambiguous depth-surface relationships.[6] I have already cited a noteworthy exception to this rule, Makino's 1928 *Chūshingura*, which contains, besides the spectacular finale, numerous, briefer instances of oblique 'deep-field' shots, especially in the opening sequence, evocative of Mizoguchi's future masterpiece. Apart from this film, the very exceptional work of Kinugasa and the films of Futagawa Montabe (the epitome of the academic neo-Western director), the depth potential of Japanese architecture is neglected in all of the other films of the 1920s that I have seen. Even the faculty of the *shōji* (sliding partitions) for revealing sudden depth as they are

SURFACE AND DEPTH

4. Drexler, Arthur, *The Architecture of Japan*, p. 176.

5. ibid., p. 179.

6. Budgetary considerations no doubt often played a role in this over-determined phenomenon.

drawn back, widely explored in later years, was enlisted in aid of the general emphasis on surface. When a *shōji* fills the frame at the beginning of a shot (first perceived less as 'door' than as detail of the general rectangular pattern), then opens to reveal a character about to enter a room, the depth which we *know* to have been revealed by such an action is contradicted by the head-on, rectangular flatness of the final image, with its neutral, 'distance-less' background behind the human figure framed in the opening. An expectation of depth is met by flatness. This effect is directly related to a procedure employed in *kabuki* on-stage interior sets: a sliding door is drawn back by an unseen hand to reveal a new *tableau*, adding a rectangular vignette to the picture plane of the stage. And often in these early films the framing is such that there is the same feeling of separation between the actors' appearance and the opening of the *shōji*; it is almost as if a stage-assistant had performed the effective gesture. In the films of the 1920s, this type of entry soon became fairly frequent, together with the complementary mode of exit. The shot either began or ended with an 'empty frame', as the camera focused on the austere rectangles of the exposed wooden ribbing. The 'wipe' effect by which characters thus appeared or disappeared was a further factor in confining these ambiguous images to the two-dimensional screen surface. The systematic use, by the mature Kurosawa, of the hard-edge wipe is a significant echo of this practice.

The acknowledgement of the surface is most strikingly and significantly exemplified in Japanese films of the silent era's last decade by the practice of *super-inscription*, which seems to have spread with the development of titling itself.[7] It became common for the so-called spoken titles to *overlap* with the image which preceded and/or followed them, and for explanatory titles to overlap with establishing shots at the beginning of certain sequences. In Makino's 1928 *Chūshingura*, when a bonze-in-waiting (*chabosu*) warns Lord Asano that the all-important ceremony has begun without him, an allusive cutaway to the ceremony in progress serves as background for the titles conveying the bonze's speech. Later, immediately after the assault on Kira, a 'voice' calls the bonzes to assemble in titles which appear in the centre of a long shot of the scene and which, by an animation effect, increase in size as they seem to advance toward the spectator. This highly emphatic device – and it may be observed that this super-inscription does often have a dramatic function – produces an effect of volume, but it is *on the near side of the screen*, as it were, in a space which is not that of the diegesis.

In Inagaki's *The Mother He Never Knew* (*Mabuta no*

7. Super-inscription was used in only a very few European experiments, such as *L'Homme du large*, partly because Western films, unlike those of Japan, were to be shown to audiences in many different countries. This consideration does not diminish the positive significance of this remarkably widespread practice in Japan.

*haha*, 1931), the hero's challenging shout uttered during the rescue of an ally 'echoes across the valley' in the form of an exclamatory group of characters super-inscribed on the pan shot of a landscape inserted into the editing scheme. In Fuyushima Taizo's *Double Suicide on Mt Toribe* (*Toribeyama shinju*, 1928), the cry for help of a damsel tied up in a closet is super-inscribed on a fragment of the design painted on the closet door, offering a two-fold emblem of surface.

One of the loveliest examples of this practice is found in a very late silent film by a famous director of the following decades, Gosho Heinosuke, one of the Japanese to master the Western codes of editing and to exploit them unstintingly throughout his career (within a narrative framework correctly regarded as uniquely Japanese, however). Gosho's *The Dancing Girl of Izu* (*Izu no odoriko*, 1933) tells of the travels of a group of entertainers making their way to Izu, the traditional island gathering place of their trade. A medium long-shot showing the group's arrival in the village is overlaid by an extensive, extra-diegetic, 'documentary' title giving particulars of the tradition which brings them here. Later, as the brother of the female lead holds her in his arms to comfort her over the loss of the student who had been sharing their travels but has now gone his own way, the embracing figures are shown framed in a doorway *at the far end of a corridor*, and the image is overlaid by a *tanka* related to the film's theme and mood. This *composite* image, in which one of the depth-producing strategies, by then commonplace in the Japanese cinema, is combined with that of super-inscription, is typical of the continuing acknowledgement of surface, however incidentally, in Japanese film. It is also worth stressing the fact that these extra-diegetic super-inscriptions, all the more striking as they are the only ones in the film, neither open nor conclude it. In the sound film of the West, super-inscription has long been tolerated in credit titles, scroll prologues and the like, as an intermediate stage between 'reality' and full absorption in the diegesis; the diegetic effect becomes fully operative when such titles end and ceases to be so when they return. In the Japanese view, the diegesis was not taboo; already the *benshi* was 'writing on it'.

Even today, this relative indifference towards one of the vital premises of Western illusionism is instanced daily on commercial television channels, since at any moment, particularly during peak viewings, in the midst of the most thoroughly encoded gangster serial or samurai drama, large, often ingeniously animated characters may invade the lower portion of the screen to remind us of the merits of a deodorant or a Korean barbecue. The procedure of super-inscription, which has many precedents in Sino-Japanese culture, from the sutra-inscribed mirrors of the Fujiwara period to the 'painting-poems' of later eras, provides us with a remarkably enduring example of the manner in which the notions of *surface* and *writing* reveal essential affinites within the text-which-is-Japan.

# 13. Kinugasa Teinosuke

Nearly all of the films made during the 1920s by those who were to become the major figures of the 1930s – Ozu, Mizoguchi, Shimizu – must unfortunately be regarded as lost. Knowledge of their early work might well inflect this attempt to reconstruct the *tableau* of the representational modes of the period as determined by the conflicting currents previously described. To what extent, we can only surmise on the basis of the earliest known films (1929 and after). These indicate that Ozu and Mizoguchi had gone further than most of their contemporaries in assimilating the Western mode and codes, and articulating them in modern subjects. Their lost films might fill a peripheral area of the *tableau* which remains blank. In them, imported codes were probably exploited for their stylistic potential, as in the work of Murnau or Sjöström at their average best.

From all available evidence, however, it seems that only one director active in the 1920s assimilated the Western mode (according to the norms of the most highly Westernized period or modern dramas) and went on, albeit briefly, to work *beyond* it as in the advanced cinema of Europe. There the mode was being stretched to its breaking point, 'undermined' by the introduction of basic ambiguities, ultimately 'de-constructed' systematically (Vertov, Dreyer) by the inscription of its basic mechanisms within the film, so that one could read the filmic text *relative to the mode as such, considered in its historical dimension,* and not merely *through* it, as if it were a 'natural language'. The only director who assumed this task, utterly thankless in Japan at that time, was Kinugasa Teinosuke.

Of course, the socio-economic and political circumstances which no doubt determined the work of the first French avant-gardes, the 'Expressionist'/Kammerspiel movement in Germany (not to mention the more radical gestures accomplished marginally in both countries in connection with dada, surrealism and the modernist movement in general) had, I have indicated, echoes in Japan. Strikes, inflation, the rise of a radical working-class movement (the clandestine Japanese Communist Party was founded in 1921), attested to Japan's development from agrarian feudalism to a form of Imperialist Monopoly Capitalism in only half a century. The fate of her economy was already inextricably bound up with that of the capitalist powers. Yet, of course, the non-conformity characteristic of important sectors of the capitalist cinemas of France and Germany was further determined by super-structural phenomena, i.e. ideological or 'cultural' factors. The critical undertakings initiated by Gance, L'Herbier and Epstein, by Mayer/Wiene and Robison (and by Man Ray, Léger and Richter) may be characterized in the larger context of art history, by reference to the change which took place during the first quarter of this century and which is described in the following terms by Gaëtan Picon.

Prior to modern art, a work appears as an expression of previous experience . . . the work tells what was conceived or seen, so that between the experience and the work there is only the application of a technique of execution. In modern art, the work is not expression, but creation: it bodies forth something which had never been seen before, it is formation rather than reflection.[1]

We will recognize in this view the representational/presentational contrast between *kabuki* and the Western theatre as described by Earle Ernst and which is typical of the antinomy of Japanese and Western arts in general. However, we must also recognize that today, in the West, more than ever before it contains the key to what is most fundamental in the distinction between cinema as cultural activity and cinema as profit-earning commodity.

Given these premises, it might seem legitimate to deduce an elegant symmetry, whereby Western directors applied themselves to a critique of the codes of Hollywood illusionism – associated or not with a critique of the existing social order – while Japanese demolished with equal gusto the 'codes', derived from traditional arts and attitudes, which had achieved undeniable stability by 1920. While the Western avant-garde, in this symmetrical scheme, would be flirting with Eastern presentationalism, a Japanese élite, seeking to formulate a more-or-less virulent social critique, would be assimilating Western representational developments – at best looking to the German and French social realists, at worst copying Hollywood.

This double profile is correct as far as it goes, but it is

---

1. Picon, Gaëtan: *L'Usage de la lecture*, Vol. 2, p. 289.

2. The social cinema of Western Europe, with very few exceptions (Phil Jutzi, Vigo) took over the codes *as they were*, regarding them as a natural language, 'innocent' of an ideology which was regarded in turn as *pure signified*, totally enclosed by the *diegetic vehicle*. Already challenged in practice by cubism, dada, surrealism . . . and the Soviet film-makers, this position has become theoretically untenable today.

symmetrical only because it does not go far enough. Although Japan's attitudes towards representation are historically and socially determined, it is very difficult to speak of such widely shared values simply as part of the ideology of the dominant class, even though they have been confiscated in recent years by a certain bourgeois intelligentsia, at least in their purest forms (traditional theatre, cinema of the 1930s). A basic, inter-class consensus on these matters had existed since time immemorial, illustrated by the rapid and direct development of the aristocratic *nō* from the theatre of travelling players and *kabuki* from its early associations with the Edo underworld. A situation which contrasts sharply of course with the irreversible social segregation in all the arts which came about in capitalist society during the eighteenth and nineteenth centuries.

The political and economic upheavals of the eras of Meiji and Taisho (1912–26) had begun in some important respects to disrupt that feudal unity in Japan and to produce the need for the development of a specifically middle-class ideology, that of industrial capitalism in its most general form.

At different moments in the development of class struggle on the one hand and art on the other in the West, the working-class movement and its petty bourgeois allies have been led to appropriate the modes of representation originally developed by the bourgeoisie to suit its own needs. In capitalist countries, this often enough produced films which furthered the progress of radical ideas, but which very rarely took that critical position *vis-à-vis* the dominant modes which is the hallmark of a century in which radical art has become the mainstream of art – and in which the struggle of the avant-gardes *runs parallel to but quite separate from that of the proletariat*. In the first country where the balance of class-power was reversed, these two struggles met, only too briefly, to 'produce' Maiakovski, Vertov, Tatlin, Dovzhenko...

All of these developments, however, were enmeshed with the whole history of representation and signifying practice in the West. Our most radical denials of the dominant modes can be understood only in relation to the history of their rise and domination; in short, to their genealogy.

In the Japan of the 1920s, a few film-makers were bent on reforming the Japanese cinema. Most represented the needs of a middle class fighting to achieve dominant status, though, a few years later and for a brief time, some did speak for the growing proletariat. And the triumphant return to the values of feudal Japan in the films of the 1930s is, as we shall see, the sign of the temporary defeat of both these classes.

In view of the objective need of a rising class for greater realism, in view of the fact that the West, with its much older tradition of class struggle in an industrial society, had produced a system of representation which it accepted as realistic, it was understandable that the advanced Japanese directors should have adopted that system. They were all the more drawn to it as it was in every way opposed to a traditional mode which, however popular, was also intimately bound up with the image of the dominant cast of 'feudal capitalists' who still controlled Japan. Whatever the objective needs of their class, however, the gulf that had to be bridged by these film-makers was such that it produced the displacements and condensations already described.

It would be foolish to expect that the process of assimilation of such an alien mode could go hand in hand with a practical critique of that mode, to presume, in short, that the major gestures of European film-art could be repeated on such a fragile basis. We must, however, bear in mind that a century of radical innovative art in the West has shown that the arts of Japan and of the Far East in general can be allies, as witness encounters made by such figures as Degas, Debussy, Pound, Eisenstein and Brecht.

A similar experience may be said to have been granted, only too briefly, to Kinugasa Teinosuke.

Two significant films by Kinugasa have come down to us.[3] They prove him to be the one Japanese director to have made a successful attempt to transform the Hollywood codes in accordance with what he may have regarded as the advanced European approach. As we shall see, the execution of this project, whether or not it was consciously influenced by European film,[4] was ultimately determined by many native factors. However, at this level of interaction and mutual transformation, the traditional modes were unrecognizable for an audience that 'lived' in them.

Kinugasa Teinosuke started to work in films as an *oyama* in 1918. He began his directing career in 1922. To my knowledge, only a twenty-minute fragment of one of his silent *chambera – Benten, Apprentice* (*Benten kozō*, 1928) – can still be seen, and it is indistinguishable from the bulk of similar productions known to us. Kinugasa, however, former *oyama* though he was, apparently played a leading role in the movement to oust the *oyama* from the cinema, and quickly came to share the views of those who wished to Westernize Japanese films. In 1926, he founded his own independent production company, a rare and difficult venture in Japan at any time, and equipped his own make-shift

---

3. With these two major and two or three minor exceptions, the many films directed by Kinugasa before 1945 were destroyed by fire in that year. However, Kinugasa himself feels that these were his only two 'avant-garde' productions.

4. Kinugasa has no recollection of having seen the few advanced European films shown in Japan during the early 1920s (e.g. *Caligari*, *La Roue*), yet most Japanese authorities feel that he must have seen and been influenced by them. On the other hand, Kinugasa's decision not to take *Page of Madness* with him on his tour of Europe in 1929, to take only *Crossways*, a far more academic 'Western-style' film, might indicate that he was not, indeed, aware that his masterpiece would most likely have been hailed as such by critics and an élite audience who accepted and admired *Caligari*, *La Roue* and *Potemkin*, all of which had gone much 'further' than *Crossways*. Perhaps he feared that he had not done justice to his Western 'models', if such indeed they were. Or perhaps he had not indeed been 'influenced'. Perhaps this film is simply the result of a cultural encounter, in a particularly sophisticated mind which had mastered the codes of the West at an early date, between these and the general potential of Japanese culture vis-à-vis that of the West.

5. Kawabata is known in the West for his later novels, *The Snow Country*, *A Thousand Cranes* and *The Master of Go*.

6. '... it is difficult for us to render perfectly the posture of the noble figures of the Court ... since we do not have access to them. However, we must enquire as best we can of their habits of speech, their manners, and pay attention to the observations of persons of quality.' Zeami in Siefert, René, *La Tradition secrète du Nō*, p. 70.

studio and laboratory in Kyoto, a city which remained, until the Pacific War, a film-making centre as important as Tokyo. That same year he produced the film which was to be his masterpiece and which, though lost for many decades, has recently been revealed again to audiences in the West and in Japan.

The scenario of *Page of Madness* (*Kurutta ippeiji*, 1926) was written in collaboration with the young novelist Kawabata Yasunari,[5] at that time a prominent member of a group of advanced liberal writers with whom Kinugasa had close relations. Kawabata's original setting was a circus, but Kinugasa changed this to an asylum for the insane, and significantly spent several months studying this kind of institution, a tribute to Western naturalism which was not, however, incompatible with the working methods of the traditional Japanese theatre at its most presentational.[6]

The resulting film, as we shall see, is notably closer to that specifically Western twentieth-century phenomenon defined by Gaëtan Picon as creation than to the eighteenth/nineteenth-century concept of expression. While ultimately this approach had been Japan's since the dawn of her culture, it was the intellectual work of a collectivity, rather than of a series of 'original geniuses'. And although the Japanese cinema has known, especially since

SURFACE AND DEPTH

Fig. 4. Kinugasa Teinosuke, *Page of Madness*

the Pacific War, independent artists who correspond to the Western image of the original creative temperament, Kinugasa was undoubtedly the first of these.

The use of women rather than *oyama* in female roles, a contemporary setting and a subject which the 'poetic realists' of France and Germany would certainly not have rejected, gave Kinugasa's and Kawabata's project an up-to-date aspect. They quite naturally tried to complete it by eliminating the *benshi*. Their 'modern' aims also determined their decision to eliminate titles as well, an exceptional experiment in a 'Western-style' film for that period.

It is fascinating to observe that in Japan as well, at least one director of cultural ambition was seeking, with respect to the presence of inter-titles on the screen, 'to turn back the clock'. As we have seen, the films of the West, like those of Japan but not for as long, were originally untitled, with a 'lecturer' filling the role of *benshi*. I believe it can be shown, however, that in the one Japanese example of this 'revival' which is known to us, the result is often diametrically opposed to that of such European experiments as *Der Letzte Mann, Ueberfall* or *Ménilmontant*; despite obvious important differences, it is ultimately related to certain aspects of Dovzhenko's *Earth* or to the most seminal of all the untitled films of the 1920s, Vertov's *The Man with a Movie Camera*.

The opening montage sequence of *Page of Madness*, striking for its visual stylization, could easily have graced a German or French film of the late 1920s. Indeed, I feel that Kinugasa's film was slightly 'ahead of its time' on the Western scale; the narrative sophistication which this film shares with *The Wind, Spione* and L'Herbier's *L'Argent* (all 1928), was characteristic of the last two or three years of the silent era.

– rain at night; dissolve to . . .
– close-up of a window
– a door bangs in the wind
– a car's headlights come towards camera
– the car's tyres pass in close-up
– two barred windows in *chiaroscuro* interior (lightning)
– water swirling in gutter
– the silhouette of a man steps out of the rainy night into a pool of light
– repeat of previous window-shot; overlay
– water lapping against a wall
– close-up of man's feet climbing rain-swept concrete stairs
– close-up of single barred window (interior)
– a larger view of the same
– a telegraph pole, scarcely visible in the dark

– previously seen stairs, from a different angle with water pouring down them

Gradually, these and similar elements are blended in rapid montage and increasingly elaborate overlays, until this veritable swirl of images dissolves to . . .

– a row of water-spouts and a huge, glittering tinsel ball, in front of this a lovely variety entertainer is dancing in a fancy costume (the dance is shown in a series of staggered overlays); the camera tracks back and bars appear in black silhouette in the foreground; the screen goes black
– an off-centre iris unmasks first a barred window, then a barred doorway; beyond the doorway, projected on a wall, is the shadow of the dancing girl *in her stage costume*; dissolve to . . .
– close-up of the girl dancing in the rags of her hospital gown

This mood-setting, 'impressionistic' introduction was, in its general outlines, already part of the codes of sophisticated European films (such as those of the great Lupu-Pick or Delluc). After Murnau, Sjöström, Lubitsch and Leni had arrived in America, it made its way into the Hollywood codes proper.

When we examine the development of this sequence, we observe, however, a number of singularities profoundly incompatible with the standard Western approach. 'Normally', when a man appears on a rainy night after a series of inanimate details to 'set the scene', it marks the introduction of the *human centre* of the diegesis. Here, however, the man – like the car before him, which brought a similar suggestion – immediately vanishes, never to return. The man's disappearance is emphasized by the shot of the empty stairs. The automobile might be linked to the vehicle, seen several reels later, in which patients are brought to the asylum, or even to the car which appears in the old janitor's delirium towards the end of the film. Though we never see his face, it is just possible that the man in the rain is the janitor's briefly glimpsed son-in-law or one of the shadowy doctors. These are merely vague possibilities, however, and the ambivalence remains intact, as it does not in the narrative editing of the 'brick-by-brick' Pudovkin tradition. This 'false start' with its ambivalent echoes later in the film is fundamentally at odds with the impressionistic chain which ensures a gradual approach to continuity and the human centre at the beginning of Sjöström's *The Wind*.

Moreover, while this portentous introduction might seem to indicate that the main narrative line deals with whatever drama led to the dancer's internment, this 'beginning' is still another strategy of deception. For the dancer's past is *present* again only through a glimpse of a torn photograph on the wall of her cell and in recalls of her stage costume, to be dealt with shortly. The very simple main narrative is also predicated on a past/present relationship which, viewed superficially, seems perfectly linear: an old man's devotion to his schizophrenic wife has led him to take menial employment in the asylum where she is interned; memories of their happy past mingle with scenes of their present misery, culminating in the husband's pathetic attempt to flee with his wife. However, the principles of spatio-temporal ambivalence suggested in the compressed evocation of the dancer's drama – black bars in front of the night-club stage, the costumed shadow on the cell wall – are brought into play throughout the film, continually challenging, on the level of articulation, the inherent linearity of the coded narrative matrix. Close examination of the complex articulation of temporal narration in this film reveals procedures which are fundamentally opposed, for example, to Kirsanoff's time-lapse sequence of grass growing on a mother's grave articulated by successive dissolves to signify that her two daughters have grown up. Nor do the 'memory shots' function at all like those in, say, Pudovkin's *The Mother*.

The image of the dancer's costumed shadow provides an outstanding example. It may be described as a conjunction of 'past' and 'present' within a single instant of diegetic space-time which, to the extent that it is neither 'past' nor 'present', is *extra-diegetic*.[7] Now this conjunction was ultimately assimilated as a flashback signal by the Western narrative codes in films where a connotation of theatricality made it possible to exclude ambiguities – Benedek's *Death of a Salesman,* Sjöberg's *Fröken Julie* (both 1951).[8] In such a context, this particular semantic contradiction became a coded sign, replacing the iris, the dissolve, the wipe, close-up with surging music, sound-track wind-down, etc., all of which, at various periods, have had the same function.

In this passage of Kinugasa's film, on the contrary, the interpenetrations of past and present do not function on a coded level only. It is true that the bars which appear in front of the stage and the shadow on the cell wall are ultimately coded to the extent that the one may be read as 'premonition of the future', the other as 'remnant of the past'. However, they can be read as such only from a point which 'commands a view' of the entire sequence. At the moment of immediate perception, these messages are uncertain, deferred by ambiguities or misleading indications. They are pinned down only as subsequent images

7. But in no sense is this image *extra-narrative*. This, I feel is a clear illustration of the fundamental distinction to be made between diegesis and narrative.

8. Significantly enough, both these films were originally plays, and Arthur Miller's original text called for this very device.

appear. When first seen as fuzzy, black bands, the bars do not look like bars at all, and when they become sharp, they might easily be prison bars. And the possibility exists that the girl, whom we have not yet seen in her inmate's rags, is actually wearing her costume in her cell (an image which actually appears later in the film). These circuitous transmissions of what are, at best, messages of low semantic density – lacking, in particular, any subjective dimension: memory, here, is anonymous – result in the partial expulsion of these images from the diegesis (where instantaneous transmission is the rule) and in their *rising to the surface of the film*.

The shot of the shadow on the wall bears a significant relationship to the pivot-word (*kakekotoba*), central to Japanese traditional poetic forms; like the pivot-word, it is the point of junction of two separate systems which 'overlap' at that point, and it functions simultaneously as a part of each system. In *Page of Madness* this procedure never becomes a coded 'punctuation', for though it is used twice more, each time it assumes different forms with different results.

The girl dancing in her cell is a theme that frequently recurs, but only twice again does the costumed figure from the girl's 'past' appear in her drab present: once 'in the eyes' of the male inmates, frantic with sexual excitement, as they crowd against her cell door to watch her dance; and once in conjunction with the old man's memories of a festival attended with his wife and daughter. In the latter sequence, the image is contrasted with a 'reality' in which she is not dancing but lying bound hand and foot on the floor of her cell, following the near-riot caused by her exhibition; in the former, it works against shots of her dancing in her inmate's garb. Here too we encounter ambiguities and deferments, but the itineraries are very different. The first shot of the costumed girl dancing in her cell has optical distortion and is preceded by a track-in on an inmate's face pressed to the bar: at that moment it appears as a libidinous, first-person fantasy vision, *yet at the same time* it is an anonymous memory of the original night-club shot in the prologue and of the 'pivot-shot' which introduced the scenes of life in the asylum. This shot too is a pivot-shot but the over-lapping systems are of a different order and are related in a different way. The second appearance of this shot brings a third type of pivot structure: when it first appears, it 'rhymes' by analogy with the father's recollections of the festival and his happiness with wife and family. When it is followed by a shot of the bound dancer on the floor, it acquires, for the first and only time, the cast of subjective memory.

CROSS-CURRENTS

We are dealing with an approach to semiosis not unrelated to that encountered in Tanaka's *The Red Bat*, but of a much more sophisticated kind. The patently random, unorganized circulation of free-floating signifiers characteristic of Tanaka's (and Ito's) films – and more generally of a particular cultural filter – is replaced, in *Page of Madness*, by a systematic exploration of the combinations offered by similar types of polyvalence. It is in this sense that we may speak of Kinugasa's film as containing *play* (i.e. creative work) *on the codes* directly related to the masterworks of Vertov and Dovzhenko cited above.

The film does not, of course, consistently maintain this level of complex tension with respect to the narrative codes. The shots of mental evocation – and there are many – are often unequivocally subjective, such as that of the insane wife's face as a young woman, seen in a mirror, a shot which is cut into a sequence of demented primping. However, Kinugasa's preoccupation with conjoining the de-constructing and structuring processes, still extremely rare at that period even in the Soviet Union, is evident in many other instances.

Three times in the film the old man looks out of the window of his shabby room at the asylum. In two of these episodes, what he 'sees' is ultimately designated as his 'memory': the festival referred to above (confused with an 'actual' festival to such an extent that it takes many viewings to discover the 'seam' between them) and his wife's dramatic arrival at the asylum. The first of these 'flashbacks' is presented in a 'deferred' version of a standard form – a shot of the old man looking out of the window is followed by the shots of the daylight ('actual') festival which will lead to the nocturnal ('past') one. The wife's arrival has an even more ambiguous status, since it is preceded by a shot in which the old man leaves his room, and since the association looking-out-of-window/old-man's-memories is confirmed only in retrospect (a shot of the old man at the window immediately *follows* the arrival scene). By now it seems established that the association is a coded one: what the old man sees out of the window are, ultimately, his memories. Whence the ambiguity of the third episode in this series, since this time he looks down on what we can only perceive as an 'actuality': children mimicking the behaviour of the patients. And while it is precisely the theatrical nature of this scene which is the key to its 'reality', at the same time this theatricality relates it to the fantasy-exploration of the film as a whole.

'Acted out' fantasies – seldom those of the patients, most frequently those of the old man – occupy an important place in the film. However, while the climactic hallucinations – in which the old man sees his daughter in wedding dress, presumably driving off on her honeymoon with the bearded inmate who lusts after her – is a visually impressive bit of bravura, its 'surrealist' mentalism is perfectly coded. A European reference would be Mosjoukine's *Le Brasier ardent* (1923), with which this sequence compares favourably. On the other hand there are many less spectacular sequences which offer remarkable non-linear structures, related to those already described.

Early in the film, at the end of the first dancing episode referred to above, the old man appears on the screen for the first time, coming to visit his poor mad wife. This section, too, is worth describing in some detail.

– repetition of the earlier shot of barred windows back-lit by lightning; the old man makes his initial entrance, in a knee-length shot, silhouetted against the windows
– the girl rises from her prone position on the floor and resumes her dancing
– the old woman is lying on her stomach, seemingly watching the dance ('Kuleshov effect':[9] the women are in separate cells and cannot see each other)
– another shot of the old woman from a different angle
– a titled shot of the grill; the old man enters in *overlay* wearing a 'splendid' uniform; he puts his hand on the grill *which opens in the overlay but remains closed in the original image*
– the woman looks up *to her left* and speaks to her husband

There ensues a correctly matched reverse-field series as they exchange a few words. Then the woman gazes around her.

– image of a baby crying overlaid by that of a ventilation grill
– close-up of the woman; she seems to have a moment of absence, then looks up again, but this time *to the right*
– the original shot of the barred doorway: there is no one there
– the woman turns her head slowly to the right again, then drops it to her chest
– in the empty cell corridor, the camera tracks towards the large grill which closes off the end; a very slow dissolve (in fact, for a time, an overlay) combines this forward movement with a backward movement in the same set so that, at the end of the shot, the camera is in its original position; the old man comes down the corridor peering into the cells (Fig. 5)

SURFACE AND DEPTH

9. Imaginary spatio-temporal juxtaposition through 'deceptive' use of matching procedures.

Fig. 5. Kinugasa Teinosuke, *Page of Madness*

Ultimately, he comes face to face with his wife as in the fantasy, but clearly she does not recognize him, is only dimly aware of his presence.

Retrospectively, to be sure, the first 'visit' is designated as fantasy by the second, and the secondary signs (the tilted frame, the uniform, the overlay, the incorrect eyeline-match) as indices of the movement into and out of fantasy. However, the actual process of understanding is far less direct. In the first place, we must remember that this action occurs at a moment in the film when a veritable orgy of overlays and dissolves has just established these two procedures as the signs of a purely visual simultaneity, in which such distinctions as past/present, absent/present, real/imaginary are absorbed by a single, polyvalent surface relationship. This polyvalence is echoed throughout the sequence just described. Not only does the previous context have a 'dissolving' effect on these first strongly narrative gestures, but each use of simultaneous images, to the extent that it is perceived as coded, brings into play a different system of contradistinctions.

The first overlay, in fact, introduces two systems simultaneously: reality/fantasy and past/present. It is clear that the old man is much younger and happier in the overlay, and the uniform he wears is presumably associated with his past station in life. The ventilator-over-baby shot brings in the presence/absence dichotomy, and for this very reason constitutes a momentary suspension of the fantasy, even though, from a linear viewpoint, we are still 'in it'. The dissolve on the empty grill clearly marks the 'return to reality', thus giving possible meaning to the disconcerting eyeline match that marked the start of the encounter. As for the double dolly movement in the corridor, its remarkable ambiguity comes from being 'superfluous': it is the second or the fourth time (counting the baby and the mismatch) that the return to reality has been announced, and here it is done with such extravagance (the movements are slow and the shot is long) that for a while we seem to have returned to the system of pure surfaces which characterized much of the earlier imagery.

This sequence as a whole is made more ambiguous by the fact that while the fantasy of the old man's uniformed appearance at the grill is ultimately designated as the woman's fantasy, its appearance on the screen is also determined by the husband's 'actual' intention to visit her, as conveyed by the shot of him passing the windows. This situation precludes any simple mentalist reading of the fantasy and its indices; both it and they are over-determined.

This non-linear approach to the signification process is not confined to fantasy sequences. One of its more remarkable instances is the sequence that follows the daughter's departure at the end of her first visit and the ensuing near-riot caused by the dancer.

– the old man has been called into the office of the head-doctor, who rebukes him for his involvement in the riot; dissolve to . . .
– close-up of a spinning railway-ticket rack; overlaid on this, the daughter in a medium close-up takes a ticket from one of several such racks
– close-up: she punches the ticket
– she hands the ticket through a window to an invisible customer; in overlay, the wheels of a train start to turn; very slow dissolve to a coin lying on the sidewalk; clogged feet pass
– detail of curtain and wall-paper; truck back to full view of apartment where the young woman lives with her husband[10]

Now, Kinugasa made a sound version of the film after his accidental rediscovery of the negative and a print among his personal belongings in 1971. Among the very few sound-effects added to an almost exclusively musical track were a train-whistle over the close-up of the spinning ticket

SURFACE AND DEPTH

10. The rest of this sequence contains an ambiguity so startling that one hesitates to attempt analysis: the young woman looks through a door and appears to see herself talking to her husband, who is lying on a sofa.

rack and the sound of a train gathering speed over the ensuing images of the ticket office and the wheels turning. These are clearly intended as reinforcements of temporal linearity and to re-establish semantic 'clarity'. The whistle helps to pin down the visually ambiguous image of the ticket rack, while the ambiguity of the following images (is that train merely an associative image, or does the girl take it to go home; and what, if any, is the 'meaning' of that coin on the sidewalk?) is *overridden*, so to speak, by the impetus of the train sound. Posthumous correction of early films in this way often points to what is still today most subversive about them.

In Japan, sophisticated freedom with the codes of narrative linearity disappears until the late 1950s and early 1960s. It is all the more remarkable that the structures of such advanced Soviet films as *The General Line*, *Earth* or *The Man with a Movie Camera*, all of which are slightly later than *Page of Madness*, may be considered to be prefigured in this remarkable film.

Kinugasa, however, was discouraged by the hostility of nearly all the critics and by the film's commercial failure. His next independent venture, *Crossways* (*Jūjiro*, 1928), was far more faithful to the Hollywood and European codes. Although the film's imagery has been compared with Japanese traditional ink-painting (*sumi-e*), it is far more obviously related to that of latter-day Expressionism/Kammerspiel. One long and very impressive sequence does, however, recall the complexities of *Page of Madness*: the hero, a poor *rōnin* who has been temporarily blinded in a quarrel at the Yoshiwara over a famous courtesan whom he loves, has feverish visions of her (Fig. 8) and of the gaudy revelry of that famous 'entertainment quarter'. His fantasies are often joined *seamlessly* with sequences which are, in fact, not 'visions' at all but parallel action ('While our hero is raving, this is what is happening at the Yoshiwara'). In this film, the hallucinations, like those in the final sequence of *Mabuse* or the vision of Moloch in *Metropolis*, affect at times the material appearance of the set, as in the scene in which the hero's poor hovel becomes a field planted with jars containing boiling water, which burns his parched throat (Fig. 9).

The mastery with which such structures are manipulated in these sections of *Crossways* is equal to that displayed throughout *Page of Madness*. However, in confining this type of ambiguous articulation to passages designated as hallucinatory, Kinugasa was making the decisive concession to codicity which ultimately brings this film into line with the psychologism of the dominant Western cinema. Any violation of the principles of illusionism must automatically

Figs. 6, 7. Kinugasa Teinosuke, *Crossways*

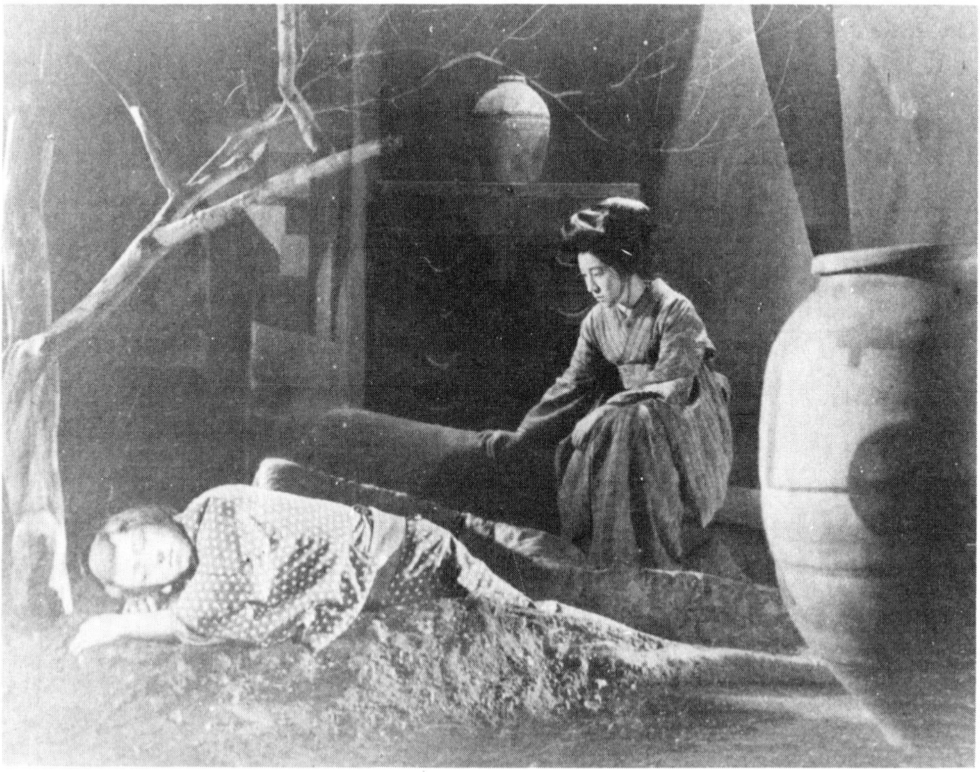

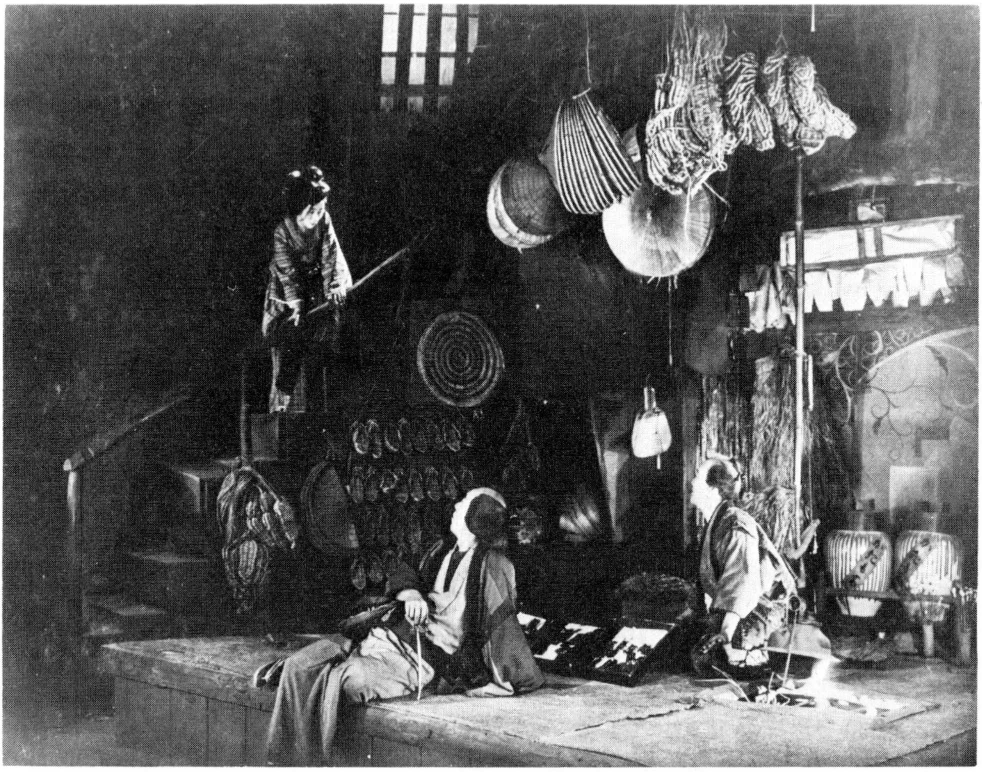

Fig. 8. Kinugasa Teinosuke, *Crossways*

be equated with the representation of dreams, fantasy, madness, etc. It might be argued that this 'concession' was already present in *Page of Madness*, insofar as an 'expressive' alibi for even the most sophisticated disruption of coded linearity was provided by the asylum setting. In that film, however, as in *Caligari* before it, the setting acts rather as a catalyst, and any reduction, *by the reading spectator*, to linear 'expressiveness' is precluded by the film's actual syntax.

The fundamental and, from an historical point of view, capital contradiction of *Caligari* occurs at the end of the film; it is the contradiction between the alleged finality of the scenes showing the Doctor and his patients in their 'real' roles, and the persistent presence of settings whose 'unreality' has until now been regarded as the guarantee of 'fantasy'. The Expressionism of *Caligari* cannot be reduced to the expression of a mental state. Similarly, in *Page of Madness*, aside from the fact that the bulk of hallucinations and fantasies *are those of the sane protagonist*, the non-linear procedures described above affect the narrative at every 'level of reality' and cannot be accounted for as mere descriptions of mental states in 'impressionist' or 'expressionist' modes.

This film, then, is significantly close in a way which is

Fig. 9. Kinugasa Teinosuke, *Crossways*

anything but anecdotal, to *Caligari*, one of the earliest, basic experiments of the European avant-garde, and to the Soviet films which were the highpoint of that entire period of experimentation. However, such an undertaking was so alien, so meaningless in the Japanese context that Kinugasa could only return to *chambera* and other acceptable genres.[11]

He became an academic master in a mildly traditional vein, as is evident from *The Actress* (*Joyu*, 1947) or *The Gate of Hell* (*Jigokumon*, 1952). What are the merits of a film like *The Summer Battle of Osaka* (*Osaka natsu no jin*, 1932) seen by Robert Florey during a trip to Japan and described by him as a masterpiece?[12] We will probably never know.[13] But as Kinugasa himself has said in an interview, published in the Paris weekly, *Les Lettres Françaises*, in 1972: 'My work has consisted mainly in finding ways of making actresses laugh or cry, of getting characters killed in artistic circumstances.'

11. Kinugasa was so shaken by this incomprehension that, as I have indicated above, he took only *Crossways* to Europe with him in 1928. It was the first Japanese film seen abroad by Western audiences and, quite understandably, had a considerable *succès d'estime* in Europe. It was in Germany that the film was rediscovered in relatively recent years.

12. *Japan Film Yearbook*, 1938.

13. The very recent discovery of his 1938 version of *Yukinojo henge* (*The Ghost of Yukinojo*) should provide some grounds for appraisal.

# Part 4   Iron Trees
# Golden Flowers

# 14. The Weight of History and Technology

The two major traumas of the post-war period had been inflation and the Kantō earthquake of 1923, which shattered much of the country's industrial structure. Conjointly, they produced two complementary and not unexpected results. On the one hand, class struggle began to develop rapidly, with Marxist ideas penetrating the urban proletariat and certain fringes of a liberal bourgeoisie which, by the late 1920s, had acquired some political weight. The political parties, led largely by middle-class civilians, had succeeded in creating a new balance of power and were pressing for an even more complete 'Westernization' of Japanese political and social norms, indispensable, they realized, to the 'healthy' growth of capitalism. On the other hand, there was a spectacular rise in the activity of the so-called 'patriotic societies', radical right-wing clubs some of which had existed since Meiji times, all of which now displayed an unprecedented virulence. The conditions that gave rise to these societies and the motives of the men who formed or radicalized them have been summed up thus by an American historian.

The growth of industry ... was helping to undermine the attitudes proper to a disciplined and dedicated people, for its profits tempted those who shared them into new forms of extravagance, nearly all imported from the West, while their unequal distribution led to 'dangerous thoughts', also of Western origin, like socialism, pacifism and democracy. Similarly, modernization of the economy could be blamed for rural distress and hence for weakening the position of the farmer, society's staunchest upholder of traditional behaviour. In fact, dance halls, luxury, political corruption, big business, trade unions, strikes, agrarian unrest and debased standards of every kind, all could be lumped together as results of an overindulgence in foreign ways. They thus became a focus for the resentments of men of many different kinds: those who felt that the new order of things gave them less than their proper station; those who genuinely respected the past and the values it represented; and those whose sense of inferiority in the face of the West's achievements brought a hatred of factories, as well as ambition for empire. The resulting movement embraced conservatives, professional patriots, agrarian idealists, advocates of state ownership and social revolutionaries, all contributing in some measure to the aggressive 'ultranationalism' of the nineteen-thirties.[1]

Whatever their diverging social origins, these men were all bent on reactivating what we clearly recognize as the official ideology of the Tokugawa *bakufu*, with its distrust of commerce, industry and science and of all that was not Japanese. A belated feudal ideology was stubbornly determined to stem the tide of history, the accelerating rise of the bourgeoisie and the development of proletarian consciousness. The elected enemies of all these groups were the *zaibatsu*[2] who continued to determine the realities of economic power in Japan and who were increasingly aware of the need to strengthen the attributes of bourgeois democracy in order to consolidate their political power. During the early and middle 1930s, the extremists virtually paralysed government through a campaign of systematic assassination and intimidation. Their goals came to coincide with those of a traditional military cast, who received support from young officers of peasant origin, embittered by the desperate plight of the country folk, and who were bent on widening Japan's foothold on the continent. The Mukden 'incident' and the annexation of Manchuria in 1931 (followed, significantly, by Japan's withdrawal from the League of Nations in 1933) coincided with a serious trade slump, due, in particular, to the Wall Street crash and the collapse of the world silk market.

From that time on, Japan began, economically and psychologically, to withdraw into herself, to reject Western ideas and fashions. She began to see these through the eyes of the patriotic extremists.

Foreign visitors were accused of spying on the flimsiest pretexts. There were arguments about the use of foreign words and whether nameboards at railway stations should read from right to left (Japanese style) or left to right (Western style). Much of this chauvinistic atmosphere was injected into the schools and universities. Many foreign books used in them were proscribed by the police – often without a very clear idea of their contents – and text-books were rewritten in nationalist terms.[3]

By the mid-1930s, the jingoist propaganda had found fertile soil in a country under economic pressure. Shakai

---

1. Beasley, W. G., *The Modern History of Japan*, p. 237.

2. *zaibatsu*: the financial and industrial clans, largely of aristocratic origins, formed during the Meiji era.

3. ibid, pp. 225–6.

THE WEIGHT OF HISTORY AND TECHNOLOGY

Taishuto remained the only moderately left-wing opposition party after the physical elimination of the Communist Party and the rest of the radical left by 3,000 arrests in October of 1932. It made record gains in the elections of 1937, but this reaction on the part of the urban masses, while attesting to a very real current of dissenting opinion, came too late to prevent the impending tragedy.

I have dwelt at some length on the political and ideological climate of the period because it is directly relevant to our subject. Yet this relevance is problematic, to say the least, since the most fruitful, original period in the history of a nation's cinema coincided with the rise of a régime and a national ideology akin to European Fascism. It was between 1934 and 1943 that Ozu and Mizoguchi produced their finest work, and that Naruse, Shimizu, Ishida, Yamanaka and many others helped to perfect an approach to film-making that was not only uniquely Japanese but was equal, at its best, to the finest achievements of the traditional arts of previous centuries.

A comparison with Germany, where Nazism quickly and effectively strangled anything resembling a living cinema, is of no value, since Hitler's putsch caused the wholesale and immediate exodus of both celebrated and budding talents. Had liberal intellectuals like Ozu, Mizoguchi or Ishida ever wanted to leave (and this is quite unlikely) there was no place for them to go. The linguistic and cultural barriers to departure were insurmountable.[4] However, most of the major figures of the Italian industry also went on working in their native country under Fascism, and the slick, conformist films of Blasetti and Camerini give certain evidence of the sterilizing power of Fascism, observable in every other art.

It is here that we observe a significant difference (not, of course, an intrinsic 'superiority') which sets Japanese military Fascism apart from its Western equivalent. For while what we may legitimately regard as the 'golden age' of Japanese cinema was certainly overdetermined, one factor is that withdrawal of Japan into herself, the rejection of Western values *by the nation as a whole*. The nationalism of the 1930s was a mass phenomenon to an extent and in ways which that of the European Fascist countries was not,[5] and at the cultural level it struck particularly sensitive chords in both the masses and the intelligentsia. The relations between film history and the political history of that period are of course complex; as we shall see, themes of mild social protest do appear in the work of the masters. One thing, however, is quite clear: *the social pressure to adopt Western modes undoubtedly abated* during those dark years. As we have seen, in

4. To my knowledge, no Japanese director has ever made a career abroad, as so many Europeans have in America, or a few Americans in Europe. The contemporary director, Hani Susumi, who has shot several Japanese-produced films in the West, is as close to an exception as one can find.

5. There was no equivalent in Japan either to the physical elimination of an important part of the German population or, conversely, to the Italian resistance movement.

so far as cinema was concerned, those modes had never really taken root in the mass audience. There was ample room for the growth of a specifically national cinema.

It is to the credit of Mizoguchi, Ozu and most of their noted contemporaries that the politically nationalistic film seems to have remained rare in their work until the end of the 1930s.[6] The maintenance in so many films of traditional values, in both narrative form and mode of representation, is nevertheless clearly consonant with the ideological indoctrination organized by the caste that was rapidly taking over Japan at that time.

We must not forget that in Japan this concept of a specifically national cinema takes on a meaning unknown in the West, since it implied the development of a *non-Western*, specifically *Asiatic* film. And of course it is no accident that the tacit refutation of the Hollywood codes and of their claim to universality (as opposed to the 'passive resistance' of the 1920s) was sustained in the background, so to speak, by the pan-Asian ideology which the Japanese Right had gradually been forging to justify their imperialist aims. The doctrine known as the Greater East Asia Co-Prosperity Sphere was a deadly threat to China's fragile and still largely formal democracy and independence; it was also, nonetheless, a reaction to an equally important historical reality: the colonial exploitation of Asia by the Western powers over the past four centuries.

Let us now turn to the situation of the film industry proper. The major event of the early depression years was the appearance of talkies from the West. The sound film produced two fundamental changes everywhere. First, it immediately showed that it was potentially capable of greatly broadening the film-going audience. At the same time, of course, it called for much heavier investments, ultimately justified by its greater box-office potential, but which in Japan raised problems less easily solved than in Europe or the United States. These problems derived mainly from the small profit-margins of Japanese cinema and the need of investments from banks and big business, a practice which was not normal in Japan and which was not established for many years. The result was a situation which was practically unique among the developed film industries of the world. In Japan, silent films were still being produced as late as 1937, and in 1934 they still represented the bulk of production.

In Western Europe and the United States, on the other hand, they had disappeared by 1931, in the Soviet Union by 1934. This technical advance had a fundamental effect on the composition of the film-going audience of the West. In France, polls taken by trade papers showed that in 1927,

6. However, Mizoguchi's early film, *The Dawn of the Founding of Manchukuo and Mongolia* offers a striking contrast with the 'tendency' films that had preceded it, a contrast emblematic of the ambivalent status of cinema in Japan of the 1930s.

over three-fourths of the population never went to the cinema at all. And it is common knowledge that the French audience was overwhelmingly urban and proletarian – a situation which was reflected to a degree in all developed capitalist societies. It was not until the coming of sound that the bourgeoisie began to attend films *en masse*, for the obvious reason that films had at last begun to talk. Edison's project was fulfilled, films had at last attained the status of the ultimate performing art, the 'realistic' theatre. And, of course, the aspects of cinema that did not meet with this expectation were rejected. The pressure to produce 'canned theatre' for the new spectators, who could pay more and attend more frequently, was tremendous; few directors were in a position to resist. The 'poetic licence' of the silent film, its non-realist stylizations, its lack of the Word, had become acceptable to a predominantly proletarian audience, not yet thoroughly formed by an ideology of transparent representation, simply as a result of cultural segregation, still so complete at that time. Reflecting, no doubt, this 'open-mindedness', even the hack critics of the day seem to have taken that freedom in their stride (witness their calm reception of bold works, such as *Caligari*, *Potemkin* and the French 'Impressionists'). It was, however, to be brutally eliminated from the professional cinema of the United States and Europe for some thirty years. As we view in retrospect the ostracism that stifled Dreyer after *Vampyr*, Stroheim after *Queen Kelly*, and brought about the more or less involuntary resignation of such major figures as Gance, L'Herbier, Dulac, Epstein and perhaps above all, Fritz Lang, in work of desperate conformity, we see that the late 1920s and early 1930s constituted the final and most spectacular stage in the saturation of Western cinema by the modes of representation of the dominant class.

Paradoxically, it was during the 1930s that the Japanese cinema, wholly out-of-phase with this Western pattern, 'comes into its own'. Three major factors contribute to this apparent anomaly. One has already been discussed: the 'return to Japanese values' which marked the political and social scene. Secondly, the bourgeoisie which indeed began to attend the cinema more frequently as films began to talk, remained a Japanese bourgeoisie, with its heritage of traditional culture. We may compare their need for 'realism' to that of their forebears under the Tokugawa *bakufu*. It still involved attitudes unlike those which we associate with the bourgeois ideology of representation in the West. Thirdly, there was the economic and technological factor, i.e. the decade required for the spread of sound.

According to the novelist Kishida Kunio,[7] the first

7. In *Japan Film Yearbook*, 1937.

IRON TREES,
GOLDEN FLOWERS

Japanese sound film was Osanai Kaoru's *Reimai* (*Dawn*, 1926?), a faithful rendering of a *shin-geki* production. Osanai, the co-director with Murata of *Souls on the Road*, was primarily a man of the theatre. His film was presumably shot by the De Forest Phonofilm process, which had been demonstrated in Japan the year before. However, as I have said, the talkie did not completely supplant the silent photoplay on Japanese screens for more than a dozen years, and nothing resembling the regular production of sound films was begun until 1932. The first commercially and 'artistically' successful venture, all authorities seem to agree, was Gosho's *The Neighbour's Wife and Mine* (*Madamu to nyobō*), made in that year.

This extremely gradual introduction of sound is interesting in a number of ways. The longest period of resistance to sound occurs at both ends of the cultural scale. Ozu and Naruse did not make their first sound films until 1936. Gosho, after the film cited above, returned to silent production until 1935. Mizoguchi, after 1930, alternated sound and silent films, the last of which dates from 1935 also. So that on the one hand, silence – and the *benshi* – still strongly tempted well-established film-makers, who already had a cultural reputation. Their attitude might seem to reflect that of the many Western directors who resisted sound to the point of temporary retirement. Consider, however, that in 1936, when 259 regularly operating theatres out of a total of 1,627 in Japan proper were still showing only silent films, at least one company, the Daito Motion Picture Co. Ltd, a subsidiary of Shochiku, was producing *only* silent films (this was still the case the following year); and that in that year it produced 101 films out of a national total of 531! Moreover, and most important, these 101 films were 'principally cheap, second-rate pictures'.[8]

In other words, the resistance of the most sophisticated film-makers to the coming of sound also corresponded to the surviving popularity of the silent film. Whatever the ideological reasons for the former and whatever the socio-economic reasons for the latter, both facts, clearly over-determined, constitute a single complex historical situation of considerable significance. They also clarify the lingering survival of the *benshi*, who apparently did not vanish completely from commercial theatres until shortly before the Pacific War. The *benshi* played an active role as a pressure group in the persistence of the silent film. The 1932 strike of Nikkatsu *benshi* is a celebrated episode. However, it is also clear that while film-makers like Ozu and Mizoguchi were unlikely to have been outspoken partisans of the *benshi*, they accepted his virtually inevitable presence beneath the silent screen *rather than convert to sound*. In other words,

8. ibid., Ichikawa Sai, 'An Outlook of Motion Picture Industry in Japan' [*sic*]. The figures cited here are from this source. Actually, the company may well have been the Shinkō Kinema Co. Ltd, another Shochiku subsidiary which produced 99 films that year (the doubt arising from a regrettable tendency among the translators of that otherwise invaluable Yearbook to confuse 'latter' and 'former'). The Yearbook's publication in 1937 for the first time is significant of the fact that, as Ichikawa points out, 'the experimental period for talkies [was] at last terminated' and 'a remarkable tendency of businessmen to invest capital in the motion picture business [was] looked upon as a foreboding of dawn upon the motion picture industry.' Unfortunately only one further issue of the Yearbook appeared in the following year. It presumably succumbed to the lack of interest abroad in Japanese productions and to the country's developing war economy. (Rare copies of both issues are preserved at the BFI Library (London) and the Cinémathèque Royale de Belgique.)

they made use of the *benshi* and his distancing role during the formative period of their mature styles. They postponed coming to grips with sound until they felt capable of maintaining, in and through their mature styles, a 'traditional' distance with respect to Western representationalism as reinforced by synchronous sound.

This hypothetical explanation suggests another: if any period of European film may be regarded as its Golden Age, it was the five years between the first commercialization of synch sound recording in 1927 and the ultimate, stultifying spread of 'canned theatre' under the combined pressure of German and American capital via Tobis and Western Electric, in 1932. Has any other comparable period of time seen such an extraordinarily rich harvest? It includes Epstein's *La Glace à trois faces* and *L'Or des mers*, Gance's *Napoléon*, L'Herbier's *L'Argent*, Renoir's *La Chienne* and *La Nuit du carrefour*, the complete works of Jean Vigo, Buñuel's *Un Chien andalou* and *L'Age d'or*, Cocteau's *Le Sang d'un poète*, Dreyer's *La Passion de Jeanne d'Arc* and *Vampyr*, Lang's *Spione*, *M*, and *Das Testament von Doktor Mabuse*, Sternberg's *Der Blaue Engel*, Dudow and Brecht's *Kuhle Wampe*, Vertov's *Man with a Movie Camera*, Eisenstein's *October* and *The General Line*, Dovzhenko's *Earth* and *Arsenal*, Barnett's *The Thaw*.[9] Even such minor figures as Pabst (*Westfront 1918*, *Kameradschaft*) or Kuleshov (*The Great Consoler*) produced at that period what were far and away their crowning achievements. Not only were the silent films named here among the ultimate attainments of the silent period, but these very early sound films remain to this day among the supreme examples of the 'creative use' of sound, thanks to the three-year delay before the triumph of 'canned theatre' with the absolute priority it gave to dialogue and its increasingly pervasive back-drop of 'movie music'. During the first few years of the sound period in the West, a relatively large number of film-makers were able to extend their experiments with images and graphic signs to the sound-stage. It seems reasonable to suggest that in a country where this transitional period lasted over ten years, and despite our relative ignorance of the films made during this period, that the interregnum had a similarly stimulating effect in Japan.

There is one fundamental difference between the achievements of the great Japanese directors of the 1930s and the great Western directors of the 1920s. As I hope to demonstrate at length, this was a period in which the aesthetic values of Japan's past came to be fully reincarnated in cinema. We have observed that *originality* was never a primary value in Japan, particularly in art. The individual artist's contribution was not evaluated, by himself

THE WEIGHT OF HISTORY AND TECHNOLOGY

9. In the Soviet Union, too, sound ultimately brought a complete change in the scope of cinematic creation, partly for reasons related to Western developments. The political cadres suddenly found themselves confronted with a medium which involved spoken discourse, i.e. the very substance of their political practice. Their competence to intervene far more directly than before was suddenly legitimized. The results are only too familiar. In particular, the decision to replace 'typage' and the mass-hero by a star system and the positive socialist hero is curiously parallel to similar developments in Western Europe and the United States.

or by his society, in terms of his aptitude for inventing new forms, or the 'revolutionary' quality of his work. On the contrary, the subtlety with which he recombined elements that had served for generations, the way in which he introduced cunning changes, fresh but slight, into the work of his predecessors, was valued above all else. Originality, as such, was inconceivable except when fused with evident mastery of the methods and spirit of tradition. Such was the character of Japan's cinema during its first half-century. During the 1930s and 1940s, this character was developed to its highest degree.

Supreme as the individual achievements of Ozu and Mizoguchi may appear to us today, *there is no break in continuity* between their work and that of a large body of directors working in similar genres. Despite the ready adoption of the Hollywood codes of *découpage* by Gosho and Shimazu, for example, their work, considered collectively, is nearly as remote from that of the dominant cinema of Europe and America as that of Ozu, Mizoguchi and Shimizu, whom I view as no more nor less than the supreme masters of a unified cultural practice. They are to the cinema of that period what Ki no Tsurayuki was to Heian poetry, Sōtatsu and Kōrin to seventeenth-century screen-painting, Zeami to the *nō* or Chikamatsu to the doll theatre. None of these can be said to have towered over their period or their art as Shakespeare, Beethoven or Cézanne did.

Although this fundamental distinction may be challenged by Western (and Japanese) adepts of the '*auteur* theory', at least one Japanese observer of the period was fully sensitive to it. Katumoto Seiitiro was clearly aware of the profound community among Japanese directors of the period, of the importance for them of the Japanese past, and of the deep gulf that separated the cinema of Japan from that of the West. In a remarkable article, he not only recognizes but briefly describes the Japanese mode of filmic representation.

The attitude of these film directors is something like the mental position assumed by Japanese poets of the *tanka* and *haiku* schools since ancient times. Not all of them, of course, are conscious of the notion that their own particular art might have a close connection with the traditional poetry of their country. They evidently believe that they are striding youthfully along the path of modern art [i.e. Western art]. Judged dispassionately and objectively, however, there is a surprisingly good deal of the ancient Japanese poet in them, their modern appearance to the contrary notwithstanding . . .

These historical circumstances have also affected the Japanese cinema today. Our film directors and actors have, of course, seen American and European pictures here in Japan and been influenced by them. They have even employed certain effects that outwardly appear to be similar to those of the foreign film. Nevertheless, the tradition back of the technique that has been followed in this country and, accordingly, the innermost artistic sense, are entirely at variance with those of Europe and America. This difference is clearly revealed everywhere in the general run of pictures produced in Japan . . .

. . . the Japanese cinema is no other than a means which provides images to the story-telling performance of the feudal age and the popular novels of today. *A continuity of illustrations as it were, that revolve on an axis consisting of a typical narrative tale –* such is the essential nature of the Japanese cinema today.

Obviously the constructive method of the Japanese cinema which has pursued this narrative medium is a somewhat different thing from the so-called 'pure movie constructive sense', such as is employed by American and European directors and which is considerably removed from the [traditional Japanese] literary narrative method. Whether or not the difference between the two can be explained away by the simple statement that the American and European schools constitute an advanced step in the making of film plays, and that the Japanese school is a step behind the times, is a moot question indeed. The dual aspect of the Japanese cinema, namely that on the one hand it has as its central factor the constructive method as indicated above and that, on the other hand, it is conceived along lyrical and suggestive lines, is fostered by the principle of reciprocal causality. Moreover, they are both characteristics which will cling tenaciously to the core of the film plays of this country, and whether our directors will in future attempt to elevate the quality of their pictures by cutting loose from those fetters, or whether they will strive all the more to develop these features and attain a higher level – this, indeed, is a serious problem which is pregnant with interest.[10]

To complete this contemporary corroboration of views which I will develop in the following chapters, a few words are in order about the difference, also pin-pointed by Katumoto, between the development of cinema and theatre in Japan, on the one hand, and music, painting and literature on the other. I actually know little of the social place of *shin-geki*, but it seems quite clear that unlike such resolutely élitist, neo-Western forms as the 'serious novel', classical music and oil-painting, which developed in an isolated, almost artificial world, cut off from any mass audience, the cinema was, from the very beginning, a popular art, appealing to the concrete reality of Japanese taste,[11] formed by a unique historical experience.

All the contributors to the 1937 *Yearbook* concur in

THE WEIGHT OF HISTORY AND TECHNOLOGY

10. Katumoto Seiitiro, 'Characteristics of the Japanese Cinema', in *Japan Film Yearbook*, 1936. The italics are mine.

11. This may seem contradictory in view of my claim that the development of Western cinema after 1909 was not simply a response to the tastes of a mass audience but, ultimately, an imposition upon that mass audience of the tastes and conceptions of the ruling classes. This contradiction does not obtain, however, given the relative unanimity of taste in Japan until very recent times. The cinema of the 1930s reflected tastes which were shared more or less equally by the producing and consuming classes. Or at least they were *on the most basic level of representation*. We cannot assume that all films appealed equally to all classes, regardless of genre and subject-matter.

IRON TREES,
GOLDEN FLOWERS

12. Uchida Kisao, 'The Motion Picture Theatres in Japan', *Japan Film Yearbook*, 1937, p. 53. Several other contributors stress the fact that a movement towards mixed programmes had begun (presumably because of a scarcity of native sound films). Today the segregation principle is completely restored in the cities; some theatres have two or more halls, one of them reserved for foreign films.

substance with Uchida Kisao that 'the minority of the public who prefer foreign pictures to Japanese ones are of a higher intellectual level than the majority who are satisfied with pictures made in Japan. Indeed, some critics have gone so far as to state that the former form a class all by themselves. Such being the case, one may well understand why it is there are to be found in every important city in Japan theatres which make it a business of screening only imported films'.[12] And it was of course the same élite which was reading Western or Western-style literature, listening to Western or Western-style music. However, a very large majority in every walk of life were watching Japanese films. And until the mid-1930s a majority of these films were 'all the more Japanese' as they were silent.

# 15. Some Remarks on the Genre Syndrome

Before turning to the cinema of Ozu, so firmly anchored in a single genre, we must consider one important general aspect of the Japanese attitude towards cinema. Although present since the beginning, its relevance to our theoretically oriented investigation begins in the 1930s. As all observers of Japanese cinema have pointed out, numerous strict genre classifications were set up and maintained at all costs, in production and programming as well as in publicity and criticism. The distinction between *jidai-geki* and *gendai-geki* (period as against modern 'plays') may appear identical with the genre distinctions of the West, costume-drama, gangster film, etc. However, there are, I believe, two important differences.

Japanese genre taxonomy has been developed and used, not to establish hierarchies of differentiation, as so often in the West, but in order to emphasize an objective unity/plurality relationship. This is achieved partly through linguistic effect, by the repetition of a root word (though an occasional departure from the norm may not imply a break in the series), but undeniably reflects a very real attitude. *Jidai-geki*, *gendai-geki* and also *ken-geki* (sword plays, a more pedantic term for *chambera*) were simply variants on a single object, the film: Tanaka's *The Red Bat* was *jidai-geki*, Mizoguchi's *Sisters of Gion*, *gendai-geki*, and his *Tale of Late Chrysanthemums* a *Meiji-mono* dealing as it does with the Meiji period that comes 'between' *jidai* and *gendai*. Indeed the Japanese divide their films as rigorously as they divide the periods of their history or the many natural seasons of the year. Historical criteria are not the only ones that are used, of course, but the *jidai-Meiji-gendai* series may be regarded as primary to all the others. Like all the others, these categories are purely descriptive, not hierarchical; and they are far more widely used by both critics and general public than any hierarchical distinctions (such as B-picture and main feature, or art-film and pot-boiler) which dominate our Western discourse on film.

IRON TREES,
GOLDEN FLOWERS

The other major type of genre classification is based upon what we might call 'subject-matter'. However, in this case the term covers much more than the general plot outline and setting. *Seinen-eiga* or *haha-mono* are not simply films about youth or about a mother, they are films set in quite specific social milieux, developing a very similar ideological message, with more or less the same set of character types and more or less the same narrative structure. To take a more recent example, practically all of the *yakusa-eiga* ('bad-guy movies') made in the late 1960s and early 1970s – and this means over a hundred films a year – resemble each other closely in setting, subject-matter, structure, pace and tone; they present, in particular, the same actors in the same typed roles with only a change of name.[1] Them *chambera* of the 1920s and the *shōmin-geki* (films about 'townspeople', i.e. the lower middle-classes), which were the dominant genres of their respective periods, also share this extraordinary homogeneity, which of course can also be traced back to the poetry of the Heian period and indeed to almost every Japanese artistic practice. It is often said that Bresson, for example, makes the same film over and over again under different guises; this is the hard core of the *auteur* theory. From a Western point of view, this may be true, but any comparison with the *shōmin-geki* of Ozu or Gosho makes his work seem a veritable zigzag of eclecticism. And despite the important ideological and above all formal differences between the films of these two men, and between their films and those of Shimizu, Shimazu and countless others, they constitute a remarkably unified genre. They maintain a conformity inconceivable in, for example, the gangster movies of Hollywood, with their self-conscious and unrelenting search for a 'new twist'. As stated earlier, the essence of Mizoguchi's or Ozu's films is not originality, but a supremely refined contribution to a continuum.

There appeared towards the end of the 1920s, however, an important genre which to an extent seems to have escaped from this homogeneity, no doubt because it was the first to reflect class struggle rather than the 'unanimist' ideology of traditional Japan. It lasted about five years, and then succumbed to the repression that hit the whole radical movement.[2] This new genre, called *keiko-eiga* ('tendency film') reflected the impact upon the liberal petty bourgeoisie of such pregnant ideas from the West as 'democracy', 'socialism' and even Marxism.[3]

*Gendai-geki*, to which the *keiko-eiga* of course belonged, had developed through the 1920s as an effort to master and to *naturalize* the codes of the Western film.

---

1. Of course, many of these films are also part of a series, which further heightens the sense of sameness.

2. After the Pacific War, the genre may be said to have revived in the films of such directors as Imai Tadashi and Yamamoto Satsuo, though the development of class struggle was such that these films reflected far more often than in the 1920s the aspirations of the proletariat.

3. At about the same time, the Communist Party was able to create a special committee called *Prokino*, for the distribution and production of films for workers. There were some forty productions. Of the five surviving films, I have seen only *May Day* (1925) by Iwasaki Akira, a film of newsreel format, predominantly consisting of long shots of demonstrators and police.

Insofar as they bore strongly the stamp of traditional attitudes the results remained out-of-phase, de-centred with respect to those codes. We are about to examine the consequences of this. However, when it came to emulating the social cinema of Europe in films inspired, on one level or another, by class struggle in Japan, a fresh need was created for better assimilation of codes so closely associated with realism in the West. And, of course, diversification is one of the Western models. Iwasaki Akira, the celebrated left-wing critic, has described the two main sub-genres into which these films seem to have been divided:[4] some 'took the alternative of depicting in a very real way the miserable petit bourgeois outlook of the unemployed and wage-slaves euphemistically called [the] salary-man. Others chose to handle serious problems into satirical comedies. The former [i.e. the latter] group is represented by Ozu Yasujiro who directed *The Chorus of Tokyo* (1931) and *I Was Born, But . . .* (1932); the latter [former] by Uchida Tomu, the director of *The Champion of Revenge* (1931), and Itami Mansaku who directed *The Unrivalled Hero* (1932).'[5]

Besides this general subdivision, it seems that at least the 'serious' tendency films were more differentiated *individually* as well, if only in accordance with the stereotypes of Hollywood and Europe. The half-dozen films of this sort which I have seen including Ozu's *That Night's Wife* and Mizoguchi's *Tokyo March* seem to confirm this hypothesis.

Richie and Anderson explain that the tendency film reached its peak in 1932 and then, due to frequent censorship, degenerated politically into bedroom farces about the lower classes. Others took the form of *rumpen-mono*, films about the lumpen proletariat, a less dangerous topic than bona fide and possibly organized proletarians, less subversive than holding a mirror to the exploited lower middle classes. This genre produced, however, important works of art, including Ozu's *An Inn in Tokyo* (1934).

The entire history of Japanese cinema, like the whole of Japanese art and life, is intricately patterned by genres and sub-genres.[6] We will return to them incidentally, even though the main thrust of this study is in the direction of the deeper structures of Japan's cinema. For, as I have been at pains to insist, Japan, viewed in and for herself, is an assemblage of just such surface patterns.

SOME REMARKS ON THE GENRE SYNDROME

4. See *Japan Film Yearbook*, 1937. It is significant of more than one contradiction in the Japan of those years that nearly all of the articles in that very official publication have, overtly or between the lines, a Left bias. Such a situation would have been inconceivable in Nazi Germany or Fascist Italy.

5. These films of Uchida and Itami (*Adauchi senshu* and *Kokushi musō*) have not survived, but Uchida's *Police* (*Keisatsukan*, 1933) is a perfect pastiche, well ahead of its time, of the post-war Hollywood police investigation film with social overtones.

6. For a fuller listing and description, the reader is referred to Richie and Anderson (particularly Chapter 13). On this subject they are quite informative, if whimsical.

# 16. Ozu Yasujiro

Ozu began making films in 1927. With the exception of his very first film, *Sword of Penitence* (*Zange no yaiba*, 1927), he is known to have specialized from the start in *gendai-geki*. Only six of the first eighteen films which he had directed by the end of 1931 survive today in part or in whole. I have seen only three of these, but *Days of Youth* (*Wakaki hi*, 1929) and *The Lady and the Beard* (*Shukujyō to hige*, 1930) are no doubt good examples of a naturalized form of the Western bourgeois comedy, subtly off-centre by virtue of its very slightness, as it was widely practised in Japan at that time.[1]

Whether or not *That Night's Wife* (*Sono yo no tsuma*, 1930) resembles other early Ozu, whether or not it resembles other films of the Western 'social' tendency, I have no way of knowing. The film is, however, fascinating evidence of the impact which American films and Western culture had, not only upon Ozu but upon a sizeable portion of the Japanese middle and lower middle classes. It is an adaptation of a piece of American pulp fiction. An unemployed office-worker commits a robbery to bring food to his starving wife and medicine to his sick child. That same night, a plainclothesman comes to arrest him but the wife manages to get her hands on his revolver and the trio spend the night in tense confrontation, with the detective held vigilantly at bay. Overcome by fatigue, the couple doze off and awake to discover the detective has the upper hand again. However, his heart has been softened by his glimpse of the man's personal tragedy and he gives him a chance to escape. The husband nobly prefers to pay his debt to society; he and the detective march off side by side into the dawn.

In addition to this familiar pattern[2] the film, though clearly set 'in some Japanese city', scarcely shows us a single traditional artefact (the couple's tenement room has Western beds, chairs, etc.), and the few studio exteriors show an anonymous concrete metropolis, close to the settings of *The Crowd* or *Spione*. The film reveals, moreover, a

---

1. I have not been able to see the recently discovered *Be Cheerful* (*Hogaraka ni susume*, 1930) or *I Flunked, But...* (*Rakudai wa shita keredo*, 1930), nor have I seen the twenty-minute fragment of the earlier *I Graduated, But...* (*Daigaku wa deta keredo*, 1929).

2. As familiar to the Japanese as to us. Unjust suffering, revolt and penitence before the social order are an established theme in Japan (cf. the *Chūshingura* theme). Ozu's choice of this obscure piece of hack-work clearly repeats the pattern of Japan's discovery of Western literature according to a principle of *recognition*.

thorough mastery of the Western system, with only an occasional false eyeline-match (though we shall see the importance of this apparently insignificant detail). There are a great many descriptive pan-shots, aimed at stressing the squalor of the principal set. There are also, however, close-ups of objects which do not possess the same connotative weight, which appear rather to serve as *sheer transition*. The most typical example is a series which, near the beginning of the film, affords a transition between the sick child in her bed and the father crouching in the shadow of a building prior to the robbery.

- close-up of the ceiling-lamp above the girl's bed
- potted flower on the window-sill
- tree foliage and a street lamp
- high-angle shot of shadows of foliage projected on the balcony with the sidewalk in the background below

Though this procedure is somewhat simplistic in its linearity, it very directly prefigures a strategy that soon became essential to Ozu's film-making.

There are also a great many 'spoken titles', but the film paradoxically pays tribute to that significant avatar of dominant ideology in the West, the doctrine that 'the picture should tell the story'. For these titles are totally redundant, so explicit is the imagery, so carefully *spelled out* in visual terms is the narrative. Not, of course, that directors such as Murnau, Leni or Lubitsch, despite their frankly condescending attitude towards a public judged capable of perceiving only one idea at a time, actually doubled the silent pantomine with equivalent titles. On the contrary, the films which best illustrated the ideology of the pictorial narrative – such as *Der Letzte Mann* and *Ménilmontant* – eliminated titles altogether.

In Ozu's film, which otherwise reproduces the codes of the Western all-picture narrative, titles re-enact, at the surface of the screen, the pre-emptive role of the *benshi* (who was certainly part of the performance). Possibly the great explicitness of the images and tautological character of the titles were intended as '*benshi* repellents'. Whatever the case, the narrative saturation of these images situate this film at an opposite pole from Ozu's mature works of the mid-1930s.

Of Ozu's silent films, those best known in the West today are three comedies made during the next three years: *Chorus of Tokyo* (*Tōkyō no gasshō*, 1931), *I Was Born, But...* (*Umarete wa mita keredo*, 1932) and *Passing Fancy* (*Dekigokoro*, 1933). These films were experiments for the masterpieces to come. In them Ozu appears to be eliminating gradually a certain laxness in shot composition (particularly noticeable in *That Night's Wife*). It is also in these films that the systematic low-angle frontality, which has elicited so much comment from critics, begins to appear. More generally and more significantly, we witness the gradual abandoning of that narrative density so typical of the West, that relentless chain of diegetic events codified by Griffith's generation and brought to the peak of perfection by Lang in the first *Mabuse*. To Westerners used to that narrative density, Ozu's films, like so many Japanese films, will seem increasingly 'halting', 'aimless', 'vague', full of 'dead spots'. Abandoning certain Western codes, however, did not constitute for Ozu an end in itself. He does not stop at refusal, at a formless 'de-construction'; he organizes the resulting gaps and ambiguities with a refinement attained by none of his contemporaries. The dilution of narrative is associated with a growing stylization of editing procedures. Camera movements are subjected to a swift radicalization through numerical reduction, specialization and geometrization. The pan-shot, in particular, was soon to be eliminated completely. Ozu's comedies of this period, while perhaps recalling American silent comedy, are significantly closer to the Soviet school (*Mr West, Bed and Sofa*). They display certain attitudes towards editing (an awareness that the cut was not to be 'taken lightly') and towards camera movements (an urge to use them sparingly) which were common to some of the most advanced French and German as well as Soviet directors during the late silent period.

By these Western norms, *Chorus of Tokyo* – a portrait of a white-collar worker and his family – is the most patently *recherché* of these three comedies; it is also the closest to slapstick. The celebrated gag of the wad of banknotes that falls into the gentlemen's urinal and then is spread out all over the office to dry is not entirely typical of the film, whose overall structure does, nonetheless, hinge on a succession of gags, however slight in some instances these may be. Far more discreet, and at the same time representative of the editing subtleties which already point to the future, is the following gag sequence that takes place in the main character's home as he is dressing to go out.

– close-up of a table-top with a hat and mirror; the man's hand enters the shot and picks up the mirror
– medium close-up of mirror as he polishes it on his trouser leg, crossing the room
– 180° reversal: medium close-up as he stands knotting his tie, then looks off-screen left
– low-angle shot of factory chimneys against the sky
– medium shot of main character from behind; the ball is thrown into the shot from the left

- close-up of ball bouncing on *tatami*
- repeat of previous shot; he picks up the ball and throws it out of shot again (left)
- medium shot of child catching ball from off-screen left ('wrong' direction match)
- return to shot of father; child enters shot from left

Now, while the 'one-idea-per-shot principle' is still maintained in this brick-on-brick editing scheme, the sequence is revealing in several ways. First, it attests to a tendency to dilute narrative consistency, which becomes increasingly noticeable in Ozu's work. Late silent films like *An Inn In Tokyo* and *A Story of Floating Weeds* will be almost exclusively composed of such 'mood pieces'. Secondly, the shot of the sky with chimneys, though tenuously 'justified' by a glance at what retrospectively may be assumed to have been a window, prefigures, by its composition, placing and quiet disruptiveness, the kind of de-centering through more or less unsituated, off-screen elements which will soon develop a complex semi-autonomy, as we shall see. Although the incorrect direction match may seem an insignificant lapse, it heightens the autonomy, the 'otherness', of the space in which the cutaway shot places the child; it is also related to the function of the exterior cutaway and has a similarly premonitory significance with regard to future films.

*I Was Born, But . . .* and *Passing Fancy* are both pitched in a somewhat lower key than *Chorus of Tokyo*. The plot lines are even more slender and the gags far less gross. Both are centred around children. The former shows the tribulations caused their lower middle-class parents by a pair of particularly obstreperous but delightful brothers. The latter deals with the relationship between an unemployed labourer (played by Sakamoto Takeshi, one of the most remarkable members of Ozu's growing troupe of actors) and the young son whom he is trying to raise in precarious circumstances. All of these films show Ozu's preference for strict formalization which will develop into the unparalleled beauty of the films of the later 1930s and early 1940s, before its gradual petrification in academic rigidity during the post-war era. Yet he is still, one senses, casting about for new strategies. The limitation of camera movement, for example, produces interesting attempts to use tracking not merely as a descriptive device, but as an organizational procedure. The barber-shop sequence in *Passing Fancy* is bracketed by slow, contrary tracking shots combined with sophisticated ellipses through dissolves. All such punctuating 'opticals' will soon disappear completely for reasons to be discussed later, but this architectonic use of lateral tracking will recur again in *A Story of Floating Weeds*, where it has much the same function, but as part of a sustained pattern articulating the film as a whole. Similarly, the use of a repeated gesture associated with a recurring frame (the main character in *Passing Fancy* putting on or taking off his coat) to give rhythmic pattern to a series of brief sequences, is another type of structure that will reappear in later films, though much less obtrusively and, again, as part of their basic structure.

Although *Passing Fancy* is said to have been made a few months after *Woman* (or *Women*) *of Tokyo* (*Tōkyō no onna*, 1933) I find it difficult to believe, on internal evidence, that this was actually the case. True, the rather sudden change of genre with this film may have accelerated Ozu's development. Whatever the case, *Woman of Tokyo* is the earliest film in which two important components of Ozu's system of representation are completely in place, and they will remain constant in his work until the very end of his career.

Although its theme is thoroughly Japanese, the film constitutes a rather strange return to the type of plot and characterization of *That Night's Wife*. A poor student and his sister share a flat. He does not know that in order to finance his studies, she supplements her meagre secretarial earnings by working nights as a taxi-dancer/prostitute. The young man's fiancée accidentally discovers the truth (*her brother is a police official and the police seem to have been particularly concerned with private morality at that time*) and unthinkingly blurts it out to him. Unable to bear the shame, he commits suicide.[3]

Two major aspects of Ozu's systemics[4] figure prominently for the first time in this film. Their theoretical implications are of great importance.

The reverse-field figure with matching eyelines (and an acute angle of incidence to camera axis) was not merely the last component of the dominant Western editing system; it was, as well, the most crucial. It was this procedure which made it possible to implicate the spectator in the eye contacts of the actors (and ultimately in their 'word contacts'), to *include* him or her in the mental and 'physical' space of the diegesis. Clearly such a procedure was basic to the illusionist fantasy/identification situation. For many reasons, as we have seen, the Western representational system as a whole had gained very slow acceptance in Japan. Reverse-field editing, in particular, was still being awkwardly and sparsely used by a large majority of Japanese film-makers when Ozu began his work. He himself assimilated the Western codes of *découpage*, handling them with increasing ease as he went along. One anomaly,

3. According to Sato Tadao, author of a major study on Ozu and his work, the 'original' script indicated that the girl worked nights .'. . to pay her membership dues in the (outlawed) Communist Party. Ozu preferred to avoid a clash with the censors. While this might have made the film a good deal more 'original', not to say bizarre, I cannot see that it would have made it a greater step towards *An Inn in Tokyo* or *Only Son* . . . nor furthered the interests of the working-class movement.

4. An association of inter-related but semi-autonomous systems. The concept is also useful in dealing with such Western directors as Dreyer or Godard.

however, persists all through the comedy period; he seemed never quite 'sure' about or 'properly' concerned with eyeline and screen-direction matching. Sometimes these were 'right', sometimes not. Since this was still common in Japan and not uncommon in Europe and even America, this might not seem extraordinary. In 1933, however (in my opinion, and despite the lost films, it was in *Woman of Tokyo*) he began systematically to set up his camera in such a way as to produce invariably incorrect eyeline matches. *Moreover, he continued this practice until the end of his career.* The angles of incidence nearly always match; the directions never do. Once one is aware of this trait, one necessarily sees it as the consequence of a deliberate choice, *as part of a fundamental textual economy*. This conclusion is borne out, with a disarming directness, by the following anecdote, reported by Sato Tadao.[5] At some point during Ozu's later career (after 1938; unfortunately, the exact date seems unknown), Ozu's editor, Hamamura Yoshiyasu, decided it was time to call the master's attention to the fact that his eyeline matching was 'wrong'. In order to settle the argument which naturally ensued, Ozu decided to try it – both ways. He shot a two-person reverse-field sequence as he normally did, matching the eyelines 'incorrectly', then shot it again the 'right' way. When the two montage sets were screened, Ozu's only comment is said to have been, 'There is no difference.' Hamamura could only let the matter drop, while Ozu went on imperturbably setting up reverse-fields 'the wrong way'. I will not presume to interpret Ozu's cryptic 'There's no difference.' He had already, at a crucial stage in his career, made a definitive choice between the two procedures, after using them interchangeably. The choice must be regarded, therefore, as part of a coherent economy within which *there was a difference*. The fact remains that by this choice Ozu *symbolically* (in the strongest sense of the word) challenged the two basic principles of the dominant Western mode of representation. He challenged the principle of *continuity*, for the 'bad' eyeline match produces a 'jolt' in the editing flow, a moment of confusion in the spectator's sense of orientation to diegetic space, requiring a moment's readjustment. The resulting effect of hiatus emphasizes the disjunctive nature of the shot-change, which the developed 'editing rules' had perceptually obliterated.

Even more fundamentally, by undermining the verisimilitude of face-to-face reverse-field situations, Ozu challenged the principle of *the inclusion of the viewer in the diegesis* as invisible, transparent relay in the communion of two characters. Once the spectator is unconsciously obliged to rectify with each new shot-change his mental position

5. Unpublished English translation of his *Ozu Yasujiro no gei-jitsu*, Asahi Shinbun, Tokyo, 1971.

with respect to the players, the trap of participation no longer functions in quite the same way.

Various explications of this development have been proposed by Japanese critics. Most of them are postulated upon the idea that it is a device meant to express 'incommunicability' or some such neo-Western cliché. Sato Tadao offers, somewhat guardedly, a slightly more sober version, suggesting that Ozu's characters speak to themselves rather than to their partners. No single 'explication' can satisfactorily account for Ozu's decision. Its full implications can be grasped only by situating it within the whole set of seminal choices which subtend Ozu's mature work. Once described, they are seen to offer a discreet but devastating critique of the fundamental tenets of the dominant cinema.

Apart from the young Naruse, no other Japanese director seems to have imitated Ozu in his systematic disregard for eyeline matching, not even those who, like Shimizu, were otherwise indifferent to the Western codes. One cannot therefore simply claim that linear spatial orientation is not 'natural' to the Japanese as it is to Westerners. It has, however, been suggested that for the Japanese 'the entire experience of space in the most essential respects is different from that of Western culture.' In the Ryoanji rock garden in Kyoto, 'the grouping is such that no matter where one sits to contemplate the scene, one of the rocks that make up the garden is always hidden'; the Japanese 'believe that memory and imagination should always participate in perceptions.'[6] This implies that any spatial arrangement is a 'text' that requires a reading; it is not simply *given and received at face value*. Ozu's approach, not only to eyeline but also to screen-direction and -position (the 180° match was to become increasingly prevalent in his work) does express a typically Japanese approach to the perception of three dimensions by stressing that *their representation is not to be taken for granted*.

We shall see how this reading tallies with other aspects of Ozu's work. For the present, we must examine the second feature of Ozu's systemics, which had reached full development in *Woman of Tokyo*: the very particular use of 'cutaway still-lifes'. (At times, landscapes fill the same function, and in the silent films, the 'still'-lifes are occasionally filmed by a moving camera, as in the opening shot of this film.) The particularity of these shots is that *they suspend the diegetic flow*, using a considerable range of strategies and producing a variety of complex relationships. With some hesitation, I will call these images *pillow-shots*, proposing a loose analogy with the 'pillow-word' of classical Japanese poetry.[7] As we shall see, they also play at times

---

6. Hall, Edward T., *The Hidden Dimension*, p. 153.

7. '*Makurakotoba* or pillow-word: a conventional epithet or attribute for a word; it usually occupies a short, five-syllable line and modifies a word, usually the first, in the next line. Some pillow-words are unclear in meaning; those whose meanings are known, function rhetorically to raise the tone and to some degree also function as images.' (Brower and Miner, op. cit., p. 508.)

the role of 'pivot-words' and for this reason the term I have chosen is not entirely adequate.[8]

The pillow-shot may also be regarded as an expression of a fundamentally Japanese trait. Like Ozu's mismatching, it is not simply a signature, an individual stylistic trait, but a culturally and complexly determined sign of dissent from the world-view implicit in the Western mode. This mode, of course, is profoundly *anthropocentric*, as demonstrated by the rules of centering applicable both to composition within the frame and to the whole camera/diegesis relationship. Prolonged or 'unmotivated' absence of human beings from the screen in a fiction feature film[9] functions as a departure from the codes. In Antonioni's *Eclisse*, this departure is received as a sophisticated poetic statement. In a more advanced film like Paulino Viota's *Contactos*, it has a critical, aggressive effect.

Ozu's pillow-shots have a similar de-centering effect when the camera focuses for a moment, often a long one, on some inanimate aspect of Man's environment.[10] People are perhaps known to be near, but for the moment they are not visible, and a rooftop, a street-light, laundry drying on a line, a lampshade or a tea-kettle is offered as *centre of attention*. It is the tension between the suspension of human presence (of the diegesis) and its potential return which animates some of Ozu's most thoughtful work, making these shots anything but decorative vignettes. It should be emphasized that while Ozu developed the pillow-shot to a degree of unparalleled refinement, it was used by other film-makers of the period. Naruse, Shimizu and others introduce these shots into their films. And from the evidence of Tasaka Tomotaka's earliest surviving film, *Town of Love* (*Ai no machi*, 1928),[11] Ozu did not invent the procedure; the future director of *Five Scouts* anticipated the master's later uses of the pillow-shot by some three or four years.

Ozu's approach to the pillow-shot cannot be reduced to a simple, endlessly reiterative assertion of a single truth – that Man is not the centre of the Universe – however fundamental it may be. These shots intervene in a certain kind of discourse, and each de-centering effect possesses its own specificity. These shots cause a suspension of the diegesis;[12] this statement requires qualification. For, as analysis will demonstrate, while these shots never contribute to the progress of the narrative proper, they often refer to a character or a set, presenting or re-presenting it out of narrative context. The *space* from which these references are made is invariably presented as outside the diegesis, as a pictorial space on another plane of 'reality' as it were, even when the artefacts shown are, as is often the

OZU YASUJIRO

8. A Japanese critic of the 1940s (Naubu Keinosuke) has called these shots *kāten shōto* ('curtain shots'), comparing them with the punctuating function of the stage curtain in the Western theatre. This term has not been generally adopted in Japan and I feel that it is a misleading oversimplification. The traditional technical term 'cutaway', though materially correct, is also unsatisfactory by itself, as it does not do justice to the complex specificity of this figure in Ozu's work.

9. Unless it conveys some such clear, unambiguous message as 'Sunday' or 'spooky house'.

10. The half-dozen films made by audio-visually 'illiterate' Navajo Indians under the non-directive guidance of the semiologist Sol Worth and the ethnographer John Adair offer a striking similitude with the non-anthropocentric pillow-shot. In nearly all the films, on-going human action is frequently inter-cut with 'gratuitous' shots of the surroundings (a stone, a door, a landscape). The makers' general lack of concern with matching, as well as the actual editing context, precludes any reading of these shots as 'clumsy' continuity-saving cutaways. We are clearly dealing with a cultural and ideological attitude much closer to the Far-Eastern view of the relations between man and his surroundings than to our own. (See Worth, Sol, and Adair, John, *Through Navajo Eyes*.)

11. A print is preserved in the Cinémathèque Royale de Belgique.

12. The suspension of the diegetic flow is not unrelated to that *suspension of the production of meaning* which characterizes the practices of Zen Buddhism. Roland Barthes (op. cit., pp. 97–101) has set forth the premises of this materialist reading, while commenting upon the annexation of Zen by neo-Christian ideology as an 'answer', proposed by a certain Anglo-American bourgeoisie, to the unbearable tensions associated with the crisis of State Monopoly Capitalism. Paul Schrader's *Transcendental Style in Film* is a recent attempt to conscript Ozu's films into this neo-spiritualist trend.

IRON TREES,
GOLDEN FLOWERS

case, seen previously or subsequently in shots that belong wholly to the diegesis. This exteriority, the result of many factors, cannot be defined in simple terms. One of its primary signs is the stillness of these shots in a context whose movement ensures diegetic continuity, tells us that the imaginary referent is a *living world*. The shots also imply exteriority because they lack a compositional centre. This is why the phrase 'still-life' so often seems apt. They cannot be correctly described as merely shots of lamp-posts or of laundry hanging on the line in the same manner that a diegetic shot can be described as 'close-up of John' or 'long-shot of Sally'. Unmoving, often lasting a long time (seldom less than five seconds, which we at least experience as long for an 'unpeopled' shot), fully articulated from the graphic point of view, they demand to be *scanned* like paintings, not like *inhabited* shots which, even in Ozu, are relatively more centred around characters.

The complex structural function of the pillow-shot is best understood through the opening sequence of *Woman of Tokyo*. Admittedly not one of Ozu's mature films, it nevertheless already provides excellent illustration of the use of this figure, crucial to his objective break with the linear approach that had dominated the cinema of the West

Fig. 10. Ozu Yasujiro, *Woman of Tokyo*

162

for twenty years and of which *That Night's Wife* had provided such a reasonable facsimile.

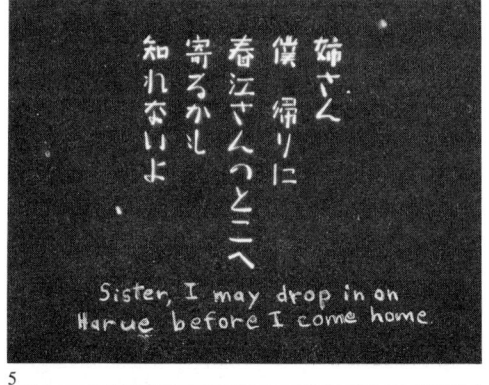

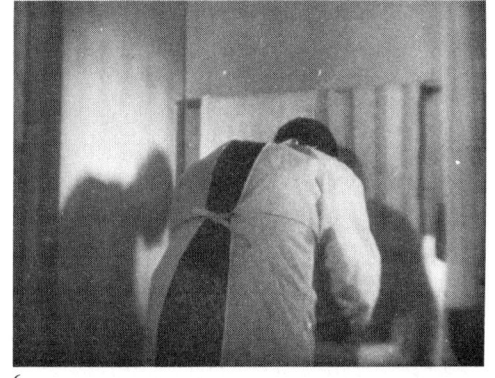

Like all of Ozu's films, *Woman of Tokyo* opens with a pillow-shot.[13]

- very slow dolly-back from a close-up of a gas-burner to a larger shot of the corner of the room (Fig 10, Pl. 1); the shot is held for several seconds
- *apparent* PS[14] of a low table (on it are breakfast remains) seen at a rather low angle (actually, what might be the leg of a pair of trousers hanging in the background is the *perfectly motionless* leg of the brother) (Pl. 2)
- waist-length shot of the sister washing up; she turns towards the camera and speaks (Pl. 3); incorrect eyeline match with the following
- knee-length shot of brother answering (Pl. 4)
- title: 'Sister, I may drop in on Harue before I come home' (Pl. 5)
- medium shot: sister goes back to work (Pl. 6)
- brother continues to dress (Pl. 7), then sits down; match on movement
- 180° reversal: brother starts to put on his socks (Pl. 8)

13. In transcriptions pillow-shots are subsequently indicated by the initials PS.

14. As defined above: absence of people, of pro-filmic movement, etc. However, as this example shows, a shot will often be *composite*, beginning or ending 'pillow', ending or beginning 'diegetic'.

9

10

11

12a

12b

13

*Fig.* 10. Ozu Yasujiro, *Woman of Tokyo*

– 180° reversal: close-up of leg and foot (hole in sock) (Pl. 9)
– title: 'Are there any socks?' (Pl. 10)
– PS: outside the window, socks are hung up to dry (Pl. 11)
– medium shot of sister looking out of window (Pl. 12a); she turns to brother (Pl. 12b); incorrect eyeline match with following
– medium shot of brother (Pl. 13)
– close-up of foot; he has removed his sock and is massaging it (Pl. 14)

14

15

16

17

18

19a

- PS: near-repeat of window with socks (Pl. 15)
- exterior shot of socks and window; window slides back but it is five seconds before the sister appears, looking not at socks, but past camera (Pl. 16)
- PS: tree silhouetted against sky with rooftops (Pl. 17)
- return to sister; she turns and reaches for a pair of socks (Pl. 18)
- long-shot of room, brother in foreground, sister at window in back (Pl. 19a);

165

Fig. 10. Ozu Yasujiro, *Woman of Tokyo*

– she brings him socks (Pl. 19b) (incorrect eyeline match with next shot)
– title: 'You have to pay your tuition today?' (Pl. 20)
– 180° reversal: medium shot of brother, kimono of sister in foreground (Pl. 21)
– reversal: knee-length shot of sister (incorrect eyelines) (Pl. 22)
(The brother's answer, not shown, is: 'There's no hurry')

The very first shots of this sequence illustrate perfectly one of the most frequent *modus operandi* of the pillow-shot, particularly in the silent films: a *gradual* transition from the inanimate 'universe' of the pillow-shot to the animate world of the diegesis. This type of transition is frequent in this film and in *An Inn in Tokyo*, *A Story of Floating Weeds*, *A Mother Ought to be Loved*,[15] and in *Only Son*. The opening of *Woman of Tokyo* provides one such transition through four successive frames, of which the first two are linked by a slow, brief tracking movement.[16] Each of the first three, while they present artefacts suggesting human presence, give no hint of the actual, off-screen presence of human beings. In other words the flat, obviously inhabited, might be empty. In the non-diegetic, frozen time of the pillow-shot, it *is* empty. This fundamental uncertainty (are

15. These are the four remaining silent films accessible to us.

16. In later films these would be separate shots. The ultimate elimination of these camera movements probably corresponds to Ozu's growing awareness that the essence of the pillow-shot, its extra-diegetic character, lay precisely in its *stillness*. Nonetheless, these brief, rigorously controlled movements through the frozen space of the suspended diegesis tend to intensify the stillness of these pillow-shots – an effect remarkable in *A Story of Floating Weeds*: the camera tracks past absolutely motionless spectators prior to a performance.

there or are there not people 'present' off-screen; if so, where? how many? who?) is an essential dimension of the pillow-shot. The third shot in the series contains, moreover, an element of ambiguity, likely to be *read* only in retrospect. Such effects of *trompe-l'oeil* are not uncommon in Ozu's films. As motionless as those that precede, the *tableau* that appears here also seems 'uninhabited' at first; it, too, seems to present 'abandoned' artefacts, like those of the previous shot. Yet the trouser-leg in the background is actually 'alive'. Or rather, and here is the crux of the matter, it comes alive in the next shot, so that the previous shot is perceived retroactively as ambivalent, as an interlocking pivot or transition between the stasis of the pillow-shot and the 'life' of the diegesis.

This use of the procedure is particularly remarkable in *An Inn in Tokyo* (*Tōkyō no yado*, 1935), another portrait of an unemployed worker (again played by Sakamoto Takeshi), this time with two boys to raise. It is probably the masterpiece of Ozu's silent period. Very near the beginning of the film, after a brief sequence in the industrial wasteland which is the rather abstract main setting of the film, there occurs a pillow-shot of a lamp-post with a poster on it advertising 'Rabies-prevention week'. This announcement plays a role in the future development of the slender narrative but no one is seen looking at the poster, either before or after its presentation. For this and other reasons adduced below in discussing the narrative function of certain pillow-shots, it must be considered, at one level, as equivalent to the next shot in the series, which shows the signboard of the inn, occupying a discreetly peripheral position in a beautiful window composition with a lantern. The next shot continues with the utter stillness of a pillow-shot, but while the centre of the screen is occupied by one of Ozu's 'signatures' (a certain form of glass lampshade), in the lower right-hand corner and completely out of focus (it is the lampshade which is sharp) is the motionless face of a small boy asleep. We next cut to a closer shot of the same boy, still asleep and still absolutely motionless. The next shot shows a man on a bed, also asleep and motionless, but in the foreground and in focus, while in the background, out of focus, are the father and his two sons, equally unmoving. At last, one of the sons almost imperceptibly moves his arm, but it is not until the sixth shot in the series – the first of several close-ups which follow – that full movement finally returns, and the diegesis acquires its usual consistency.

The crucial role of the hard-and-soft focus relationship within such 'pillow-structures' is further illustrated by the last three shots of the opening sequence in *Woman of Tokyo* described in part above. After her brother has gone,

1a  1b

1c  2

3a  3b

Fig. 11. Ozu Yasujiro, *Woman of Tokyo*

17. And all emblematic of the Japanese home. Nearly all the pillow-shots carry with them the cluster of incidental symbolism traditionally attached to nearly every object – plant, tool, decoration, etc. – which is part of the traditional way of life.

the sister potters about the room (Fig. 11, Pl. 1a), removes her smock (Pl. 1b) and finally settles down at the far end of the room before her make-up box (Pl. 1c). She is quite out of focus, but the camera remains in this position for nine seconds. We note the looming presence in the foreground of objects such as tea-kettle and rice-cooker, all typical pillow-shot objects.[17] They have figured, or will figure, in pillow-shots in this film. Their presence here and the fact that the sister can scarcely be seen to move during the final nine seconds (her apparent stillness is heightened by the scale and low definition of her image) make this one of those 'semi-pillow-shots'. This 'pillow-status' is further

168

emphasized by the fact that the focus is such as to blur the human centre of the diegesis (soft-focus in the pillow-shots is often used for this kind of de-centering).

As pillow-shots come in series, this ambivalent image is a prelude to the sequence's closing shot. After an intervening close-up in which movement, definition, etc. ensure 'normal' diegetic production (Pl. 2), there is a close-up in the mirror of the sister completing her make-up (Pl. 3a). We now see how an 'animate', fully diegetic shot can *become* a pillow-shot: the sister leaves the shot, the mirror remains empty (Pl. 3b) and this out-of-focus, reflected image is held for five seconds, so that the shot is quickly transformed into an inanimate pillow-shot – an effect facilitated, of course, by the lack of any off-screen sound. The next shot is separated from the previous one neither by dissolve, fade nor other 'punctuation'. Even at this early stage, Ozu's elimination of such devices was essential for developing the full ambivalence of the pillow transitions. The next shot in the series, then, seems entirely unrelated to the empty mirror: we are still in the frozen space-time 'outside' the diegesis. Only in retrospect does this 'still-life with gloves' (Pl. 4) evoke a narrative 'elsewhere and elsewhen' as we discover the presence and profession of the man who has just shed them: a policeman come to see the sister's employer (Pl. 5).

4    5

The evocative role of the pillow-shot is rich and varied. It may refer to a character, as in this instance, or to a setting, as with the gas-burner and tea-kettle which serve throughout as introductory emblems of the brother's and sister's flat. It may also be used as authorial signature; such are the glass lampshades which appear in so many Ozu films (two are to be seen in Fig. 11, Pls. 1a–c, although in this film the object does not appear in a pillow-shot until the very end). One very sophisticated use of the pillow-shot as recurring emblem of a family and its house is found in one of his last masterpieces, *Toda Brother and Sister* (*Todake no kyōdai*, 1941). A motif of potted plants and a caged bird reappears in a variety of compositions throughout the film. In this instance, particularly close to the actual pillow-word of poetry, the emblematic function is more general, more ambivalent than that of the gloves in *Woman of Tokyo*, or of the sword in its scabbard which introduces the sequences in the home of the fiancée's policeman brother.

And indeed, from the early to the later films, the relations of the pillow-shot to the diegesis evolved and became less specific. It might be objected, for example, that the shots of drying socks (Fig. 10, Pl. 11) and of a tree against the sky (Pl. 17) are not pillow-shots at all but an integral part of the diegesis. In terms of visual style, both of these shots are pillow-shots. However, unlike the 'purest' pillow-shots, which transmit no diegetic information beyond the suggestion of a timeless place or presence, these shots do participate in the diegetic movement: they *respond* to what preceded ('yes, there are socks', 'the sister sees that it is a fine day'). Moments in which 'the picture tells the story' were already rare enough in Ozu (the only other one in this sequence being the close-up of the hole in the sock, Pl. 9). Yet we do find a few more such instances in the silent films, such as the bicycle in a house entrance, indicating the son's presence in his foster-mother's house, in *A Story of Floating Weeds*, and this later narrative annexation of the pillow-shot is actually more systematic than the examples in *Woman of Tokyo*. The shot of the socks, in its second appearance (Pl. 15), is diegetically superfluous, and is thus partly expelled from the diegesis. The bicycle, on the contrary, while it conveys each time the same message of presence, brings fresh temporal data to the progress of the narrative ('this is another visit'). However, this direct narrative function was gradually phased out, and disappeared completely in the sound films, which is not surprising.

Another sequence in *Woman of Tokyo* seems worth citing here, precisely because of the way in which semi-narrative functions are incorporated into a pillow-structure: at the end of the film, when the sister has come to the fiancée's flat to find out if she has seen the missing brother, a child appears to tell the fiancée that she is wanted on the phone. The fiancée goes out and the sister is left alone.

– she glances to her left
– PS: kimono hung up to dry, framed in the doorway to an adjoining room
– she looks up
– PS: in the right foreground, out of focus, one of those 'signature' lampshades and in the left background, in focus,

a clock indicating 8:20 (The information offered as to the time of day is the diegetic centre of the shot – the presumed object of the sister's gaze – but while this is made explicit by the focus, it is contradicted in part by the predominance in the composition of the lampshade)
– PS: interior of a watch-maker's shop: clocks all over the wall and, in the foreground, a telephone receiver off the hook; the fiancée enters the frame, smiles a thank you at someone off-screen and picks up the receiver
(A titled, cross-cut sequence sets forth a conversation with her brother in which he tells her of her fiancé's suicide)
– numbed, she slowly hangs up the receiver
– PS: composition of clocks on wall
– fiancée standing by phone with hand still on receiver
– PS: clocks on wall (different shot)
– PS: clock and lamp seen earlier in fiancée's flat (this time the composition is laterally reversed, and the lamp on the left is now in focus, while in the background to the right, the clock, still indicating 8:20, is blurred)
– PS: (actually a 'false' one, not unlike the second shot of the film) shows the traditional charcoal brazier with tea-kettle and, in the foreground, the motionless pattern of the sister's kimono
– in front close-up, the sister looks up as the fiancée opens the door

Several observations are in order here. The shot of the kimono drying and that of the first lamp-with-clock composition are both, through the sister's off-screen gaze, related to the diegesis. Visually, however, they partake of the timeless stillness of the pillow-shot, and their diegetic relationship is in no sense part of a chain of necessary meaning, like the socks-shot analysed earlier. Thus, for a moment, the diegesis is suspended, only to 'recover' as we cut to the telephone-with-clocks. The cutaway to the clocks on the shop-wall as the fiancée hangs up acts as a diversion; we seem to have entered another transitional suspension, but the action is then resumed exactly where we had left off. The shot was in fact a suspensive *parenthesis*. However, the appearance at this point of a very similar pillow-shot is, on the contrary, the first in a transitional series which constitutes a double variation on the earlier series. The cut from clocks on shop-wall to clock-and-lamp is a *signifying* (diegetic) reversal of the earlier transition (it 'takes us back' to the flat) while the second of these shots is a *non-signifying* reversal of the first shot in the earlier transition (reversal of positions and focus relationship). The third of these pillow-shots, moreover, is a reference to another 'pillow-structure' (the tea-kettle and brazier have been emblematic of the fiancée's room throughout the film). In this particularly dramatic sequence the suspension of meaning itself acquires the weight of pathos and, thereby, a second meaning, a connotation. Such rhetoric was soon to disappear completely – together with scenarios like this one. Structurally, however, these early pillow-shots function according to a model which was to remain essentially unchanged for thirty years.

The final shots of Tokyo exemplify the pillow-shot at its purest, as a *satori*-like[18] suspension of meaning; they prefigure its use in the most mature films. Scandal-mongering reporters try to interview the sister and fiancée over the brother's corpse; then we see them back in the street, going about their business; they come upon a piece of 'real news' posted on a telegraph pole; they go out of the frame, chatting merrily. After a few seconds there is a cut to a close-shot of the nondescript base of the telegraph pole, then to a dolly-shot along the kerb-stone, in the course of which the image fades out. Not even the ironic tone of the first of these pillow-shots (the news-bill, the 'emptiness' left by the reporters) can be said to survive in the semantic void of the last two, which provide a paradigm of de-centering and meaninglessness, the filmic equivalent of the Zen-master's stick-blow answers to his disciples' earnest questions.

I shall cite further significant instances of the pillow-shot in dealing with Ozu's later films, but first we must examine the other aspects of his systemics.

Camera movements, severely restricted in number and specialized in *Woman of Tokyo*, were gradually to disappear almost altogether. The successive stages of this disappearance are of considerable interest in themselves. I have already referred to the occasional moving semi-pillow-shots in *A Story of Floating Weeds*. In the subsequent *An Inn in Tokyo*, there is still a surprisingly large number of track shots, but these, without exception, are used to 'freeze' apparent screen-movement; they are follow-shots or reverse follow-shots that accompany the wretched father as he wanders aimlessly through the industrial suburbs of Tokyo with his two boys, occasionally making a half-hearted attempt to find work. The same frame is maintained throughout each given shot. Camera movement is used to reproduce, at moments when a relatively ample pro-filmic movement is indispensable to the narrative, that principle of immobility central to the pillow-shots and which came to dominate Ozu's work as a whole, especially after he began to work with sound. Paradoxically, this gradual absorption of the diegesis into the static world of the pillow-shots, though essential to Ozu's development,

18. 'Satori... which Westerners can only translate with vaguely Christian words like *enlightenment*, *revelation*, *insight*...' Barthes, Roland: op. cit., p. 99.

ultimately contributed directly to the frozen academicism of the films that followed *There Was a Father*, made in 1942.

In *Only Son*, Ozu's first sound film, the first and almost the only camera movements appear as a sudden, startling departure from the principle of camera fixity which characterizes the opening section of the film. These are a series of gently weaving low-angle shots taken from behind the mudguard of a taxi which, we soon learn, is conveying the old mother and her son, whom she has come to visit for the first time in the city. In *Toda Brother and Sister*, only a single camera movement appears, in the film's penultimate shot, a very brief pull-back when the sister is disagreeably surprised not to find her brother in his room and realizes that he has not kept a promise of marriage he has made. The poetic aptness of this effect is completed by a long shot of the brother running on the beach. In his last masterpiece, *There Was a Father*, he eliminated camera movement altogether.

This development is not to be explained by any single reason; these directorial positions form a coherent whole. However, even as early as *Woman of Tokyo*, camera movement is used to contribute to the effect of quietude. And one reason why Ozu's richest period is that of the late silent and early sound films, is because of their dialectical structure in this respect whereas the systematic exclusion of movement in most of the post-war films seems, ultimately, an impoverishment.

We must now consider the low-angle camera position which has come to be identified with the films of Ozu. Of course, many Japanese film-makers often adopt a low level for their camera, if only because the Japanese, in their traditional interiors, spend much of their time on the floor. Unless one wishes a constantly high angle on seated characters (like Mizoguchi in his late silent and early sound films) a shortened tripod is indispensable. Ozu did, however, use this approach more systematically than any of his contemporaries. Many 'expressive' explanations have been offered, of which the most pertinent is Sato Tadao's suggestion that this angle endows all pro-filmic activity with a 'ceremonial quality'. This peculiarly Japanese reaction is perhaps difficult for us to appreciate fully, except insofar as religious and other ceremonies in Japan do take place close to the floor and involve low bows and prostration. However, the key to Ozu's specific, radical use of this procedure lies in more theoretical considerations. In order to understand it, we must examine the films subsequent to *Woman of Tokyo*. For while the camera in this film is often very low, the type of composition produced often involves an emphasis on deep space relatively untypical of Ozu's work.

This is partly due to the nature of the lodgings – one-room flats – in which the film was set. It is also quite clear that the principles of *flatness* and *frontality* had not yet been added to his gradually evolving systemics. From *A Story of Floating Weeds* onwards, it will become increasingly apparent (and overwhelmingly clear in *Toda Brother and Sister* and *There Was a Father*) that a set of converging strategies is at work. Not only is the camera unusually low, but it is systematically placed at right angles to the back wall and in the centre of the rectangular 'vault' of the room or set. The characters are usually filmed head-on and in long shots. They generally occupy only the lower part of the frame when they are seated. This, in combination with the low-angle frontality, is a further flattening factor, since one perceives that which is behind the characters as above them. Also, as Sato Tadao points out, in the later films the converging borders of the *tatami*, insofar as they are visible at such a low angle, are carefully obliterated by the placing of flat cushions.

Now, all of these strategies produce a single effect: the elimination of depth indices, the flattening of the image, its reduction to the two-dimensional surface of the screen. We have already discussed the surface-oriented character of traditional Japanese art and architecture and the unconscious tendency to ignore the Western strategies of depth representation in earlier films. It seems obvious – and an examination of Figs. 12–16 will prove helpful here – that Ozu uses every technique at his disposal *to produce the filmic image as picture plane*.

Stillness, which was becoming increasingly predominant in his films, is important in this development, since movement (and especially axial movement, which rapidly became rare) is basic to the illusion of depth. Once we understand this preoccupation with a picture plane, other aspects of Ozu's systemics begin to take on importance. Series of reverse-angle shots in his mature work are seen as a succession of flat surfaces, side by side rather than face to face; there is no imaginary space between for the spectator to be inserted, as it were. There is no encounter between eyelines, *the necessary complements in Western cinema of the receding and converging parallels of deep space*. Similarly – and this is particularly true of *A Story of Floating Weeds* and *Only Son* – the systematic neglect of direction-matching (of frame exits and entrances) tends to prevent successive shots of a given interior from flowing into one another 'naturally'. The mental reconstitution of a three-dimensional space on the basis of these 'badly joined', flat images, requires a considerable effort of memory and imagination, i.e. a *reading*.

Another strategy of editing related to the overall flatness of image is Ozu's fondness for 180° cuts, in particular without change of shot size. *There Was a Father* is rich in matches of this kind, rigorously proscribed by the film-school primers, which produce the disconcerting effect of a picture that has been abutted to its photographic reversal – the shot seems to 'flip over'.

Finally, though it would be absurd to reduce the pillow-shot to any 'ultimate' function, the pictorial quality which it almost inevitably displays may be regarded as the epitome of Ozu's surface imagery.

Though such metaphors have their limits this visual flatness has a diegetic 'equivalent', for incidents soon grow rare in the Ozu narrative. These portraits of family life, or lessons in family relationships, become increasingly *eventless*. This phenomenon, which touches a whole sector of Japanese film-making, will be discussed later. As concerns Ozu, particularly important are the developments after his belated conversion to sound. The early sound films (from *Only Son* to *There Was a Father*) quite naturally relied more on dialogue, but while this did facilitate characterization (within, however, very narrow culturally and socially determined limits), it also soon tended to reduce the narrative incidents to *spoken* events, and the relative autonomy of the imagery, mostly of people talking, increases greatly. Here one may observe an unexpected similarity with the doll theatre. The wildly contorted features and almost unbearably expressive vocalization of the *gidayu bushi*, the slow succession of the all but frozen *tableaux* formed by puppets and manipulators (the puppets often remain motionless for minutes on end, with only an occasional bob of the head and flick of the hand to indicate the identity of the 'speaker') suggest indeed a parallel: a division of labour between presentational image and representational voice in both the performance of the dolls and the films of Ozu.[19]

*Only Son* (*Hitori musuko*, 1936), the master's first sound film, is not only his most radical experiment with this division between the verbal and the spatio-temporal parameters; it is also, in my opinion, his supreme achievement. It is difficult to describe with written words and still photographs this principle of disjunction, as it is most commonly and *reiteratively* presented in long dialogue scenes. In the analysis that follows, this disjunction may be taken as the fundamental basis on which Ozu has built a system of 'pillow-structures' and other relationships.

The sublimated plot of *Only Son* is a far cry from the melodrama of *That Night's Wife* or *Woman of Tokyo*. It tells of a widowed working-class mother who, at the insistence of her son's schoolteacher, makes every sacrifice to

19. I have already mentioned one film by Antonioni in connection with the de-centering function of the pillow-shot, and it is not without interest that his first – and finest – film, *Cronaca di un amore*, is based on a comparable dissociation of text and images (see my *Theory of Film Practice*, Ch. 5).

send the boy to high school. Years later, when she visits him in Tokyo, she finds that he is one of the vast city's army of unemployed, barely able to keep alive on part-time night-school teaching. Realizing that his mother's disappointment is justified and a source of profound shame, he promises to apply himself to getting ahead in the world. His mother goes back to her province and the silk-mill where she has toiled all her life; nothing remains for her but to die.

One of the pillow-shot emblems used frequently in this film is the traditional head-rest or mounted bolster which, in accordance with polite custom, the son has bought for his mother's use during her stay in his house. Its use in one brief sequence, mid-way through the film, is worth describing here. A pillow-shot of the sleeping mother's kimono hung on the wall, attesting as part of its function to her general presence in the house, is followed by a shot in which the bolster occupies most of the foreground (in focus). In the background, completely out of focus, the son and his wife discuss the problems (in particular, the financial ones) caused by the mother's visit, happy though they are to have her. The conversation is pursued in a pair of medium close-ups of the couple (with the 'incorrect' eyeline match which by now was standard), followed by a slightly larger shot taken from the same angle, showing as before the bolster with husband and wife in background. This time it is they who are sharp while the bolster is out of focus. In this shot, their conversation is ultimately interrupted by the arrival (off-screen voice) of the mother.

This remarkably elegant visual structure is derived so directly from the 'pillow' concept that it seems almost to develop in a different space from the dialogue, even though the couple are actually on the screen. In contrast with the soft focus in the relatively deep sets of *Woman of Tokyo*, there is no effect of depth at all. So close are characters and bolster that the effect is more like that obtained in the French silent films of the 1920s by artfully smearing vaseline on a sheet of glass in order to blur certain areas of the picture. Here, too, the fuzzy patches do not appear as 'incidental' background or foreground, but as soft areas sharing the surface of a composition with the hard areas (a trait to be observed in many pillow-shots, beginning with *Woman of Tokyo*).

It is in *Only Son* that the organization of the pillow-shot reaches its ultimate degree of sophistication. The opening sequence of the film, which I have illustrated photographically, is a remarkable case in point, involving an interesting variant on the hard-and-soft-focus motif:

– PS: 'still-life with oil-lamp' (Fig. 12, Pl. 1)

1   2a

2b   3

4   5

– PS: 'village-street with oil lamp' (the same or another?); the lamp is fuzzy (Pl. 2a). After a few seconds, the deserted pillow-shot acquires a new dimension as a woman worker carrying a bundle of silk appears in the roadway (Pl. 2b), followed by another, and another
– in the background, the women workers, out of focus now; in the foreground, a notice referring to the presence in the village of a silk mill (Pl. 3)
– inside the mill: a woman working (Pl. 4)
– another woman working (Pl. 5)
(The second of these women is the mother, the first her best friend; their conversations subsequently provide com-

Fig. 12. Ozu Yasujiro, *Only Son*

Fig. 12. Ozu Yasujiro, *Only Son*

mentary-interludes between the film's three sections)
— PS: spinning machinery (Pl. 6)
— PS: long shot of the village with only the Japanese flag stirring faintly in the evening breeze ( a remarkable displacement of the conventional 'establishing shot') (Pl. 7)
— PS: another 'still-life with oil-lamp' (Pl. 8)
— the mother in her house grinding rice-flour with a millstone (Pl. 9)

The organization of this *approach to the centre of the diegesis* is quite complex: it develops from stillness to movement and back to stillness before the definitive entrance of full diegetic movement. Parallel to this, we are introduced first to the *anonymous figures* of the women porters, then to *characters presented* as anonymous and, finally, to the mother *in her role*.

These visual structures were completed by a discreet progression on the sound-track, evidence of experimental attentiveness to sound throughout. The first shot is silent for a moment; then the chimes of a clock are heard, carrying over into shot 2 (lantern with street). There is another pause, followed again by chimes, heard briefly until the appearance of the notice-board. We then hear the muffled noise of mill machinery, a motif that will recur throughout (a factory near the son's house in Tokyo provides a subtle variant). This sound grows louder during the three shots in the mill, is still heard very faintly during the long shot of the village; it gives way to another long silence during the last lantern shot. The series ends with the synch sound of the grinding stone over which the film's first dialogue will soon be laid. In this sequence a new dialectic of sound/silence is added to the visual movement/fixity relationship which already informed the 'pillow-structure'.

It is used remarkably well towards the end of the mother's stay in Tokyo, immediately after the film's one 'dramatic' moment – a nocturnal conversation in which the mother pours out her disappointment to the mortified son while his wife sobs bitterly on the other side of a *shōji*. Following a close-up of the couple's sleeping baby (wife's sobs continue off-screen), we cut to a pillow-shot which has been a constant motif: a rather wide view of one corner of the sitting-room. On the wall, placed upside down as tradition prescribes, is a good-luck scroll given to the son by his old teacher, and beneath it the usual charcoal brazier and tea-kettle, along with the baby's empty bottle. The wife's sobbing continues for a while longer, then silence. After some thirty seconds (the shot lasts fifty and is the longest pillow-shot I have seen) there is a barely perceptible change in the lighting, followed by the emergence of a distant mechanical throb. Then there is a pillow-shot of the mother's bolster and quilt, another of silk skeins drying on a rack and finally (as the background sound grows slightly louder) a shot of the mother herself holding her grandchild in her arms and chatting gaily to it as she ambles back and forth in a vacant lot.

This extraordinary sequence is one of Ozu's most radical. The implicit meditation on film-time and the ellipsis, the interweaving of so many different motifs essential to the film's diegesis (the sequence is a veritable nerve-centre in this respect) are typical of this, his most mature period.

Ozu made *Only Son* when he was thirty-three years old. Apart from the obvious pressures of the political situation, the master's two long periods of 'silence' – 1936–42, broken only by the totally atypical and negligible *What Did the Lady Forget?* (*Shokujyō wa nani o wasureta ka*, 1936), and 1942–8 – clearly mark basic divisions in his development: growth/plateau/decline.

*Toda Brother and Sister* (*Todake no kyōdai*, 1941) together with *There Was a Father* form indeed the plateau/peak of Ozu's mature development. Both are characterized, in particular, by an unparalleled predominance of long-shots. These are often de-centered, as in Mizoguchi, when the characters are seated. The closer

Fig. 13. Ozu Yasujiro, *Toda Brother and Sister*

Figs. 14, 15. Ozu Yasujiro, *There Was a Father*

20. It should be stressed that this theme of 'shame', so common in Ozu's films, must not be regarded, as Western commentators tend to do, as a personal one but as one of the principal cultural themes of Japanese history, fundamentally related to the individual's sense of social solidarity (see Doi Takeo, *The Anatomy of Dependency*). On the other hand, Sato Tadao's remarks on the biographical and psychoanalytical origins of the widowed-father theme seem very plausible.

21. Ernest Callenbach points out to me the 'great pathos Japanese people attach to children being brought up without the normal complement of parents'. And he is quite right that while this may be 'a characteristic Ozu theme' [cf. *Passing Fancy, Only Son, An Inn in Tokyo*, etc.] it is widespread in Japanese films and in Japanese society.

shots, introduced in accordance with a pattern also found in films by other, minor directors, often seem almost arbitrary. They appear to obey principles of symmetry or geometry, rather than any dramatic code. *Toda Brother and Sister* and *What Did the Lady Forget?* are the only films from Ozu's mature period to deal with upper-middle-class family life. The Toda family is especially well-to-do. I expect that this is related to the ideological pressures of the period as well.

Ozu's last masterpiece was *There Was a Father* (*Chichi ariki*, 1942), the almost excruciatingly sublimated study of a widowed schoolteacher, masterfully portrayed by Ryu Chishu, another famous member of Ozu's troupe, who played the schoolteacher in *Only Son*. In *There Was a Father*, the schoolteacher abandons his career after a fatal accident, on a school excursion, for which he feels indirectly responsible.[20] This father too has a young son to raise, and the film follows their relationship over some twenty years, until the father's death.[21] The beautiful scene of the boating accident is a fine example of Ozu's faculty for de-dramatization. The father glances out of an off-screen window and asks the students relaxing in the hall of an inn: 'Who went boating? I forbade it.' One of the students gives a name and the games and conversations resume. After a

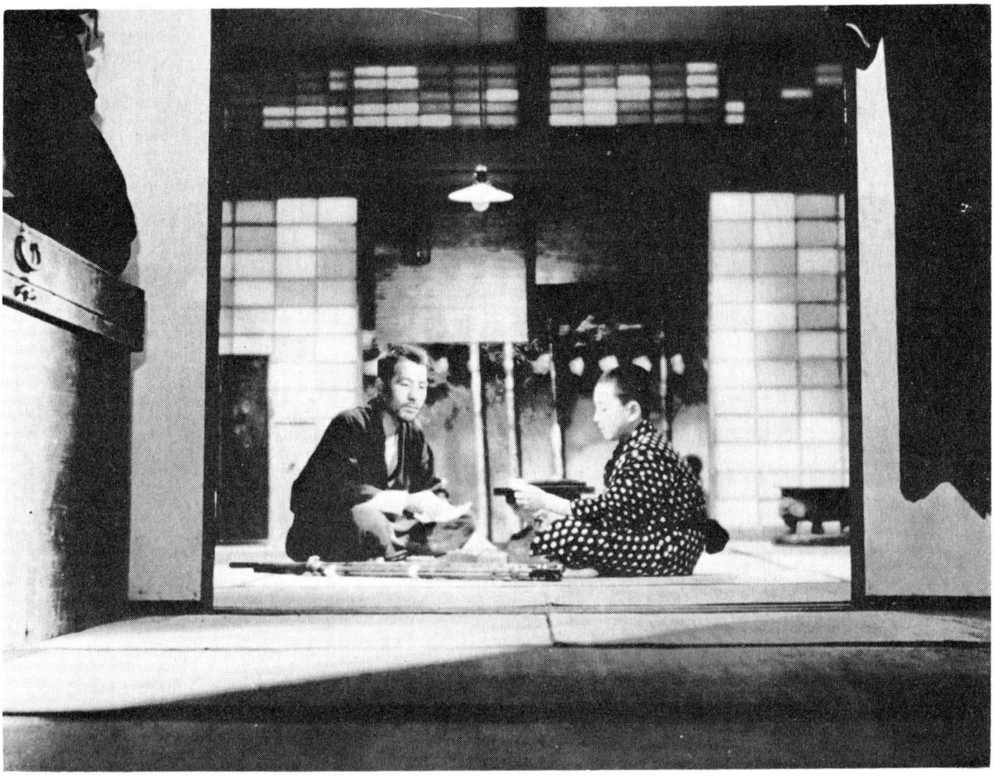

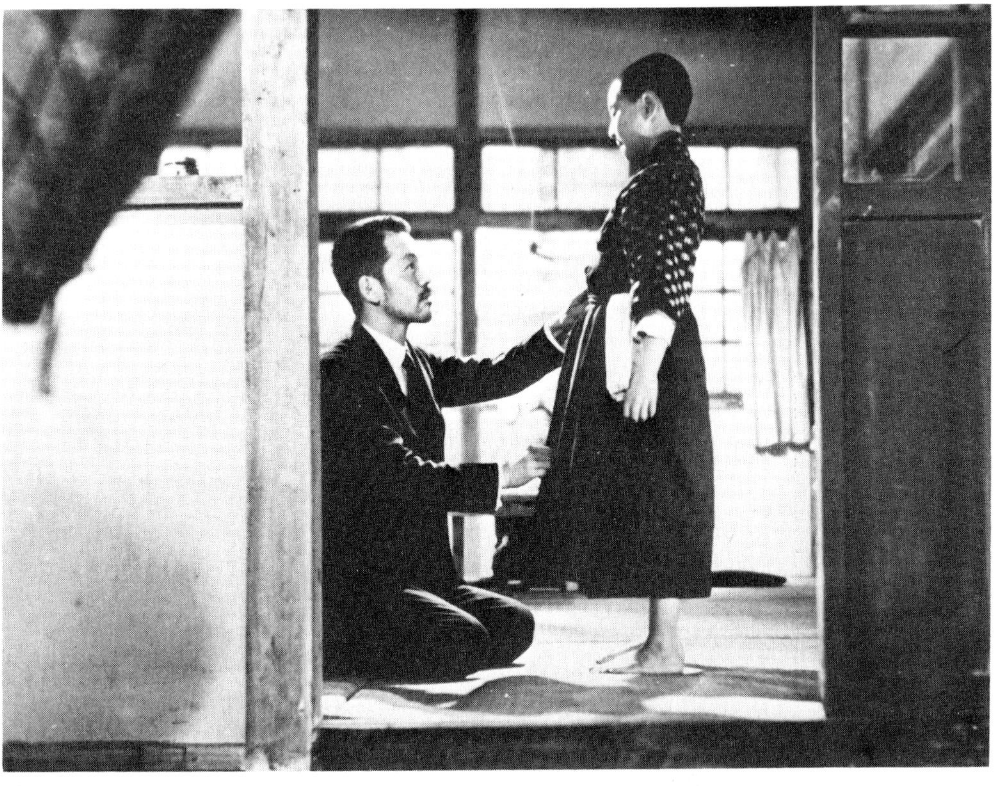

Fig. 16. Ozu Yasujiro, *There Was a Father*

few minutes, a breathless student rushes in with news of the accident. Students and teachers all hurry out, past the row of drying umbrellas (an image which served as introductory pillow-shot to this sequence). On the wharf, the children's cries of 'ahoy' echo pathetically across the lake, and the sequence ends simply with a shot of an overturned row-boat, drifting. The funeral which follows is probably the most remarkable ceremonial sequence in a body of work which abounds in them.

One of the most beautiful of all the pillow-shot series occurs during a weekend spent by the father and his grown son in a mountain hotel. A long dinner conversation is followed by a fifteen-second pillow-shot of the empty bath-house in which we have seen them bathing before dinner (Fig. 16) (and the frame is exactly the same in both instances). There follows a seventeen-second shot across the top of the bath-house roof, with the hotel and vague signs of human presence in the distance and, finally, a ten-second shot of the empty dining-room in which the meal was taken. The return to 'diegetic plenitude' is gradual, since the next sequence is completely wordless; father and son stand fishing side by side in a mountain stream.

The very perfection of this film contains the seeds of that

academicism to which the master succumbed soon after the war. His refined system was imperfectible by then, and departure from it was certainly not encouraged by the alternatives which he saw around him.

Ozu is known to have rehearsed his actors for hours in order to work every bit of 'spontaneity' out of their acting; in this, his approach is related to Bresson's. Sato Tadao also points out that his characters constantly behave as though they were being observed by others, that their behaviour is at all times 'public', we might say 'presentational', and that Ozu's 'psychology' is systematically *superficial*. I would add that Ozu's films, whatever their subject, whatever their formal organization, always evoke the traditional tea ceremony and what the celebrated tea-master Okakura called its 'moral geometry':

> Be sure you know
> That the tea ceremony, in essence,
> Is nothing
> But to boil water,
> Make tea and drink it.[22]

This didactic poem by the sixteenth-century tea-master Rikyū, is one more reminder of the essentially earthly character of all Zen-related disciplines, epitomized by *cha-no-yu*, the Japanese name for what we call the tea ceremony (it means simply 'hot water for tea'). The emphasis, in Ozu's work, on the quotidian, the here-and-now, on everyday gesture and everyday objects (among them, precisely, the tea-kettle and charcoal brazier) and on their *fine appreciation* – by both characters and 'camera' – is clearly related to *cha-no-yu*. Many famous accounts of such 'ceremonies' read like an Ozu script, replete with pillow-shots and seamless ellipses. Here is a passage from a description of a private 'ceremony' offered by Rikyū to a fellow tea-master, Sōkyū.

The host and the guest had exchanged a few words, when they heard the sound of the kitchen door open. As Rikyū explained, a servant he had sent to Samegai for its noted water had just come back. Saying he would now get that fresh water, Rikyū lifted up the kettle and went into the kitchen. Sōkyū drew near the fire and looked at it, now that the kettle was gone. The charcoal, so arranged as to fit the time of the dawn, was beautiful beyond words. Looking up, Sōkyū noticed reserve charcoal neatly kept in a container on the shelf. He brought some down, added it to the fire, and cleaned the fireside with a feather brush. When the aged host reappeared from the kitchen with the kettle in his hand, Sōkyū explained that he had added more charcoal to the fire as he thought it would be needed for boiling the fresh water, even

22. Quoted in Ueda, Makoto, op. cit., p. 96.

though he was sorry to impair the beautiful arrangement the host had originally made. Rikyū was deeply moved and complimented Sōkyū, saying that he was delighted to entertain such a thoughtful guest. As the winter night was long, there was still a bit of time until daylight. Rikyū, saying that he would like to serve tea while the fire lasted, brought out a light meal. As they sat eating, the morning bloomed out.[23]

However, Ozu is not to be read in the light of a single historical aspect of the Japanese 'text', Zen/haiku/cha-no-yu. As we have seen, essential traits of Japanese painting and narrative arts, and of typically Japanese social behaviour, are always present in his films. The Japanese, of course, are fully aware of this quintessential quality of his work, and for many years steadfastly refused to make any effort to export his films, or those of his major contemporaries. It was assumed that these films were 'too Japanese' to be understood by Westerners. I reserve discussion of the élitist and equivocal admiration his works have aroused in the West for a later occasion.

What is one to make of Ozu's known admiration for American films? However much they may have affected his earliest work, absolutely no such influence is detectable by the mid-1930s, and one is inclined to feel that his relationship with the films of Hollywood and Europe (he particularly admired Ophuls and Lubitsch) was purely subjective. However, two of his key films, *Woman of Tokyo* and *Only Son*, contain very strikingly used citations from Western films. In *Woman of Tokyo*, the brother and fiancée watch a fragment of Lubitsch's sketch in *If I had a Million*, while in *Only Son* the young man takes his mother to see a Viennese operetta. In the first of these interpolated sequences, Charles Laughton at his desk is given a message that the boss wants to see him. He climbs long flights of stairs and passes through endless offices on the way to the inner sanctum. This sequence is used by Ozu as a subtly metaphorical transition (ironical in its attitude to the Japanese sense of hierarchy) between two pillow-shots, one of the sister's humble typewriter, which closes the sequence of the police investigation in the office where she works, and one of the fiancée's brother's sword and scabbard, symbol of his social authority. In *Only Son*, mother and son watch a scene from a germanic operetta: a coy plump 'peasant girl' is pursued through a field of wheat by a dashing, amorous cavalry officer to the accompaniment of syrupy music and spectacular tracking. This sequence is offered as the antithesis of Ozu's manner, and yet the sequence ends with a close-up of a fallen locket which Ozu contrives to integrate into his editing *as if it were a pillow-*

23. ibid., p. 98.

*shot*, for it is immediately followed by the shot of the mother's kimono, opening the sequence built around the bolster, as previously described. In this sequence, Ozu seems more aware than is commonly admitted that his departure from the language of *That Night's Wife* was in fact a departure from Western approaches. It is as though he introduces a reference by which to measure the distance covered, while recalling the cosmopolitan enthusiasms of his youth.

Rediscovery of the three or four lost films made between 1933 and 1937 is not likely to add greatly to our understanding of the work of Ozu Yasujiro. Judging from the incomplete version now available *A Mother Ought to be Loved* (*Haha o kowazu ya*, 1934) is a moderately interesting compromise between family melodrama (*Woman of Tokyo*) and the more subdued profiles of the later work, with handsome uses of the pillow-shot. It also has some curiously Sternbergian sequences in a water-front bar, in which the elder son tries to pry his younger brother away from the clutches of a prostitute. These scenes are probably the last traces of any actual Hollywood 'influence' on Ozu.

Barring the unlikely emergence of a lost masterpiece, the mature work of Ozu may be said to consist, then, of five films: *An Inn in Tokyo, A Story of Floating Weeds, Only Son, Toda Brother and Sister* and *There Was a Father*. This body of work is incommensurable with that of any other Japanese film-maker except perhaps Kurosawa. (Too much of Mizoguchi is still missing for a meaningful comparison.) As a contribution to Japanese culture, however, it is comparable only to that of the great poets, painters or sculptors of the past. For like theirs, Ozu's *oeuvre* is not merely an individual achievement but, more significantly, that of an historical and national collectivity.

# 17. Naruse Mikio and Yamanaka Sadao

Japanese cinema in the 1930s is predominantly characterized by latent and overt conflict between the dominant representational modes of the West and emerging Japanese modes. The uneven career of Naruse Mikio (whose work has, in large part, survived) embodies the intensifying contradictions between Japanese and Western culture, contradictions which were not confined to the cinema, but which were to have decisive consequences in cinema after the 1945 defeat.

Japan's general historical development at this time was overwhelmingly determined by the rise of the militarist clique and the approach of the war they were soon to wage against the Western Powers. Yamanaka Sadao represents, through his political commitment, his premature death on the Chinese front to which he had been assigned in punishment for his political activities, and through the tragic loss of all but two of his twelve films, the heroic martyrdom of a tiny minority of politically conscious democrats.

As we shall see, both men also contributed substantially to what is probably the only lasting achievement of that bleak era in Japan.

Naruse Mikio began directing in 1930, and his earliest films known to me, both of them silent, date from 1933: *After Our Separation* (*Kimi to wakarete*) and *Nightly Dreams* (*Yogoto no yume*). Both are essentially what we know as melodrama, although the melodrama never seems to have acquired classified status as such. Japanese genre classifications, as we have seen, are based on class distinctions, historical period or even narrative structure, rather than on hierarchical distinctions of content and tone such as have come to be implicit in melodrama, slapstick, etc. Most *ken-geki* had strong melodramatic themes as we understand them. So did many *rumpen-mono* (a genre to which *Nightly Dreams* can be attached).

NARUSE MIKIO AND
YAMANAKA SADAO

*After Our Separation* tells of an unhappy love-affair between a geisha's son and a younger geisha, culminating in her attempted suicide and their separation. *Nightly Dreams* is a portrait of a young woman who works as hostess in a waterfront bar to support her indolent, perpetually unemployed husband and their child. The husband's sense of guilt towards his wife ultimately drives him to attempt a robbery. He then commits suicide by drowning in the harbour, near the bar where his wife is immersed in the forced gaiety which constitutes her 'nightly dream'. In both these films, Naruse casts about somewhat desperately to achieve a personal style. The manner in which he uses his double heritage, Western and Japanese, is interesting, however. It was, of course, the heritage of his generation. He had thoroughly assimilated the Western system but unlike Gosho, for example, he was not content to apply it literally. In *Nightly Dreams* he carries the use of the dramatic track-in to such frequent extremes that one sometimes almost feels a parody is intended. At the same time, he uses, in both films, a device closely akin to Ozu's pillow-shot, although three times out of four, his cutaways are produced by the wandering gazes of his protagonists and are given more explicitly narrative functions than is ever the case in Ozu's work. In the same film, when we first see the young woman returning home, she embraces her child, then glances at the clock.

– close-up of motionless pendulum with clock-face half out of frame
– close-up of faded flowers
– close-up of calendar indicating the 12th of the month; the woman's hand enters the frame and changes the date to the 23rd

Similarly, when the husband comes home after still another unsuccessful job-hunt, he sees:

– kettle on brazier
– pot on stove
– child's toy car on table

Naruse's approach to the Western codes could be a simple magnification of cliché, as description of the rest of this scene can show. The father winds up the toy car and it falls off the table. At that very moment, his child is being struck down by a real car, a scene which is recounted a few shots later in flashback by neighbours' children.

IRON TREES,
GOLDEN FLOWERS

On the other hand, there are several much more ambivalent cutaways which act as ellipses within conversation sequences; these anticipate later Ozu as well as Naruse's own masterpiece. A charming sequence in a vacant lot, with the father playing baseball in his stockinged feet while his child uses a caramel to 'mend' a hole in one of the abandoned shoes, is somewhat more baroque than Ozu (a very decorative use is made of unburied cement conduits); it nonetheless anticipates *An Inn in Tokyo* to some extent.[1] The film's aping of Western codes is not always as inept as I have implied. The bar scenes, in particular, are pleasantly reminiscent of some of the more effective films of the late 1920s and are quite successful in the genre. One suspects that Sternberg's *The Docks of New York* made a strong impression on more than one Japanese director.

*After Our Separation* contains typical excesses due to a fascination for the most explicitly pseudo-linguistic aspects of the Western codes. Among them is a feverish suicide attempt cross-cut with dancing at a party next door. However, the film also contains the first stage in the development of a system of matching on foreground movement which becomes a principal strategy in Naruse's first sound film, his single masterpiece, *Wife, Be Like a Rose* (*Tsuma yo bara no yo ni*, 1935).[2]

– a city street seen through a window (frame in foreground): a blind descends and blacks out the picture
– view of rush-hour sidewalk at street level; the crowd is moving towards and past the camera
– tall office buildings, again seen through a window, but here the frame is not visible; a blind descends and blacks out the picture
– again the camera is at sidewalk level: now the crowd moves past the camera and away from it
– a crowded railway platform, the train arrives
– a girl stands waiting on a street corner
– high-angle shot of a train going by; a blind descends and blacks out the picture (end of opening musical sequence)
– long shot: inside a large office, the office boy is pulling down one last blind, whistling the theme of the musical sequence; he picks up a tea-tray
– a smartly dressed young woman says good night to him
– in the street, we find her whistling the same tune as she walks along

In this splendid sequence, Naruse plays with the potential ambiguities of 'pillow time and space' (non- or 'weakly' diegetic time and space) with consummate virtuosity. It is

---

1. Both films also illustrate what were clearly the limits which film-makers faced in dealing with such matters as unemployment, presentnted as a conjugation of social fatality and individual resignation.

2. The lost *The Girl They're Talking About* (*Uwasa no musume*) which dates from the same year (described by Richie and Anderson, presumably according to contemporary accounts, as 'something of a triumph of technique over old-fashioned material') is one of the films one would especially like to unearth.

3. Is this why it was one of the very few films of that period to have been distributed abroad? Or was it mistakenly assumed that the theme would seem close to Westerners?

4. The contrast is significant with respect to Naruse's role in Japanese cinema.

the opening sequence of a film which at that time undoubtedly stood out as one of the masterly examples of the new school.[3]

*Wife, Be Like a Rose* is pure *shōmin-geki*, dealing with the very down-to-earth problems of a middle-class family. A young woman (the office-worker seen in the first sequence) resolves to draw closer to her father, who is estranged from his poetess-mother and lives with his mistress. Having decided that it was actually her mother who was responsible for the separation, she undertakes to bring about their reconciliation and her father's return home.

The first sequence, as described, is emblematic of the entire film's formal texture, with its cuts on foreground movement. The window blinds, however, will never appear again; the Western setting of this prelude is followed by a film in a purely Japanese setting, where the blinds will be replaced in their formal function by kimono sleeves, teakettle, etc.[4] Every one of the many conversation pieces which form the body of the film, is shot in a reverse-field set-up, generally involving systematically unorthodox eyeline matching, like that of Ozu. In these, Naruse also uses a technique of cutting on movement which is quite original and implies an interesting *displacement* of the encoded norms.

NARUSE MIKIO AND YAMANAKA SADAO

Fig. 17. Naruse Mikio, *Wife, Be Like a Rose*

IRON TREES,
GOLDEN FLOWERS

In the classical reverse-field set-up, the 'over-the-shoulder' shot is the chief alternative to the 'one-shot'. In the usual Western approach to this set-up, the 'live' element in the foreground (a shoulder, an arm, the back of a head or an object held in a character's hand) remains discreetly motionless. As a passive presence, it anchors the shot, fully establishing the signs of confrontation (generally before the move into close-up) but is never allowed to intrude, never, except in sequences of violence, used to play a key role in the shot-change.

Naruse's development of Ozu's radical attitude towards the mechanics of matching is of considerable interest, as evidence of Naruse's participation at that time in the collective work of his generation. It also helps to confer upon this film a singular stylistic authority. A great many shot-changes are articulated around relatively brusque and ample movements of these foreground elements, movements which occur perceptibly just before or just after the shot-change proper. These are not, strictly speaking, cuts on movement. Even when a direct match is implied (for example, a character's kimono sleeve is seen to move in the fuzzy foreground of an 'over-the-shoulder' shot and again in the sharp background of the reverse angle), the extreme disproportion of perceptual breadth[5] is anything but an expression of continuity. Consequently, most shot-changes within otherwise 'transparent' exchanges such as reverse-field conversations are *signalled*,[6] just before or after the caesura, by a *disproportionate* foreground event which pulls the spectator's eye abruptly back to the surface of the screen, in the manner of the descending blinds in the opening sequence. This procedure must be regarded as doubly 'anti-illusionist'; it emphasizes the discontinuity of the shot-change and exposes one of the essential depth-producing procedures of dominant cinema. For in the last analysis, such is the goal of the 'over-the-shoulder' shot. It produces an effect of depth by the contrast between an unfocused foreground presence, peripheral to the spectator's consciousness, and the distant, sharply focused *centre of the diegesis*.

The film also contains remarkable uses of the cutaway, closely related to Ozu's use of the pillow-shot, though generally more disruptive. At one point, during the running debate between the father's mistress and his daughter, who is determined now to bring her father home, the mistress starts to rise from a seated position, presumably to break off a painful conversation. On her movement, Naruse cuts to the outside of the house, so that the movement is continued by that of her shadow projected on the paper wall. This shot is part of a series of cutaways from this long

---

5. A hand moving in close-up may cross the screen in half a second, whereas the same hand seen from a distance may traverse only one tenth of the screen in that time. Hence a radical and ultimately irreducible discrepancy in surface velocities. Irreducible but not undiminishable: Naruse was on the contrary contriving to make this effect *fully visible*.

6. Though we must not forget that continuity is already challenged by eyeline 'mismatching'.

dialogue to the adjoining garden.

Unlike Ozu, Naruse never abandoned the use of camera movement, but he had discontinued a grossly expressive use of it, as in *Nightly Dreams*. It was now used for a sophisticated organization of pro-filmic movement, exploiting entrances, exits and empty frame to good advantage, both dramatically and decoratively.

The approach adopted in this film involves not only a specifically Japanese refusal of certain norms of Western cinema, but also a budding sense of formalization based, *in the Western manner*, on the transgression of norms. Unfortunately, Naruse seems not to have seen it as a point of departure for future work. One feels today that *Wife, Be Like a Rose* might have had a place in his work comparable to that of *Woman of Tokyo* in Ozu's career. His next surviving film, *Tōchūken Kumoemou* (1936), a turgid biography of a famous Meiji performer who sacrifices everything for his art, scarcely seems to be the work of the same director. One is irresistibly reminded of the *chroniques filmées* which Marcel L'Herbier was reduced to making in those very same years. Naruse's is a laboriously academic, slightly over-edited film, with a preponderance of medium close-ups, perfectly correct eyeline matching, and the actors have obviously been ordered to remain perfectly still when providing foreground support for an 'over-the-shoulder' shot. *Tsuruhachi and Tsurujiro* (*Tsuruhachi Tsurujiro*, 1938), a 'family drama' about a brother and sister team of traditional concert musicians, is somewhat less painfully familiar to us, if only because of some very fine music, used at times in conjunction with sound-effects in a manner similar to later experiments of Mizoguchi. There are some decorative pillow-shots as well.

Even what is generally regarded, and rightly, I should say, as the director's most endearingly successful film of that period, *The Whole Family Works* (*Hataraku ikka*, 1939), is, on the level of editing, a thoroughly 'Western' film, however 'Japanese' it may be in other respects. It inaugurates the delicate dramatic style of Naruse's post-war films.

As one reviews the Naruse films of this immediate pre-war period, one concludes that he had made some kind of 'agonizing reappraisal'. He seems to have had serious personal problems around that time, no doubt aggravated by the war; from 1941 to 1951 he was almost completely silent. The films which he made during the 1950s, and to which I shall refer briefly later, are wholly responsible for his reputation in the West. They are certainly as fine as anything he made after *Wife, Be Like a Rose*; they are, in fact, excellent narratives in *shōmin-geki* form, on a level with the best of

Becker or Lattuada. By this time, however, the specifically Japanese mode of filmic representation and the formal innovations which had characterized that early masterpiece seemed to be no more than a forgotten memory.

The very remarkable promise shown by Yamanaka Sadao in the dozen films which he made in the 1930s also went unfulfilled, for very different reasons; he was killed on the Chinese front in 1938, at the age of thirty-one. Yamanaka is often called the Vigo (or the René Clair) of Japanese cinema. It is difficult to analyse or evaluate his work with any assurance, since only two of his films have survived.[7] Both of these are happily representative in many ways of what is most Japanese in so much of the cinema of that period. At the same time, they have a special, personal tone and style that corroborate Yamanaka's reputation as an *auteur*.[8]

The earliest of the two Yamanaka films known today, *The Pot Worth a Million Ryō* (*Hyaku-man ryō no tsubo*, 1935), is a delightful low-key comedy, a delicate mixture of pathos and satire probably rare in that period of social tension. Set in the late Tokugawa period, the plot is a variation on a universally familiar theme. A large, very plain earthenware jar is valued, for unfathomable reasons, at the astronomical sum of one million *ryō*, and a powerful lord is determined to add it to his rich collection. Unfortunately, one of his vassals, believing it to be worthless, has offered it, in a gesture of contempt, to his brother as a wedding present. Genzaburo, an easy-going, quite unmartial samurai, immediately sells it at his bride's behest to some rag-pickers, who give it in turn to a little boy, Yasu, the son of a rice-vendor. The rice-vendor is murdered by ruffians, and the child is taken in by Okami, who runs an archery range and tea-room, and her lover, Tangekazen, a one-eyed *rōnin*, a traditional figure in *chambera* (Fig. 18). Having discovered the value of the jar, Genzaburo's shrewish wife sends him out on a full-scale search for it, and he begins to spend most of each day in the archery range, making eyes at Okami's lovely assistant. The plot is thickened by the ceaseless attempts of Genzaburo's brother to find the jar, which is, of course, right under the noses of everyone concerned. (Yasu keeps his goldfish in it.) Genzaburo and his new friends finally discover the truth, but agree to keep quiet, giving Genzaburo a pretext to stay away from home 'looking for the jar', in other words continuing to enjoy himself at the archery range.

We are clearly a far cry from the austere narrative of the *shōmin-geki*, or the grandiloquence of the average *jidai-geki*. We are, in fact, startlingly close to René Clair, or even

7. According to Donald Richie, in private conversation, a third film was located in a private collection a few years ago. The films were dispersed on the death of the collector and the Yamanaka has yet to be found.

8. In contrast, I am afraid, with Itami Mansaku, the other best-known radical director of the 1930s. *Akanishi Kakita* (1936), his one surviving film as a director ( he scripted films for Inagaki and others), may be an effort to renew the content of the *jidai-geki*; it is in no sense a contribution to the visual and narrative style of the period, as were the films of Yamanaka.

Fig. 18. Yamanaka Sadao, *The Pot Worth a Million Ryō*

Renoir. It is interesting to see how, working with – and in the spirit of – certain fundamental traits of the Japanese cinema of the 1930s, Yamanaka produces a film which is not only original in the Western sense but which, on the strictly diegetic level, is close to certain Western patterns. These Japanese traits are the following: (a) overwhelming preponderance of long-shots and medium long-shots; (b) a correlative rarity of close-ups and reverse-field figures; (c) use of prolonged empty frames for a variety of effects strange to Western eyes; and (d) systematic use of a kind of pillow-shot, mainly as transitions between scenes.

In the masterpieces of Mizoguchi and Shimizu, in particular, the camera is nearly always placed further from the characters than in the Western cinema after 1910. It is also often held there throughout a scene. Though the works of these two masters provide extreme instances, this is an absolutely basic trait of Japanese cinema in general, whose possible origins and overall theoretical implications are discussed elsewhere. In this film, Yamanaka extends in such wide shots his playing area to the whole screen surface in a lively way. When little Yasu, hoping to end the bickering between Okami and Tangekazen, writes a farewell note, picks up his huge goldfish jar and steals out of the house, the half-dozen wide-angle set-ups which constitute the child's itinerary are *explored* thoroughly, one after another, by Okami and Tangekazen as they look for him.

The European silent cinema, particularly that of Germany, did on occasion create dramatic tension through the use of the empty frame, as in Lang's *Mabuse* and Dupont's *Variety*. The procedure had always been, and is still, more frequent in Japanese films. This willingness to stress the existence of a frame, to leave the shot uncentered (or with an imaginary, 'off-screen centre'), is related to aspects of traditional painting, as illustrated by an anecdote recorded by H. P. Bowie.

The artist Buncho being requested to paint a crow flying across a *fusuma* or four sliding door-like panels, after much reflection painted the bird in the act of disappearing from the last of these subdivisions, the space of the other three suggesting the rapid flight which the crow had already accomplished, and the law of proportion (*ichi*) or orderly arrangement thus observed was universally applauded.[9]

The Western system abhors a vacuum; the frame empty of people, a quite ordinary event in the Primitive cinema, with no special expressive value, was rapidly codified. It came to signify various forms of suspense and was particularly valuable in horror films. More rarely, off-screen action was productive of a style of understatement (e.g. Nicholas Ray's *They Live By Night*, Bresson's *Les Anges du péché*).

As we have already seen, these were not the attitudes that dominate the use of the off-screen/on-screen relationship in most of the films of that period in Japan. It was a non-committal, 'arbitrary' de-centering that was practised by Ozu, meaningless except in so far as it emphasized the materiality of the frame, the picture as design and the diegesis as a circumscribed space. This spirit is present in the 'empty frame' strategies of most of his contemporaries.

At one point in *The Pot Worth a Million Ryō*, Shuchibei, the rice-vendor, has been attacked and mortally wounded by ruffians. Tangekazen has found him and brings him back to the archery range. Inside, the women are clearing away for the night. There is a knock at the door. Cut to the street outside; Tangekazen stands at the door, with the wounded rice vendor on his back; the women let him in and close the door; the camera continues to 'gaze' at the closed door *for eight seconds*, as we hear faint voices, then silence from inside. There follows another long shot of an empty street, before the cut back to Shuchibei's pathetic death-scene, *shown in full*. In other words, it is not possible to detect any *ellipsis*, any significant time-lapse *inside* while the camera was *outside*. The empty shot has no coded, rhetorical function whatsoever. Simply, Yamanaka shows the bird *and* the

9. Bowie, Henry P., *On the Laws of Japanese Painting*, p. 48.

empty space behind it. Like most Japanese artists, he saw representational space/time as an association of fullness and void, of event and non-event.

Yamanaka's use of 'cutaway transitions' in this film is frequent and systematic, but on the whole more simplistic than the example above or than Ozu's pillow-shots. Many are of the still-life variety, but the image is *centred* on the *manekineko*, the good-luck china cat, which is a continual object of contention in the archery range, or on other props peripherally related to the narrative strands. The repeated shot of *omochi*, a white, gummy savoury associated with the New Year season, swelling over the charcoal brazier during the sequence of Yasu's runaway bid is a somewhat more developed instance. In every case, the procedure demonstrates the cultural concern with objects and environment also obvious in the long shot and common to so many films of that period.

*Humanity, Paper Balloons* (*Ninjō kamifusen*, 1937), the young director's last work, is far more pessimistic in mood. Set in approximately the same period in Japanese history, it is a portrait of a poor section of Edo, with its itinerant pedlars, shop-keepers and artisans, its petty intrigues and private tragedies. The slender main plot is concerned with an impoverished *rōnin* and his mistress, who makes and sells paper balloons. Desperate for money, he ultimately becomes involved in a hare-brained kidnapping scheme. When it fails, his mistress, in despair, kills him in his sleep, then takes her own life. It should be added that the narrative structure is 'circular', since the film had opened with news of the suicide of another poor *rōnin*.

Among the most remarkable sequences are those which take place in the narrow, crowded alleyway in which the *rōnin* and most of the main characters live (Fig. 19). The camera angle usually coincides with the axis of the alley, and the editing takes us up and down it in a series of concertinas that can hardly be said to match at all; each shot is at once separate from and identical to the previous shot. The overall result is quite the contrary of one's expectation of an effect of depth; it is as though new characters were continually appearing on the self-same 'screen-proscenium'. In these sequences the *découpage* has a rough-hewn refinement which points ahead, towards the mature style of Kurosawa.

Concertina articulations are developed to a high art in the most beautiful sequence in either of Yamanaka's surviving films.

The setting is a street much wider than the alleyway referred to above. It appears to be a more affluent neighbourhood, though close to the slum where most of the film

Fig. 19. Yamanaka Sadao, *Humanity, Paper Balloons*

is set. It is the day after the suicide of the first *rōnin*, which opened the film. The goldfish vendor meets the *rōnin*'s (and his own) landlord and another, fat man; they carry on a running conversation the central theme of which is who is going to buy *sake* for the evening's wake. The sequence is composed of five shots joined by four concertinas, each one taking us one 'station' further along the street as the three men, with their backs to the camera, slowly advance according to a rather complex pattern. Each shot involves various entrances and exits, and with each concertina one or two of the protagonists is left behind. This bypassing, as well as various small diversions, structures their weaving conversation. The fat man turns his ankle and has to remove a clog to repair the strap. This event causes him and the landlord to lag behind the goldfish vendor, in keeping with the structural needs of the *découpage*. The vendor intersperses his part of the dialogue with cries of 'Goldfish for sale', while the last shot is underlined by a charwoman who appears in a doorway and empties a bucket of water over all their feet, so that again the fat man must remove his clogs.

To find an equivalent of the geometrical poetry of this jewel-like scene, one must return to the great period of the Soviet cinema, or go forward to Kurosawa. And indeed, this film as a whole is closer to the post-war cinema than to that of the 1930s.

Yamanaka, as I say, was drafted and sent to the front in reprisal for his left-wing convictions. It is regrettable that more of the films of the handful of politically progressive film-makers of the 1930s have not been brought to light. As it is, we have only a very partial view of their contribution to the film-art of the period, of the difficulties encountered, the strategies used in that period of intensified repression.

Fig. 20. Yamanaka Sadao directing *Humanity, Paper Balloons*

# 18. On Architecture

Implicit in my account of the Japanese cinema is a recognition of the importance of the country's traditional architecture. Already fully apparent in Ozu's films, it will appear again in those of Mizoguchi and Ishida. I therefore turn to a consideration of some aspects of domestic design.

The traditional Japanese home has been and continues to be designed in a manner common to all, rich and poor.[1] Its principal characteristics are by now well known to Westerners: semi-mobility of the partitions which separate rooms, and separate interior from exterior. The internal organization of space is, within certain limits, quite flexible. Similarly, interior and surroundings (generally a landscaped garden, however narrow) may be related in a variety of ways. The possibilities include complete separation (wooden shutters drawn over the paper doors (*shōji*) during storm or absence); communication of light only (shutters removed, *shōji* closed); 'framed' communication (for both exit and entrance and the creation of 'natural pictures'); and relatively free 'flow of space' between indoors and outdoors, obtained by drawing back *shōji* as much as possible.[2] The range of inter-room communication is equally varied, especially if we consider the existence of another kind of sliding door, the *fusuma*, covered with opaque (often decorated) paper. It is also important to note that whatever fixed surfaces there may be – particularly the flat false ceilings – they echo the bare ribbing of the *shōji*. In fact the concern with apparent structure is so great that many elements of house architecture are in fact *falsely structural*.

Some critical consideration of that notion of the 'flow of space' in Japanese dwellings is necessary at this point. Heinrich Engel, one of the foremost Western scholars of Japanese architecture, takes as one of the general premises for his analysis that 'the eye accepts space architecturally, i.e. as being defined in character and purpose, as long as the remaining space-making elements are pointed enough to optically suggest controlled space' and that 'since life in

1. Modern flats, whether 'mansions' (two-level constructions) or full-blown apartment houses, are usually fitted with non-connecting windows that do not reach floor-level. They do, however, conform in most other respects to the traditional model: *tatamis*, sliding partitions, few pieces of furniture, quilts spread out for sleeping and stored away during the day, etc. A surprisingly large number of Japanese still live in individual houses (hence the huge surface area of a city like Tokyo).

2. The *shōji* are often replaced today by sliding windows of translucent glass, but many houses, especially in the country, are equipped with shutters, glass windows and *shōji*, providing an even greater range of practical and aesthetic combinations.

the dwelling is essentially "immobile" ... rather than "mobile" ... sensitive residential space in its most appropriate substantiation is arresting rather than driving; it is static.' Apropos of the Japanese house, Engel maintains, contrary to the usual view that its architecture is one of free spatial flow, that 'the two different orders of space definement and space control – the vertical planes for marking the individual rooms, the horizontal planes for marking the house interior – are the keys for understanding Japanese space. In spite of all openness, the quality of space, though easily transformable, remains static and crystallinely defined. There is no interchange of space between exterior and interior, nor does space flow from room to room; there is no "continuity of space" ad infinitum in one direction. Instead there is either a succession of space, or a fusion of space with two or more units being joined into one space.'[3]

Let us now suppose that we have set up a camera in a traditional Japanese house, at a medium height and equipped with a moderately wide-angle lens. We will discover that we can close off our field of view to the dimensions of a medium close-up or open it for a long shot by the simple expedient of manoeuvring the sliding doors between our camera and the far end of the house. We may also divide the pro-filmic field into several rectangular or rhomboidal cells, of different sizes and at different distances from the camera. We may open 'windows' into the garden in almost any part of the field. Characters, when we introduce them into our set, can be brought into the shot from any side and at almost any distance from the camera. In theory, at least, we are dealing with a fully developed *deep space*, far more exploitable as such than any but the most cunningly contrived Western set. It is this aspect of the space before us which corresponds to the common opinion that Japanese space is one of 'free flow'. However, if we look into our view-finder, we will find that Engel's thesis is also very relevant. In the composition as it appears, now on the ground-glass, later on the screen, the overwhelmingly dominant features are rectangles (or rhomboids, if we are not at Ozu-like right angles to the set) of all sizes and in all sorts of patterns, formed by intersecting horizontal and vertical lines: the frames and ribbing of the *shōji*, the posts and lintels, balustrades, lattice-work, etc. Even the foreshortened trapezoids of the *tatami* borders (except in temples, the mats are staggered in patterns that avoid long straight lines) are part of the system. Any Japanese film set in a traditional interior offers Mondrian-like patterns, many large or small sections of which may at any time slide back to reveal a new, *framed* element: a person, a fragment of a garden, a painted *fusuma*, etc. And although a shadow

3. Engel, Heinrich, *The Japanese House: a Tradition for Modern Architecture* pp. 246–8. I am indebted to one of my students at New York University, Barry H. Novick, for having called my attention to the importance of this study.

IRON TREES,
GOLDEN FLOWERS

projected on a *shōji* may occasionally designate the segment which is about to open, no purely architectural trait marks it out as 'door' or 'window'.

Most often, especially in *jidai-geki* (where 'period etiquette' calls for kneeling and other ritual gestures for opening and closing, exits and entrances), these new vistas are produced not as adjuncts to an infinitely extensible deep space, but as *cellular sub-divisions of the screen-surface*. For, despite its plasticity, the dominant aspect of Japanese architecture is, as Engel puts it, the 'static and crystalline' definition of space. In the projected image of it, depth cues, such as axial character movement and receding, converging lines are, in the most common instances, *over-ridden* by the effect of surface, due primarily to the predominance of the quadrilateral. Thus, the filmic image becomes, *predominantly*, the planar projection of the three-dimensional cells, static in each of their successive arrangements, which constitute the pro-filmic dwelling-space. Predominantly, but seldom exclusively: movement of characters and camera, as we shall see in the films of Ishida and Mizoguchi, introduce an effect of spatial flow, in contradiction, we might say, to the primary character of Japanese dwelling-space, and which is an important source of formal and dramatic tension in the work of these and other masters.

The fact that a closed 'door' or 'window' is not designated as such until the moment of functioning – nor an opening as a potential 'wall' – also gives the traditional interior a kinetic potential which directors are often at great pains to exploit. One of the most radical instances of this kind of work is found, curiously enough, in Kurosawa's *Lower Depths*,[4] shot in a quite untypical interior (the collective space of a theatricalized flophouse), exploited nonetheless according to the mode of traditional domestic architecture.

The general predilection of Japanese film-makers for the long shot cannot be explained merely by the particularities of their native architecture. Yet architecture has undeniably played a role, together with attitudes towards narrative representation at variance with Western ones, as analysed earlier. Ozu, considered the most 'montage-conscious' of all the classical masters, rarely used true close-ups, and was always careful not to lose the geometrical, planar character of the traditional interior, even in his closest shots.

On the other hand, we cannot ignore the importance of other kinds of architectural setting, and especially the closed, corridor-like verandas in which head-on shots produce a predominance of converging diagonals and a familiar effect of perspective. The film-makers most sensitive to

4. See Chapter 24.

this issue – among the classics, Ozu; among the contemporaries, Yoshida Yoshishige – use such shots as dialectical 'break-throughs', as suspensions in *that projection of cellular space as tessellated surface* that is otherwise so typical of interior shots.

One final observation on the 'standardization' of Japanese architecture is in order.[5] In Western cinema the set-designer has primarily been given the task of *setting the scene*, of 'expressing' not only the social status but even the inner psychology of the characters, and 'reflecting' the mood of the narrative. Only rarely or incidentally does he produce a framework designed to suit a specific mode of image composition. This, however, is the main function of the Japanese set. Variations on an expressive register are severely limited by standardization, so that the designer's effort is chiefly devoted to the linear and planar composition. He can deal more freely with the abstract elements of architecture than his Western counterpart, and because of the very nature of architectural abstraction, he will think in *framed* terms. Modern film-makers, especially Kurosawa, have sought to introduce expressive possibilities into Japanese set-design, often by adopting Western-style interiors (as in *The Idiot*). The standard Japanese films – and many which are not standard at all – continue, however, to use the traditional interior as an all-purpose form, as a basis for surface design. The Japanese interior has, without doubt, inflected the nation's cinema as a whole, in an entirely unique manner, confirming it as a cinema of surface.

5. For this insight I am also indebted to Barry H. Novick.

# 19. Ishida Tamizo

I know almost nothing of Ishida Tamizo except that he began his career in 1926, made eighty-three films and retired from the Toho Company in 1947. I know, too, that he was Ichikawa Kon's 'teacher' and had close relations with a Western-style theatre company called *Bungaku-za* ('Literature troupe'), politically less radical than other similar troupes (it seems to have functioned right up to the Second World War) and specializing in the art-theatre of Europe (Tchekhov, Strindberg, etc.). Ishida may even have staged productions for the *Bungaku-za*. Both films discussed here were originally plays, performed by that troupe and written for it by Morimoto Kaoru. They also have in common the fact that they are set against major, interrelated political upheavals of the nineteenth century: the Meiji restoration war of the 1860s and the Satsuma rebellion a decade later.

*Fallen Blossoms* (*Hana chirinu*, 1938) is set in a geisha house in the Gion quarter of Kyoto, and the action takes place (as an opening title specifies) between the evening of 17 July 1866 and midnight of the following day. During those two days, soldiers of the Chōshū clan, who formed the military spearhead of the Restoration movement, turned back the *bakufu* troops sent to punish the rebel clans, and entered Kyoto. This was to be a turning-point in that sporadic civil war. Ishida's film is one of the most remarkable *community portraits* ever filmed.[1] It has half a dozen major characters plus a kind of chorus, consisting of all the other inmates of the house, and any résumé of the narrative is bound to be misleadingly reductive. Characters are not, strictly speaking, of equal importance. However, so exceptional is the formal/dramatic integration of the whole, that the 'main character' really is the social group, rather than any individual. The prominence of the two characters who are most often on the screen is due as much to their rank in the hierarchy of the house as to the need to centre the diegesis around an individual. These two characters are the house madame (*okāhan*) and Akira,[2] the new

---

1. And, of course, the form has mushroomed in every Hollywood genre, from *Grand Hotel* and *Stagecoach* to the catastrophe films of the 1970s.

2. Normally Akira is a man's name. Like those of the other characters, it is a sobriquet. These were customary in geisha houses, but at the same time Akira displays independence and indeed aggressiveness which in Japan are still exceptional for a woman.

'star' of the house (and one strand of narrative is the deepening embitterment of Harue, the former 'star', who has turned to drink). Akira has fantasized a great love for a young samurai of the Chōshū clan. On the basis of a brief and not very recent affair, she is convinced, despite general scepticism, that one day he will pay her debt and perhaps marry her. This obsessive fantasy rises to fever pitch as news reaches Gion that the Chōshū men are entering the city. As the fighting develops, it becomes clear that the women will have to leave; already, the other houses in the district are being abandoned. Most of the film takes place after the decision has been made but before it is carried out. This sense of 'dangling' is developed at every level throughout. Finally, the moment of departure comes, but Akira refuses to go. Alone in the house with a dead-drunk Harue, she gazes out at the battle-torn city, at last aware, perhaps, that her 'lover' will never come.

This résumé, however, is extremely misleading insofar as it creates the impression that the film is centred about Akira. This is not ultimately the case. There are many characters with long scenes centred about them, in which Akira either does not appear or appears only incidentally. There is Matsuba, who had left with a man and now, tired of him, wants to come back; Miako, a plain-looking servant, jealous of the geishas' beauty, while lucidly pitying them; Kichiya, a lovely, sentimental lesbian, forever worried about her lover, Michyo; and, of course, *okāhan* and Harue, already mentioned.

The mood and construction of the play are reminiscent of Tchekhov, which is not surprising considering the work of the *Bungaku-za*. Tchekhov, it should be stressed, was one of the most popular European dramatists among the Japanese intelligentsia. This was probably due to the formal relationship of his plays with the narrative tradition that ultimately produced *shōmin-geki*, to their household settings and low-key dramatizations, rather than to the psychological and philosophical subtleties which endear them to Westerners.

Yet although *Fallen Blossoms* is much more authentically a film about a community than the comparable Western product – in which the 'community' is nearly always an allegorical ersatz, à la Vicki Baum – it is certainly a much more 'psychological' film than, for example, any by Ozu. This is so if only because the author's decision to describe a moment of temporary breakdown in the social system has a dissolving action on the group and is a 'revealer' of personality. (The characters of classical *shōmin-geki*, on the other hand, are signs in a system of behaviour before they are psychological individuals.) It is this conflict between unity and diversity which provides one of the keys to the film's formal organization.

Three very strict, seminal choices characterize Ishida's work. Two of them clearly derive from theatrical production; one is specific to film. First, the camera never leaves the geisha house and its garden; all of the on-screen fiction develops within them, while the historical action (street-fighting, etc.) takes place off-screen. It is evoked through sound-effect or dialogue-description, and appears only briefly and dimly across the rooftops at the very end of the film as distant flame and smoke. Second, *no man ever appears on the screen*. This is a universe of women, and when, as in the film's opening sequence, there are still patrons in the house, they are kept off screen; their presence is signified only by voices. The specifically filmic choice, maintained in close dialectical relationship with the other two, consists in the absence of any *single repeated shot in the entire film*.[3] (It contains 371 shots, which is quite average for a 'normally' edited film of less than an hour and a quarter.) This combination of a restricted, unified setting and continual renewal of the imagery, through camera movement, as well as editing, is to my knowledge unparalleled in the history of the conventional narrative or strongly diegetic film.

In Western cinema the repeated shot has a number of sources and implications. It is economical. Shooting a single take, which, in the editing, will become half a dozen shots as in the classical reverse-field series, saves time and money. In this sense, the long, non-repeating reverse-field sequence described below represents an enormous waste. However, the repeat must not be seen merely as a consequence of the law of profit. In the reverse field (or the cross-cutting figure from which it derived) and the equally classical recurrence (often throughout a film) of a given shot associated with a given pro-filmic location, the repeat has its own special efficacy, dialectically related though it is to the principle of material economy.

In the Primitive cinema, where each setting corresponded to one and only one frame, the recurrence of a given setting mechanically produced the recurrence of quasi-identical images, and this mechanical quality of the repetitions in Primitive films had to be eliminated from the new art in order to achieve organic 'transparency'. And the introduction of narrative editing (by Hepworth, Griffith, *et al.*) did not mean simply the more-or-less arbitrary variation of angle and shot size; it meant that each successive composition was endowed through angle and size with a given function (or set of functions) in the *chain of signifiers* (the 'situational' long shot, the 'presentational'

3. With three or four patently random exceptions, due almost certainly to contingencies unforeseen during shooting and which had to be coped with in the editing by stop-gap means.

medium shot, the 'introspective' close-up, etc.).[4] The messages thus conveyed are, of course, rudimentary. The burden of elaborating upon them is entrusted to the actor's pantomime and words, spoken today, but originally printed on the film. This rudimentary character is related to the fact that a relatively sharp contrast between shot-sizes is required to produce pertinently discrete, i.e. meaningful, differences. The poverty of this code, due ultimately to the fact that it is a *reductive transposition* of a 'natural', in other words cultural, code, is an important factor in the rationale of the repeated shot. The tendency to repeat a given frame literally, rather than to introduce minimal variants, below the threshold of pertinent differentiation and therefore diegetically redundant, corresponds to a principle of semantic economy which meshes admirably with the selective *thrift* of that bourgeois creed, the law of profit.

Objectively, Ishida's strategy is a rejection of this parsimony. It is the introduction of a surplus of signs, useless for the transmission of the diegetic messages. These signs form a parallel mode of discourse – parallel because 'over-rich' – but also one rooted in the primary signifying process, since the shot-changes as such continue to convey the elementary spatio-temporal messages essential to the constitution of the diegesis.

Another function of the repeated shot, within the economy of the dominant cinema is to reinforce the *centering* of the diegetic effect. A repeated shot, especially in the reverse-field or cross-cut contexts, carries this message: 'You have been here before; pay no attention therefore to what you have already seen (i.e. in a medium or long shot, the quasi-totality of the iconographic signs) but only to what is *new* (i.e. possible changes in the actor's expression, and of course the dialogue) since this is where the message is concentrated'. It is against this perceptual alienation that some recent European film-makers (Kurt Kren, Jean-Daniel Pollet in *Méditérranée*) employ strategies of repetition *ad nauseam*. Ishida, in absolute contrast, offers some 500 systematically and often minutely differentiated *tableaux* (one arrives at this figure if one takes into account the fact that a single shot often involves several fixed compositions). Each of these develops an entirely fresh itinerary through the multiply articulated space of the geisha house. The film's spatial progression is a labyrinthine circuit in which we repeatedly go over the same ground, without ever being provided with the compositional cues that are the guarantee, in film, that 'we have been here before'.

*Fallen Blossoms*, then, like the doll theatre or the films of Ozu, constantly elicits a double reading. This, of course, cannot be merely reduced to two parallel lines. Nor is the

4. For a discussion of the codifications of social distance which is very relevant to film theory, see Hall, Edward T., 'A system for the notation of proxemic behaviour', in *The American Anthropologist*, 65, 1963, pp. 1003–26.

IRON TREES,
GOLDEN FLOWERS

relative autonomy of the *découpage* as great as in Ozu's systemics. In many respects we are dealing with a formalization of the signifier of the type to be encountered, for example, in the most sophisticated films of Fritz Lang. In the Japanese context, the film is closer to *Page of Madness* or the films of Kurosawa than to Mizoguchi or Ozu.

In order to clarify Ishida's working method, I shall review the film's first twenty-three shots (see Fig. 21) and describe two or three later moments which present refining elements of that method.

Fig. 21. Ishida Tamizo, *Fallen Blossoms*

— Pl. 1a shows the main entrance of the house, much less

1a  1b

2a  2b

3a  3b

clearly demarcated as such than is the Western doorway – for nine seconds the frame remains empty (we hear the strumming of a *shamisen* and laughter off-screen); two women enter from the right (Pl. 1b); they are Akira and a young servant from a neighbouring house, where Akira has been helping out for the evening; Akira removes her clogs, the servant crosses and goes out right

– she lays the clogs in their proper place (Pl. 2a), turns to say 'Good night' (Pl. 2b) and exits right

– she reappears again in the background of the next shot (Pl. 3a) before her final exit; pan with Akira to the left; she meets Ochio, *okāhan*'s assistant, and they kneel to exchange greetings (Pl. 3b); Akira then turns *to the left* to greet someone off-screen (Pl. 3c)

– in a long-shot of *okāhan* (on left) and herself, Matsuba greets Akira (off-screen *left*) (Pl. 4); all this time the music off-screen continues as before and the cries and laughter grow louder

– Akira, still on her knees, inquires what the noise is and Ochio tells her that it is the girls upstairs (Pl. 5a); Akira stands up and moves towards the back of the shot (Pl. 5b)

– she starts up the stairs (more loud laughter); Akira: 'How gay they are!' (Pl. 6)

– she continues up the stairs but is stopped by an even

3c

4

5a

5b

Fig. 21. Ishida Tamizo, *Fallen Blossoms*

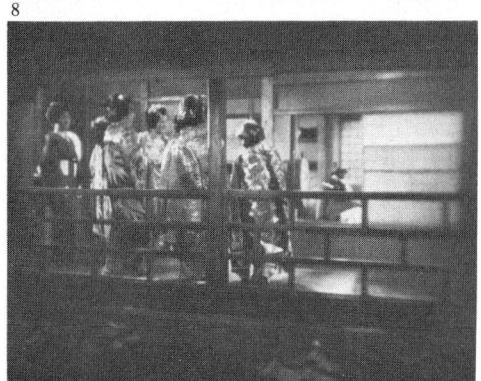

louder burst; Akira: 'Sounds like festival time!' (Pl. 7)
– long shot of the sitting-room (left to right: Ochio, okāhan, Matsuba and Miako); Ochio: 'The guests from Nichijin . . . a textile magnate!' (Pl. 8)
– On an upper-floor veranda, three girls are standing near a room in which we glimpse more girls sitting (this is the place of merriment, and the sounds are much louder now) (Pl. 9a); a group of giggling girls (the 'chorus') come bursting out of the room; a servant enters the shot and scolds them, 'Not so much noise: *okāhan* will be angry' (Pl. 9b); bantering exchanges; then men's voices are heard from within

208

10b    10c

11a    11b

– reverse field: the camera is inside the room, off-screen dialogue with patrons (Pl. 10a): 'It's so hot in here,' someone says, 'let's move up to the watch-tower'; 'It's haunted up there', says a guest; the girls in the background scream with laughter and dash away (Pl. 10b); one girl remains alone in the frame (Pl. 10c); music and badinage continue . . .
– they may still faintly be heard over the close-up of a mosquito-repelling incense-burner placed before an opening in the *shōji* perimeter (Pl. 11a); the camera slowly pulls back; we discover Akira, wearing a different kimono, examining bolts of silk (Pl. 11b); she stands up, still holding

Fig. 21. Ishida Tamizo, *Fallen Blossoms*

some material (this composition is held for twenty seconds: Pl. 11c); the off-screen voices are silent now

– in a knee-length shot, Akira is still examining the material; now she comes across a folded paper, bobs her head to it affectionately, starts to put it away, changes her mind, unfolds it and reads a poem, *sotto voce* (Pl. 12): 'Even the moon is transmigration of life and so, in this life, I do not complain of my past'; she glances through the rest of the letter, smiles to herself (a *shamisen* is heard: this time someone is performing to a silent audience)

– medium shot of Miako, still seated on the *tatami* (Pl. 13a); the camera pans with her gaze to the right: *okāhan* (on the right) and Matsuba are deep in conversation (Ochio is in the background) (Pl. 13b)

During this and the nine subsequent shots (Pls. 14 to 22) – one of which (Pl. 18) is another cutaway to Miako, but from a different angle – Matsuba tries to convince *okāhan* to take her back, explaining how badly her husband treats her, how unattractive he is and how she hates housework. *Okāhan* is very patronizing ('You should have listened to me!') and scolds her for not even knowing whether the man has taken her as his legal wife rather than merely his concubine. The music ends. This event draws *okāhan*'s atten-

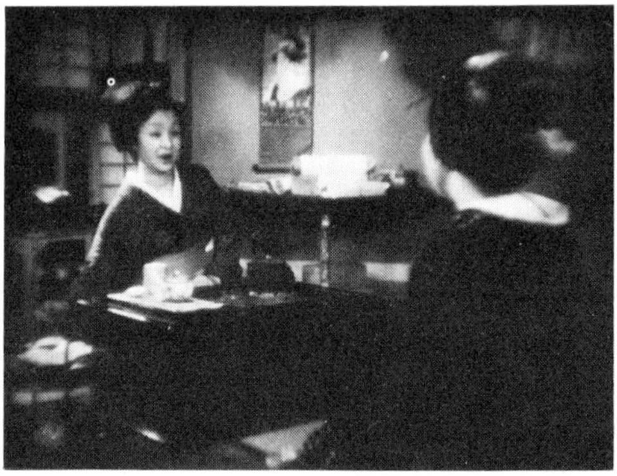
14

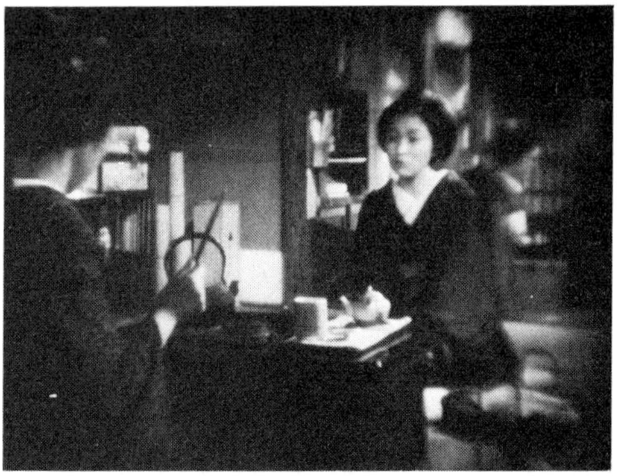
15

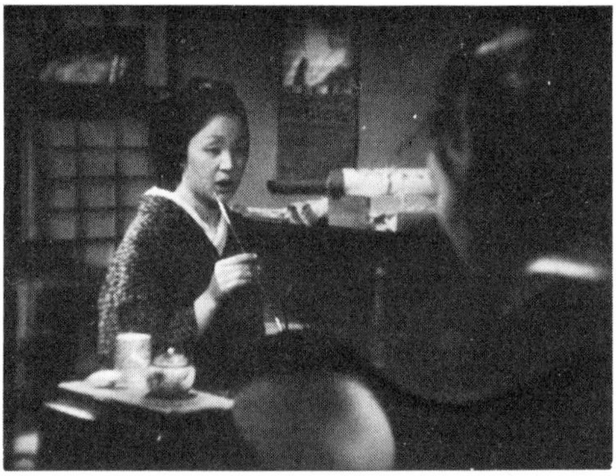
16

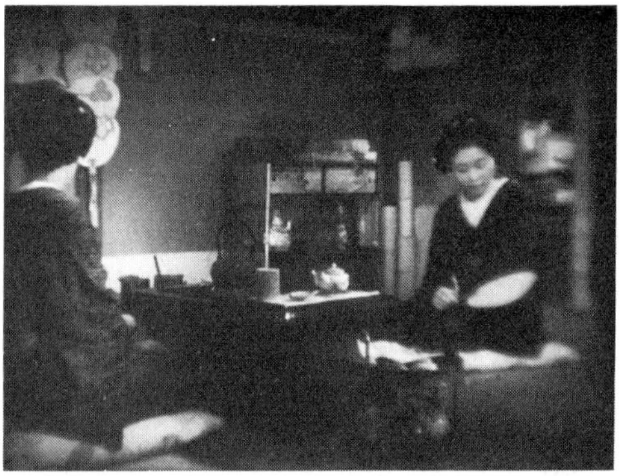
17

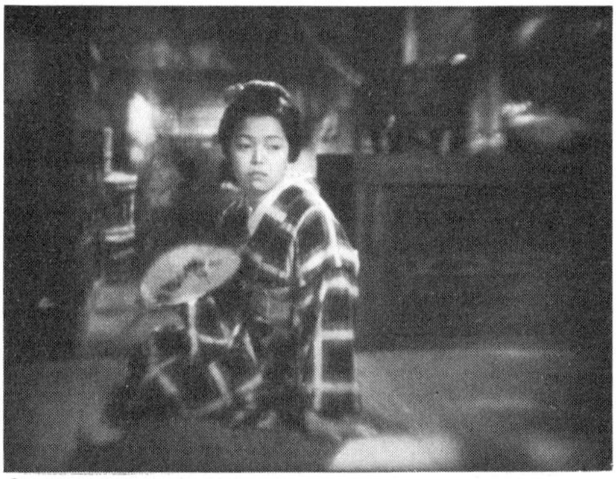
18

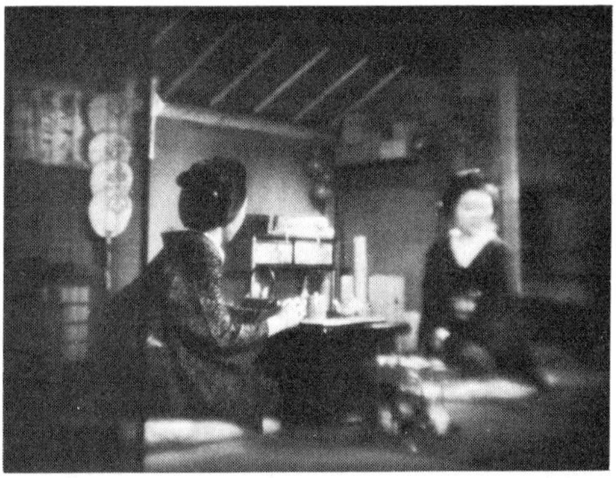
19

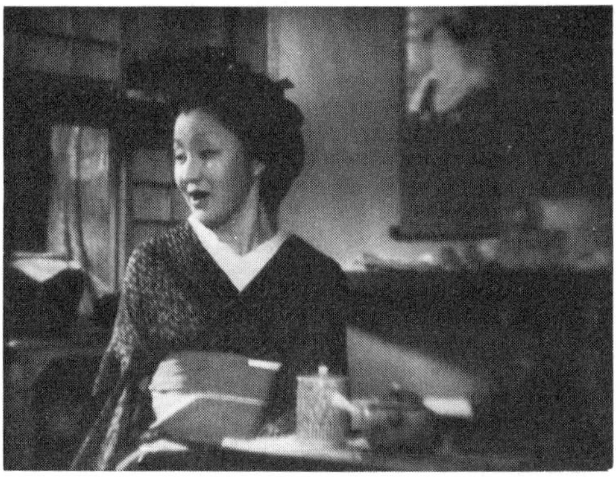
20

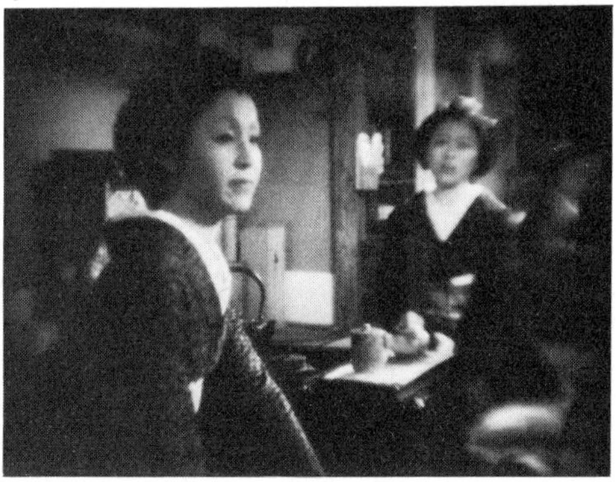
21

Fig. 21. Ishida Tamizo, *Fallen Blossoms*

tion and she orders Miako to take *sake* to the guests (Pls. 20 and 21). The conversation ends on a close-up of Matsuba: 'I've made up my mind . . . It's the last time' (Pl. 22).

– At the foot of the stairs leading to the watch-tower, the 'chorus' are applauding gaily: they have been doing *kabuki* take-offs to amuse themselves (Pl. 23); a servant comes down the ladder and scolds them: 'Aren't you going to the tower? You mustn't leave the guests!'

This first 'sequence' actually contains at least five. Temporal continuity is treated very freely, through 'invisible' ellipses, while the principle of narrative continuity, rigorously respected, creates an illusion of temporal unity. We shall examine this matter shortly. Of considerable importance is the admirable illustration of the principle of perpetual renewal by the one protracted reverse-field series in the film (Pls. 13b to 17 and 19 to 22). It will be observed that considerable care has been taken so that no two of these nine shots should be exactly alike (while Pls. 15 and 21 are more or less the same size, the second is framed further to the left and since *okāhan*'s position – throughout the shot – is quite different in 21 from what it was in 15, the principle is maintained even here).

However, it is the first eight shots which are perhaps most significant here, for they provide a key to Ishida's articulation of space. It will be noticed that the shots in Pls. 1b and 2a, though presumably 'communicating' with each other, offer no common features enabling them to be immediately perceived as such, except of course for the presence of the servant. However, as her screen directions – right-left in the first shot, left-right in the second – are not matched, the disjunctive quality of this cut is all the more emphatic. And although the next cut (2b/3a) involves a correct direction match, the effect of spatial disorientation is again strongly present for lack of a clearly common architectural element. The transition from shots 3 to 4 produces perhaps the strongest spatial hiatus thus far, since the lack of any common architectural reference is maximized by an 'incorrect' eyeline match (3c/4).

The return to Akira and Ochio in Pl. 5a involves a 180° reversal which certainly does not help relate the spaces associated with the two groups. The next three shots match 'normally', but the return to the long shot (8) re-introduces the previous ambiguity, since the staircase is off-screen. The cut from 9 to 10 introduces another hiatus, less radical but quite real, due to the sharp contrast in shot sizes and 180° change. Match 12/13a introduces an ambiguous eyeline relationship, since at first it appears that Miako is watching Akira read her letter.[5]

Belonging to a different but nevertheless related mode of disjunction, the cut to the girls at the foot of the watch-tower stairs (22/23), coming shortly after the end of the music and applause, also frustrates the viewer's expectation in a manner common to all these disjunctions. We might have supposed that this group (whom we discover as they applaud Kichiyo's *kabuki* imitation) is the source of those sounds, yet no instrument is present and the guests are elsewhere ... and, as we are told, alone. Either an ellipsis has occurred, or else the guests have been making music for themselves. A similar ambiguity occurs in connection with cuts 8/9a and 10c/11a: Akira's change of kimono implies that she has taken a bath, but there has been perfect temporal continuity in the sound-track since she first started up the stairs (to go where? in shots 11 and 12 she is on the ground floor again).

The compact flow of the diegesis itself – the illusion of temporal unity – is repeatedly articulated around disruptive breaks, spatial or temporal or both, reinforced by the labyrinthine use of architecture as in the first five shots. These ambiguities are not an absolute rule; there is, in fact, remarkably free interplay between the various possible modes of shot-change, including the most classical ones, and this freedom counterbalances the almost simplistic strictness of the three basic strategies enumerated above.

The refusal to demonstrate any pro-filmic communication between successive shot spaces is, as we have already seen, particularly characteristic of Ishida's disruptive editing procedures. In a later scene, Ochio sits in the kitchen listening to the quarrel that is building between Akira and Harue in an adjoining hallway and which finally degenerates into an abortive fight. A truly hallucinatory tension is created between the two spaces which the sound-track suggests as proximate. For, although the architecture does implicitly situate them in a right-left relationship, they are

5. It would certainly be of great interest to analyse this film from the point of view of Eisenstein's concept of the *montage unit* as set forth in his teaching and explored to some extent in *Potemkin*, i.e. a dialectic of correct and incorrect direction/eyeline/position matching and a division of the filmic discourse into units determined by these parameters and conceived as sub-divisions of (and of a different order from) the sequence properly so-called. (See Nizhny, Vladimir, *Lessons with Eisenstein*, Chapter 2.)

Figs. 22, 23. Ishida Tamizo, *Old Songs*

6. The feminist implications of this film are remarkable for the period and for Japan. In this respect, the authors were more 'radical' than Mizoguchi, whose women, on the whole, are far less conscious of their condition.

never seen to communicate. No shot ever shows both Ochio listening and the two women quarrelling, nor does Ochio's blank gaze into space provide an eyeline tie.

Another, somewhat different use of off-screen space, occurring at the film's first important climax, illustrates the relation between the decision to confine action to the house and these de-centering strategies that are frequent at the level of *découpage*. A skirmish is taking place in the street just beyond the garden wall. The women rush to the gate and listen tensely as a wounded and pursued soldier pounds on it to be let in. Akira in her delusion is convinced that her 'lover" has come for her at last and wants to unbar the gate. The others drag her back and hold her until it is clear that the soldier has been mortally wounded by his enemies. A transposition of a theatrical mode ('history taking place in the wings'), also used as a basis for the film's shot-by-shot organization, provides the unifying principle of the entire film. The exclusion from the screen of men, patrons or soldiers, the other principal factor of formal unity, is also a meaningful corollary of the exclusion of Japanese women from the history of their country.[6]

Ishida's graphic use of the architecture of his fine set provides another element of unity. The cellular construction of the *découpage* is related to that of traditional architectural space and its rendering on the screen surface, a relationship stressed by frame composition and editing.

This film is exceptional by both Western and Japanese standards. The sophisticated relationship of unity to diversity is typical of Western musical form, for example, as opposed to the reiterative forms of Eastern music — a contrast homologous to the Ozu/Lang opposition. The film, nevertheless, has traits essential to the Japanese cinema: prevalence of long shot, 'irrational' approach to matching, tenuous plot-line. The film's most fully Western aspect is its dramatic form, the somewhat hackneyed device of placing history 'in the wings' and presenting it through the eyes of those who are in the wings of history. Japanese writers, playwrights and film-makers, when attempting to describe history in scientific categories (e.g. as powered by class struggle) have systematically resorted to Western forms, often in appropriately metaphorical terms. Here, the impotence of these women, witnesses of a cataclysm, was that of an entire generation of Japanese intellectuals, including the emperor himself, long since relegated to his beloved marine biology. The background for the credit titles provides a rich emblem: goldfish in an aquarium.

*Old Songs* (*Mukashi no uta*, 1939) seems to have been Ishida's very next film. It bears, curiously enough, the same relation to *Fallen Blossoms* as Antonioni's second film, *La*

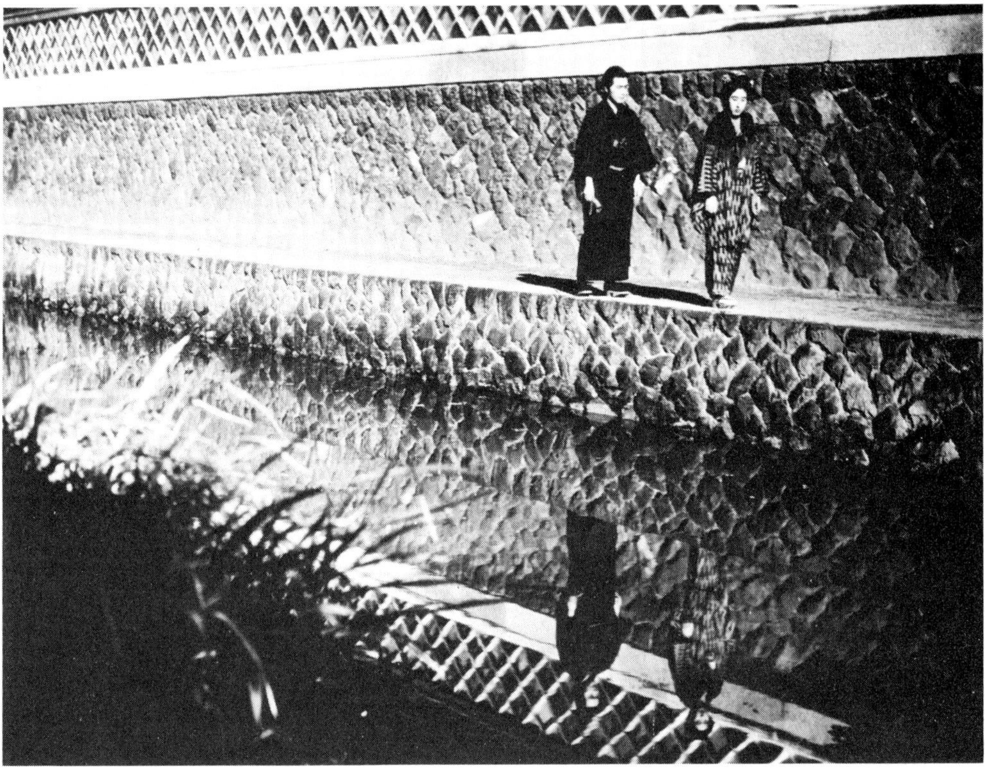

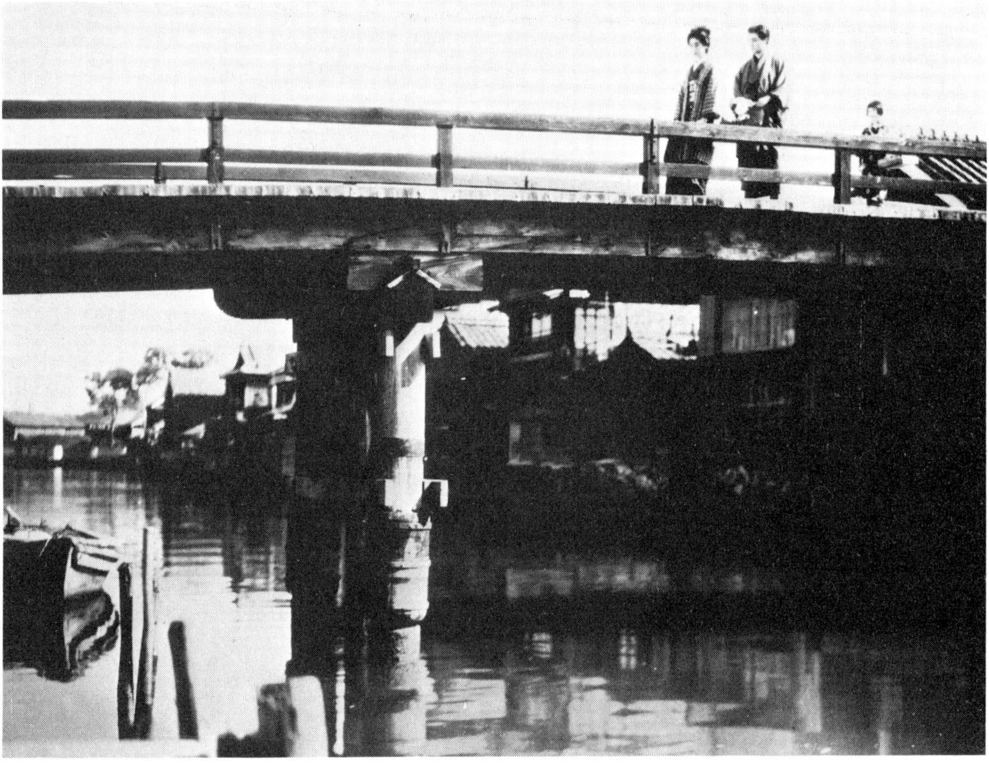

Fig. 24. Ishida Tamizo, *Old Songs*

*Signora senza camelie*, did to his first and finest work, *Cronaca di un amore*.[7] The main components of the respective, original, achievements are, on the whole, still present: in Antonioni's film, the long takes, the stylized framing, even the same star, and in Ishida's the non-repeating principle (here more often violated), a comparable political (off-screen) background, and also the same actors and author. Like *La Signora senza camelie*, Ishida's film completely fails to 'jell'. The plot involves two families, representative of the contradictions that developed after the opening of the country and the Restoration. One is an oil merchant, prosperous and moving with the times, the other a glorious samurai whose despair at the decline of all the values he has lived for drives him to join the ill-fated Satsuma rebellion. Melodramatic complications involving a secret affiliation between the two families spoil what might have been an elegantly sparse narrative construction. And despite a number of visually fine sequences which make skilled use of typically de-centred panoramic compositions (Fig. 22–24) the film simply cannot be compared with the masterpiece that preceded it. Is Ishida, as was generally believed, the maker of a single great film? This view is difficult to credit, considering the qualities of that film. One hopes that further evidence will clarify the issue.

7. See my *Theory of Film Practice*, Chapter 5.

# 20. Mizoguchi Kenji

Mizoguchi is known to have made no less than forty-one films between 1922 and 1929. He is said, in particular, to have made in 1923 an 'expressionist' film, *Blood and Soul* (*Chi to rei*), influenced by *Caligari*, but we are entirely dependent on hearsay and a few stills concerning this period of his development. Judging by the subsisting fragment of *Tokyo March* (*Tōkyō koshin kyoku*, 1929),[1] he had by that time thoroughly assimilated the Western codes of film-making just as he had those of painting (in his late teens, he had studied briefly at the Aoibashi Institute for European Painting in Tokyo). As already indicated, *Tokyo March* was a 'tendency film', in which, for example, distance between classes is symbolized by a raised tennis-court overlooking a slum area. The film does contain faint promises of preoccupations to come. The camera is quite mobile and shots are relatively long, but all of the basic principles of the Western system are observed; a long shot is never without its 'complementary' close-ups, although the awkwardness with which these are inserted inclines one to feel that they already 'bother' Mizoguchi, that he would prefer to keep his distance, as it were. Camera movements are properly 'invisible', they cleave faithfully to the diegetic movement (descriptive tracking, follow-shots, expressive dolly-ins, etc.).

The first complete work available for study is *White Threads of the Waterfall* (*Taki no shiraito*, 1933). This silent film is an adaptation of a *shimpa* play and tells of the stormy and ultimately tragic love of a beautiful stage-performer whose specialty is water-jet juggling (*mizugei*),[2] and a timid, rather proper young man. Taki No Shiraito (for this is also the heroine's stagename: a freer translation of the title would be something like 'Miss Waterfall') is the prototype of Mizoguchi's rebellious women. Of dubious morals by Meiji standards, she strives for financial and social independence in a phallocratic society, takes the initiative in sexual relations, etc.

1. *Koshin Kyoku*: 'march' in the sense of a piece of music.

2. Literally, 'water art'.

IRON TREES,
GOLDEN FLOWERS

The film is sophisticated dramatically, and while it develops within the framework of the Western editing codes, the camera tends increasingly to remain at a distance and to neglect, as it were, the requirement of shot-change. The sequence in which Taki is beaten and kidnapped by a scheming procurer is seen entirely in a single *tableau*-shot, while the very lovely scene in which she seduces the young Kin-ya is shot from beyond the *shōji* delimiting a 'boudoir'. A screen masks half the acting area; Taki retires behind it to ask Kin-ya to love her. (The film is generally remarkable for its intense eroticism, unparalleled even in Mizoguchi's last films.) Another striking example, of both the film's socio-psychological sophistication and Mizoguchi's emerging tendency to shoot dramatic moments in long shot, is a scene in which a rival performer begs Taki for money to go to her dying mother. Taki refuses, and the woman grovels at her feet: 'Then kill me,' she says. 'Why should I?' is the brittle reply, 'and why should I give you money? It's mine!' After a long pause, however, Taki goes to the back of the shot to get the money. The woman scampers after her and again grovels at her feet. This last part of the scene takes place quite far from the camera, and absence of any shot-change is perceived as a clear departure from the norms of narrative editing.[3]

Japanese and Westerners generally agree that *White Threads of the Waterfall* is a finer achievement than Mizoguchi's other complete surviving silent film, *O-Sen of the Paper Cranes* (*Orizuru O-Sen*, 1934). The earlier film is certainly less rambling and more sophisticated as literature. At the same time, *O-Sen of the Paper Cranes* is so remarkably inventive, and such a vivid instance of Mizoguchi's system of representation at a critical formative stage that it is for our purposes far more significant than *White Threads of the Waterfall* and we will examine it at some length.

Based on a novel by Izumi Kyōka, *Baishoku kamo namban*,[4] the film tells a very involved tale which can be only briefly summarized here. A young man, So-Kichi or So-Chan (Little So), sets out from his village to enter medical school but is diverted from his path by circumstances and is befriended when on the verge of suicide by O-Sen, a lovely prostitute, played by Yamada Isuzu, the remarkable leading actress in all of Mizoguchi's films between 1934 and 1936. O-Sen is the somewhat reluctant accomplice of a particularly unscrupulous antique dealer cum pimp named Matsuda and his band of hoodlums, whose principal con-game consists in 'selling' O-Sen to a customer and then simply taking her back by force. So-

3. Needless to say, in these late silent films of Mizoguchi, a shot which is interrupted by a title but resumes its course afterwards is legitimately regarded as a single shot, conceived, that is, as a whole.

4. Untranslatable title, involving a presumably symbolic reference to a duck dish of non-Japanese origin that was popular during the Meiji period.

Kichi is given menial work by O-Sen's protectors, who treat him with sadistic brutality. At the crucial moment of a particularly involved swindle, concerning a lascivious bonze and a lost temple treasure, O-Sen betrays the whole gang to the police and flees with So-Kichi. Her ambition is to send him to medical school. To do so, she must (unbeknown to him) return to prostitution, and is finally arrested for stealing a customer's watch. Years later, when So-Kichi has become a prosperous doctor, he accidentally comes across O-Sen who has fainted in a crowded railway station: he takes her to hospital, only to discover that she is hopelessly tubercular . . . and hopelessly mad.

This narrative material is worlds apart from the quotidian banality of Ozu, Shimizu and the other masters of *shōmin-geki*; it is, however, not far from the narrative substance of the masterpieces to come, *Sisters of Gion* and *Tale of Late Chrysanthemums*.[5]

Throughout his career, Mizoguchi was concerned not only with tense emotional conflict, with pathos in the strongest sense, but with emphatically dramatic narratives illustrating such conflicts. However, as we shall see, his development over the next decade was characterized by a progressive abandonment of the Western mode of representation and its dramatic functionalism. During this period he developed a systemics which, in his supreme (surviving) masterpieces, *Tale of Late Chrysanthemums* and his version of *Chūshingura*, functions as disjunctively as the doll theatre or the films of Ozu. It is in this respect that the work of these two masters, though almost altogether different, may be said to converge in a manner specifically Japanese.

The narrative construction of *O-Sen of the Paper Cranes* is quite complex, involving at least two levels of flashback and a rather allusive and elliptical handling of antecedental material; as already noted, a film of this sort would hardly have been conceivable without the *benshi*'s constant 'reading' of the diegesis.[6] It begins in that railway station where the mature doctor who was once So-Chan is waiting for a delayed train. This sequence follows close-ups of waiting passengers, among them people wearing festival masks.

– close-up of the doctor
– medium-long shot of what appears to be a misty garden (apparently a reverse field)
– close shot of dead leaves blown across the ground by the night wind; the camera pans with the leaves and we see the young So-Kichi, his head bowed in misery, leaning against a tree in a park

5. It must not be thought that we are dealing solely with the influence of, say, Balzac or Dickens. The popular literature of late Edo already had much of the same flavour.

6. A print of this film has recently been rediscovered to which was added, in 1935, a *benshi* track complete with horrible Western music. It may be assumed that this was done in order to play the film before the better-class audiences of the sound-equipped theatres.

IRON TREES,
GOLDEN FLOWERS

— profile close-up of the doctor
— 'close-up' of the moon; the camera pulls back and we are in So-Kichi's grandmother's hovel, from which he originally set out ('So-Kichi, study hard!' his grandmother exhorts him)
— So-Kichi propped against the tree
— So-Kichi adult, then track along the platform to people on a bench in a shelter
— close-up of a woman (O-Sen), then swish-pan to people on platform
— return of 'misty garden' shot
— close-up of O-Sen, who appears to see the same shot
— 'garden' shot
— close-up of O-Sen running backwards from the camera, terrified: she begins to climb a flight of stone stairs; the hand-held camera follows, losing her face but keeping her kimono in close-up
— close-up of O-Sen at the station
— camera retreats now before the fleeing girl; the frame is filled with falling leaves; she hides behind a tree . . .

Soon she comes upon So-Kichi, realizes he is in some trouble himself (Fig. 25). She then is attacked by her latest 'husband' and his domestics, bent on dragging her 'home'.

Fig. 25. Mizoguchi Kenji, *O-Sen of the Paper Cranes*

They are driven off by the formidable swords of Matsuda and his men who arrive in the nick of time.

This very remarkable commingling of two sets of memories, overlapping as if by 'pivot-word' in that enigmatic 'garden' shot, is the last sophisticated editing pattern in any subsisting film until *The Love of Actress Sumako*. The film as a whole shows that Mizoguchi's mastery of narrative editing was as great as that of any European director. This is important when we consider his gradual disaffection for the editing codes and the shot-change in general. As the saying goes about Picasso, 'he knew how to draw'. This first sequence also gives some indication of the freedom with which Mizoguchi was using camera movement by that time – often, it is true, as exclamatory signifier, but also, as we shall see, in a baroque spirit reminiscent of Ito and anticipating his own *Chūshingura*.

The fact that Mizoguchi should have evolved from the sober efficacy of *White Threads of the Waterfall* to the frankly extravagant tracking of this film, paradoxical as it may seem, is highly significant. For he was clearly moving away from his camera's simple subservience to expressive and/or functional requirements of pro-filmic action. In this film the subservience is still largely intact of course, but it is manifested with such a frantic excess of fidelity, with such a plethora of waste motion, that the result was a partial *dismantling* of the Western codes of movement. We will consider one representative sequence, which takes place soon after O-Sen's return (with So-Kichi in tow) to Matsuda's house.

– A fade-in reveals a succession of architectural planes occupying two-thirds of the screen: through a gap on the right, we glimpse O-Sen reclining in her room: she turns towards the camera (title: 'I'll do nothing of the sort!') then turns away again. The camera pulls back and we discover Matsuda in the foreground; he goes towards her room and pauses on the threshold (title: 'It's a big job, it could put you on easy street'). She rolls over again (title: 'If you cheat a bonze it's seven years bad luck!'), then leans forward and shuts the *shōji* in his face. He jerks it open violently and we see that O-Sen is now sitting on her haunches (title: 'Still being stubborn, eh?'). Matsuda quickly exits left; the camera dollies after him, loses him for a moment, then catches him again in the far-left corner of another room, where he seizes a sheathed sword. Pan back to the right as he goes through a hitherto unseen gap in the *shōji* and disappears. The frame remains empty for several long seconds; dancing shadows appear on the far wall, then the girl comes running towards the opening, leans against the left-hand *shōji* (she is only partly visible to the camera) and then, as Matsuda appears with drawn sword, sinks to the floor. He glares at her, sheathes the sword and coming into the foreground (but still in head-to-foot shot) sits by a low table and pours some *sake* (title: 'You'd better do as you're told!'). As he drinks, the camera pans suddenly and quickly to the right: in the entrance-way, one of Matsuda's henchmen is welcoming the bonze. He turns and calls towards the interior (title to the effect that the bonze is here). A silhouette passes in front of the camera, exits and enters again on the far side of the low entrance-way screen which separates us from the bonze; it is Matsuda. He greets the bonze and all exit to the left. Pan away from them to an old servant and So-Kichi peering out from behind a *shōji*. She turns to the boy and shoos him away: it's none of his business.

Now, this scene, as I have suggested in my description, was clearly conceived and most likely executed as a single shot, even though Mizoguchi knew in advance that it would be intercut with titles. This is indicative of the interest, of the *pleasure*, he already seemed to take in organizing long takes.[7] Moreover, not only could any and all of these movements have been easily 'replaced' by cuts, but two of them, the 'gratuitous' pan-aways to a different action, would automatically have been so replaced in classical Western practice. This is all the more interesting, as there is absolutely no 'gain' in spatial coherence. Through most of the film, the camera continually pans and tracks around the house, and yet the correlation of the various frames thus presented is no clearer than in the opening shots of Ishida's *Fallen Blossoms*. Certain shots shift from interior to exterior with no indication of the 'actual' articulation of the two locations. This is particularly remarkable in a labyrinthine nocturnal scene in which O-Sen, instead of admitting the bonze into her bed as she was expected to do, has taken So-Kichi. Long mysterious camera movements through the dark house and garden culminate in the dramatic centre of the entire film; in a gesture which momentarily seems to destroy the structure of non-communicating cells (linked in abstract chains by camera movement), Matsuda and his men break down the *shōjis* of her room.

The characters tend to desert the frame, or the camera to desert the characters in accordance with a de-centering principle which will assume other, less obtrusive forms in the mature work to come. It is, however, already a fully developed element of Mizoguchi's systemics, corresponding to Ozu's pillow-shots and the tradition of 'uninhabited' shots associated with the Japanese cinema throughout the 1930s. One of the most striking instances of this de-

7. It is hoped that the reader will take these and other traces of an intentionalist ideology which still occasionally informs this study as inadequate metaphors for certain textual evidences.

centering, all the more radical to the present-day analyst's eye as it is unusually mechanical even for this film, occurs in the sequence in which Matsuda's henchmen send So-Kichi, whom they have been sadistically starving, to buy delicacies for them. Though of course he is not supposed to spend any of the money on himself, So-Kichi cannot resist the sight of some inexpensive food in a stall which he passes on his way, and he enters to buy. When he leaves the stall, the camera remains with the vendor for a few seconds, then sets out *to catch up with So-Kichi* (pan and truck), and we find him gulping down his food and crying for shame (title: 'Forgive me, grandmother'). From a differently angled shot of So-Kichi, the camera now pans to a blank wall and tracks along it, finally coming to rest on another stall where people sit eating. After a moment, So-Kichi enters the frame again and makes the purchase he has been ordered to make.

Here, even more clearly, where a transparent editing scheme normally *cuts*, camera movements have been used, spelling out that scheme in such a way as to assert the physical presence of the camera.[8]

Uneven though it is, this film is not simply a laboratory experiment, a formal curiosity. Often enough, it is a splendidly baroque poem. It contains in particular some beautifully *outré* sequences, such as O-Sen's arrest when, standing in the street with her hand bound by the policeman's traditional rope, she tugs a paper crane out of her kimono with her teeth and blows it to her lover as a parting kiss. Another such gem is the final hospital scene in which she leaps from her bed to protect once again So-Kichi from his persecutors, laying about her with a razor; then, when the vision has vanished – and there is a poignant insert of leaves blown across the ground – she returns to her room, climbs serenely back into the bed and draws the covers to her, utterly oblivious of her former lover kneeling with bowed head at the foot of the bed.

The recently rediscovered *Poppies* (*Gubijinsō*, 1935), first seen in Europe in 1976, shows that the range of Mizoguchi's experimentation at this period was great indeed. In the first place, this film, shot just before *The Elegy of Naniwa*, is closer, perhaps, than any other Mizoguchi, to the narrative norms of the *shōmin-geki* of the period, even though Mizoguchi's tale of an ambitious young man torn between a self-serving *mariage de raison* with a sophisticated older woman and the pure love of a delicate virgin, characteristically involves a more bitter approach to the traditional social structures than does any pre-war Ozu. Above all, however, the film constitutes a radical departure from what already appeared to be the main thrust of Mizoguchi's developing stylistics, for it was shot almost entirely

8. This is something of an over-simplification. 'Authorial presence' might be a better description, as I suggest in an analysis of Dreyer's *Vampyr* (Roud (ed.), *Dictionary of the Cinema*) with which Mizoguchi's film offers certain parallels.

with a fixed camera and attempts, on the contrary, to exploit to the full the possibilities of Western style dramatic editing: reverse-field figures and medium close-ups abound, while in one instance rapid-fire cutting is used to stress a moment of special tension. The film is by no means a negligible piece of work and was clearly the object of considerable thought and care. It is as if Mizoguchi felt the need to give the Western mode one serious, thoroughgoing try before striking out resolutely in his own, Japanese, direction.

*O-Yuki, Alias Maria* (*Maria no O-Yuki*, 1935), not seen by me till 1978, shows that *Poppies* was not unique. However, this adaptation of Maupassant's *Boule de Suif* does not seem to have interested Mizoguchi very much, and his use of the Western codes is, on the whole, passive and uninventive.

Mizoguchi's next film, *The Elegy of Naniwa* (*Naniwa erejī*, 1936),[9] is, in my view, rather problematic. Considered by most Japanese critics to be Mizoguchi's first masterpiece (on account of its socially significant subject, involving a young switchboard operator whose employer sexually exploits her need for money), by the criteria adduced here it is a prefiguration of Mizoguchi's post-war decline. Presumably his first sound-film since his initial experiment with the new medium five years before, it cleaves remarkably closer than *O-Sen of the Paper Cranes* to the Western codes of editing, and the occasional long take falls into the established pattern of the virtuoso follow-shot (like those of the *Dreigroschenoper*, for example). While the carefully stylized shot composition gives hints of the work to come,[10] camera distance is almost always reduced early in a scene and on the whole the film is densely edited. In short, Mizoguchi seemed to be hesitating not between originality and conformity – the classical Western choice – but rather between East and West, in this era the crucial choice facing the Japanese.

His very next film made it clear what the option was to be: *Sisters of Gion* (*Gion no shimai*, 1936)[11] sets forth Mizoguchi's mature systemics *in all its pertinent traits*, even if *Tale of Late Chrysanthemums* must be regarded as a more radical, possibly its most radical, instantiation. The principal characteristics of this systemics are widely recognized: exceptionally long takes, systematic rejection of editing in general, of the reverse-field figure in particular, and of the close-up.

The role of the long shot in the origins of the Western cinema, its preponderance in Japanese cinema, not only through the 1930s but to this very day, has been made clear.

---

9. Naniwa is the old name for Osaka. The film has a contemporary setting, and the use of the old name suggests the permanence of tradition in what was already by then a modern industrial metropolis.

10. Of course, for the ideology of transparency this is already a *defect*: 'It [*The Elegy of Naniwa*] sounds melodramatic in description but was actually very quietly told, its realism being only slightly vitiated by Mizoguchi's eternal concern for pictorial beauty and atmosphere.' (Richie and Anderson, op. cit., p. 103).

11. The character for 'sisters' in this title is sometimes read *kyodai*.

we find in the dominant Western system, be it the edited, reverse-field variant (eminently suitable, 'on paper', to such a scene) or the 'Bazinian' single-take sequence, with the subtle displacement/variation of the codes that it implies. The pro-filmic space depicted here offers a complex iconographic syntagma, i.e. a large section of a specific room equipped with specific artefacts, etc., and these signifiers are at all times simultaneously represented on the screen. The actors' movement and gestures, however 'expressive', are at all times meshed with a set of visual signs which the eye must also sort out and decipher, all the more so as in this shot – as so often in Mizoguchi – the characters are not centred, there is 'too much room over their heads', as a Western studio cameraman might put it. This is a decisive factor, for these relatively small, distant figures are thereby designated as part of a framed totality, one which includes and is visually dominated by a profusion of other signs. The whole of this procedure, the distance, the de-centering, underlines, moreover, the ultimately non-anthropocentric quality of Mizoguchi's mature style. Most important is the fact that no editing pattern, in either a narrow or an extended sense, reinforces the semantic pattern of the dialogues as they unfold over the low table; picture and text become virtually detached from one another. To all intents and purposes we are watching a slide show or, again, the doll theatre.

As for the role of camera movement, in what may both literally and figuratively be called a *distancing system*, it does, in several instances, serve simply to maintain distance. Omocha's other 'big scene' with an older man (which takes place in the same room and in which she seduces the merchant who is the boss of her young suitor) is a case in point. When the merchant enters the parlour with Omocha, they sit down near the door (the camera is in the middle of the room, at a slightly elevated angle, and the figures are in the lower left-hand corner). As they discuss the clerk's dereliction, it becomes increasingly clear that the merchant would not be averse to obtaining the favours he assumes have been granted his employee. Omocha proposes tea and rises. At this point, the camera draws back to a second position at the back of the room, so that the frame now includes the low tea-table. Omocha sits behind the table (only her shoulders and the back of her head are visible, low and small in the frame). After a 'decent interval', the merchant comes and sits facing her; the camera is nudged slightly as he advances, so that in the final composition, the two of them still occupy the lower left-hand quarter of the frame. Soon, Omocha rises and goes to sit on the same side of the table as the merchant, and here the camera moves slightly forward, again so as to maintain their eccentric position in the frame. Here, then, camera movement serves to maintain both distance and the de-centred composition which is its essential complement.

More importantly, we begin to see here that Mizoguchi's systemics often involves as well a particular kind of 'montage within the shot'. In contrasting his method with the cunning adaptation of the narrative editing codes to the long take as practised at various periods in the dominant cinema of the West, I do not mean to deny the obvious; in all of his major films, from *Sisters of Gion* to *Utamaro*, each given shot consists of a series of very precisely determined and distinctly differentiated compositions. In *Tale of Late Chrysanthemums*, as we shall see, he even contrives to avoid camera nudges of the kind mentioned here.

In *Sisters of Gion*, Mizoguchi's montage method, in both the narrow and extended senses, is not entirely worked out. However, a variety of modes are already at work, and while their interaction is more haphazard than in later films, the principle of diversification is there. Occasionally, a single reverse-field cut will be introduced into a sequence, never seeking to isolate a character or to bring him or her into close-up, but rather simply to introduce a caesura within the sequence (for reasons, one suspects, which are often purely practical). The sequence in the automobile during Omocha's kidnapping is shot entirely in close-up, and is dramatically remarkable; Mizoguchi succeeds in singularizing the sequence in such a way as to 'justify' what is undoubtedly another concession to practical circumstances (how do you shoot long shots inside a car?). One feels sure, nonetheless, that the maker of *Tale of Late Chrysanthemums* and *A Tale of Loyal Retainers of the Genroku Era* would have contrived to eliminate this sequence altogether rather than introduce the emphasis on personalization which such an editing scheme invariably carries with it.

One of the most important modes of 'montage within the shot' which first appears in this film can, despite the precaution which should accompany parallels of this kind, be compared with the painted hand-scroll (*e-makimono*). The two clearest instances of this procedure occur at the very beginning and the very end of the film, a sign that Mizoguchi was working towards an organization of the 'modes of montage'. The opening is a lateral truck shot through which successive aspects of the auction which finalizes the unfortunate merchant's bankruptcy are unfurled, as it were. From a frame filled with screen panels, the camera tracks past a recess in which the auction proper is being held. It then passes another, in which assembled creditors are waiting, then a third (seen through a wooden grille) in which men are preparing objects for sale. A pan takes us past a thick post, revealing another man carrying a bibelot and we finally dissolve to a dolly-in on the merchant sitting with his friends. The second shot, which appears as a kind of vertical penetration into the surface of the 'scroll', also has a symmetrical relationship with the final dolly-in on Omocha, a shot which in turn follows another major 'scroll-shot' of a somewhat different conception. This is a slow, circular pan around the interior veranda of the hospital, starting with the elder sister's entrance on the right, following her to the door of the operating-room in the centre and then, as Omocha is carried out on the back of a nurse, continuing slowly to follow the little group around the veranda to Omocha's 'room', an enclosed space which is almost invisible behind a bamboo curtain ... and yet where the action goes on without a shot-change for several minutes longer.

In both these 'scroll-shots', the pro-filmic organization of architectural space is such that the passing lens produces successive tableaux which appear as both discrete and inter-penetrating. This is a major effect of the *e-makimono*. In these shots Mizoguchi achieves a corresponding fusion of the two fundamental and opposite aspects of lateral camera-movement as such: successive stages versus steady flow.

During most of this film, the camera is slightly higher than the usual (Western) eye-level. This may be due to the fact that the rudimentary dolly used simply could not be made lower. Considering Ozu's floor-level dolly shots in *A Story of Floating Weeds*, made two years earlier (by another production company, it is true), this is a bit hard to believe. Whatever the case, this relatively high angle will recur fairly often in the masterpieces to come, and it evokes the traditional Japanese representation of interiors in *e-makimono*. Receding verticals to the picture plane are drawn at 45° to the horizontal, producing a high-angle effect to our eyes, though in fact other elements in the image are not foreshortened, are seen head-on. The result, in painting but also in film, is an ambiguous presentation of the depth/surface relationship. For while the placing of the figures low in the frame tends (in Mizoguchi as in Ozu) to flatten the image, the high-angle camera, which emphasizes the receding lines of the *tatami* borders, *shōji* rails, etc., has the opposite effect. Moreover, while fixed frames in Mizoguchi give the classical effect of tessellated surface, his camera movements tend to produce sliding effects of plane against plane between the successive, fixed positions. Here again the articulation of the surface/depth issue is exemplary. Yet striking and frequent as the illustrations of these

IRON TREES,
GOLDEN FLOWERS

principles are in *Sisters of Gion*, their development in this film is only embryonic, by comparison with the monument that was to come.

The presumed loss of the three films which Mizoguchi made in 1937-8 is the most unfortunate loss in Japanese cinema. We may never be able to trace the development from *Sisters of Gion* to that supreme work which is *Tale of Late Chrysanthemums* (*Zangiku monogatari*, 1939). Of course, judging from his earlier career, we have no reason to suppose that this development was linear. Nevertheless, the links between the two films are many and direct; indeed, the systemics that first crystallized in the earlier film finds its ultimate development in the later one.

*Tale of Late Chrysanthemums* runs just over two hours and contains, according to my count, 140 shots – as against an average 400 to 600 in a 'normally' edited film. While relatively few sequences actually consist of a single take, very few contain more than three or four shots. And while the overall average shot-length is over a minute, this figure is considerably higher (nearly two minutes) if we exclude the three *kabuki* sequences, densely edited in accordance with a system completely different from that which otherwise prevails throughout (fifty-three shots for less than half an hour of screen time).

The narrative, slender by Western standards for such a long film, is set in the Meiji era[15] and concerns the life of a *kabuki* actor, Gombei Kikunosuke, the adopted heir[16] to a celebrated dynasty of actors. He falls in love with a servant, Otoku, partly because she is the only member of his entourage who dares tell him to his face what a bad actor he is. When the family forces her to leave him, Kikunosuke decides to leave his 'father's' Tokyo troupe and to polish his acting in the hard school of obscure provincial tours, with the support of Otoku, who becomes his mistress. After five years, Kikunosuke is 'discovered' again by his family. He has become a truly great actor and all is forgiven. Kikunosuke is invited back to Tokyo and Otoku, realizing that she is henceforth an obstacle to his career, again steps out of his life. This is a blow to Kikunosuke, but he makes no effort to find her again. Finally, during the river procession at which the public traditionally paid homage to their *kabuki* idols, Kikunosuke learns that Otoku is desperately ill and goes to her side. She sends him back to the procession and breathes her last while Kikunosuke is bowing to the crowd from a flowered barge.

The film's thematic substance has been described as 'escapist' by the celebrated critic Iwasaki Akira[17] who, nonetheless, rightly regards Mizoguchi's concern with oppression of women as an objectively committed theme.

15. This was a period of predilection for the maturing Mizoguchi. *White Threads of the Waterfall*, *O-Sen of the Paper Cranes* and other films of that period were *Meiji-mono*.

16. Still quite common in Japan is the practice of the head of a family adopting a grown man as son, either because he has none of his own or because he feels the young man is especially apt to continue his name, art or trade.

17. Iwasaki Akira, 'Kenji Mizogushi' in *Anthologie du Cinéma*, Vol. 2, p. 463.

It is my opinion, on the contrary, that *Tale of Late Chrysanthemums* is one of his most deeply 'feminist' films. Otoku is typically the Mizoguchi heroine; more intelligent and stronger in character than any of the men surrounding her, she too is sacrificed on the altar of male supremacy, and the success of the irresolute Kikunosuke's career (as an *oyama*!) is at best an ambiguous triumph.

In this film, Mizoguchi's sensitivity to the importance of privileged departures from his systemics is particularly evident. While the diegetically representational passages almost entirely exclude intrasequential editing in the strict sense (there is only one direct match in these sequences), the presentational *kabuki* scenes follow quite a pure Griffith line, so to speak. It is also in this film that the Mizoguchi system of montage within the shot achieves its supreme development, and a sharp, structurally operative contrast is provided by this kind of movement as against the 'scroll' approach. In addition, the representational passages as a whole are striking evidence of the camera-distance principle, sometimes applied with almost obsessive strictness.

A thorough analysis of this long, complex film would require countless detailed descriptions and make tiresome reading. One can merely provide brief illustrations of its principal traits in so far as they are peculiar to this stage in the development of Mizoguchi's systemics.

One nine-minute take admirably illustrates the principle of 'station-by-station montage'.

– The family have just sent Otoku away from the house and Kikunosuke is about to confront his adoptive father. In a typically bare room with an opening in the *shōji* at frame right, Kikunosuke and his mother are for the moment alone (Fig. 26, Pl. 1). Kikunosuke crosses in front of his mother and the camera pans with him to where the father is sitting; Kikunosuke kneels before the father. The camera pursues its circular movement while the mother re-enters from the

Fig. 26. Mizoguchi Kenji, *Tale of Late Chrysanthemums*

right and the elder son from the left; they sit down on either side of the father (he and the mother are momentarily hidden by the elder son: Pl. 2). As the movement continues the group as a whole appears (Pl. 3). The father tells Kikunosuke that he must behave himself in accordance with his station, the mother that Otoku has ulterior motives and the elder 'brother' that he mustn't trust women. The latter rises now and walks out of frame to the right, soon followed by the mother. Father and son are left face to face.[18] There is a long silence. Then Kikunosuke rises and walks to the right; pan with him to the opening in the *shōji*: in the adjoining room, mother and brother are again seated on the *tatami*. Kikunosuke joins them (Pl. 4) (though no longer visible, the father's continued presence off-screen is unmistakable) (Pl. 5). The discussion now becomes more heated, *as if the father were not within ear-shot*: Kikunosuke announces his intention of marrying Otoku, and when the elder son reminds him of his career, his admirers, his obligations as an adoptive son, he declares he would prefer to earn a reputation on his merits rather than owe it to his family status. Unable to maintain his conventional reserve, the father storms into the foreground (Pl. 6), furiously orders his son out of the house and goes out of shot again. The mother begs Kikunosuke to go and apologize to the father (Pl. 7). There is a long silence; then Kikunosuke rises, comes into the near foreground, kneels again and very formally asks permission to marry Otoku.[18] Silence. We hear the father's pipe knocking against his tobacco tray. Kikunosuke rises, exits left, kneels again off-screen (rustling kimono, crackling *tatami*) and, as his brother and mother listen aghast from the next room (Pl. 8), starts to repeat his request. 'Don't speak,' his father shouts. 'I won't listen!' We hear Kikunosuke rise and stride across the room: sound and a play of shadows on the *shōji* tells us that he has opened the outside door and left the house. The mother and brother rise and the mother comes forward, gazing off-screen (Pl. 9). Mother goes out of frame, brother goes to follow her, and the camera pans ahead of him towards the door. The father is still sitting on the floor on the far right, while we find the mother standing in the doorway, calling Kikunosuke's name (Pl. 10).

The demarcations in this shot between movement and fixity (of both camera and characters)[19] define some dozen separate *tableaux*. Moreover, the dramatic structure proper is such that the cellular division of space evident in the *découpage* seems to be 'acknowledged', one might even say it is *taken literally* by the diegesis when the quarrel shifts 'out of the father's presence' (Pl. 5), at the moment of the

IRON TREES,
GOLDEN FLOWERS

Fig. 26. Mizoguchi Kenji, *Tale of Late Chrysanthemums*

18. Neither of these two important stations could be included in the series of illustrations.

19. During the circular movement which opens the shot, these stations are defined only by character displacement, but are nonetheless quite distinct.

3

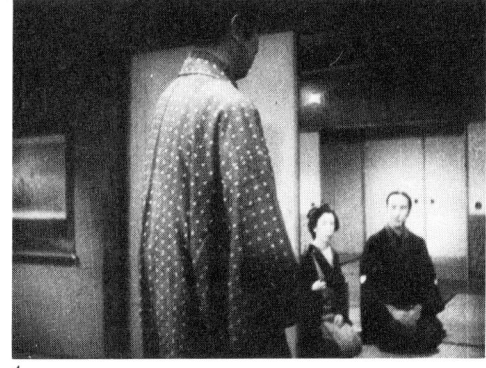

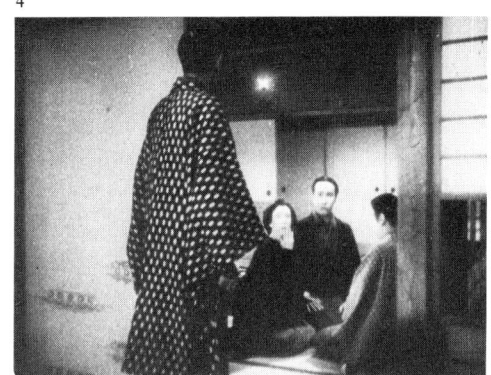

4

5

6

7

8

9

10

father's angry intervention (Pl. 6) and Kikunosuke's double plea (the second off-screen in Pl. 8). Furthermore, and this is a trait of Mizoguchi's which is particularly noticeable in this film, camera movements are plotted in such a way that minimal displacements bring about maximal renewal of frame, both in terms of content and composition. And though this principle, along with that of a clear opposition between movement and fixity, is abandoned in *A Tale of Loyal Retainers*, it was partially maintained through the immediate post-war period, and traces are to be found even in the most academic of the late films, by which time, however, it had become an incidental ingredient of that 'flowing elegance' which has been so admired in the West.

Earlier in this film, there occurs what I believe is the most remarkable instance of the 'scroll-shot' in Mizoguchi's known work. Depressed by what he knows was a bad performance and having wearied of the conventional flattery and futile intrigues of the geisha house, Kikunosuke has decided to return home early. Near the house, he comes upon Otoku, the servant who takes care of his brother's baby. For this scene, the camera is placed considerably lower than the road, at the bottom of an embankment. It is characteristic of the scroll-like nature of this shot that the characters never occupy more than the lower third of the frame in height. Considering the importance of this encounter, considering that this is Otoku's *presentation* in the film, it is remarkable that the *presence* of the characters is in fact ensured by voice alone. We first see Otoku by herself, rocking the baby in her arms. She walks slowly to the left for perhaps fifty yards accompanied by a dollying camera. Kikunosuke's rickshaw enters from the left. Seeing Otoku, he stops the runner, pays and dismisses him. There now follows the long, slow walk back to the Gombei house the way Otoku has just come. It involves several halts, in particular to buy a wind-bell (several street vendors pass them, and their cries, along with the sounds of wind-bells and clap-sticks, provide a discreet punctuation for their long conversation). This is the first real talk that Kikunosuke has ever had with the servant, and he is immediately impressed by her forthrightness; as soon as he asks for her opinion of his performance, she tells him what no one else will: that his acting is bad.

This splendid sequence, of indescribable delicacy, lasts seven and a half minutes. Moreover, the same shot is repeated in abridged form later in the film, and is echoed in another long 'scroll-shot' in the streets of Nagoya, where Otoku and Kikunosuke meet after their first long separation. The concern with cyclical figures, already observed in *Sisters of Gion*, is particularly in evidence in this film. One striking example is provided by a succession of two camera set-ups, one in the entrance of the family house, the other in the kitchen. These first occur early in the relationship between Kikunosuke and Otoku as a framework for a long conversation about his acting, They appear again in the same order near the end of the film, when Kikunosuke has finally returned to his father's house and theatre. Mizoguchi pushes the symmetry far indeed, for while Otoku was carrying the baby in the initial occurrence of the first of these set-ups, the same child is playing on the floor in the second version (Kikunosuke caresses him), while in the very same corner of the kitchen frame where Kikunosuke once cut a water-melon for himself and Otoku, a servant is now cutting what might be a loaf of Western-style bread. Aside from the general consistency with the principle of motifs, this recall has the dramatic function of belying (or perhaps criticizing) Kikunosuke's apparent resignation to his separation from Otoku.

There are three *kabuki* sequences in the film; the longest of these (forty shots, fifteen minutes) is the climactic performance in which Kikunosuke shows his uncle and cousins the progress he has made over the years. As I have indicated, these scenes are edited in a thoroughly 'conventional' way, and while both the performance which opens the film and the one which marks Kikunosuke's Tokyo triumph are almost entirely enclosed within the proscenium space, the main sequence involves a very insistent cross-cutting pattern, alternating shots of the play with Kikunosuke's impressed relatives in the wings and Otoku, tense with anxiety, backstage. I find it remarkably significant of Mizoguchi's 'dialectical sense' that it should be precisely and solely to provide a framework for this eminently presentational art that he should have seen fit to abandon utterly his own presentational systemics in favour of the Western editing codes.

Actually the film does contain one other (partly 'presentational') scene involving cross-cutting, and here the correlation of a coded editing figure from the West with what is perhaps the ultimate in 'camera discretion' offers a veritable paradigm of cultural distance, not unlike the citations from Western films in Ozu. Having been advised by Otoku's landlord that she is desperately ill, Kikunosuke leaves the riverside festival to go to her. The shot in which he finds her dying in the garret that they had shared years before is one of the film's longest (a full ten-minute reel) and certainly one of the most austere. It involves only three camera positions (disposed along the arc of a quarter circle) and even at the moment of most intense poignancy, the camera remains at such a considerable distance from the quilt-covered figure of Otoku that we can hardly see her face. And two repeats of this very same, profoundly 'primitive' shot are subsequently included in the insistent 'durational' montage of the procession on the river, with Kikunosuke bowing endlessly to his admirers on the banks: the first simply shows the landlady fanning the recumbent woman, while in the second she suddenly recoils, having realized that Otoku is dead.

It might, of course, be argued that the 'Mizoguchi distance' is a kind of rhetorical reversal of the Western code of shot size, i.e. the further the camera from the characters, the more 'intimate' the message, the more intense the emotion to be conveyed. However, this predominance of the long shot is not peculiar to Mizoguchi. What *is* peculiar to his work, at least among the important film-makers of the 1930s, is a penchant for intense pathos, and if the encounter with a specifically Japanese conception of presentational distance seems to result, to our eyes, in a kind of reverse codification, it is at best only partial. Many completely undramatic sequences are filmed at distances as great; an example is the three-minute frame in which Kikunosuke changes to street clothes after a performance in Nagoya. Moreover, the encoding process, if any, is qualitatively very different from the linearization characteristic of the Western codes of shot size, for it involves a constant surplus of iconographic signs rather than their progressive elimination (through track-in, close-up, etc.). I will not claim to settle this debate one way or the other, but as we go on to examine what is in many respects Mizoguchi's most ambitious film, *A Tale of Loyal Retainers of the Genroku Era* (*Genroku chūshingura,* 1943),[20] we may discover further evidence to the effect that camera distance in Mizoguchi's mature work involves much more than a purely 'dramaturgical' option.

Before dealing with Mizoguchi's film, a few words are in order concerning the *Chūshingura* theme which provides its narrative fabric. The place which this theme occupies in national legend is roughly equivalent to that of Joan of Arc in France. Above all, however, it is typical of that fund of narrative and symbolic material with which every Japanese is so familiar and upon which the popular cinema (and the traditional arts before it) have so heavily and repeatedly drawn.

The events upon which the various theatrical versions of *Chūshingura* are based took place, as I have indicated, at the very beginning of the eighteenth century. On the occasion of the arrival of two imperial envoys at the Shōgun's palace in Edo, two *daimyō* (provincial lords) were appointed to oversee the festivities. One of the *daimyō* thus

20. The common title in the West, where the film has never been distributed, is *The Forty-seven Rōnin*, but this conventional translation of the classical title, *Chūshingura*, does not render the historical specification of Mizoguchi's title.

honoured in the year 1701 was Asano-Takumino Kami, Lord of Akō. Ignorant in the ways of Court, Asano was reluctant to accept, but was assured that an experienced courtier, Kira-Kōzukenosuke, would advise him. Kira was a courtier of relatively low rank who relied on advisory positions of this sort to round out his income. As Asano failed, half out of naiveté, half out of pride, to offer the customary bribes, not only did Kira deliberately misinform him, but repeatedly insulted him during the three-day ceremony. One final insult was too much to bear, and Asano drew his sword and assaulted Kira. Although the wounds were only superficial, Asano was sentenced to commit ritual suicide for having drawn his sword in the Shōgun's palace, potentially an act of treason. As further punishment, all of Asano's property was seized and his retainers were stripped of their legal attachment to the house and forced to become *rōnin*. A group of these, however, led by Oīshi-Kuanosuke, chief councillor in charge of the castle of Akō, secretly swore vengeance against Kira, and for months they plotted, going to extravagant lengths to put Kira off guard. Finally, exactly one year after Asano's death, the *rōnin* stormed Kira's residence during a New Year's tea ceremony and executed the villain. They then made their way to a nearby temple; after a month of house-arrest in the mansions of four *daimyō*, they were allowed to commit ritual suicide instead of being executed like common criminals. For already their courage and loyalty had fired the imagination of the entire country.

This saga exemplifies the typically Japanese conflict of personal loyalty and national obligation, but its interest lies less in the forty-seven's actual choice than in the fact that they dramatized publicly a dilemma which, to the 'Japanese mind', is in any case inextricable – Oīshi would have discreetly died of shame had he not avenged his master. It is this detour through spectacular violence which explains why *Chūshingura* still stirs the Japanese heart.[21]

More important to us, however, is the fact that aside from the numerous eighteenth- and nineteenth-century stage versions of this theme, *Chūshingura* has been filmed at least twenty times. One of the most celebrated versions was a 1931 film by Kinugasa, unfortunately lost. The familiarity of the theme no doubt helped to determine the specific narrative modes adopted by Mizoguchi for his version, the most sumptuous and ambitious of them all. It is also an essential dimension of the Japanese cinema as a whole and, in particular, of *jidai-geki*, which even today occupies a large place in both cinema and TV production. For the political and social struggles, the values and the symbolism, and even the individual characters of the

MIZOGUCHI KENJI

21. The disturbing effect of both the suicide of the novelist Mishima Yukio and the bloody exploits of the 'Trotskyite' Red Army on most Japanese radicals is no doubt attributable to this feeling.

IRON TREES,
GOLDEN FLOWERS

Figs. 27, 28. Mizoguchi Kenji, *A Tale of Loyal Retainers of the Genroku Era*

Tokugawa period (and, to a lesser extent, certain earlier periods) are so familiar to Japanese audiences that a great deal more 'background' can be taken for granted in *jidai-geki* than in its Western counterpart. Most important of all, however, is the endlessly repetitive quality of such films, grounded as they are in this shared heritage. Though this is a ticklish subject on which to make definitive pronouncements, it would seem that in a new film on an old theme the average, untravelled, unsophisticated Japanese film-goer still seeks *not* startling twists or even any novelty at all, but rather a *confirmation* of the permanence of certain values, certain symbols, certain structures.

*A Tale of Loyal Retainers*, which lasts nearly four hours, is entirely devoid of anything remotely resembling spectacular action, if we except one *nō* performance and an abortive combat described below. Its sumptuous austerity, its hieratic stateliness border at times on academic formalism. In some respects this is one of the few Japanese films which reflects to any serious extent the mood and rhythm of the classical *nō*, although at the same time its lyrical scope would almost incline one to a more exotic comparison with Wagner's *Parsifal*.

Though played against elaborate reconstructions of vast mansions and castles, nearly every scene in the film is either a long discussion over such subjects as dividing up the Asano fortune, the ethics of the vendetta, the politics of the period (Fig. 27), or else is devoted to pure ritual: preparations for suicide (Fig. 28), ritual hair-cutting, tea-ceremony, a *nō* play, a death commemoration, etc.

One feature of the film which distinguishes it sharply from the previous masterpieces, is an emphasis on balanced, generally centred framing observable in a majority of shots and which contributes strongly to the film's hieratic quality (symmetry is regarded by Japanese tradition as suitable only to temple architecture). However, it would be a mistake to infer that this mode of composition leads to an occlusion of field and frame as does the subtle centering of the Western system, since the very nature of Japanese classical architecture, magnificently epitomized in these sets, is so committed to emphasis on frame and surface as to render such an effect unthinkable.

Perhaps most striking of all is the lavish extravagance of so many camera movements: for the first time, it seems, Mizoguchi had a crane at his disposal, though it would be trivial to reduce this radical abandonment of the principle of economy observed in *Tale of Late Chrysanthemums* to this mechanical contingency. For when these movements occur they adhere to a remarkable inner logic. The successive camera angles within a given shot previously tended,

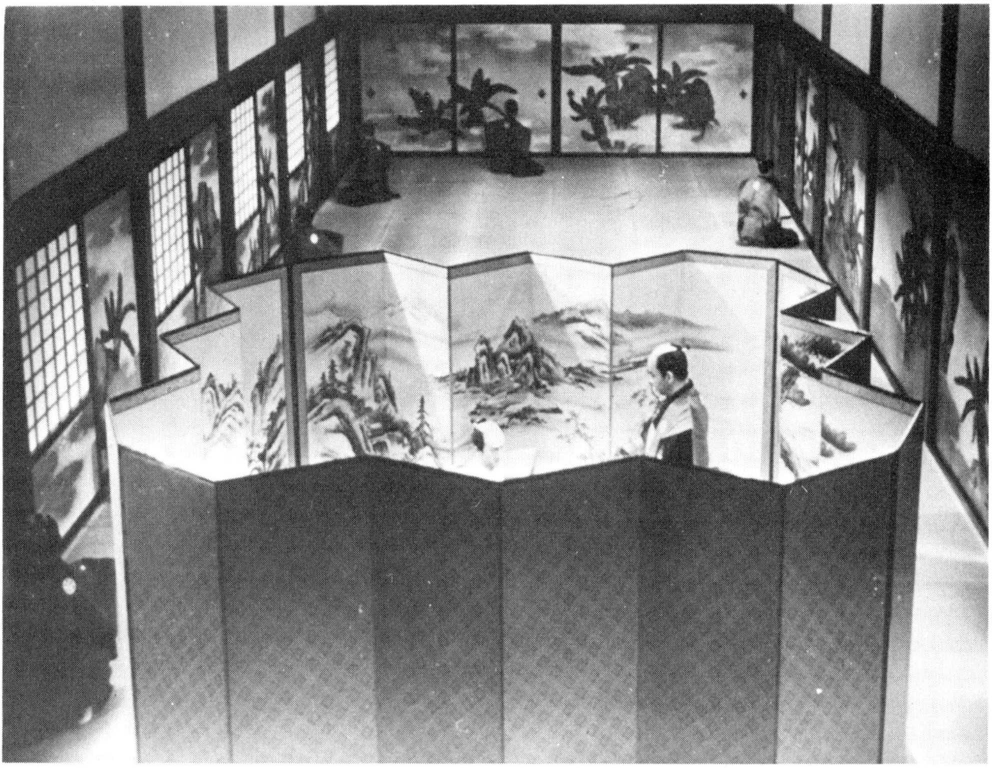

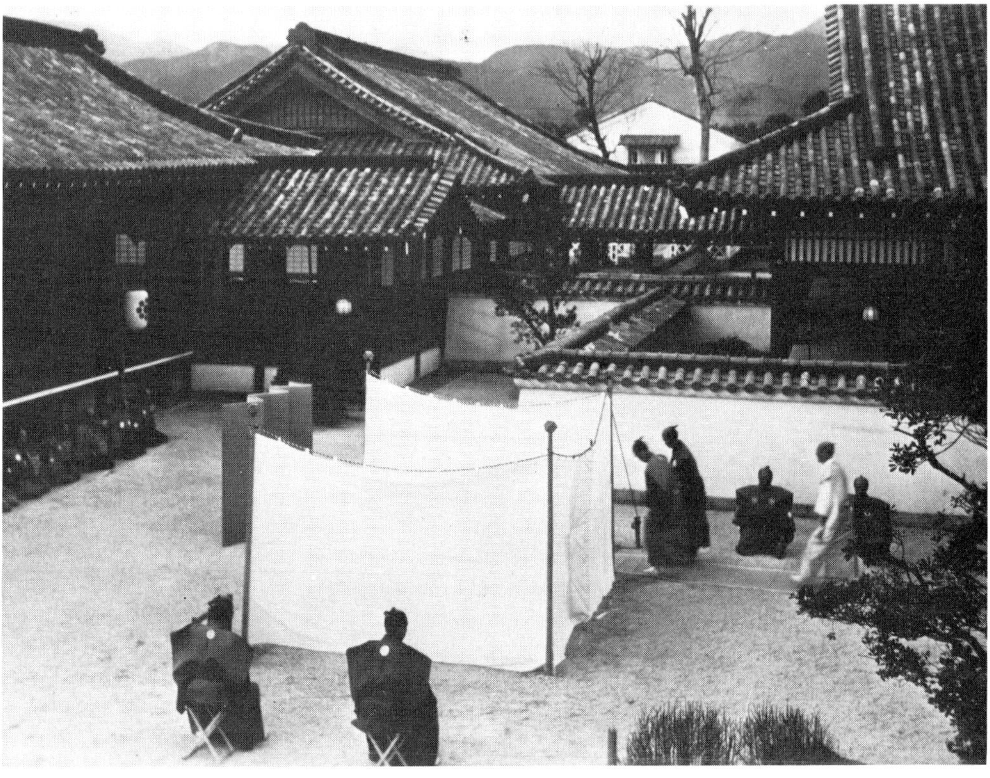

IRON TREES,
GOLDEN FLOWERS

almost without exception, to form a *centrifugal pattern* in pro-filmic space, i.e. the camera, in accordance precisely with the principle of economy of means, tended to pivot about a single point or line. In *A Tale of Loyal Retainers*, on the other hand, the pattern tends to be *centripetal*, i.e. the camera tends to circle about the characters and often in fact effects one or more complete reversals during a single shot. And while this analysis certainly does not account for all of this monumental film, one does detect a systematic tendency to introduce the two main figures of dominant narrative editing – the concertina and the reverse field – into the camera movements but at the same time to *unfold* them with ostentatious slowness. As a result, there is absolutely nothing of that 'organic' embedding in the diegesis achieved by a comparable adaptation of the editing codes to movement in the West. In fact, the extravagance of these movements is such that ultimately they may be said to offer an absolutely unique *ceremonial commentary* on the representational system of the Western film.

One of the most spectacularly beautiful instances of this procedure is the sequence in which Asano's wife sacrifices her hair preparatory to entering widowhood. This five-minute shot begins with a distant rear view of the lady, with two of her ladies-in-waiting visible on her right. The only sounds to be heard are the tolling death-knell and the women's sobs. After a long moment, one of the women rises carrying a knife on a tray and goes towards Lady Asano. The camera starts to circle to the right and soon we see that there are many other women in the room all bowed and sobbing. One of the servants wraps the long hair in a sheet of paper, the other cuts the tresses with the knife. The camera completes its semi-circle. Facing the camera now, the widow remains erect and dry-eyed while all the servants prostrate themselves and sob even more desperately.

A far more elaborate example of this approach, almost bordering on the pedantic, is to be found in the long confrontation between Tokugawa Tsunatoyo, a relative of the reigning Shōgun but who secretly sympathizes with the plotters, and Tominomori Sukeyemon, a young retainer of the late lord. The conversation in which Tsunatoyo affects to persuade Sukeyemon to give up the vendetta, is set in a large audience-room in Sukeyemon's mansion, and consists mainly in two very ample circular movements which produce the equivalent of two reverse-field 'cuts' spread out over a period of five minutes! Similarly, slow forward tracking movements seem to reproduce the concertina, but within such restricted limits on the shot-size scale that the principle of camera distance is at all times respected, altogether eliminating the close-up, motor and target of the concertina in the classical Western *découpage*. When Oīshi comes upon two vassals of Asano, the commoner Izeki and his son, dying of self-inflicted wounds in front of the castle of Akō, the first part of the scene is filmed from an extraordinary distance; when Oīshi whispers to the dying Izeki that he intends to avenge their lord, the camera dollies in to a head-to-foot shot, which might be said to *stand* in this instance for a cut to a dramatic close-up. Taken on its own, this example might of course suggest that there is an 'innate' Japanese code of shot sizes, parallel to our own and merely less extended, but such procedures are too rare in the Japanese cinema to explain such work in purely cultural terms (not to mention the fact that this film was a commercial failure). We seem rather to be dealing with a specific transformation of a set of Western codes, comparable, at the level of the individual artist, with those cultural modes of transformation observed earlier.

Another remarkable example of distance, 'resolved' in this case by an actual concertina, is the scene in which Sukeyemon hot-headedly attacks Tsunatoyo as he prepares to perform in a *nō* play (Fig. 29, Pls. la, b, c, d, e, f, g, and 2). The tiny face of Sukeyemon's wife appearing from time to time in the background is typical of the way Mizoguchi demands that an audience *read* the image. A concertina occurs in the midst of the two men's struggle (Pls. lg, 2) as a prelude to the dialogue in which Tsunatoyo explains that he in fact favours the vendetta and that Sukeyemon must follow Oīshi's lead and bide his time. It is indicative of the displacement effect of Mizoguchi's basic distance option on the editing codes in their literal use; but it also demonstrates the director's new concern to introduce established editing figures. For although very long takes are again the rule in this film, the dilated analysis of the editing codes through movement is matched by a relatively frequent use of the actual figures (more predominant in the first part of the film than in the second, however). What is significant here is that their use usually seems to be *deferred*: often a scene will take place in very long shot for quite some time and then, at a point in the narrative which may seem quite arbitrary, a concertina (or other type of match) will occur (of course, the example illustrated above was not of this type).

Was it because audiences were disappointed in the complete lack of violence? Was it because of the extreme austerity of the narrative – for long inter-titles recalled the episodes not shown (among them the attack on Kira's mansion and the suicide of the forty-seven) and the diegesis was almost exclusively discursive or ceremonial? These explications are difficult to accept, because so many

1a

1b

1c

1d

1e

1f

1g

2

242

successful films made until then had been equally eventless and austere, and this continued to be the case for years. Whatever the reason, this inordinately expensive film was a financial disaster. Possibly, of course, this lavishly austere presentation of basic 'feudal' values did not mesh with the historical mood and the material conditions which determined it.

The film was made during the Pacific War, in response to government demands that Shochiku increase their production of patriotic films ... and Mizoguchi seems to have volunteered. He was always prepared, it seems, to respond to this type of demand; in 1932 he had made *The Dawn of the Foundation of Manchukuo and Mongolia* (*Mam-Mō kenkoku no reimei*) and he collaborated during the last months of the war in an all-star production, *Song of Faith in Victory* (*Hissho ka*, 1945). These facts help us to relativize the 'progressive' content of so many other of his films. More generally, if one were to examine the political records of most of the major film-makers of the 1930s, it seems fairly clear that the suggestion made earlier that the fusion of traditional values and militarist ideology was a major factor in the development of a specifically Japanese cinema, holds true at the level of the individual as well.

Mizoguchi's first post-war films were already increasingly inflected by that fascination with the efficiency and 'effectiveness' of the Western codes, an aspect of his career which will be discussed later. *Five Women Around Utamaro* (*Utamaro o meguro gonin no onna*, 1946) – the first *jidai-geki*, it seems, to be authorized by the American censors – is a remarkable exercise in dramatic efficacy, as are so many of Mizoguchi's films. The long take is largely subservient to the Western codes and there are frequent close-ups. In general, it gives an impression of hesitation, not unlike that observed in his work in the mid-1930s: one observes both the temptation of the codes from the conquering West and the nostalgia for an exemplary past of personal and national rigour.

*The Love of Actress Sumako* (*Joyu Sumako no koi*, 1947) is probably the last of Mizoguchi's films to extend his work of the pre-war era. It, too, deals with the theatre. This theme seems important to Mizoguchi, though many of the films illustrating it are lost – one especially regrets *Woman of Naniwa* (*Naniwa onna*, 1940), shot with the collaboration of the Bunraku Theatre. It tells of the love and of the death of an actress and a director (Shimamura Hogetsu) who were among the founders of *shin-geki*. Among many remarkable innovations, this film displays a radical, quasi-pedagogical contrast between the first reel – seen as a universe of men – and the rest of the film which is the

Fig. 29. Mizoguchi Kenji, *A Tale of Loyal Retainers of the Genroku Era*

domain of one woman. The introductory sequences show Shimamura lecturing to a drama-school class, then holding a conference with his colleagues. They are shot entirely according to the reverse-field concertina mode. The characteristic Mizoguchi systemics is then abruptly introduced in a five-minute take in which Sumako thrashes her husband and makes the acquaintance of her future lover, who has been watching the scene. As in *Tale of Late Chrysanthemums*, an effort is made to contrast the theatrical scenes with the rest of the film, but here the use of editing is more rigorously restricted; performances are shot either in very long shot, with the stage barely visible at the far end of the hall, or in medium close-ups which exclude the proscenium arch. Dramatically, too, the film is one of Mizoguchi's most accomplished, though it cannot compare, on this score or any other, with the chiselled perfection of *Tale of Late Chrysanthemums*.

Following *The Love of Actress Sumako*, which represents a plateau of excellence in the work of Mizoguchi, the quality of his films declined in much the same way as the standards of Ozu's films had fallen away. With what might be regarded as a typically Japanese opportunism, he appears to have discovered that his systemics were perfectly compatible with one of the dominant tendencies in Hollywood at that time: the long take *à la* Wyler. The social dramas which he made in the late 1940s are perfectly in keeping with the general tone of that tragic period. By the time he returned to *jidai-geki*, he had become a virtuoso stylist. The elegance of a film like *The Life of a Woman, by Saikaku* (*Saikaku ichidai onna*, 1952),[22] with its sensitive adaptation of an eighteenth-century classic, though incomparably more sophisticated as literature than, say, Wyler's *The Heiress*, is not to be compared in any way with his earlier masterpieces. In particular, one observes in this film and in the others of the 1950s such an utter absorption in the aesthetics of the long take, its organization and composition, that it is as if shot-changes simply did not exist. Each cut gives the same impression of perfunctorily 'turning a page', as in, say, Visconti's *Il Gattopardo*. When the end of a shot has arrived, we pass on to the next, and the spatio-temporal event constituted by that change seems to be regarded as non-existent, whereas even in *Tale of Late Chrysanthemums*, where cuts were rare and were not the object of any special effort, they were almost always *produced as caesura*. The camera in these later films was, of course, as supple and free-moving as it had ever been before, but totally subservient to a stylized version of the dominant code. To the extent that there is 'editing in movement' at all (for nudges are commonplace by now), it is

Fig. 30. Mizoguchi Kenji, *Five Women Around Utamaro*

Fig. 31. Mizoguchi Kenji, *The Love of Actress Sumako*

22. Distributed in the West as *The Life of Oharu*.

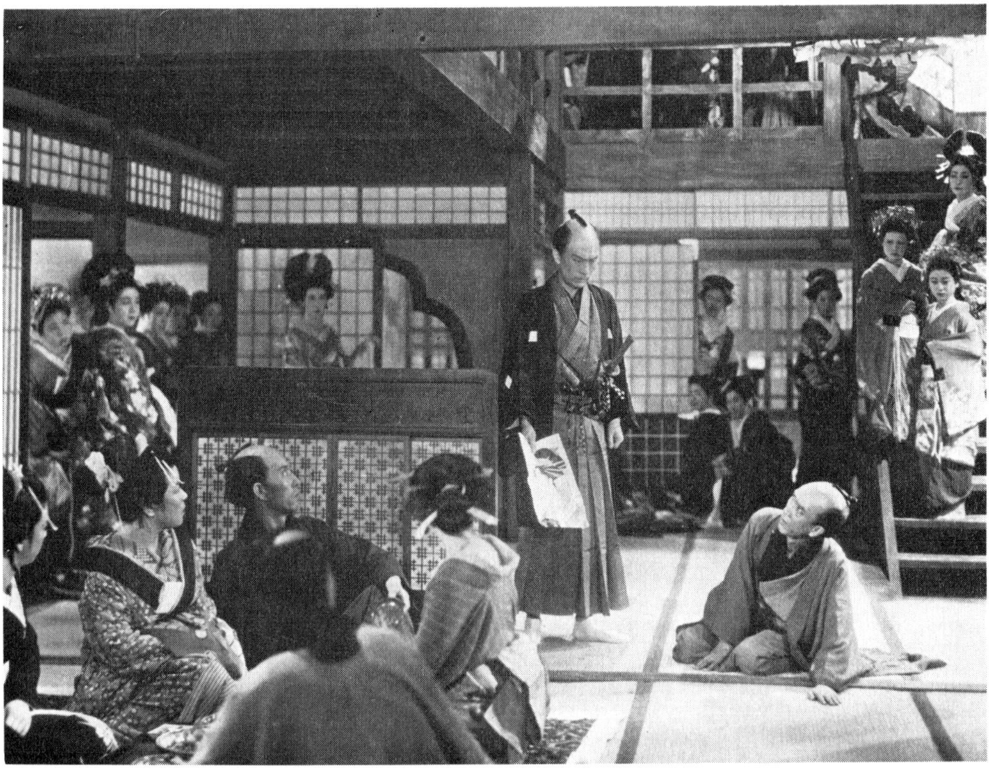

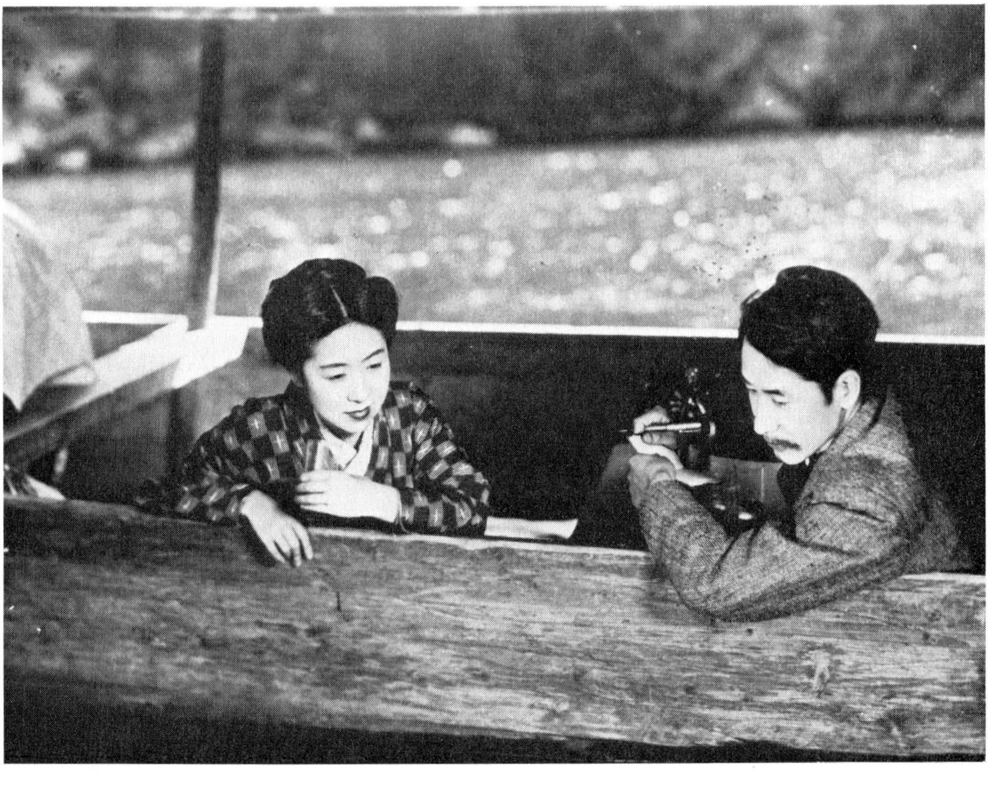

practically identical with, say, that of Samuel Fuller in *Pickup on South Street*.

One film, *A Story by Chikamatsu* (*Chikamatsu monogatari*, 1954), stands out among the films of Mizoguchi's last years – for reasons, however, largely unrelated to the main issue of his pre-war work. I have described elsewhere and at some length how Mizoguchi and the composer Hayazaka Fumio explored in remarkable fashion the 'sound-track continuum', establishing frequent *relays* between music, sound effects (noise) and the spoken word.[23] Though none of his later films contains sustained work in this area, it was prefigured by certain passages in *Tale of Late Chrysanthemums*.

Mizoguchi's last period will be given some consideration in the context of post-war cinema and its critical reception, for I am fully conscious of the extent to which my evaluations run counter to accepted judgements. Lest there be any misunderstandings, I claim that the Mizoguchi of *Sisters of Gion*, *Tale of Late Chrysanthemums* and possibly, too, other films of that period is no doubt the greatest of all Japanese directors, in the way that we as Westerners judge such matters.

Mizoguchi was throughout his career a master of dramatic narrative in a sense that Ozu was not. And judged according to the stylistic criteria of dominant criticism, *The Life of a Woman, by Saikaku* or *Sansho the Bailiff* (*Sanshō da yū*, 1954) are no doubt in all respects the equal of *Sisters of Gion* or *Tale of Late Chrysanthemums*. But from our historically and theoretically oriented standpoint the importance of these early films is incomparably greater; their superior internal rigour is due in large part to the director's fidelity to the otherness of his native culture – just as his ultimate decline must be understood within the context of Japan's historical situation and that of her cinema after the 1945 defeat.

---

23. See my *Theory of Film Practice* (p. 44 ff.), in which I also discuss some of the implications of Japanese music and theatrical sound with regard to modern Western music and cinema. The Japanese musical sensibility, which has never made the distinction between music and noise which conditions the Western ear, seems admirably suited to coping with the problems of formalizing the total track, while the organization of the Japanese film-crew, in which the same man records, edits and mixes the track, would seem the ideal condition to promote experimentation of the kind undertaken by Mizoguchi in that exceptional film. Yet to this day it remains almost unique in Japan.

# 21. Shimizu Hiroshi and Some Others

Shimizu Hiroshi seems the most 'spontaneously Japanese' director of his generation, unscientific though this judgement may be. His 'work on the signifier' has none of the advanced complexities of Ozu, Mizoguchi, Ishida or even Naruse at his best. His was a privative rather than an elaborative systemics. It is, however, unrivalled as an emblem of the essence of this golden age. More radically than any of the more generally recognized masters of *shōmingeki*, Shimizu came to reject the concept of the linear, unified narrative. His 'spontaneous' insistence on camera distance is in some ways more startling even than Mizoguchi's, if only because his *découpage* (save for an occasional geometrical patterning, which we shall examine in a moment) is not otherwise remarkable.

Furthermore, Shimizu is the one Japanese director who has produced a body of work which offers meaningful comparison with the writings of the great seventeenth-century poet and 'novelist' Ihara Saikaku. And Saikaku's prose writings are, in turn, the epitome of a specifically Japanese approach to narrative, often the most startling aspect, to Westerners, of the Japanese cinema. There has always been, in Japanese literature, a tendency towards an agglutinative conception of narrative which finds expression in the very early long poem (*chōka*) by Hitomaro presented in Chapter 3, and in the *uta-monogatari*, those collections of brief tales built around *tanka*. It is very much in evidence in the large scale *monogatari* such as 'The Tale of Genji' which, despite the unifying factor provided by the central characters, has a rambling non-cumulative quality about the narrative which sets it totally at odds with what the Western world for two hundred years has commonly termed the novel.

Saikaku devoted most of his life to *haikai*, or chains of brief verses (*hokku* or *haiku*). He was, moreover, a product of the rising merchant class, and not the least interesting aspect of the prose writings to which he devoted the last seven years of his life, is their portrayal of the minds and manners of the merchants and other city-folk of the Genroku era.

For our purposes, the most significant among his writings is *The Japanese Family Storehouse* (*Nippon eitai-gura*), a collection of thirty 'short stories' with an ostensibly didactic purpose: advising the ambitious merchant on how to get rich. However, as the most authoritative Western specialist on this author, G. W. Sargent, has put it.

> Saikaku does not labour his points... He proceeds rapidly from topic to topic, expecting his readers to follow as best they can – and if his readers were already schooled in the twists and turns of rapid *haikai* verse, they probably experienced very little difficulty. The moral is there for the curious, but it does not seem likely that either Saikaku or his readers were interested in it for its own sake. It is part of the pattern.[1]

Indeed, many of the most representative pieces in the collection echo in microcosm the fragmented form of the book itself (derived, it seems, from the chatty travel guides which were a popular genre in the sixteenth and seventeenth centuries) by a disjunctive, multi-polar structure derived from the associative/dissociative techniques of *haikai*.

> The thought is not logically progressive... each brief section is permitted to develop in a way which has no direct bearing on what is to follow, and the transitions, when effected, are brought about abruptly and almost casually, sometimes by mechanical means... A *haikai* short story is less closely knit, less compelling to the reader, than one constructed on dramatic principles. It is basically a succession of related digressions.[2]

One of the better examples of this construction is 'Making a clock in slow motion'[3] which unfolds its disjunctive discourse against two unifying elements: the city of Nagasaki and what is in fact the overall theme of the book, 'the proper approach to making a successful living.'

First, the wrong – the unpractical Chinese – approach is given. Then follows an example of how inventiveness should be turned to practical use, to the making of a fortune in a single generation. Next, after a brief introductory description of trading at Nagasaki, come stories of Nagasaki dealers, illustrating the point that ingenuity is essential for making a fortune. Then there is a short conclusion giving the right and wrong methods of buying imported goods at Nagasaki.[4]

However, an analysis of the English text alone reveals remarkably sophisticated 'mechanical' articulations, antithetical to that of the classical Western novel, which seeks

---

1. Sargent, G. W., *The Japanese Family Storehouse*, p. 210.

2. ibid., pp. xxxv and xxxvii.

3. ibid., pp. 105–8.

4. ibid., pp. 209–10.

precisely *to 'compel' the reader* and rejects obtrusively mechanical transitions.[5] It appears closely related to the practice of some of the most advanced Western literature of our century (Joyce and the French novel since Robbe-Grillet), which require readers no less schooled in the twists and turns of language play.

Shimizu is known to have directed over 150 films between 1924 and 1959, most of which are not considered 'personal' films. I cannot verify this assumption, since of the Shimizu films which have been unearthed so far,[6] I have been able to see only a few. Of these, the film which best illustrates the 'agglutinative' narrative is *A Star Athlete* (*Hanagata senshu,* 1937). The five episodes that compose this film do involve the same characters and subtly converge to point up a fundamentally Japanese – and, at this date, *patriotic* – moral: No matter how good you are individually, it is the group that comes first. These episodes are, however, primarily autonomous as to structure of *découpage* and mode of narration. They contain cyclical motifs not unlike those observed in Saikaku. Moreover, two of them are frankly farcical, while the other three are, in different ways, contrastingly serious.

The first 'cameo', for it is hard to think of these sections under any other category, tells how the 'star', Seki, is roused from a nap on the high-school lawn by Tanni, the serious athletics monitor who resents the other boy's lackadaisical attitude and challenges him to a foot-race. Seki wins ... and goes back to his nap (I shall deal with this sequence in detail when considering Shimizu's approach to *découpage*). The second section, the most elaborate in the film and certainly one of Shimizu's most brilliant achievements, presents the students on a two-day march as part of their obligatory military training. Seki and Tanni are only incidentally present in this scene which, for most of its eleven minutes, consists of thirty consecutive dolly movements, forward or backward along a country road, with the camera always preceding or following the students. The action consists of encounters which they have along the way and is treated in a mode of cyclical humour closer to that of the French master, Jacques Tati, than to that of American silent comedy. They overtake a group of small boys who fall in behind the double column, pass three pretty girls with parasols, then three peasants wearing broad rainhats. Holding their noses all at the same time, they leave a wide berth for a wagon-load of manure passing between their ranks; they overtake and pass a group of girls on a hike ... but soon a truck overtakes them, and the same girls wave merrily at them from the back. The truck is soon out of sight and now the sergeant orders his men to proceed 'on the

SHIMIZU HIROSHI AND
SOME OTHERS

---

5. The occasional exceptions found in Dickens merely confirm this rule.

6. Most of them since I was last in Japan (see Appendix 2).

double'; the jogging students overtake the truck, which has had a breakdown; the girls watch the students jog by (still followed by the little boys) and after a whispered consultation, fall in behind; however, the sergeant cuts out across country. The students scatter in battle formation and ford a shallow pond; the children follow bravely, but the girls are left looking foolish and disappointed at the edge.

The play of the camera up and down the road, taking subjective and objective roles by turn, is a constant source of gentle humour, while, at the same time, coupled with reappearances of characters and visual themes, it contributes to a truly musical dimension. The third section of the film is, 'musically' again, a kind of double interlude, one of its sub-sections pursuing the central theme, the other being a complete diversion: during a rest-period in a clearing, Tanni almost comes to blows with Seki, whom he again feels is 'putting on airs'. Then, when the troop moves out again, one of the boys has stomach cramp and his buddy stays behind to help him. A peasant passes in a cart and takes them aboard; they pass the marching troop, in an echo of the previous section.

Section four is a veritable nocturne; it takes place in and around a commensal country inn (*yado*) and involves several brief portraits and vignettes. It is centred, however, around a woman traveller with a sick little girl: a doctor comes, a *shinto* priest officiates over the child and Seki runs afoul of some card-players whom he tries to quieten down for the child's sake. Finally, there is the faintest beginning of a flirtation between Seki and the mother. This is more than Tanni can take (Seki has broken training, as it were) and he knocks him down 'so that the Sergeant won't have to do it'. Seki readily admits that he was in the wrong and in the courtyard of the inn he and Tanni make peace before the assembled students.

Next day, they are back on the road, and the fifth and last section of the film, the only one which is frankly farcical, is built on an extravagant misunderstanding: the *shinto* priest, who has resumed his journey, seeing the soldiers coming down the road on the double, imagines that they are out to get him, and flees. Catching up with another of the characters from the previous night at the inn, he passes on his panic, and this process continues until a whole ludicrous group are fleeing down the road with the soldiers apparently in hot pursuit. (The structure of this gag echoes a fragment of the earlier marching sequence: the hiking girls were also strung out along the road and as the students approached they gradually joined together in much the same way.) The frightened travellers strike out across the fields but are relentlessly followed by the students; they plunge into a river but when they reach the opposite bank, they don't even have time to wring their clothes out, but must dash on half-naked, terrified by the distant spectacle of . . . exhausted students wading their way through the water (and of course these last stages of the pursuit are a variation on the earlier sequence as well). After a short rest, the students go on their way singing . . . and the film is over.

The date of the film and its underlying political moral are clearly not unrelated. Yet, in a balanced historical perspective, it is impossible to reduce it to a mere contribution to the coming war effort. From a textual point of view, we may say, as Sargent puts it apropos of Saikaku, that the moral is not there for its own sake, that 'it is part of the pattern'.

As a further example of the modest and yet exemplary way in which Shimizu envisages 'patterning,' let us look in some detail at the opening sequence, illustrated in Fig. 32.

– on the shady school lawn, students are cleaning rifles (Pl. 1); dissolve to . . .
– the same frame, rifles are stacked (Pl. 2); after eight seconds, dissolve again to . . .
– the same frame; the rifles have disappeared and far in the background three boys are asleep (Pl. 3)

Fig. 32. Shimizu Hiroshi, *A Star Athlete*

Fig. 32. Shimizu Hiroshi, *A Star Athlete*

– on the playing field, the energetic Tanni, seeing three boys sleeping during gym period, leaves the track and comes towards the camera (Pl. 4)

– concertina: in passing, he remarks on Seki's laziness to two other boys (Pl. 5) then exits frame right on the double

– concertina: he comes towards the sleeping boys and stops by Seki: 'Why aren't you out there? You're a good runner!' (Pl. 6)

– concertina: Seki gets up: 'This spring, I don't feel up to it' (Pl. 7a); however, he turns and walks towards the field; Tanni has a scathing word for the other sleepers (Pl. 7b)

– concertina: they pay no heed; he turns to run after Seki (Pl. 8)
– reverse angle of the other two sleepers, who sit up and gaze after them (Pl. 9), then go back to sleep
– Seki reaches the field, stripping off his sweat-shirt as he goes (Pl. 10); Tanni joins him and both go out frame-right
– they take position on the starting line, a student on the far right gives the signal (Pl. 11); a circular pan, the only movement in the sequence – broken only by a jump cut – follows them twice around the track to the accompaniment of a sprightly bit of music

SHIMIZU HIROSHI AND SOME OTHERS

7b

8

9

10

11

Fig. 32. Shimizu Hiroshi, *A Star Athlete*

—another fixed shot of the track (Pl. 12); Seki, followed by Tanni, comes into the frame and they sit side by side on a wooden platform
- 90° match: they start to dress (Pl. 13), exchanging a few words, but before Seki has even finished, he gets up and exits to the left
- Seki lopes away (Pl. 14)
- Tanni watches him with a smile (Pl. 15)
- Seki jogs back to where his companions are asleep under the trees (Pl. 16a); he lies down beside them (Pl. 16b) and goes to sleep

Now, in this sequence, Shimizu has used only the most classical editing figures – primarily concertinas and 180° reversals; however, the insistent mechanical repetition of these, their geometrical arrangement with regard to profilmic topography and the radically singularized use of movement, give to this section a geometric rigour which is rooted in traditional art and architecture and prefigures Kurosawa. Also remarkable, and typical of Shimizu, is the steadfast refusal to aestheticize any of these choices; in this respect his handling is very different to Ozu's.

Special attention should be paid to Shimizu's strict avoidance of close-ups. The tightest shot in this series of seventeen is Pl. 7a, a thigh-length two-shot. In Shimizu's films generally, close-ups are extremely rare. However, unlike Mizoguchi, for whom the long shot soon became part of a refined aestheticism, Shimizu seems to have regarded it simply as a privative rule, to be followed as a matter of course. Even his very last post-war films retained this 'prosaic' use of camera distance, and among the film-makers of his generation he is, in fact, one of those who remained most faithful to his own style. His last films are certainly less austere than *A Star Athlete*, but their formal homogeneity, determined by the same principles, remains remarkable.

In fact the choice of camera distance is perhaps carried to its ultimate consequences in *Children of the Great Buddha* (*Daibutsu-sama no kodomotachi*, 1952) set in Nara and centred upon a group of war orphans who serve (or aspire to serve) as tourist guides. The central figure is a precocious boy, deeply enamoured of the temples and their statues, and who acts as mentor for the other children, teaching them by rote the guide's sing-song spiel, the substance of which he actually gets from the little son of a bonze. This film too is 'no more than' a collection of 'cameos': a conversation with an American girl of Japanese ancestry who has come to visit the land of her parents now that the war is over; touching scenes of the boy listening outside different houses everyday at noon until he can catch the midday radio news with its list of returning war-prisoners (his father is a missing soldier); his conversations about art with a professor from Tokyo. The film is composed predominantly of huge long shots, taking in the giant statues, the towering temples, and with the characters often little more than tiny silhouettes scurrying along the edge of the frame. At times, the fictional dimension of the diegesis seems to be almost completely dissolved in favour of a 'documentary' *experiencing* of Nara. Even the scenes which are not set inside the city proper, and in particular the picnic with the *nisei* girl, are shot almost exclusively in long shot, with at most one or two medium shots inserted here or there.

Fig. 33. Shimizu Hiroshi, *Children of the Great Buddha*

Shimizu's reputation in Japan rests on his films about children. He loved children and, being independently wealthy, founded a home for orphans after the war ended. This home provided actors and subjects for two of his last films, *Children of the Bee-hive* (*Hachi no su no kodomotachi*, 1948) and its (never released) sequel, *So no go hachi no su no kodomotachi* (1951). Perhaps his most famous film is *Children in the Wind* (*Kaze no naka no kodomo*, 1937). Yet although the typically discreet sense of *mise en scène* and the attachment to camera distance are already in evidence, the film has a more linear anecdotal structure than that of *A Star Athlete* and some of its successors. It tells the story of children whose home is broken up when their father is falsely accused of forgery. They ultimately manage, by accident, to prove his innocence. The scenes with the band of village children are certainly very delicate and reveal the sense of cyclical construction which was to become so prominent in some of the later films. A dramatically articulated scenario, however, simply did not suit Shimizu's very special gift.

Nonetheless, Shimizu Hiroshi remains an admirably representative figure, precisely because of the manner in which he remained so faithful and for so long to what we may regard as a combination of basic Japanese traits.

I do, however, wish to insist that these traits – which can be summed up as camera-distance and exceptionally low-key narrative – seem to appear in a very large number of Japanese films indeed. Random soundings among the films of directors of the 1930s of lesser standing than those already discussed, as well as some of no standing whatsoever, have convinced me of the validity of certain cautious generalizations. Here are a few examples.

In 1939, the director Inoue Kintaro made *Crow in the Moonlight* (*Tsukiyo karasu*), a curious story, with sado-masochistic overtones, of the relationship between a woman musician and her handsome young pupil, in which insistently academic reverse-field scenes alternate in seeming arbitrariness with amazingly long takes, the camera often remaining at a considerable distance on the far side of a garden or at the end of a street, for minutes on end.

Toyoda Shiro's better-known *The Bush Warbler* (*Uguisu*, 1938), though ultimately no more distinguished, associates a curiously uncentred narrative (portraits and vignettes in a village police station) with an even greater proclivity for long takes and camera distance.

Going back to the very beginnings of sound in Japan, a film by Tanaka Eizo, *Namiko, the 'Cuckoo'* (*Hototogisu Namiko,* 1932), a really trashy *gendai-geki* in a patriotically edifying, melodramatic vein, is shot entirely in single-take sequences. This was certainly due in part to the sound-editing difficulties experienced also in the West, but despite an occasional track-in for dramatic emphasis, close frames are extremely rare, and the camera tends to take in an entire room from the outset, with the characters gradually occupying the film as they arrive. The film may well have been adapted from a play, like so many of its Western contemporaries, but the 'theatricality' of its *découpage* is specifically Japanese. It contains, in particular, a single five-minute take marking the hero's participation in the war with China, a besieged smoke-filled interior crowded with soldiers (throughout with their backs to the completely motionless camera) shooting out of the windows until the whole set literally comes down around their ears. One would not be likely to find this sort of shot in a comparably obscure Western film, even in that period of technological constraint.

The films of the 1930s which descended from the original *chambera* also seem to have perpetuated quite naturally the tradition of camera distance which had been so intrinsic to the genre during the 1920s. *The New Tangezasen* (*Shinpen Tangezasen – Sogan no maki*, 1939) by Nakagawa Nobuo, an eclectic 'B-picture' director who has the esteem of today's younger generation of critics, is a clear-cut example. The opening sequence, involving a running combat of one against many, is shot from an extravagant distance throughout and is intercut, moreover, with decentering 'pillow-shots' of reeds. In this film, the reverse-field system does appear from time to time (as it did in most films of the period). It no doubt took an Ozu to subvert it radically, a Mizoguchi or a Shimizu to banish it entirely, and this, of course, is one measure of the ultimately exceptional character of their accomplishments. One senses, however, that even a Nakagawa has no special 'feeling' for the system, since he too introduces it rather arbitrarily into certain conversation pieces while often treating other equivalent scenes in a single long shot.

However, just as the action film often accommodated a rare use of the editing codes, so too the most 'eventless', low-keyed, typically Japanese genres related to *shōmin-geki* accommodated those same codes in all their perfection. And at one level *shōmin-geki* is undoubtedly informed by a Western ideology of realism – Western in scope but not entirely foreign, of course, to a realist bias present in Japanese cultural patterns since the time of Saikaku, Chikamatsu and Hokusai.

The coded, academic quality of what was probably a majority of films in the new modern genre is an observable fact. The outstanding instances are two highly respected specialists of 'family drama', Shimazu Yasujiro and Gosho Heinosuke. The quotidian banality and radical under-dramatization of such films as *Our Neighbour Miss Yae (Tonari no Yae-chan,* 1934) or *Family Meeting (Kazoku kaigi,* 1936) are astonishing when one considers that they are contemporary with and most comparable to *It Happened One Night, La Belle Equipe* or *Storm.*[7] Shimazu's rather clumsy fidelity to the Western codes, in spite of an occasional 'pillow-shot', makes his work 'typically Japanese' only in a very limited sense. However, critics insensitive to the ideological and cultural determination of modes of representation and who therefore fail to see that the Hollywood codes are not a natural language, tend to place a high value on it.

On the other hand, while Gosho's very real mastery of Western-style *découpage* demonstrates the subtly pervasive action of the Hollywood system as clearly as Shimazu's pale imitation, his scripts are so admirably representative of a genre that a brief discussion of a typical film is in order.

*The Burden of Life (Jinsei no onimotsu,* 1935), like nearly all pre-war Gosho films, is set in a merchant-class family. The middle-aged father has just married off his third daughter but still has Kan-Chan, a nine-year-old child, to raise. Kan-Chan is resented by his father, as he was an

---

7. Comparable by their typicality. Such exceptional Western films as Barnett's *By the Blue Sea* or *Menschen am Sonntag* are the references which make even the most run-of-the-mill *shōmin-geki* appear avant-garde in the West.

unwanted baby, and the boy is aware of this. Finally, the mother, who disapproves of her husband's attitude towards Kan-Chan, takes him away to live with one of her sons-in-law. Kan-Chan, however, is not really happy in his new home and one day unthinkingly goes back to his own house after school. He has a meal with his father for the first time in many years, and this embryonic reconciliation brings the mother home as well. Needless to say, this slender central narrative is filled out with portraits of the various family members, all of whom are equally 'three-dimensional' in sharp contrast to the dominant Western model of graded characterization (see Chapter 23). It is not that there is no dramatic conflict or underlying narrative movement; only such extreme films as Naruse's post-war *Mother* really achieve this 'void'. It is simply that the fundamental diegetic economy is not centred around a plot-line or a character of privileged 'density' in any way comparable to the dominant Western model. There are, in particular, many 'irrelevant' events which are offered as being equal in importance to those articulated to the 'main theme', and the diegetic space-time of the film as a whole is offered as being of no more importance than what 'preceded' or 'will follow' in the family's life-stream. If ever the ideology of the 'slice of life' were realized in cinema, it is in such films as this. The combination of follow-shots with cutaways to the sleeping Kan-Chan in the sequence in which mother and father come home late from the wedding ('What a relief to be rid of the three of them . . . but there's still Kan-Chan') anticipates and equals the most successful moments of Italian neo-realism. The Japanese need for confirmation that when all is said and done 'everyone is like everyone else', indeed their willingness to accept such confirmations as sufficient basis for communal spectacle, is perhaps nowhere so clearly instantiated as in these films. Despite the realist bias of Edo, it is not absolutely certain that 'illusionist' representation is, in the Japanese view, necessarily *better* suited to satisfying this need than the 'presentationalism' associated with the traditional arts. Whence, the persistence of the *benshi* and the relative popularity, in their day, of the films of Mizoguchi and Ozu. The conviction, presumably shared by Gosho, Shimazu and others, that the 'right way' to make films involved the dominant Western approach to shot-size and editing followed from a gesture that had become typical among the liberal intelligentsia. For them, Western and especially American 'know-how' had a decisive prestige; they quite rightly associated it with the bourgeois conceptions of liberalism and democracy. At the same time, of course, a film like *The Burden of Life* served quite directly the interests of the reactionary forces at work in Japan. The traditional cohesion of the family cell is preserved against the 'individualistic' (antisocial) bias of the father, while the balancing influence of middle-aged women, allotted considerably more power within the family than when they were young and desirable, is an essential element of the social fabric. We shall return to these contradictory aspects in the next section.

Aside from these fairly numerous films depicting the family life of what was essentially the petty bourgeoisie, the galaxy of 'plotless' genres also provided occasion for somewhat more independent directors to depict the lives of the poor 'as they really were', though not of course to offer dissenting criticism of the social and political developments of the late 1930s. Uchida Tomu's *Earth* (*Tsuchi*, 1939) is a famous portrait of peasant life made under difficult conditions; it anticipates films like *Farrébique*. Naruse's *The Whole Family Works* (*Hataraku ikka*, 1939) is somewhat more interesting: this sketch of a sorely pressed, very large working-class family is remarkable for its use of the long shot to present a social group. Its systematic and often very lovely recourse to the pillow-shot and its constant concern with money and material difficulties are equally noteworthy. It contains, of course, and for obvious reasons, not a word against capitalism or militarism, and one has the curious impression of reading a Chikamatsu play, expressive of the hard times of the Edo merchants under the *bakufu*, and yet full of feudal loyalty, as well.

One further remark about what seems to be the specific scope of the low-key diegesis is in order. For while *jidai-geki* have predominantly been reserved for fantasy production, rampant with supermen, ghosts, erotic violence, etc.,[8] *gendai-geki* have traditionally been as far removed as possible from the imagery and constructions of fantasy. The importation of Western genres such as the spy film has somewhat modified this picture over the past few decades, but in the 1930s the dichotomy seems to have been quite rigorously respected.

It is also striking to a 'distant observer' that nothing whatsoever comparable to the *shōmin-geki* existed in popular Western films during the period under consideration (compared with Gosho's *The Neighbour's Wife and Mine* or Ozu's *A Story of Floating Weeds*, *Toni* or *Marius* are Elizabethan tragedies). The coming of television, however, in both Europe and the United States has produced an audio-visual genre[9] astonishingly similar to 'family drama'; although these programmes emphasize such values as marital fidelity rather than filial obligations, for example, they do often bear a remarkable resemblance of tone to the

8. The reputations of Yamanaka and Itami rest largely on their having gone counter to this tendency.

9. Prefigured in the United States by the 'daytime' radio serial, and a certain type of women's magazine story.

*shōmin-geki*, both in the cinema of the 1930s and today's TV, insofar as they attempt to portray the everyday lives of the 'average' viewer in a way that Western cinema had almost never done. Of course, the relative unity, even today, of Japanese society is such that all classes could, to some degree, recognize themselves in the characters of Ozu and the others, whereas in Western television we most often have the middle class imposing its own image of itself or of the dominated classes. This unanimistic dimension of *shōmin-geki* is an important aspect of its specific social role. However, without exaggerating the importance of McLuhan's glib insights into the new dimensions given capitalist society by television, it does seem that this convergence does point to the rise of an ideological need which is relatively new in the West ... but not in Japan. A comparative study here, provided it does not give way to positivistic sociologism, might shed light on the changing nature of ideological domination through the media.

## 22. Epilogue to a Golden Age

Although Japan's 'withdrawal into herself' after her annexation of Manchuria was a determining factor in the maturation of a specifically Japanese cinema, we cannot forget that this decade of relative cultural and ideological seclusion was above all the crucible of a quasi-Fascist militarism. Domestically, this generated a police state far surpassing that of the Tokugawa *bakufu*, and ultimately brought death and destruction to most of South-East Asia. The objective complicity of nearly every Japanese film-maker of the period is a fact – *especially to the extent that his films extolled, implicitly or explicitly, those traditional values which constituted the ideological basis for the new authoritarianism.* For while it is true, for example, that some of Ozu's early films, such as *An Inn in Tokyo*, treat discreetly progressive subjects, it is equally true that his entire effort, from the mid-1930s onward, constitutes a single anguished query as to the possible disappearance of that pillar of Japanese society, the traditional family system. And it is no accident that his most important film made during the Pacific War is almost the only film in which he seems to see hopes for the system, in the lifelong camaraderie of father and son. Although absolute judgement, cultural or political, on the Japanese family system is impossible, we know that it was essential to the ideology of militarist Japan. Just as, I might add, the development of a 'language' which fed upon traditional aesthetic and ethical values went hand in hand with the reinvigoration of *shinto* and other ideological strategies. And while certain films by Mizoguchi may be said to convey a progressive message (especially on the condition of women) we have also seen that he did not hesitate, either after the annexation of Manchuria or during the Pacific War, to make his contribution. Setting aside the patently militarist directors, such as Yamamoto Kajiro, Kurosawa's 'teacher', we may say that a vast majority of more or less forgotten directors contributed to the ideological consolidation of the régime precisely to the extent that their films aided the reactivation of traditional cultural values without which the specificity of the Japanese cinema could not have developed ... and this is a basic, irreducible dialectic. It took the courage of a Yamanaka to resist, if only passively, the economic, ideological and even physical pressures which were brought to bear. And it goes without saying that as war was resumed with China, then waged against Britain and the United States, the industry's contribution to the war effort, though in certain instances reluctant, was massive nonetheless.

When Ruth Benedict, doing 'field work' for her rather presumptuous but often penetrating study of the 'Japanese mind' commissioned by the American government[1] had occasion to screen captured Japanese war-propaganda films, she was amazed to find that by any Western standards they seemed almost anti-militarist and, in any case, scarcely corresponded to the pattern set by comparable productions from Allied or European Axis powers.

They do not play up military parades and bands and prideful showings of fleet manoeuvres or big guns. Whether they deal with the Russo-Japanese War or the China incident, they starkly insist upon the monotonous routine of mud and marching, the suffering of lowly fighting, the inconclusiveness of campaigns. Their curtain scenes are not victory or even *banzai* charges. They are overnight halts in some featureless Chinese town deep in mud. Or they show maimed, halt and blind representatives of three generations of a Japanese family, survivors of three wars. Or they show the family at home, after the death of the soldier, mourning the loss of husband and breadwinner and gathering themselves together to go on without him. The stirring background of Anglo-American 'Cavalcade' movies is all absent. They do not even dramatize the theme of the rehabilitation of wounded veterans. Not even the purposes for which the war was fought are mentioned.[2]

I might add that in these films, war is always shown as a collective endeavour, in which individual personalities are totally submerged: not only are there no heroes, but there are practically no characters.

The whole world-view of an ancient social order is of course implicit in the narrative form and substance of these films: the subordination of the individual to what Nakamura Hajime terms 'the limited social nexus' (the household, the family, the firm, the village, etc.) and its ultimate extension, the national community, symbolized by the Emperor.[3] They exalt a physical stoicism inherited from the 'way of the warrior' (*bushido*) and which has

EPILOGUE TO A
GOLDEN AGE

1. Benedict, Ruth, *The Chrysanthemum and the Sword*.

2. ibid, pp. 193–4.

3. See Nakamura Hajime, op. cit., p. 407 ff.

long since ceased to be a prime social value in the West. A film which shows what hard training it takes to become a worthy warrior for the Emperor stimulated the Japanese sense of the primacy of the social ties.

Judging by the films of the Chinese and Pacific Wars which I have seen (and I have reason to believe they are typical), the approach to representation already described as dominant in its essential features throughout the 1930s, provided the appropriate vehicle for this very specific message of morale-building propaganda. Benedict's view of these films as radically different from 'our' war films is due in large part to the fact that the Hollywood codes were still only perfunctorily and superficially assimilated. It was still felt that the most appropriate presentation of contemporary action (these films are *gendai-geki*, after all) was *a*-centric both visually and in terms of narrative structure: the persona-producing codes of narrative and the linearization of the visual signifier remained foreign.

Universally recognized as the master of the genre, Tasaka Tomotaka's films are nonetheless not unique, as a random sampling of other films of the period has enabled me to judge.[4] His best-known titles, *Five Scouts* (*Gonin no sekkohei*, 1938) and *Earth and Soldiers* (*Tsuchi to heitai*, 1939), were both shot in Manchuria on the scene of the actual battles, though apparently reconstructed with actors throughout. Although no 'better' from the point of view of the film-appreciation classroom than, say, Thorold Dickinson's *Next of Kin*, they so closely resemble certain films produced in the West at the height of the pacifist movement (e.g. *Westfront 1918*) and are nevertheless such radical examples of the dominant modes of the 1930s in Japan that they are worth brief consideration.

Both films begin with long battle sequences, in which combat is seen exactly as in the newsreels. There are innumerable long shots, incomprehensible explosions, anonymous tiny figures dashing about or flopping down in the tall grass, an occasional shot so smoke-filled as to be unreadable, etc. In *Five Scouts* this initial battle, nearly ten minutes long, is followed by interminable scenes of life in a fort; we move from one group to another, witness trivial events, such as a watermelon being cut up and shared, stare endlessly at men lying about, cooking chow, etc. At night, a dimly-seen truck pulls away with the wounded, the last soldiers leave the shot and while we perceive only the high ramparts against the night sky, an unseen soldier plays a mournful tune on a reed instrument. Finally, the 'action' gets under way: five volunteers are chosen to scout the

IRON TREES, GOLDEN FLOWERS

Figs. 34, 35. Tasaka Tomotaka, *Five Scouts*

4. Yoshimura Kimisaburo's *The Story of Tank-Commander Nishizumi* (*Nishizumi senshachōden*, 1940); Tomagaya Hisatura's *Shanghai Report* (*Shanghai rikusentai*, 1939); Yamamoto Kajiro's *The War at Sea off Hawaii and Malaya* (*Hawai-Marei oki kaisen*, 1942). These last two films use newsreel footage in a way which greatly heightens the depersonalization.

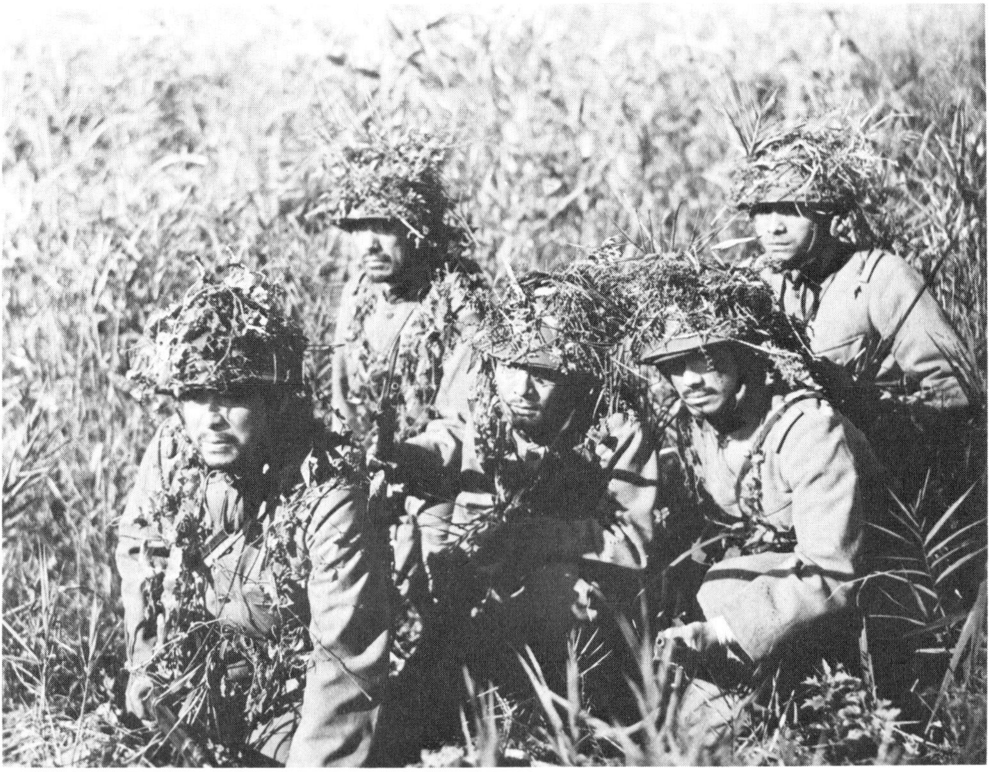

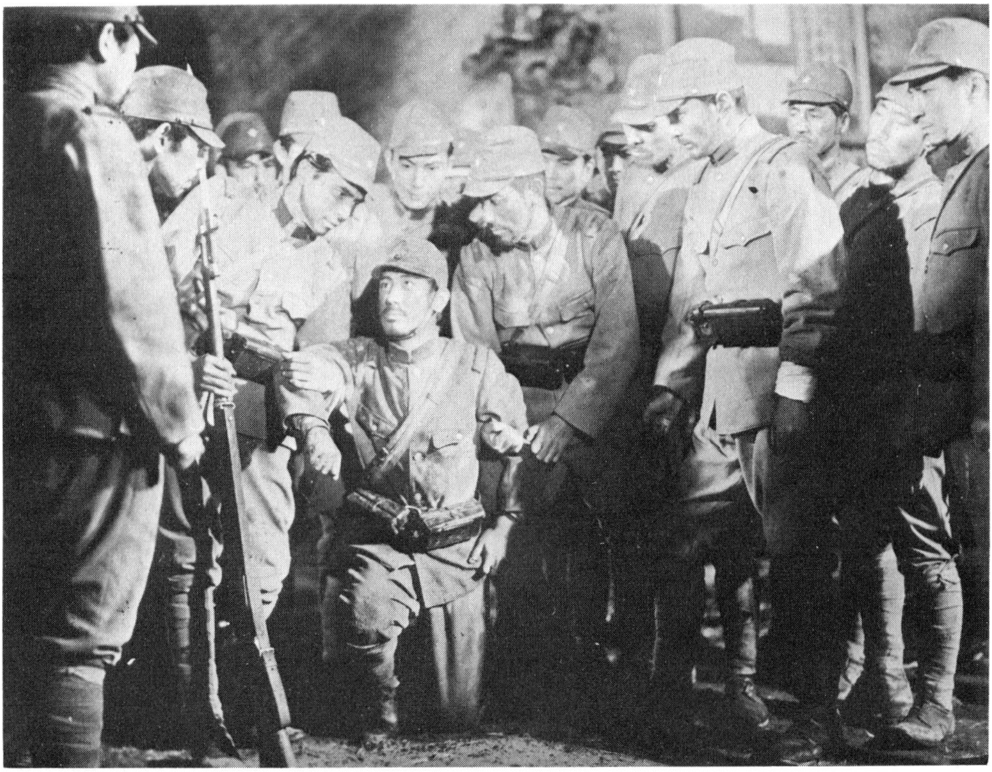

IRON TREES,
GOLDEN FLOWERS

enemy positions: for minutes on end they run through the tall grass, wade along a shallow stream, creep through more grass. Finally they glimpse the Chinese outposts at a distance and observe them through binoculars. As they are about to withdraw, they are spotted and a totally obscure skirmish takes place: seen through the slot of a pill-box, with the blazing muzzle of a machine-gun in the near foreground, the five scouts, tiny figures in the distance, dash one by one across the field of fire and somehow survive. A scout reaches the stream, hides in the tall reeds while two enemy soldiers pass. He suddenly jabs his bayonet into the reeds behind him and dashes off in the opposite direction: at the very bottom of the frame, a Chinese corpse floats by. Fade out. Back at the fort, the long wait has begun – again scenes of barracks life and its daily humdrum. When hope has all but been abandoned, one of the five staggers in, stands stiffly to attention as he barks out his report, then collapses into the arms of a dozen sympathizing companions. And the same scene is repeated almost identically three times over as one by one the scouts stagger in, report and collapse. Number five is so long in appearing that he really is given up for dead, yet ultimately he too, somewhat more the worse for wear than his fellows, returns dramatically in a driving rain-storm, makes *his* report and collapses. This last and unexpected return from the dead is cause for much tense embarrassment, gratitude and tears. Finally, there is another asssembly with an interminable speech by the commanding officer (speeches of this sort are obligatory in all these films) and the regiment marches off to battle, singing one of those melancholic Japanese warsongs.

Figs. 36, 37. Tasaka Tomotaka, *Earth and Soldiers*

It is impossible to convey in a summary the austerity of such a film, the complete lack of characterization, of 'centering', stressed by both diegetic substance and *découpage*. The thrilling, 'athletic' image of war so richly fantasized in Hollywood propaganda films is totally absent here.

*Earth and Soldiers* is, if anything, even more austere. It consists primarily of a single seven-reel battle, again shot with almost no close-ups – we are dealing with a collective hero surpassing even those of the Soviet silent cinema – and one long sequence is almost entirely focused on the *material* destruction, tile by tile, stone by stone, of a farm-house in which invisible Chinese soldiers are entrenched. The only graphic suggestion (in either of these films) that the soldiers have homes, families, etc., is a silent mood piece with musical accompaniment in which a veteran sits alone by what must have been a rather pretty lily-pond before the tanks came and, taking out his wallet, looks at a picture of his wife and children. Although this actor is recognizable

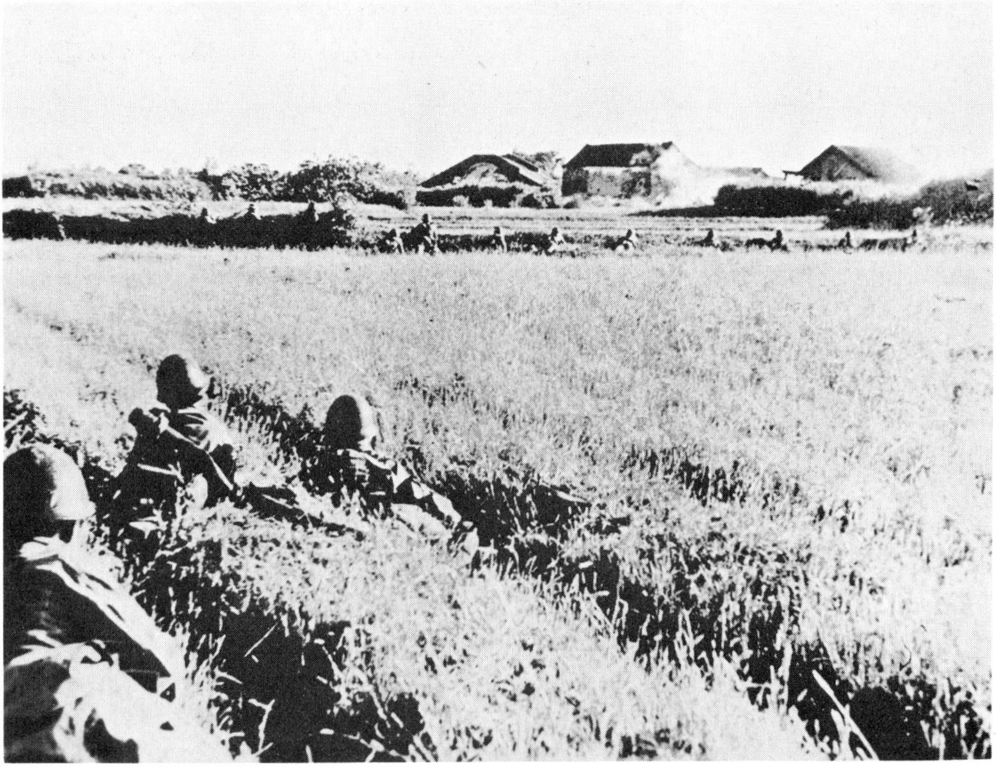

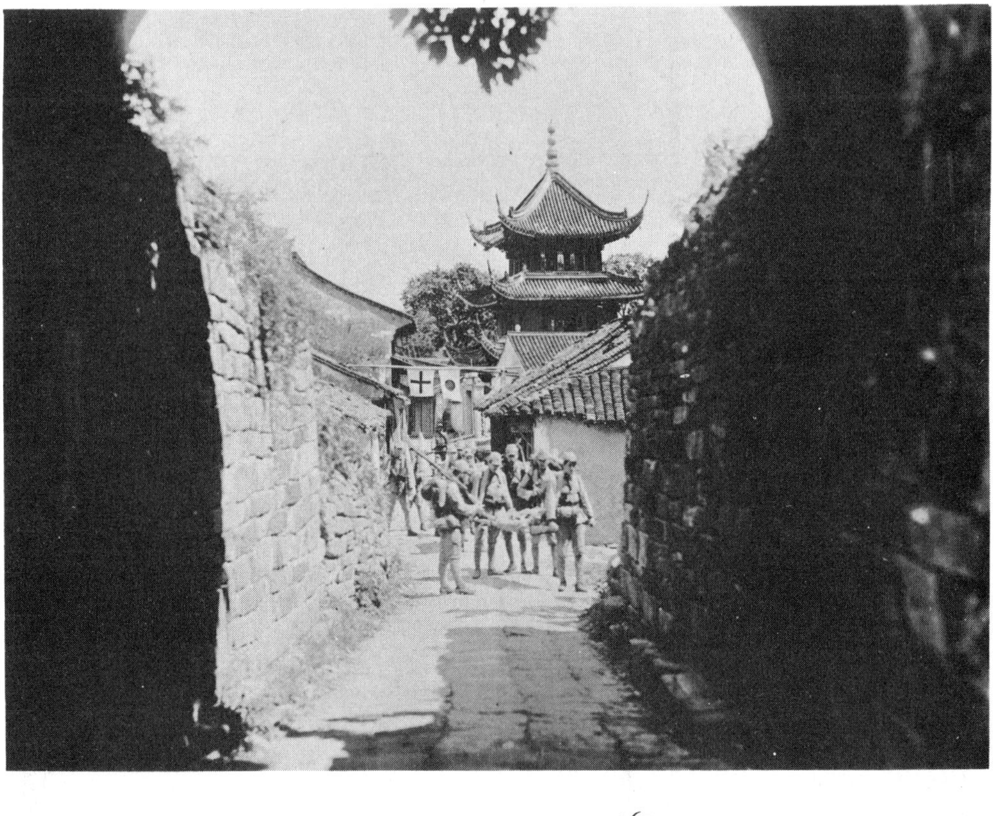

Fig. 38. Tasaka Tomotaka, *Earth and Soldiers*

again from time to time during the battle that ensues, he is in no sense the hero of the film or even its protagonist, and of course there is no question of any of his actions deciding the outcome of the battle. In contrast with this 'realism', it is not surprising to observe that death is a very quick, clean event, never accompanied by spectacular suffering or blood: in *Earth and Soldiers*, a soldier running through a field of tall grass is followed in a rapid pan (camera movement is, as one might imagine, very freely used in these films): the soldier suddenly disappears into the sea of grass leaving a shot so empty and so suddenly still that it is as if it had never been occupied by a human presence. Another soldier, fatally wounded, is immediately surrounded by a crowd of his buddies, so that only his very restrained dying words are allowed to signify his death-throes.

These films are not entirely devoid of pathos, but the dramatic emphasis is placed not on the soldier's heroic generosity, but on the tragic absurdities of the situation. The scene in *Earth and Soldiers* in which a soldier strives to save a Chinese baby's life is reminiscent of a similar incident in Isaac Babel's collection of short stories, *Red Cavalry*. And in fact, if these films have any literary parallel in the West, it is Babel's vitriolic accounts of his experiences in the Russian Civil War.

**EPILOGUE TO A GOLDEN AGE**

The importance of these war films, from the sole point of view of the development of Japanese modes of filmic representation, should not be overstressed, since they are so completely determined by socio-historical factors. It is nevertheless instructive to observe the extent to which the mode perfected during the previous period of political and ideological reinforcement of the traditional values, was directly compatible with the requirements of propaganda in a wartime situation. This is another aspect of a complex dialectical process, involving more than one uncomfortable contradiction.

# Part 5 A Chain is Broken

# 23. Film and 'Democracy'

In 1862, a decade after Commodore Perry, in the name of Western mercantile imperialism, had forced the gates of secluded Japan and five years before the political upheaval which was to enable her, in less than a century, to join the ranks of modern capitalist nations, an emissary from an English ship was murdered by samurai of the Shimazu clan. Failing to obtain satisfaction by other means, the British ordered their warships to bombard the port of Kagoshima, virtually razing part of the city. It is one of the significant paradoxes of that transitional period that this bombardment so impressed the inhabitants of Kagoshima that they immediately established close commercial and cultural ties with Great Britain, ties which lasted for decades thereafter.

Significant though this episode may seem in the light of more recent history, it would be patently over-reductive to see it as a model for the alacrity with which the Japanese people, following their defeat by the United States and their allies, not only accepted and collaborated wholeheartedly with the occupying forces, but seemed to adopt a 'way of life' which had, by the test of war, been proven, in the eyes of this supremely pragmatic people, conclusively superior to their own.

Kawai Kazuo, a journalist who has dealt intelligently with this period,[1] from the point of view of the ruling class, is himself an example of the drive to assimilate things American. He was schooled in the United States and was for a time editor-in-chief of Japanese capitalism's most successful English-language newspaper, *The Japan Times*. In his book, he invokes a dozen interrelated factors to explain the immediate sympathy of the Japanese people towards the presence and policies of the American authorities during the seven years of occupation.

The Japanese people's 'inordinate respect for authority' and their 'susceptibility to new ideas', perhaps the most widely accepted 'causes', he regards as partly true but not really adequate as explanations. He stresses instead the combined trauma and catharsis of Japan's total defeat and,

1. Kawai Kazuo, *Japan's American Interlude*.

above all, the fact that it was unexpected. The occupation caught the Japanese at a time when they were groggy, so to speak, and ready to be pushed in any direction. And the first push was bound to be decisive: 'Once they had turned to co-operation, moreover, it was furthered by the ingrained habit of always playing according to the rules of the game.'[2] This basic cultural inclination is seen as aided by secondary factors such as an historical sympathy with the United States, a 'strong sense of hierarchy', a 'warmly emotional nature', a natural 'inferiority complex' and that native pragmatism: they were 'realistic enough to see that co-operation with the Occupation was the only practicable course open to them.' All these explanations are summed up for Kawai in the national propensity to conform. He does, however, give one further explanation. It is, in his view, of limited importance, since he applies it only to 'vested interests' (i.e. class interests) but it is of great significance to us in our examination of the rapidly developing tendencies that were to dominate the cinema in post-war Japan:

Many Japanese were also attracted to the Occupation program because of their long-felt desires ... When it was seen that the Occupation program sought to restore and extend the trends which had existed in the 1920s, it naturally appealed to the Japanese elements which had supported them. While some of the Occupation measures represented a forcible imposition of alien ideas which the Japanese did not welcome, enough of the Occupation's program coincided with desirable indigenous trends to enable it to ride the wave of a substantial popular native support.[3]

And, of course, these 'Japanese elements' to whom the reforms of the Occupation appealed were, in addition to the peasantry who benefited at last by a true land reform, the two fundamentally antagonistic classes at this stage of the country's history: labour and *capital*. It must be borne in mind that although the mores and structures of a lingering feudalism favoured the exploitation of labour by Japanese capitalism in its early stages, they had also impeded the development of the forces of production and hence the growth of capitalism itself. At the same time, the overnight creation of a liberal system tailored on the American model entailed sudden, huge gains for the Japanese working class, since parliamentary democracy, trade unions, social security of a kind and state-ownership of service industries are essential to the development of the last stage of capitalism, the state-monopoly form. And while Japan's first democratic land-reform cannot really be regarded as a step towards advanced capitalism, it did at last give small peasants ownership of the land which they

2. ibid, p. 4ff.

3. ibid, p. 9.

## EPILOGUE TO A GOLDEN AGE

worked and was therefore experienced as an unhoped-for boon by a class which had traditionally been the 'revolutionary' class in Japan. However, this measure actually neutralized the peasants for only about two decades.

The sudden intensification of class struggle arising from these contradictions may be seen as the principal cause of the mutations in Japanese film production at that time.

One further historical analogy may be of help to us as we begin our investigation. We have already seen how linear perspective began, in the eighteenth century, to appear in the prints of *ukiyo-e*. This was due partly to European influence, for the Portuguese missionaries, in particular, had taught their students the techniques of perspective, and, even after their expulsion, European paintings entered Japan via the Dutch settlement on Deshima. Another factor was the need for self-representation typical of the rising merchant class. However, an additional reason, not as yet touched upon here, is of primary importance. Shiba Kōkan (1737–1818), a painter and writer of considerable eminence among the 'forebears of Meiji',

> was not really interested in Asiatic art and he wrote an essay on Western painting in which he argues that it was most useful and very superior to Chinese and Japanese painting, because it portrays light and shade, the shapes of solids, and their perspective. It is most valuable, he remarks, for illustrating in books things that cannot be explained in words. Far Eastern painting, on the other hand, is just something to amuse people at drinking parties. . . . In European painting what pleased him most was its representational side, which he called *shashin*, or 'copying truth', using the Japanese word that now stands for photography.[4]

Of course, what Shiba had discovered was that fundamental correspondence of which Leonardo, as Panofsky has pointed out, was one of the first to be aware:

> Among the qualities required of the anatomist, Leonardo mentions not only a strong stomach . . . but also . . . competent draftsmanship – and a mastery of perspective. This requirement of 'perspective', though it may at first surprise the modern reader, provides sudden insight that anatomy, as a science (and this is true of all the other sciences of observation or description), was quite simply impracticable without a method for recording the details observed, without a complete and accurate three-dimensional drawing.[5]

Although the doctrine of painting as a window on the world and the classical 'tableau' conception of the descriptive sciences were challenged in the nineteenth century, the notion of representation as transparent to perceptible reality remained the ideal of the bourgeoisie of the West. The

---

4. Sansom, G. B., *The Western World and Japan*, pp. 232–3.

5. Panofsky, Erwin, *L'Oeuvre d'art et ses significations*, pp. 117–18. Panofsky goes on to suggest that three great eras of scientific history were inaugurated respectively by the codification of perspective, by the inventions of telescope and microscope, and by the development of photography. Shiba's neologism *shashin* seems to summarize this analysis.

greater part of its art and literature were informed by this notion until photography and ultimately cinema were able gradually to assume the burden of representation and 'liberated' the other arts to some degree.

Shiba Kōkan was one of that far-sighted group of intellectuals who saw that unless Japan consented to relive at top speed not only the Renaissance, but the Enlightenment and the Industrial Revolution as well, she would perish as a free nation. Although presumably Hiroshige and Hokusai could not have explicitly provided this sophisticated rationale, the appearance of elements of linear perspective in their work parallels the actions of those clan leaders who had begun, several years before Perry's Black Ships appeared on the horizon, to smelt ore for cannon.

We may, in the light of the foregoing observations, conclude that beyond the various cultural and historical conditions operative in the striking changes that occurred in the Japanese cinema after 1945, the determining factor was the spectacular intensification and historical development of class struggle, economically, politically and ideologically. Certainly, the objectively progressive forces in the country (and these were, at this stage, principally labour and capital) required proven instruments to further their respective ideological struggles. These instruments were supplied by a system of representation which had long been geared to the needs of that liberal monopoly capitalism toward which Japan was developing. What could better favour the implantation of such a system than a benevolent Occupation by that cultural power which had been most instrumental in developing, disseminating and consolidating it on a world-wide scale?

No directives were ever issued, to my knowledge, from SCAP[6] to the film industry on 'the language of democratic films', although the manifest, diegetic substance of films was naturally subjected to strict censorship.[7]

We have seen that in the 'liberal 1920s', once the contradictions of capitalism were allowed to develop, however modestly, the need was felt by capitalist entrepreneurs to make 'Western-style' films. (This had been the origin of Shochiku as a film trust.) At the same time, liberal film artists also adopted the modes and codes of Western 'realism' in the *koku-eiga* ('tendency film') of the late 1920s and early 1930s. For, precisely because these codes are eminently suited to the propagation of the themes of liberal, 'democratic' ideology, the inherent autonomy of the individual, the natural universality of capitalist economic laws, the inevitable objectivity of 'free' media, etc., they may also articulate corresponding demands formulated in the struggle of the working class and its eventual allies. In this

---

6. The 'Allied' occupation authority.

7. Often carried to ludicrous but revealing extremes: Earle Ernst (op.cit., p. 260) tells of the censor's demanding the addition of a climactic kissing scene in a film felt to be too respectful of 'feudal formality'. The kiss has never occupied in Japanese socio-erotic etiquette the place it holds in the West, and its almost total absence from the screen, at least up to that time, was one more sign of the extent to which the Japanese cinema remained closed to the Hollywood system.

post-Pacific War period, Japan was still in an early stage of parliamentary democracy, of trade-union struggle, etc. At such a point in history, militancy classically exploits the contradictions of liberalism in order to better improve the conditions of workers and of the poor in general. And the demands formulated, whatever their historical and materialist implications, are necessarily couched in the language of liberalism: individual freedom . . . *from exploitation*, freedom of the media . . . *from capitalist manipulation*, etc. It was, therefore, almost inevitable that films reflecting or participating in the struggle of the mass organizations should whole-heartedly adopt the representational systems developed by Western capitalism and now in the service of the Japanese ruling class.

This dialectical aspect of the development of cinema in Japan during the Occupation is reflected in the attitudes of the censorship committee set up by the American authorities. It supervised all film-making from the pre-production stage to that of distribution. There was a ludicrously severe ban on period films, which were seen as vehicles of 'feudal thought'. While this ban was relaxed fairly soon – we have seen that as early as 1946 Mizoguchi obtained the first dispensation for his *Utamaro* – subjects of particular interest to the Left, such as the truth about Hiroshima and Nagasaki, remained absolutely taboo until the end of the Occupation, in 1952. While films of the newly dominant ideology were generally untouched by this American censorship, the propaganda efforts of the Communist Party and other progressive organizations were, of course, hampered.

It is significant of this contradictory situation that the bulk of films produced in Japan at this time bore traces of multiple determination. Except for the films produced by the Communist Party or other progressive forces, or films such as Ito Daisuke's Horatio Alger-like portrait of a chess champion (see below), almost any film produced during that period reveals, at the diegetic level, traces of a double class determination. On the level of both signified and signifier they reveal, as well, traces of a specifically Japanese cultural determination. This, as we have seen, derives from the traditional systems of thought and representation which, of course, continue to thrive at certain levels of Japanese social practice up to this very day.

These traces are, of course, especially noticeable in the work of the pre-war masters and near-masters who continued making films during this period – and all who were still alive seem to have done so. As I have already suggested, Ozu's, Naruse's and Mizoguchi's respective compromises with the new situation were quite different. They represent fairly well, albeit on a higher plane of achievement, the reactions of a whole generation of directors.

Mizoguchi, as we have seen, quickly adapted his representational system (radical camera distance, long takes, dolly movements) to the exigencies of the Hollywood codes. Moreover, simply by remaining faithful to what seems to have been his quasi-obsessive preoccupation with prostitutes and, more generally, with women in a situation of repression/revolt, his films also met with the new liberal prescriptions. This holds true for all the modern-dress films, from *Women of the Night* (*Yoru no onnatachi*, 1948) to his very last film, *Red Light District* (*Akasen chitai*, 1956),[8] and also for most of the period films, since the painter Utamaro, the lovers of *A Story by Chikamatsu* and the 'sacrilegious hero' of *New tales of the Taira Clan* (*Shin Heike monogatari*, 1953) are very clearly individuals struggling to assert their *natural freedom*. This was a theme present in Mizoguchi's pre-war work as well, but in these post-war films we witness a displacement. In traditional Japanese attitudes, the ultimately tragic figure was the individual caught between conflicting duties – usually between society and family, but also, often enough, between these and one's own emotions, since sexual passion had a very respectable social status. There is nevertheless a fundamental distinction between the generalized dilemma of Mizoguchi's forty-seven *rōnin* and the very personalized heroism of the principal character in the Heike tales. Omocha's final cry of revolt was a dying echo of the 'tendency film', with its awareness of social oppression, as against the stoic abnegation of the heroine of *Tale of Late Chrysanthemums*, more consonant with a war-geared revival of a 'feudal' ideology of class collaboration. Both contrast sharply, however, with the pessimistic individualism of the post-war films. Mizoguchi's ideological plasticity was no doubt even clearer in the (presumably lost) films made as out and out apologies for Japan's aggressive foreign policies. They might well help to explain his later development, his adoption of an academically decorative, opportunistic approach to *découpage*, contrived by laying certain traits of his earlier system over the framework of the Hollywood codes. It is said that the return to the spectacularly long take in *The Life of a Woman, by Saikaku* was stimulated by his having seen films of William Wyler (perhaps *The Little Foxes* or *The Best Years of Our Lives*) and wanting to prove he could do better.

Naruse Mikio had, as we have seen, long since abandoned the rigour of *Wife, Be Like a Rose*, and the difficulties which he seems to have experienced during the early years of the Occupation presumably were still related to the

8. Called *Street of Shame* abroad.

personal crisis which he had gone through during the war. *Mother* (*Okasan*, 1953), based on an essay by a schoolchild, *Floating Clouds* (*Ukigumo*, 1955), about the waning fortunes of a small geisha house, and indeed nearly all of Naruse's later productions are characteristically 'underdramatized' portrayals of modern life, so specifically Japanese, so opposed to Mizoguchi's conflict universe, and of which the cinematic prototype remains the *shōmin-geki* of the 1930s. However, these films all cleaved as closely to the Western mode of representation as had the films of Gosho or Shimazu.

It is Ozu, of course, who may be said to have remained, among all the veterans active in this period, most faithful not only to the themes and 'world' of his mature period, but to the system of representation developed at that time. However, despite the admiration which late Ozu – admittedly all that is currently available in the West – has aroused among the cultural élite of England and the United States, the great master's post-war work is in fact the history of a gradual fossilization. True, all the attitudes which so vitally informed the first version of *A Story of Floating Weeds*[9] and *Only Son* remained constantly present up to the very end: 'pillow-shots', unmoving, low-level camera set-ups, frontality and even the 'incorrect' eyeline matching. The eyelines, however, gradually come to be so close to the lens that it takes a very attentive observer to detect the 'error'. It is true that this strongly reinforced what was henceforth to be the dominant element in the systemics: the basic strategy of frontality. Nonetheless, this evolution is symptomatic. For just as this faint trace of unorthodox matching no longer significantly disrupts the production of transparency/continuity, so too the pillow-shots have become brief, perfunctory transitions with none of the radically suspensive quality or complex structural developments of the earlier films. Still much in evidence are the flat frontality of the image and the complementary surface flatness of the narrative. In the mature work, however, these traits entertained a dialectical relationship with the disjunctive matching and pillow-shot hiatuses; once these have been reduced to the status of perfunctory titles, imagery and diegesis become at best endless reiterations of a cultural constant, at worst a senile mannerism. Considering the many counts on which Ozu's work as a whole is related to the 'general text' of Japanese cinema, I am tempted to compare this final fossilization with the pattern by which the great schools of classical painting and poetry became devitalized: despite, or rather *because* of the specifically Japanese sensitivity to infinitely subtle variation within a narrow framework, a given form, a given genre, soon works itself out (in every

FILM AND 'DEMOCRACY'

9. It is a symptom of both his persistent thematic preoccupations and also of his belonging to a culture in which no onus is placed on self-quotation, that at least two of his later films, *Floating Weeds* (*Ukigusa*) and *Good Morning* (*Ohayō*), both of 1959, should have been remakes of silent films. However, this instance of 'allusive variation', though certainly not dictated by commercial motives as is habitual in the Western remake, only serves to point up the sheer exhaustion of the later years, when the only dynamic left in the films was their thematic obsession.

sense) and is thenceforth destined to be repeated endlessly in a final, frozen form through the ages, a prefabricated toy for the amusement and edification of the dilettante.

In all fairness, however, it should be pointed out that this decline, besides being gradual, was not entirely linear. *Record of a Tenement Gentleman* (*Nagaya shinshi roku*, 1948), Ozu's first film since *There Was a Father*, still makes interesting use of the pillow-shot (as in the sitting at the photographer's, with the black screen 'representing' the period of processing of the photo). This film has, as well, a remarkable sea-shore scene, unique in his work. *Good Morning* and *Autumn in the Kobayakawa Family* (*Kobayakawa-ke no aki*, 1961),[10] two of his very last works, are again faintly reminiscent of the pre-war masterpieces through an occasionally inventive use of the old systemics.

Younger Japanese critics and intellectuals have sometimes asked me why Westerners (particularly in the United States and England, where these films have been widely shown) have such a keen admiration for Ozu's late films, an admiration which they most often do not share. One element of reply surely is that these films depicting the most banal scenes of everyday life, respond to an ideological valuing of 'realism' among the cultivated strata of Anglo-American society. It is, after all, possible to see these films as the closest of all cinematic facsimiles to 'life itself', as an example of mimesis unprecedented in the West. And the academic 'transparency' of representation – which, given other cultural keys, will occasionally be perceived, in the films of Hollywood, for example, for the ideological manipulation which it so often is – allows for a very familiar fascination with these exotic products. In contrast, the overtly active formal organization of the most mature films of the 1930s is a perturbing factor; those 'images of the real' are too highly informed with artifice to permit a comfortably 'realist' reading. In some respects, one might say that the repression (in the West) of the best of Ozu (and Mizoguchi) is not unrelated to the repression for so many years of Vertov's *Man With a Movie Camera* and Eisenstein's *Strike*. In both these films, the ideologically determined definition of a certain type of image as 'documentary' is actually subverted by a Brechtian acknowledgement of artifice.

The Western ideology of realism came to Japan with the industrial revolution and, significantly enough, it was in the name of realism that the progressive post-war generation rejected the work of Ozu as a whole and in fact all of Japanese 'traditional' cinema. I have suggested that the wholesale adoption of our dominant mode of representation in Japan corresponded to a rise in the level of class

10. Shown in the West as *Early Autumn*.

struggle there. This was, in turn, a direct response to the 'social engineering' undertaken by the Americans and aimed at fitting Japan into the concert of the capitalist nations in preparation for the great confrontation with the socialist world. I have suggested, too, that to a large extent both the bourgeoisie and the growing proletarian forces needed the Western codes to develop their ideological campaigns, *considering the nature of the newly dominant ideology*. Serious attempts were made by critics committed to left political positions (and particularly by Marxists) to provide a rationale for the rejection by whole segments of the population (and, therefore, by so many directors) of the modes of representation which they saw very clearly as those of a specifically national, traditional cinema. The most remarkable critique of the pre-war generation which I have encountered was published in 1950 by Imamura Taihei.[11] An understanding of the situation of Japanese cinema during and after the Occupation demands careful attention to the ideas of this excellent critic.

Imamura's key concepts are inevitably borrowed from Western thought. His critique is addressed, first and foremost, to the Japanese 'mentality', *accused of lacking precisely those concepts*. The circularity of his argument provides the key to an eventual critique of this critique. For the Japanese, says Imamura, 'thinking is not distinct from intuition nor is a phenomenon distinct from its essence. Thinking flows along with the stream of phenomena. An object is not analytically reconstructed by thinking but is described as it appears. The essence is never explored'. Now a critique of the social order from a viewpoint which recognizes class struggle as the motor of history cannot be made in phenomenological terms alone. Seen from the new stage of class struggle in the Japan of the late 1940s, traditional forms and attitudes could only seem 'negative' and 'passive'. And Imamura sees a remarkable instance of such passivity towards the real in the cinema of Ozu and most particularly in what I have called the master's 'pillow-shots', seen here as 'an escape from society into nature, and from character descriptions of events and people into descriptions of natural scenes.' Imamura perceives quite well the extra-diegetic, suspensive quality of the pillow-shot, which 'does not contribute to the development of the plot; it stops it.' This, of course, is precisely what Imamura condemns, and it is in his condemnation that we find a spontaneous theoretical designation of the very real need that is satisfied, at a certain stage of class struggle, by the representational tools of the bourgeoisie.

If conflict in drama is the reflection of social conditions, the

11. 'The Japanese Spirit as it Appears in the Movies', in *Japanese Popular Culture* ed. Kato Hidegoshi, p. 137f.

attitude which I am discussing is one which refuses to clarify the contradictions, i.e. the nature of the object. So Mr Ozu's descriptions of the environment are always static and on the fence. In his movies, society is observed indirectly through nature. Capitalist society is portrayed by such scenes as a gas tank on an uncultivated field, a small junk on a dirty canal, or a baby's diaper drying in a back alley. Society is seen only from a distance, as a natural scene, and people are but accessories.

This last remark is presumably addressed to that use of camera distance which characterizes indigenous Japanese cinema as a whole. The assertion that 'capitalist society is portrayed by ... a gas tank on an uncultivated field' is predicated on an assumption made by so many observers, both Japanese and occidental, with respect not only to Ozu's cinema but to Japanese poetry, painting, etc. 'Symbolism' in Japanese art is assumed to function according to the Western model. Imamura is much closer to a modern European viewpoint when he observes that the pillow-shot (which he calls 'natural scene') 'is not an element of the drama but an element which opposes the drama.' Japan, however, was a society in which ideological domination had never before been associated with, expressed by, or founded upon notions such as the linearity of the signifying process or the transparency of the sign. The usefulness of a concept such as the suspension of the production of meaning was therefore not likely to be evident to someone bent upon forging tools to combat capitalist domination over a society and a culture wherein the critique of representation is historically irrelevant. Irrelevant precisely to the extent that the theoretical tools which have made possible a critique of our dominant systems of representation were forged by a philosophical and scientific tradition made possible by such concepts as the transparency of the sign.

Imamura's position is perfectly tenable as far as it goes, and it goes precisely as far as it was possible and necessary for a Japanese Marxist theoretician to go in 1950. 'This [traditional] way of thinking remains attractive to the Japanese, insofar as the social oppression which produced this attitude continues to exist.' This phrase, however, indicates the theoretical limits within which Imamura was operating. It is characteristic of a 'vulgar Marxism', scarcely challenged in Japan even today, which to us appears oblivious of certain contradictions between the modes of economic and political domination on the one hand and such superstructural products as culture or ideology. In other words it regards the past as 'all bad' except insofar as the development of the forces of production made possible the objective progress of science and industry. (Needless to say, this

vulgar Marxism is by no means unknown in the West.)
Imamura takes issue with the traditionally Japanese (it is Buddhist, but not merely Buddhist) tendency to situate man *in* rather than *above* nature, to consider the life process as a continual interchange between man and his artefacts, man and the rest of the material world. Yet, stated in this way, and it is legitimate to do so, this traditional attitude clearly corresponds to the Marxist critique, initiated by Engels in the *Dialectics of Nature*, of that Western anthropocentrism, that Christian humanism which has been one of the mainstays of bourgeois ideology . . . and which is also a distinguishing feature of 'vulgar Marxism' so common in Japan even today, and of which Imamura's article was a relatively sophisticated example.

In the late 1940s, Japan was still classified by the United Nations as an 'underdeveloped country', and the stage of liberal democracy had only just begun. It was to be expected that the 'feudal past' should be rejected *in toto* by progressive social forces, especially since that other objectively progressive force, the bourgeoisie, was already making good use of the hierarchical structures inherited from traditional society. It is now becoming apparent, not only from a European point of view, that a wholesale rejection of the cultural and perhaps even ideological acquisitions of Japanese history is tantamount, in a Marxist perspective, to throwing out the baby with the bath-water.

As I have implied, Imamura's attitude towards Ozu is not simply the iconoclasm of one radical critic. It reflects the concerns of a whole generation of left-oriented film-makers whose work may not constitute a notable contribution to cinema as an art form, but whose role in the crystallization of social protest in post-war and post-Occupation Japan is far from negligible.

It is not my purpose to write the history of ideologies in post-war Japan, and for me any close reading of the films of this period as a whole could only be that. Hence my intention to cover these fifteen years in two chapters only. However, I do wish to sketch out a *tableau* of the dominant contents and styles of the 1940s and 1950s in order to provide some indication of the context in which Kurosawa Akira, the sole true master of this period, worked out his lone achievement. It is also important for us to have some understanding of a period that set the scene for the remarkable independent cinema of the 1960s and early 1970s, which constituted Japan's 'new wave'.

If we take as a starting point for our *tableau* the crude but useful distinction between films which served and films which contested bourgeois interests, we may say that on the *right* we have two principal categories: dramas of conflict in the Western style, and aestheticizations, in terms compatible with the Western codes, of traditional material. After the success of Kurosawa's *Rashōmon* abroad, these were often conceived as prestige films for export. Most of the films which Kinugasa made during this period – from *The Actress* (*Joyu*, 1947) to *The White Heron* (*Shirasagi*, 1958) and including of course the famous *The Gate of Hell* (*Jigoku-mon*, 1953) – are of this latter type. The tradition was to be carried over into the 1960s by, for example, Kobayashi Masaki, with *Hara-kiri* (*Seppuku*, 1963), *Kwaidan* (1964) etc.

As for the first category, I have already mentioned briefly the veteran Ito Daisuke's *The Chess Master* (*Oshō*, 1947), an instance of capitalist ideology dramatized. The film is a masterpiece of its kind. Splendidly acted by the great star of silent films Bando Tsumasuboro, whose eccentric, dynamic style prefigures that of Mifune Toshiro in the later films of Kurosawa, it tells of the rise from rags to riches of a famous Taisho master of a sophisticated board-game called *shōgi*. The film was shot entirely in studio, and boasts elaborate, atmospheric street-settings in the spirit of the 'poetic realism' of the French 1930s and 1940s, a style very much in favour, it seems, among film-makers of all persuasions in this period. The final shot, in which the ageing master Sakuta has returned to the Osaka slum street where he lived in poverty at the beginning of the film, and stands gazing through the fog at a great electrically lit tower in the distance, while urchins are playing *shōgi* in the foreground, is a double emblem of faith in the future of industial capitalism and of democracy, a faith so essential to the ideological edifice being hastily built during those difficult years.

The most militant films with a *left* viewpoint made during this period are probably those which looked back over recent times and examined aspects of Japanese history which film-makers had previously been forbidden to treat, by Japanese censors of the 1930s and early 1940s, then by the American censors of the Occupation. A celebrated example is Yamamura So's first film, *The Crab-Canning Ship* (*Kanikosen*, 1953). Actually, this film provides an encounter, rare and interesting for this period, of one aspect of Japan's 'traditional' cinema with an historical materialist representation of class struggle. The film tells of the savage exploitation to which workers on the crab-fishing and canning ships in the northern seas were subjected during the 1920s. In terms often reminiscent of the great period of Soviet cinema, it depicts the revolt of workers on one of these ships and the bloody repression which ensued. The allusions to Eisensteinian editing (shots of anchor chains, etc.) are stylistically atypical. However, the film cannot be reduced to the 'neo-realist' style so characteristic of the period. Much of it takes place in the workers' sleeping quarters, and here the almost absolute rule is the long shot, centripetally composed (and prefiguring Kurosawa's *The Lower Depths*). Through these 'traditionally' distanced shots, the collective hero of the early Soviet cinema is evoked.

One must also cite Yamamoto Satsuo's violent but rather laborious indictment of military brutalization, *Vacuum Zone* (*Shinku chitai*, 1952), as well as his most highly esteemed film, *The Sunless Street* (*Taiyo no nai machi*, 1954), adapted, like *The Crab-Canning Ship*, from a proletarian novel of the 1920s which tells of a long strike in a printing plant. The most famous name attached to these frankly militant films, undeniable contributions to the struggle of the working class and their allies during that period, was Imai Tadashi, a competent technician and dramatist whose best-known films are *Rice* (*Kome*, 1954) a study of conflict and change in rural areas, and *Shadows in Sunlight (Mahiru no ankoku*, 1956),[12] the autopsy of a miscarriage of justice that was still a *cause célèbre* in Japan when the film was made. The film consitutes a scathing indictment of class justice.

Far more ambitious, stylistically, than any of these films was the eclectic Shindo Kaneto's *Children of the Atom Bomb* (*Genbaku no ko*, 1953). This was the first fictional feature film to reveal the true horrors of Hiroshima and Nagasaki after the American ban on the subject had been lifted with the end of the Occupation. Generally speaking, of course, it is no accident that this militant cinema developed chiefly after 1952. Shindo's film played a considerable role in the campaign which resulted in Japan's solemn renunciation of nuclear weapons. Its grandiloquent lyricism, also reminiscent at times of early Soviet imagery (*Arsenal*), as well as its semi-documentary nature and fragmentary construction, make it one of the most effective films of the period (on a par with Kinoshita's *Japanese Tragedy*). In some ways it even anticipates the films of Oshima and his contemporaries.

The single film which perhaps exemplifies most forcefully the adoption of the Hollywood codes by the progressive Japanese cinema is Kobayashi Masaki's monumental *The Human Condition* (*Ningen no joken*, 1959–61). This film epitomized and ended this whole tendency of Japanese film-making during the 1950s. Its running time of nine consecutive hours makes it probably the longest commercial feature ever made.[13] It typically associates a violent

12. Tendentiously translated in the West as *Darkness at Noon*.

13. The film is actually divided into six hour-and-a-half episodes, but its structure – that of the Tolstoian novel – is such that the ideal viewing is in one sitting.

indictment of militarism (and only incidentally of capitalism) with an extraordinarily graphic illustration of the ideology of humanist individualism. The hero – and rarely in the Japanese cinema had a character better deserved this title – is a personnel expert sent to Manchuria during the Pacific War to help step up the exploitation of Chinese slave-labour. However, his native 'humanist' instincts – he incarnates, of course, the heroic liberals of the 1930s – causes him to rebel against the atrocities around him and he is drafted and subjected for at least eighteen reels to the worst treatment that the particularly inhuman Japanese army of the day could inflict upon a politically suspect recruit. Eventually, however, he becomes a technically skilled soldier and lives through the nightmare of a Russian attack on Japanese positions in China, ultimately to die under a blanket of purifying snow as he attempts to make his way back to his beloved wife.

The film is an almost caricatural assemblage of the *clichés* which in the Western cinema have served for so long to determine meaning (e.g. the Rodin statue, conveniently placed in the centre of a Chinese village square during the amorous discussion between the hero and his future wife early in the film). The brusque introduction, into the first part of the film, of the acting codes of the 'traditional' Chinese cinema only serves to point this up. Of particular interest is the way in which the creation of a central character becomes in this film an overwhelming priority. Indeed, the film is a text on the notion of central character as it has been gradually codified in Western film since the turn of the century. In *The Human Condition* there is only one 'real' person, i.e. a character with psychological 'depth', torn by conflicting emotions, who can really be said to be fully *present* within the diegetic process. As we move 'outward', away from this evident centre of the diegesis, through the concentric circles of the hero's entourage, we find ourselves dealing with characters who are produced less and less as individuals, whose 'humanity' is increasingly 'incomplete'. The hero's wife is little more than a symbol of oppressed Japanese womanhood, his best friends are 'the deluded but basically good tough guy' and the 'brooding, intellectual communist sympathizer'; the company manager is a grotesquely sham humanist, while the sadistic military police and the stubbornly patriotic Chinese are cardboard silhouettes with no problems at all. This film illustrates what Oshima, just two years later,[14] was to denounce as 'the consciousness of being victimized' (by militaristic feudalism and then by American imperialism) and which can be said to characterize not only most of the films of the left during that period, but also its propaganda as a whole.

14. See below, Chapter 25.

15. The original title means both 'the tragedy of Japan' and 'a tragedy in Japan.' It is not insignificant that while the accepted English translation is 'A Japanese Tragedy,' the preference in France should go to 'La Tragédie japonaise'.

Towards the end of the Occupation, a third category develops, distinguishable in theory at least from both these militant films and the pure vehicles of dominant ideology, though often combining in fact traces of both. An excellent example is Kinoshita Keisuke's *The Japanese Tragedy* (*Nihon no higeki*, 1953), which deals with the problems of contemporary Japan 'objectively', i.e. not from any averred class position. The problem dealt with here is the dissolution of the traditional family ties – a mother commits suicide because her grown-up children refuse to support her and display none of the traditional gratitude for the very real hardships which she underwent to rear them during and just after the war. This breakdown of basic social attitudes under the pressure of the new economic conditions and the newly dominant ideology, was indeed a fundamental historical factor.[15] The film situates it in the more general context by newsreel footage and a montage of headlines injected into a quite sophisticated narrative construction, involving unusually abrupt flashbacks. These are 'starkly realistic' in their imagery but stylized to the extent that the dialogue is spoken against absolute silence. Insofar as it is historically oriented, the film is a 'committed' one. However, Kinoshita's approach was to become more and more that of the positivistic sociologist. *Twenty-Four Eyes*

FILM AND 'DEMOCRACY'

Fig. 39. Kinoshita Keisuke, *The Japanese Tragedy*

(*Nijushi no hitomi*, 1954)[16] shows modern Japanese history (1928 to 1946) from the viewpoint of a schoolteacher on a remote island of the archipelago. *She Was Like a Wild Chrysanthemum* (*Nogiku no gotoku kimi narika*, 1955) shows an old man visiting his native village and recalling his youth. Flashbacks are signified by a stylish oval vignette, reminiscent of the tin-type and the silent cinema. *Those Dear Old Flutes and Drums* (*Matsukashiki fue ya taiko*, 1967), though little known outside of Japan, typifies not only Kinoshita's approach but the whole post-war 'slice-of-life' school, of which he has been the undisputed master. It tells the saga of another tiny island school whose proverbially unathletic students are transformed into volley-ball champions by a devoted teacher – and three full reels are devoted to the tournament which climaxes the film.

By now, of course, we have shifted imperceptibly, as we follow Kinoshita's course, into another category, and one which in a sense belongs to the *right* of our *tableau*, since this last film might easily have been scripted and shot during the hey-day of militarism. Indeed, at the centre of its 'slice of life' is the presumably immutable value-system which supports Japanese society and which is here seen to involve the virtues of team spirit, hard work, and keeping fit. Praised and practised by the dominant classes of today as of yesterday, these have effectively kept the country running. The collective callisthenics which so often begin the work-day in Japanese offices and factories are an emblem of this continuity. Of course, such practices and such values are quite legitimate in themselves, and would be perfectly at home under socialism. And it is just this fundamental ambivalence which differentiates such films as this one from, say, *The Chess Master* or . . . *The Human Condition*, each of which sets forth, though from a different class viewpoint, the new ideology of individualism.

Not unrelated to these various gradations of the sociological film as illustrated by Kinoshita is a form of populism which existed before the war, particularly in the *rumpen-mono*, referred to earlier. It is particularly interesting to us because it is the form in which Kurosawa excelled before coming into his own. Basically, it may be said to consist of 'human drama' (in contrast to Kinoshita's mood of decorous understatement) with a lower-class setting. An awareness of the actualities of class struggle in such films is on the level of 'the good little guys' versus 'the bad big guys', but often there is no such awareness demonstrated at all. A fine example, and one which illustrates the contradictions of the period, is Gosho's *Where Chimneys Are Seen* (*Entotsu no mieru basho*, 1953). It is the story of a long married but childless working couple in very modest circumstances

---

16. Literally: 'eyeballs', as the French title, *Vingt-quatre prunelles*, is able to render without incongruity.

whose lives are suddenly invaded by an abandoned child. At first they go to great pains to find the boy's mother and persuade her to take him back, but ultimately they grow attached to the boy and decide to raise him. By now, Gosho had abandoned the unaffected approach which had been his before the war and consequently, also, a certain ambiguity generally characteristic of the Japanese approach to the 'slice of life'. In this film the various stages of narrative progression are marked by an evolving symbolic device, referred to in the title. The industrial zone in which the action takes place lies in the shadow of a cluster of four tall factory chimneys, which can never be comprehended in one glance, or so it is thought at the beginning of the film. At each new stage of the narration, as the couple go about in search of the child's mother, etc. they pointedly discover different vantage points, from which only one, then two, then three, then four chimneys are seen. This redoubling of the process of 'self-discovery' and the subjectivist moral which it 'suggests' to the main character at the end ('Life is whatever you think it is. It can be sweet or bitter, whichever you are') attests to the difficulties and resistances encountered in the abrupt, partly imposed effort to shift from an old, collectively oriented ideology to the new individualism. It also points up the conflict between the need to linearize signification in order to produce such Western concepts at all and the fundamentally antithetical nature of traditional modes. Here, the age-old tendency to surface-patterning makes the chimney symbol curiously obtrusive in an otherwise coded context because, in the strict 'Hollywood' approach, such over-determination of meaning is never produced as a formal system.

We cannot leave this over-view of the post-war period without devoting a few pages to Ichikawa Kon, a director who never developed a systemics comparable to those encountered in the major films of Kurosawa, but who must nevertheless be counted as the finest *stylist* of the period, as the director who in this respect best mastered the codes of the West on their own terms.

Ichikawa, it has already been pointed out, had been assistant to Ishida Tamizo, in particular for *Fallen Blossoms*, and his sensitivity to the stylization of the *découpage* must have been stimulated by this contact. Ichikawa began his film career with animation films and in 1951 made a 'black comedy', *Mr Pu* (*Pu-san*), a satire on the 'new Japanese way of life' as it was developing at the time of the signature of the First Security Pact with the United States. The film which first won him fame in the West, *The Burmese Harp* (*Biruma no tategoto*, 1956), despite an essentially anti-militaristic theme (a fanatical officer refuses to admit Japan's defeat and leads his men to a massacre) is curiously reminiscent of the 'classical' Japanese war-film – and hence quite at odds, it might be added, with films like *The Human Condition*. However, it was apparently not entirely Ichikawa's work, and he is said to have disowned it. The earliest film, to my knowledge, which displays the stylistic mastery of *découpage* which has undeniably earned him a place apart, is *The Heart* (*Kokoro*, 1955).[17] Based on a celebrated novel of the Taisho era by Natsume Soseki, it tells of an educated man obsessed with his own 'egotism' (he has treacherously stolen from his closest friend the woman he loved and thus driven him to suicide). The film demonstrates the renewed relevance of the conflict between individualism and social responsibility, already manifest in the late Meiji period, which is the novel's setting. Ichikawa's sense of the 'through-composition' of the editing/shot set-up relationship, characterized here by minimalizing repeated shots (no doubt an inheritance from Ishida), produces a film of unquestionable dramatic vigour, although the flashback narration, divided into two symmetrical parts – the writing of the main character's suicide letter, the reading of it by a young student who was his only other friend – is laboriously academic.

However, it is between 1958 and 1963, with *Conflagration* (*Enjo*, 1958), *The Key* (*Kagi*, 1959), *Alone on the Pacific* (*Taiheiyō hotoribotchi*, 1963) and *The Avenging Ghost of Yukinojō* (*Yukinojō henge*, 1963),[18] that Ichikawa rose to his greatest heights. His best-known film, *Fires On the Plain* (*Nobi*, 1959), describes the rout of the Japanese army in the Philippines and is certainly one of the most hair-raising 'indictments of war' that has been made, involving wilfully crude representations of cannibalism, coprophagia, etc. But neither these audacities nor the dramatically impressive black-and-white imagery can hide the fact that the Hollywood rhetoric of framing and editing is not only fully present but *amplified*, so that despite the slenderness of plot we are at opposite poles from the non-centred, ambiguous presentations of the traditional war film.

*Enjo* is based on a novel by Mishima Yukio which was in turn inspired by the actual burning of the celebrated Golden Pavilion in Kyoto by a mentally disturbed youth. It is a far more 'original' film, particularly in its use of the black-and-white wide-screen image. It evokes the work of the pre-war masters through its long shots and the prominence of architecture, and also anticipates the graphic extravagances of Yoshida Yoshishige. Its use of traditional Japanese musical timbres in close symbiosis with synch-sound effects, somewhat in the spirit of contemporary Western

17. The French title, *le Pauvre coeur des hommes*, though interpretative, better conveys the connotative dimension of the Japanese title.

18. Shown in the West as *The Actor's Revenge*.

music, is also distinguished. It is not surprising, of course, that the finest stylists of the period – Ichikawa as well as Mizoguchi – should have derived their styles from typical elements of Japanese tradition. However, with Ichikawa, even more than with late Mizoguchi, these elements become, within the Western system and consonant with it, *overwhelmingly significant*. They are a coat of vivid paint which serves to define the connotative space of the diegesis. In short, they are style in the Western sense. In this film, composition involving a strong, Wellesian emphasis on depth of field and oblique angles, the dark contrasty photo, the sparse scattering of notes in musical space, all serve to determine the effect of quotidian eeriness developed by a sophisticated narrative as the boy's neurosis deepens. The comparison with Welles is not without some overall relevance, although Ichikawa's approach is less baroque.

The director's fascination with what even the Japanese would call 'abnormal' psychology is reflected also in his first colour film: an adaptation of Tanizaki's celebrated novel *The Key*. Again using the wide screen, which he was to favour almost exclusively thereafter (as did most Japanese directors – an important point, to be dealt with later), he developed an editing scheme involving great displacements on the screen from shot to shot of easily recognizable objects (at one crucial moment a bright red tin containing poison) and which can best be compared with certain procedures used by Antonioni, as in the opening hospital sequence in *La Notte*. Again, however, the style aims solely at conferring a chic, bizarre quality on this strong tale of an ageing husband who seeks to stimulate his appetite for his young wife by deliberately provoking his own jealousy. It never produces a 'geometrical surplus' as in Kurosawa or any of the various disjunctions of diegesis and signifier found in the films of both the pre-war masters and the 'new wave' of the 1960s and 1970s.

*Alone on the Pacific*, based on the actual adventure of a young Japanese who crossed the Pacific alone in a small craft, is an undeniably brilliant stylistic exercise, which makes good use of matter-of-fact 'distancing' commentary as against the pathos of the imagery. The film remained predominantly an illustration of the individualism which had been an essential theme of his work (and of his period), but this 'Brechtian' tendency was to reach a much higher development in Ichikawa's most important film, *The Avenging Ghost of Yukinojō*. Based on a tale which had already been filmed before the war by Kinugasa with the same star in the title role,[19] it related the misadventures of an *oyama* – a female impersonater both on and *off* the stage, yet who is nonetheless an accomplished swordsman –

19. A comparison of stills from the two films is at times astonishing, for the actor, in his make-up, looks identical at thirty years distance, and some of the sets also look the same. Even the work of an Ichikawa is rooted in a tradition of intertextuality. (The Kinugasa has now been found – see Appendix II – and an interesting comparison is henceforth possible.)

and of his more outwardly virile 'double' (played by the same actor, of course), who is an agile thief. The lusty, quasi-Elizabethan humour of the film, 'distancing' in itself, is subjected to an even further shift by a curiously omnipresent score of mainstream jazz. Moreover, the diegesis proper (as opposed to the *kabuki* representations contained within it) shifts from one level of 'realism' to another (a street set disappears from one shot to the next, and the ensuing combat takes place in abstract, black space; a thick yellow fog gradually dissolves to reveal a painted representation of fog on a canvas backdrop). And while it soon became clear that such experiments were of only incidental concern to Ichikawa, *Yukinojō* is certainly one of the first important instances in the Japanese cinema of the conjunction between an objective 'Brechtianism' of the traditional stage and the influence on the modern cinema and theatre of traditions as diverse as Brecht, Elizabethan drama and the comic strip. As we shall see, this encounter was to have a significant posterity.

Only two years later, in 1965, Ichikawa made the film which we must regard as self-defining. *Tokyo Olympiad* (*Tokyo Orympic*) is the stylistic exercise par excellence, a desperate attempt (Ichikawa has confessed that sport bores him) to express 'the poetic essence' of the subject in such moments as the adjustment of starting blocks for the 100 m final, through slow motion, extreme close-up, soft-focus and a stylized sound-track.

One regrets the fact that Ichikawa, like Kurosawa, has had difficulty in finding work in recent years. However, his latest film – *The Wanderers* (*Matatabi*, 1972) – is a crudely academic, pessimistic drama about youthful outlaw 'rebels' in the early nineteenth century, and one is led to conclude that the preoccupations which were briefly his during the late 1950s and early 1960s and which did indeed point to the future, have been left for others to develop.

The period which preceded the signing of the Second US Security Pact in 1959 had produced a few hints of the coming renaissance of a specifically national mode of representation. However, the films which contained them, such as *The Japanese Tragedy* or *Children of the Atom Bomb*, appear today even more abortive than the project implicit in the handful of films made by Ichikawa around that crucial date in Japanese history. For indeed, if one claim concerning that 'dark period' in Japanese film-art now appears irrefutable, it is that it was marked by only one lasting body of work, the mature films of Kurosawa Akira.

# 24. Kurosawa Akira

Kurosawa is a figure apart by virtue of the evident superiority of his work to that of all his Japanese contemporaries and to that of most of his Western contemporaries as well. He is also set apart by the very nature of his undertaking, since, after Kinugasa, he was only the second film-maker in the history of the Japanese film who, after thoroughly assimilating the Western mode of representation, went on to build upon it. He has constructed, within and beyond this mode, a formal system whose rigour and originality are comparable, on their own grounds, to those of certain Western masters: to the Lang of *Das Testament von Dr Mabuse* and *M*, to the Sternberg of *Der Blaue Engel*, to the Dreyer of *la Passion de Jeanne d'Arc*, to the Eisenstein of *Potemkin*. The following analysis of Kurosawa's development and achievements must take into account both his singularity within the Japanese cinema past and present and his place within the cinema of the capitalist world. The extent to which his work does differ fundamentally from the Lang of *M*, etc., its specifically Japanese dimension, also demands clarification.

The earliest trace of Kurosawa's apprentice years is the film *The Horse* (*Uma*, 1940), in which his assistantship to Yamamoto Kajiro became a 'co-directorship'. This bucolic evocation of the life of mountain farmers, loosely centred around children and their attachment to a horse, is, to the Western eye, a curious premonition of Rouquier's *Farrébique* — except, of course, that in the Japan of the period such near-plotless 'realism' was anything but the novelty that it represented in the post-war West. *The Horse* is generally regarded as a more 'escapist' film than Uchida's *Earth*, made the year before. And it is true that while Uchida's film depicted the real poverty of millions of small peasants, the family in Yamamoto's film is relatively better off and the treatment of their life slightly saccharine. Yamamoto, it must be remembered, was an arch-conservative who made many propaganda films for the militarist régime. Kurosawa's own position on the problem of social realism was to evolve considerably as he detached himself from his master, aesthetically and politically.

His first solo feature, *Sugata Sanshiro* (1943),[1] about the man who codified judo as a sport (in contradistinction to the traditional martial arts), has little to distinguish it from the more professional *jidai-geki* of the immediate pre-war period, though the final combat in a field of tall, wind-blown grass is a *tour de force* that already hints at the mastery to come.

*The Most Beautiful* (*Ichiban utsukushiku*, 1944), a film about keeping up the morale of women workers in a bomb-sight factory, seems to have been Kurosawa's one direct contribution to the war-effort. It is very closely related, in its glorification of the hum-drum existence of working people, to pre-war *gendai-geki*. At the same time, however, one remarkably *systematic* sequence shows that this emphasis on the quotidian and in particular on the experience of *duration*, though still grounded in the diegesis, could produce a suspensive period in the coding process which Kurosawa 'filled' with experiments in highly artificial patterning. In this sequence, the film's 'heroine', who is to remain all through the night, peering into a microscope, polishing the minute lenses, is filmed at her work in a succession of seven protracted shots, starting at the far end of the workshop bench at which she sits alone. Gradually the camera works towards the motionless girl. The increasingly tighter shots are separated by close-ups of a clock showing the passing hours, and the sequence culminates first in a 90° shift to a frontal close-up which lasts over a minute and a half. This is followed by a brief 'dream' flash as her eyelids momentarily droop.

– an enemy plane is seen through a gun-sight
– profile close-up
– return to the initial (longest) shot of the sequence
– cutaway to the empty factory
– medium close-up of the girl praying
– medium close-up of microscope
– close-up of an altar

There follow two increasingly larger shots of two other girls praying for the success of the heroine's race against time (she is the only one who can do whatever she is doing fast enough to meet a crucial deadline). In medium profile close-up, the girl returns to her work. There is music. And the sequence ends with the most inclusive shot of the workshop, with the tiny figure still at work.

---

1. The second part of this film, *Zoku Sugata Sanshiro* (1945), seems to have been lost through the intervention of American censorship.

Now it is interesting to compare and contrast this sequence with, for example, the long transitional passages in *Only Son*, representative as they are of a tradition to which this sequence owes much. Ozu's suspensions, as we have seen, constitute *true blanks*, actual suspensions of the diegesis, whether associated or not with references to it 'from the outside'. This sequence in *The Most Beautiful* is a suspension *within the diegesis*; it is in fact a moment of *suspense*. The 'pillow-shots', if indeed one may call them that – the microscope, the empty workshop, the altar – are charged with specific spatio-temporal meaning in a way foreign to Ozu. In particular, the emptiness of that workshop is the specific emptiness of those night hours in which a girl works alone in the factory. The emptiness of Ozu's pillow-shots is far more absolute, far more ambiguous, unsituated as it is in diegetic space-time. It is empty of characters because they may have left it, may not yet have entered it . . . or simply because the shot is outside the film, shows a setting or a prop in and for itself. Actually, this early Kurosawa sequence has certain affinities with a pivotal passage in the second section of *Potemkin*, which separates the action that culminates in the order to shoot the 'mutineers' under the tarpaulin, from the mutiny itself. It consists of a series of suspensive cutaways, including an exceptional one which shows the ship from a great distance. All these shots – the bugle, the life-buoy, the pope's crucifix, etc. – are borrowed from the diegesis proper. So that while the diegesis may be said to be suspended in this remarkable passage, the suspension remains within the diegesis, of which it should perhaps rather be said that it has been *dilated* here. And the sequence has in common with the one cited from *The Most Beautiful* that, independently of the formal pattern produced, it may legitimately be reduced to 'durational' editing, a series of shots constituting a single syntagma whose sole semantic function is to convey a passing of time. No such unambiguous message ever results from a series of pillow-shots in the mature work of Ozu. An objective echoing of Eisenstein, a tribute to the traditional cinema of the 1930s combined with a tendency to Westernize its modes; inscribed in this sequence are three important keys for situating Kurosawa in film history.

During the very last days before Japan's surrender, Kurosawa made *They Who Tread on the Tiger's Tail* (*Tora no o o fumu otokotachi*, 1945), an adaptation of a famous *kabuki* play and of interest chiefly for this reason. The film was dutifully banned by the American censor and not shown until 1952. It is quite irrelevant to the director's development, except insofar as it was his parting tribute to the dominant attitudes of the pre-war period.

A CHAIN IS BROKEN

In 1946, Kurosawa began his apprenticeship in the 'new way' of social thought and filmic representation. This second period was to last five years and produced seven films: *Those Who Make Tomorrow* (*Asu o tsukuru hitobito*, 1946), *No Regrets For Our Youth* (*Waga seishun ni kuinashi*, 1946), *One Wonderful Sunday* (*Subarashiki nichiyōbi*, 1947), *Drunken Angel* (*Yoidore tenshi*, 1948), *The Quiet Duel* (*Shizukanara ketto*, 1949), *Stray Dog* (*Nora inu*, 1949) and *Scandal* (*Shubun*, 1950). No linear development can be traced through these films. *Stray Dog* is probably the best known in the series and one of the best in quality. *Scandal*, which ended the series, is truly mediocre and the one wholly *anonymous* film that bears Kurosawa's signature. The early *One Wonderful Sunday* is, in many respects, the most endearing of the series, measured by the standards of neo-realism, the specifically post-war form of populist ideology common to all these films, in varying degrees. Another common denominator is a *pathos* which will remain present throughout Kurosawa's work, if we except one or two of the later *jidai-geki* comedies. This pathos can be maintained at agonizing intensity throughout a film as in *The Quiet Duel*, in which Mifune plays a surgeon, accidentally infected with syphilis during a battle-field operation, and who cannot explain to his

Fig. 40. Kurosawa Akira, *The Quiet Duel*

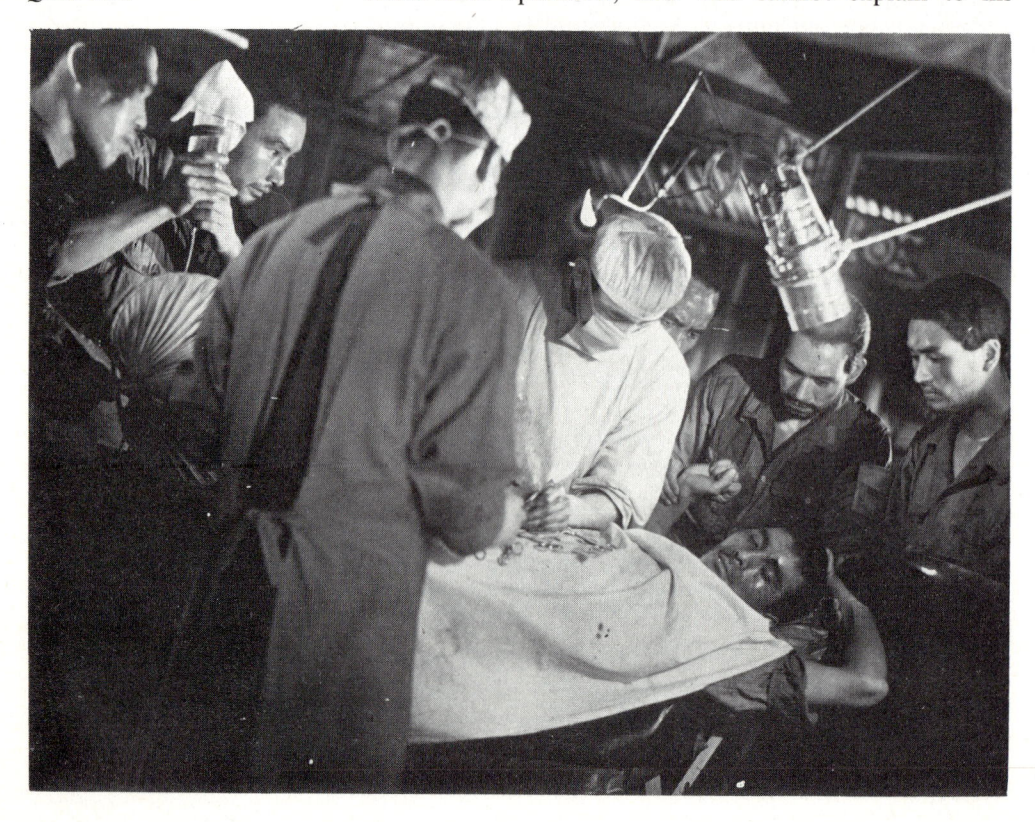

waiting fiancée, after demobilization, why he must break with her. Or it may be latent throughout most of the film, erupting only at the climax. In *One Wonderful Sunday*, the young couple, after wandering through Tokyo on a quiet Sunday, listen to the whole first movement of Schubert's 'Unfinished' Symphony, played by an invisible orchestra which the young man's 'magical' conducting gestures have conjured out of thin air, while the camera tracks about the deserted concert mall, with autumn leaves blowing in the wind. Heavily coded though these films are (from the point of view of spatio-temporal representation they are comparable with the best De Sica or Rossellini of the period), Kurosawa displayed a gift, unrivalled, perhaps, in all the history of cinema, for 'bringing off' scenes which are, on paper, totally *unacceptable* according to Western canons of taste. In *The Quiet Duel*, the protracted medium close-up in which the surgeon and the young, rather dim-witted charwoman stand face to face, shedding bitter tears over their respective misfortunes, carries a conviction which seems almost miraculous. Of course, behaviour of this sort in public is far more common in Japan than in the West; catharsis through tears or violence is a traditional, admissible element of the emotional economy of both men and women. It is, however, Kurosawa's sense of timing and framing, his mastery of editing and of the direction of actors which even at this early period renders totally convincing sequences such as this one, or the Schubert concert already mentioned or the inordinately long, silent, motionless vigil of two lovers in a dark, deserted office in *No Regrets for Our Youth*.

Related to such moments of pathos are the endings of *Drunken Angel* and *Stray Dog*, endings which offer a unique, paroxysmic break with the tone and style of the body of the film. In *Drunken Angel*, the pathos is predominant throughout, as even the most cursory synopsis makes clear: an alcoholic slum-area doctor tries to save a worthless hoodlum from tuberculosis ... and from his own base instincts.[2] The final sequence, a grotesque fight between two hoodlums amongst buckets of paint, is done in a style of sinister slapstick. It is not a parody, but the symbolic defilement of a lumpen underworld, dismissed as pathetically irretrievable. The long, minutely described investigation made in *Stray Dog* by a policeman to find the gun stolen by a pickpocket is strongly reminiscent of the American brand of post-war neo-realism (cf. Dassin's *The Naked City*). Its pathos, linked to the castration symbol of the stolen gun, remains implicit through most of the film, then bursts forth orgasmically, incongruously, during the final, frantic chase on foot, at the end of which both

2. This film brings together, for the first time, I believe, Mifune Toshiro and Shimura Takashi, who were to appear, together or separately, in every Kurosawa film for eighteen years.

pursued and pursuer collapse, side by side, panting with exhaustion.

Disjunctiveness, pathos and excess, already detectable in these early films, will be constants in the mature work of the 1950s. Kurosawa's thematic constants, as opposed to more strictly formal ones, have already been dealt with by others. One feature, however, common to many of these films, is both thematic and formal; it provides, in most of the mature masterpieces, the key articulation between the two levels. This is the characteristic *stubbornness* of Kurosawa's protagonists.[3] Indeed, 'perseverance in the teeth of adversity' is a phrase that describes nearly every one of Kurosawa's main characters. Instances of this are: the absurd single-mindedness with which Mifune, as the policeman in *Stray Dog*, pursues his stolen revolver; in *Quiet Duel* the surgeon's refusal to tell his fiancée the horrible truth and his headstrong wallowing in private misery; the stubbornness of the drunken doctor pursuing the equally pig-headed hoodlum in *Drunken Angel*. They shed some light on Kurosawa's proclivity for stubborn fantasizers in Western literature, such as Prince Mishkin or the outcasts of *The Lower Depths*. And we shall see that in at least one film, *Living*, this theme provides the entire structural support. I should add that this stubbornness syndrome is not merely a personal form; masochistic perseverance in the fulfilment of complex social obligations is a basic cultural trait of Japan, and no doubt contributed to Japan's military successes in the Chinese and Pacific Wars.

It is tempting to see the Western discovery of Japanese cinema through *Rashōmon* as something of an accident, considering both the scale and quality of Japanese production over the previous decades on the one hand and, on the other, the film's minor importance in the eyes of Japanese and (today) many Western critics. Several considerations are, however, in order: Kurosawa's place in the history of Japanese cinema; this film's place with respect to the history of Japanese cinema as a whole; the place which it so naturally came to occupy within the picture of film-culture-as-seen-in-the-West. From these it will be seen that the Japanese decision to send the film to the Cannes Festival and elsewhere, the occidental decision to consecrate its appearance as the 'birth of a great national cinema', were determined by a wide range of factors.

It has already been suggested that Kurosawa's essential achievement can be viewed as operating within and beyond the Western mode of filmic representation. In other words, it satisfied the complementary needs for originality and immediate accessibility. It is not surprising, then, that the first film in his career which fully deserves these qualifica-

---

3. This trait was called to my attention by Jacques Rivette.

tions should be brought before élite audiences of the West. *Rashōmon* was Kurosawa's first film since *The Most Beautiful* to be related to the cinema of the pre-war period – albeit in a very different way. And we must remember that at that time this cinema was totally unknown in the West and presumed by the Japanese to be inaccessible to it. The historical source of *Rashōmon* — the frenetic *chambera* of the 1920s and early 1930s, 'founded' by Ito Daisuke – was bound to attract, when translated into post-war technology, those middle-class audiences in Western Europe and the United States, for whom a certain baroque had become the sign of art in the cinema. Furthermore, Kurosawa's brilliant embroideries on a scenario constructed from two stories by the modern writer Akutagawa Ryunosuke fitted in admirably with an ideology of the 'subjectivity of truth' which had already contributed to the *succès d'estime* of *Citizen Kane*. It had been used once more, also in 1950, in Asquith's *The Woman in Question*, and only two years earlier in Jean Devaivre's *La Ferme des sept péchés*. Martin Ritt later adapted, with characteristic commercial sense, the narrative of *Rashōmon* to Hollywood dimensions in *The Outrage*.[4]

This film, not perhaps the director's finest *jidai-geki*, but certainly among the best, does establish some of the principles for that *rough-hewn geometry* of the masterpieces to come. The films which preceded *Rashōmon* had adhered to the principle of 'organic', 'natural' form overwhelmingly dominant in Western cinema. They observed, on the whole, those rules of unity of style and mood which had seldom been challenged since the introduction of sound. Significant exceptions to this rule, as already suggested, were the delirious finales of *Drunken Angel* and *Stray Dog*, and the sudden intrusion of objectified fantasy – the invisible orchestra – into the otherwise realistic context of *One Wonderful Sunday*. *Rashōmon*'s insistently artificial narrative system involves successive double flash-backs: the thief's tale, the wife's tale, the dead man's tale (told through a medium) and the wood-cutter's own tale. All these are bracketed by periodic returns to the group of travellers huddled beneath the Rashōmon Gate and are relayed through intermediary flash-backs to the magistrate's court. This is very different from the 'organic' linearity of *Scandal*, Kurosawa's preceding film. On the other hand, the artifice of *Rashōmon* is rudimentary in comparison with the geometrical complexities of *Living*, *Cobweb Castle* or even *High and Low*.

The editing in all of the previous films had been marked by an increasingly skilful conformity with the rules of 'invisible continuity' which had now come to be universally

4. The remarkable affinities between Kurosawa and the Western commercial cinema have had other illustrations: *The Magnificent Seven* of sinister memory and, above all, the entire 'spaghetti Western' series, which may be said to derive from one of the master's most evident pot-boilers, *Yojimbo*.

respected in Japan. (We have seen how Ozu himself came to comply with the spirit, if not the letter, of the eyeline match.) *Rashōmon* represents a remarkable re-activation of the freedom of the best of the pre-war Japanese cinema with respect to those rules. Kurosawa, like Ozu and his great contemporaries, spent his first years mastering the Western system of editing before he went on to develop a specifically Japanese approach to space-time. Of course, Kurosawa's style is not at all similar to that of Ozu and his generation. Gone is the predominance of the long shot, and he does not, to my knowledge, use a single *unresolved* eyeline 'mismatch' such as we find in Ozu's or Naruse's work. Yet although Kurosawa's films are original, in the Western sense, and his originality comparable in degree with that of specific Western masters, it must be emphasized that his work on the Western codes is that of a specifically Japanese sensibility.

We have considered the role of the 180° reverse-angle cut in the systemics of Ozu. This device is unquestionably more frequent in Japanese than in Western cinema, where it is still regarded as essentially perturbing. Involving as it does sudden reversals of screen direction, it is considered justifiable only in exceptional circumstances. In *Rashōmon*, Kurosawa revived this device and made it a basic element of his rough-hewn, jagged editing. He also employed frequent and sharply contrasting juxtapositions of close-up and long shot, of moving and fixed shots, or shots of contrary movement. He used, as well, the somewhat anachronistic *hard-edged wipe*.

This form of punctuation was already fairly common in the Japanese cinema of the 1940s, as in the early films of Kurosawa. However, he now began to use it much more frequently, often to the all but total exclusion of the dissolve, a development which appears especially significant when we remember that the Western trend as a whole had been exactly the reverse.

The commercialization of the optical printer in the late 1920s had precipitated an orgiastic development of the wipe in all its forms. During the 1930s, the hard-edged wipe was gradually replaced by the soft-edge version, which grew steadily softer until the vogue of 'wavy dissolves' in the late 1940s, which were in turn completely supplanted by the dissolve properly so-called. As the codes of editing reached their completion, sophisticated directors of the 1940s came to realize the *dangers* involved in a punctuation device *which caused the frame-line to actually cross the field of vision*, thereby exposing the elements most essential to the production of the strong diegetic illusion. Editing and the rest of the cinematic system had been aimed at concealing frame-line and shot-change as material discontinuities, as well as the tangibility of the screen's surface. Here is a clue to the sense in which Kurosawa's approach to 'work on the signifier' must be regarded as fundamentally different from that of, say, the late German Lang. Kurosawa's rejection of 'smoothness', his apparent disregard for many of the rules of illusionist continuity, constitute an *overall foregrounding* of all the habitually buried articulations. Independently of the geometrical structure which we shall encounter in films like *Living* and *Cobweb Castle*, his consistent use of the 180° reverse-angle match produces reversals of position and eyeline (or screen) direction which seem to reactivate, twenty years later, Eisenstein's all but forgotten dialectics of *montage units* (i.e. of 'correct' and 'incorrect' matches), exemplified in his silent films and given theoretical form in his teaching.[5] At the same time, and this is a further indication of Kurosawa's inter-cultural position, he never introduces *unresolved* 'mismatches' of eyeline into a reverse-field series; unlike Ozu, he never in any permanent way disrupts the unambiguous definition of spatial relationships. Occasionally (as in *Living*, during Watanabe's encounter with the novelist or during his meal with Toyo, his young subordinate) a cut from close-up to two-shot is 'mismatched', which is sufficient to define a change of montage unit in the Eisensteinian sense but, at the same time, instantly resolves the disruption caused by the mismatch, since now both characters are on the screen and the new orientation is a visual *fait accompli*, accepted by the spectator as such. Never do two separate close-ups fail to match, clearly because Kurosawa's approach combines a general foregrounding of articulation as such with an underlying, full-fledged adhesion to Western linearity. Ambiguity in Kurosawa – as in Eisenstein and nearly all the classical Western masters – is an element of tension to be answered by one of resolution; never is it a categorical indifference to univalence or linearity as it is in Ozu and more generally in the classical cinema of Japan.

The first of three films which Kurosawa was to adapt from Western literary classics, *The Idiot* (*Hakuchi*, 1951),[6] may also be regarded as his first dramatic masterwork. The film is probably the only adaptation of Dostoevsky to the screen which carries something of the complexity and dramatic intensity of the original. This is due in part to the film's great length (166 minutes). While Kobayashi's nine-hour *Human Condition* is an exceptional case, extensive running-times have long been more easily acceptable in Japan than in the West.[7] Another factor contributing to the supreme quality of the adaptation is the remarkable correspondence between Dostoevsky's 'universe' and certain

5. See Nizhny, op. cit., Chapter 2. Eisenstein posited that it was possible to organize the classical sequence into dramatic sub-sections by shifting into a new set of directional orientations, i.e. by 'crossing the line'. In the Odessa steps sequence of Potemkin, the falling baby-carriage shots are given a privileged status in just this way.

6. Though a minority tendency in the Japanese cinema, the transposition of Western narrative substance to a Japanese setting has been of some considerable importance, from Yamamoto Satsuo's *Denen kokyōgaku* (1938), a deliriously coded version, replete with countless close-ups of Christ on the Cross, of Gide's *La Symphonie pastorale*, to Japanese 'Westerns', complete with chaps and six-shooters.

7. This is partly because of theatrical tradition. Experience, however, seems to have shown that such films are no more profitable than they are in the West, and they have all but disappeared. Kurosawa's first version of *The Idiot* ran 265 minutes, but was apparently never released. Many of his films of the 1950s seem to have been cut, before or after release, more than he would have preferred.

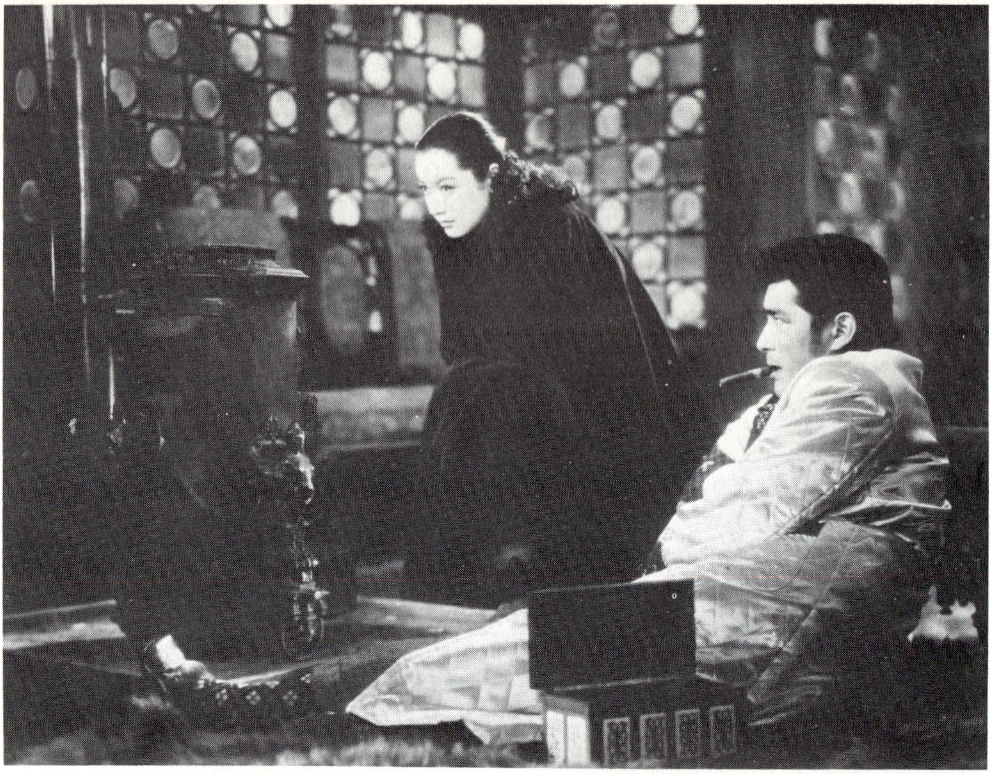

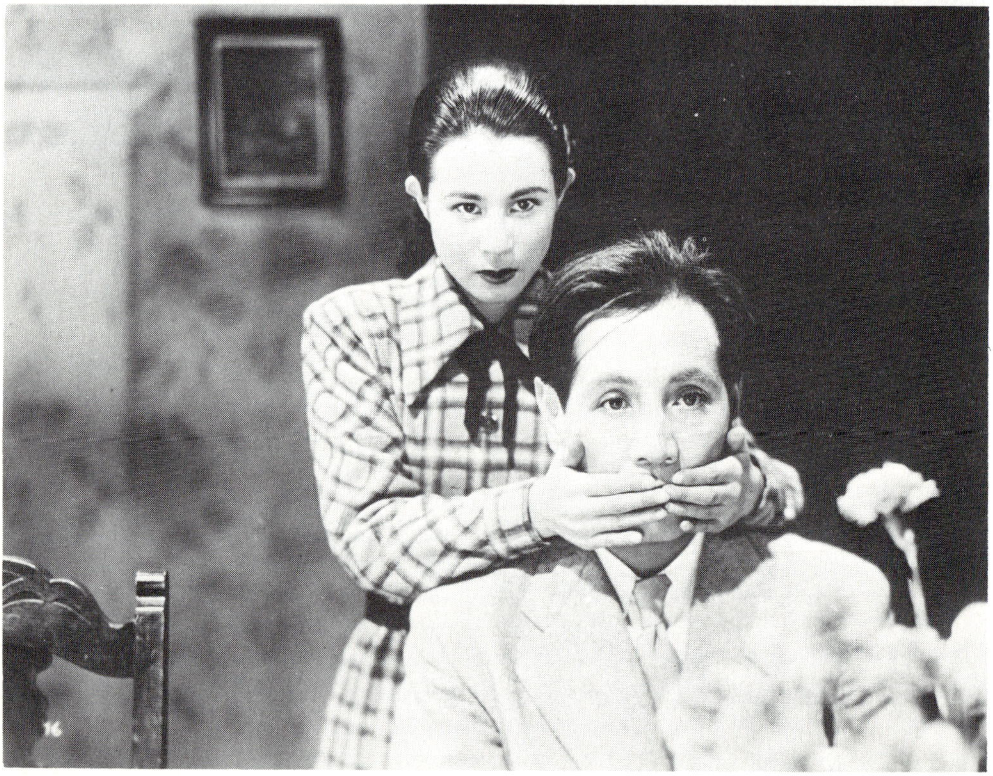

traits of Japanese society, such as the masochistic perseverance already referred to. This film, then, is far 'richer' by Western standards of psychological dramatization than either the neo-realist films or *Rashōmon*. However, the rough-hewn quality of *découpage* initiated in the previous film is considerably attenuated, less provocative, and the systematically geometrical quality of scenario organization, already apparent in *Rashōmon*, is hardly detectable here. This, I suspect, is due to the over-riding power of the novel's plot-structure, which it would certainly have been difficult to force into as formalized a mould as that which organizes *Living*.

Indeed, it was with *Living* (*Ikiru*, 1952) that Kurosawa's narrative geometry developed fully. Like Lang's *M* and only a very few other films,[8] *Living* has a 'serial' organization of signifying elements whose place is at the same time always simultaneously determined by a wholly unambiguous narrative chain. In other words we are dealing with a formalization as rigorous as that of any film by Robbe-Grillet (for example) yet which remains within the framework of linear narration. The film's entire structure may be construed as developing out of a simple, very strong (one might almost call it crude) binary opposition. The first two-thirds of the film shows Watanabe's progress from the discovery that he has cancer to the realization that he can still do something with his life. The last third shows the funeral ceremony at which he is eulogized, more or less hypocritically, by his fellow civil servants, who fill in, through flash-backs, a gap in the narrative, i.e. Watanabe's actual accomplishment: transforming an unsanitary vacant lot into a children's playground.

The two sections of the film are antithetical in prominent ways, parallel in subtler ones. The first section, which stretches over some two and a half weeks of narrative time, contains, of course, countless ellipses and makes recurrent use of the 'montage' technique (or chain of ellipses) inherited from the Western cinema of the late 1920s and the 1930s. It is discontinuous, then, as against the second section, characterized by an apparent unity of time and place – an illusion conveyed in a way to be discussed. One of the most important elements of parallelism between the two sections is the use of flashbacks in each. These flashbacks, moreover, offer one of the film's most remarkable instances of complex 'variation' patterning. In both parts of the film, flashbacks are remarkably brief. The five flashbacks in the first part may be seen to establish a pattern which is then repeated in reverse order and in expanded form in the second. In part one, we move from two isolated flashbacks (father and son riding in the back seat of a car

Figs. 41, 42. Kurosawa Akira, *The Idiot*

8. Sections of *Potemkin*, Marcel Hanoun's *Une simple histoire* (see my *Theory of Film Practice*, Chapter 5) and Oshima's *Death by Hanging* (see below) are significant examples.

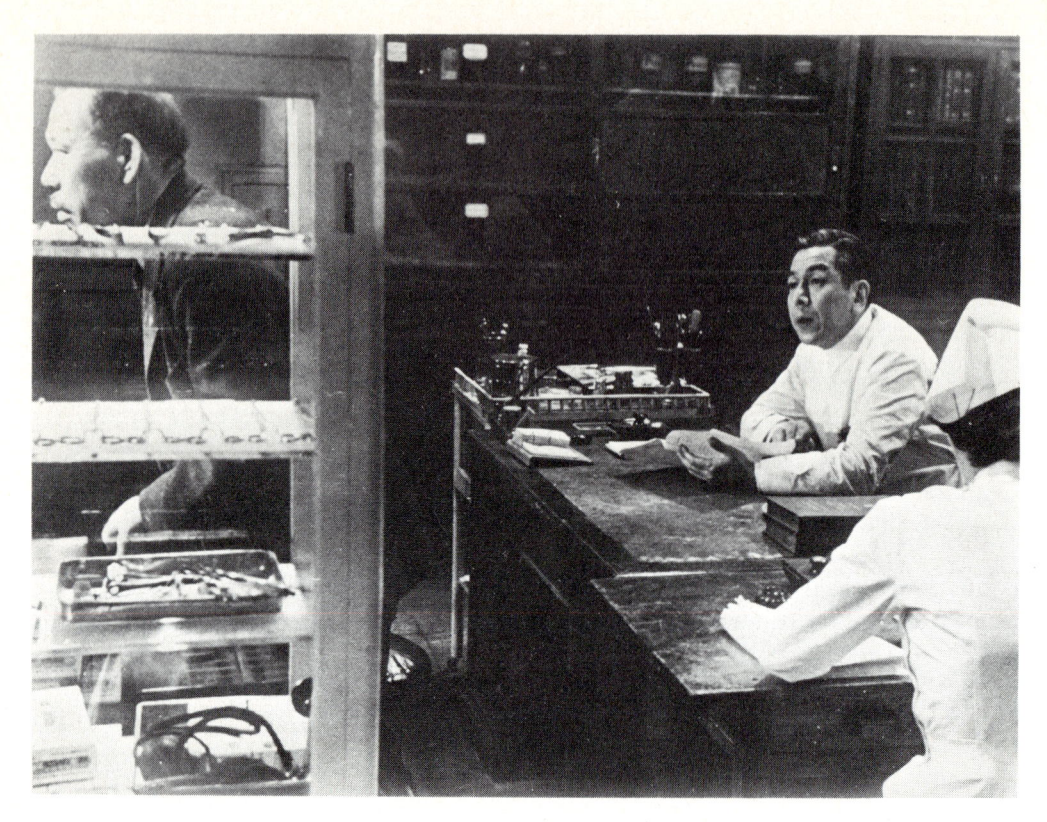

Figs. 43, 44. Kurosawa Akira, *Living*

following the mother's hearse; Watanabe discussing his future with his brother) to two related flashbacks separated by a cutaway back to the present but linked by two 'rhymes on movement' – Watanabe watching his son play baseball from the bleachers; elation at his son's 'single'; the young Watanabe rises to his feet / back in the present, Watanabe sits down / in the bleachers, Watanabe, deflated by his son's failure to 'steal' second base, sits down. Then come two narratively unrelated but directly abutted flashbacks (the boy's appendectomy, his departure for the war). In the second part of the film, the corresponding series begins with two groups of two unrelated but directly abutted flashbacks, continues with a pair of related flashbacks separated by an ellipsis, then proceeds to develop a succession of nine isolated flashbacks.

The mode of flashback employed in the first part is based solely on various forms of 'rhyme' which produce direct or indirect visual equivalents of Watanabe's mental associations: his dead wife's photo conjures up the hearse; the baseball bat which he uses to wedge the front door conjures up his son's hapless game. Then comes the double sitting-down movement which, in turn, leads to the movement of the hospital lift, also perceived as downward on the screen as the camera is inside the rising lift. Finally, Watanabe's farewell to his son entering the operating theatre evokes another farewell: to his son's departure for war. In the funeral section, on the contrary, there is no rhyming: the flashbacks are directly expository, they replace almost literally certain fragments of the mourners' verbal reminiscing, an effect reinforced by their stenographic brevity, so that the illusion of a continuous time-flow ('real time') during this part of the film is remarkably convincing. Lastly, the flashbacks in the second part are spread evenly over the final half-hour of the film, whereas in the first they are concentrated in a single ten-minute sequence and carefully knitted into the 'present tense' montage transitions (close-up of Watanabe, cutaways of the 'pillow' type) which bracket it.

The brief flashbacks which illustrate the reminiscing in the funeral room and which are designed to fill in that five-month gap in the principal narration, actually show, remarkably enough, nothing of the positive stages which enabled Watanabe to achieve his goal. We see him doggedly, mutely putting pressure on a colleague through his presence alone, pleading in a choked voice with the deputy mayor, making his way painfully down a hallway to that petty tyrant's sacrosanct office, silently resisting the intimidation of thugs – or suddenly noticing a sunset. At no time do we see decisive papers being signed, an official throwing up his hands in surrender or any other definitive stage of the struggle. We do not see the moment of completion of the playground, nor that of Watanabe's actual death: we only see him singing in the swing on the completed playground as it was *just before* his death. The great gap in the narrative, then, is bridged with moments that in themselves are merely 'bridges', *off-centered* moments which generally signify repetition ('this scene was enacted day after day until Watanabe had his way'). Hence the sense of distancing which the spectator experiences in passing from the first to the second part: 'the story is over' but the film is not; the 'story' is now being unfolded – *but not by the pictures*.

The form of the first section of the film is quite free, determined by the requirements of the narrative. However, there are a number of recurring devices and leitmotives, and although in themselves they are not unusual procedures, such systematic distribution of them is quite exceptional. They are related, moreover, to a formal attitude characteristic of Kurosawa's mature work as a whole: the tendency to singularize a given device or type of material. The very long single-take 'breathing space' in the middle of *The Lower Depths* contrasts sharply with the fragmented texture of the rest of the film and provides a dramatic and structural pivot. The pair of colour shots that intrude so incongruously upon the otherwise black-and-white context of *High and Low*, also acting as a pivot, provide a further example.

In *Living*, there are three widely spaced interventions of an off-screen narrator, each shorter than the last; they break off entirely two-thirds of the way through the film on the words: 'Five months later the hero of our story died.' These passages are not only infrequent, they are singularized in another way; they are all associated with the heavily caricatural setting of Watanabe's office in the town-hall and serve, in that context, to create a chastening effect of distancing. In this connection, one notices that the first off-screen comment is spoken over the X-ray picture of Watanabe's stomach, and announces his disease. This distancing device destroys all conventional suspense. The same X-ray picture reappears in the hospital consultation, and this double appearance is strongly singularized.

Such leitmotiv structures are common in the film. Another type, which takes two forms, inter- and intra-sequential, does not have a distancing function. However, their insistent pathos still commits these other elements to the principle of singularization. Here are some intra-sequential series: the cutaways to Watanabe's fallen overcoat in the X-ray room, echoed by a similar set of cutaways to a black dog in the drinking-place with the novelist; two shots of Watanabe starting to climb the staircase to his son's rooms on the first floor of the house and stopping each time midway. Inter-sequential series, which occur in both parts of the film, include Watanabe's new hat, symbolic of his being 'born anew', which is pointedly introduced, in close-up or accompanied by direct verbal allusion, four times in section one, is referred to verbally by his former underlings during the funeral narration and is brought back by the policeman near the end of the film. Another such series, banal enough but significant in this structural context, involves the song 'Life is so Short', used as title background, in the piano-bar sequence and in Watanabe's death-scene.

The song, the hat-motif and the echoing flashback structure are the only formal elements common to both parts of the film. Section two is as systematic in construction as section one is 'free'. Starting with a preponderance of wide-angle, fixed shots of the rows of mourners, it gradually moves towards shots which are tighter and tighter, finally breaking down into a series of lateral pans as the drunken mourners lose all sense of dignity and start crawling towards each other across the *tatami*. This overall

Fig. 45. Kurosawa Akira, *Living*

pattern is broken by recurrent elements of three different kinds. The first are close-ups of the altar photograph of Watanabe (rhyming with the photograph of his dead wife, which touched off the ititial flashback in the first part of the film), one of which opens the second part of the film and all of which act as subtly elliptical cutaways. The second is the outside interventions from people come explicitly to contest, each in their own way, the sincerity of the mourners: the reporters who put insidious questions to the deputy mayor; the mothers of the children who benefit from the new playground and who have come to pay a noisily tearful tribute; the policeman who saw Watanabe on the playground, singing and swinging in the snowstorm, and who later found him dead. The third element is the flashbacks already mentioned, of which the first is a literal repeat of the final shot from part one – and the last implies a viewpoint radically at variance with all the preceding ones, since it is introduced by the policeman and filmed in a lyrical tracking shot past a 'jungle gym', while Watanabe sings and swings on the far side. Moreover, the music in this very particularized shot is the only music to be heard in part two, whereas part one is peppered with snatches of it.

This film is Kurosawa's first full-blown masterwork and the most perfect statement of his dramatic geometry. It is also somewhat marred by its complicity with the reformist ideology dominant in that period. From the viewpoint of manifest content, which is that of ideological struggle as well, his next modern-dress film,[9] *Record of a Living Thing* (*Ikimono no kiroku*, 1955),[10] though closer on the whole to *The Idiot* than to *Living*, is one of Kurosawa's finest dramaturgical achievements. Moreover, in contrast with the reformist idealism of *Living* and its plea for the typically petty bourgeois doctrine of the heroic individual as agent of social change, *Record of a Living Thing* objectively offers a compassionate and yet critical image of the lucid social rebel, conscious of hidden historical reality and unable to act because of his isolation. An old iron-master is so terrified of the atomic bomb that he uses every means to force his family to move to Brazil, only to end by being interned in a mental hospital. This character is a curious prefiguration of what I call the Shōin complex (see below) that was to become widespread among film-makers of the next generation and which epitomized their sense of a need to appear eccentric or 'mad' in order to gain a hearing for their message. Mifune's stylized impersonation of a robust seventy-year-old (see Fig. 46) has something of the theatrical quality that was to interest many of the following generation as well. The film was ahead of its time in several ways. Its message was in conflict with the interests of the ruling

9. *The Seven Samurai* (*Shichinin no samurai*, 1954), in part because of its exceptional length and consequently leisurely pace (original Japanese version: 200 minutes), is certainly the finest of Kurosawa's minor *jidai-geki*. I exclude, of course, *Rashōmon* and *Cobweb Castle*. Such films, which Kurosawa himself tends to disregard, will not be considered in and for themselves except insofar as they illustrate, as they often incidentally do, the principles which inform the major films.

10. More idiomatically, a 'living being'. The film was released in the West as *I Live in Fear*, and subtitled *If the Birds Only Knew*.

Fig. 46. Kurosawa Akira, *Record of a Living Thing*

class and reflected popular aspirations, but the time had not come for this desperate expression of mass feeling to be recognized by the intelligentsia of Japan or of the capitalist West. The film's icy reception at the 1955 Venice Festival actually barred distribution in the West for years.

Richie and Anderson seem to be reflecting the general reaction of the Japanese bourgeois press in their attack upon it.

Actually, as shown in the film, none of the people were particularly worth saving from atomic extinction. The entire family was motivated entirely by greed for money, and the old man was plainly insane from the first sequence on. The argument against the atom bomb was never fully thought out, with the result that nothing really comes off and there is a failure – a truly Japanese failure – to bring things to a full and satisfying conclusion.[11]

The class content of this criticism, and in particular of the assumption that there is need for an 'argument' against atomic destruction, should be perfectly clear. It indicates why the film was unintelligible to all but a few critics at that time, for its readability was dependent on political education. The Communist historian, Georges Sadoul, was, I believe, the only writer to praise it at Venice. It could be read indeed only by one aware of the remarkably 'Brechtian'

11. Richie and Anderson, op. cit., p. 286.

dialectic of its didacticism; keys to the meaning of the 'unworthiness' of the family (and yet the need to save them in spite of themselves), to the lucid 'insanity' of the old man (whose sickness is health to a progressive Japanese audience) and to the realistically pessimistic 'inconclusive' ending, are provided by a reading in terms of 'epic theatre'.

Kurosawa's social concerns are reflected in all his *gendai-geki* and most of his *jidai-geki*.[12] *The Lower Depths* (*Donzoko*, 1957) might actually be called his one *Meiji-mono* except for the curiously symbiotic relationship between nineteenth-century Japanese and Russian culture already materialized in *The Idiot*. The helpless pessimism and ludicrous outbursts of Gorki's *lumpen* outcasts make them close kin to the cantankerous iron-master. This film also involves a new and important avatar of Kurosawa's basic geometry. In a thorough exploitation of the possibilities of a deceptively simple set, he lays out successive camera set-ups according to ruthlessly mechanical patterns. Moreover, in both indoor and outdoor sequences, he creates a remarkable instance of specifically Japanese centripetal composition (Figs. 47, 48). This is intimately associated with a principle of 'booby-trapped space' (*espace piégé*), whereby at any time a curtain or a door may draw back, or a face emerge from the shadows in an unexpected corner of the screen. The effect is one in which the free-floating gaze required by the centripetal composition is suddenly focused on some new and unexpected point of interest, thereby further emphasizing the centripetal potentiality of the image. The film's geometry is completed by systematically sharp contrasts between relatively long takes and brief flurries of 'rough-hewn' editing. Indeed, every cut in the film seems made with a rusty axe, so brutal are the reversals and other strategies, including precisely these cuts from wide-angle shots to the first in a given series of briefer and closer shots. Most remarkable of these wide-angle shots is a long, single take backyard scene, already mentioned as a singular suspension of the film's stylistic unity and which acts as a formal and diegetic 'breathing space'. The characters sit about warmed by a pale ray of sunlight, exchanging fantasies, while the discreetly moving camera proposes variations on a theme, as it were: a succession of different compositions all foregrounding a diagonal wooden prop (Fig. 48). In some respects, and despite the wilfulness of its spatial organization, this film is less of a model than others, since, as with *The Idiot*, the original narrative structure does not lend itself to the strict construction of *Living* or *Cobweb Castle*. In some respects, however, it deserves to be explored in far greater depth than is possible here. For this is Kurosawa's most richly

Figs. 47, 48. Kurosawa Akira, *The Lower Depths*

12. They are least apparent, perhaps, in *Three Bad Men in a Hidden Fortress* and *Sanjuro of the Camellias*.

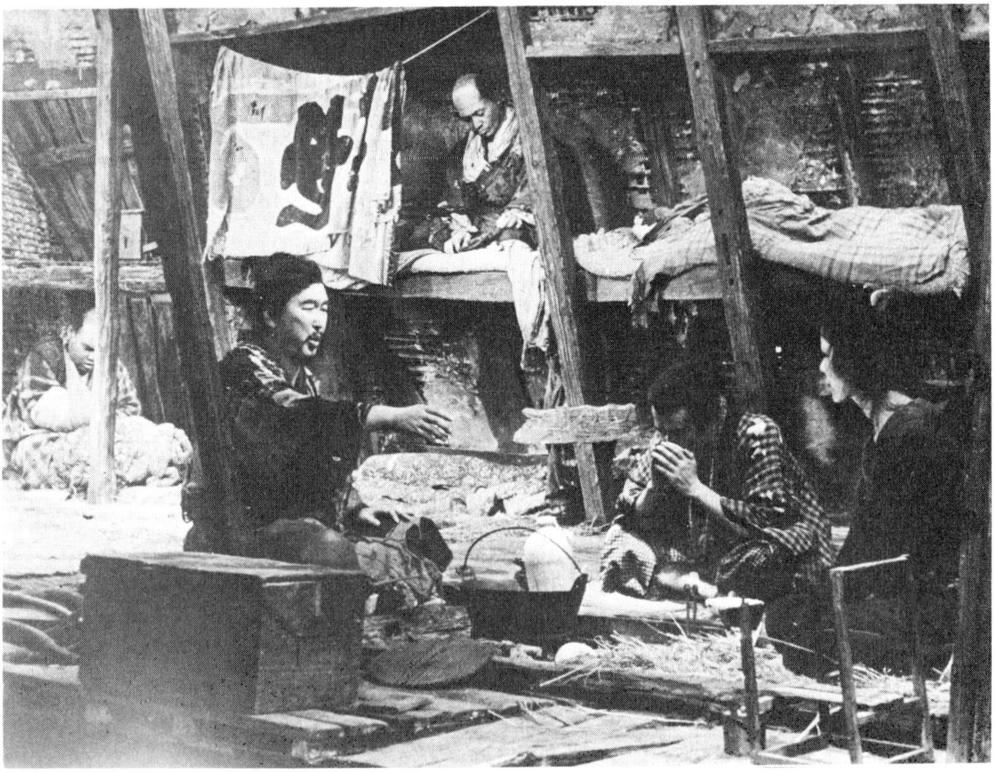

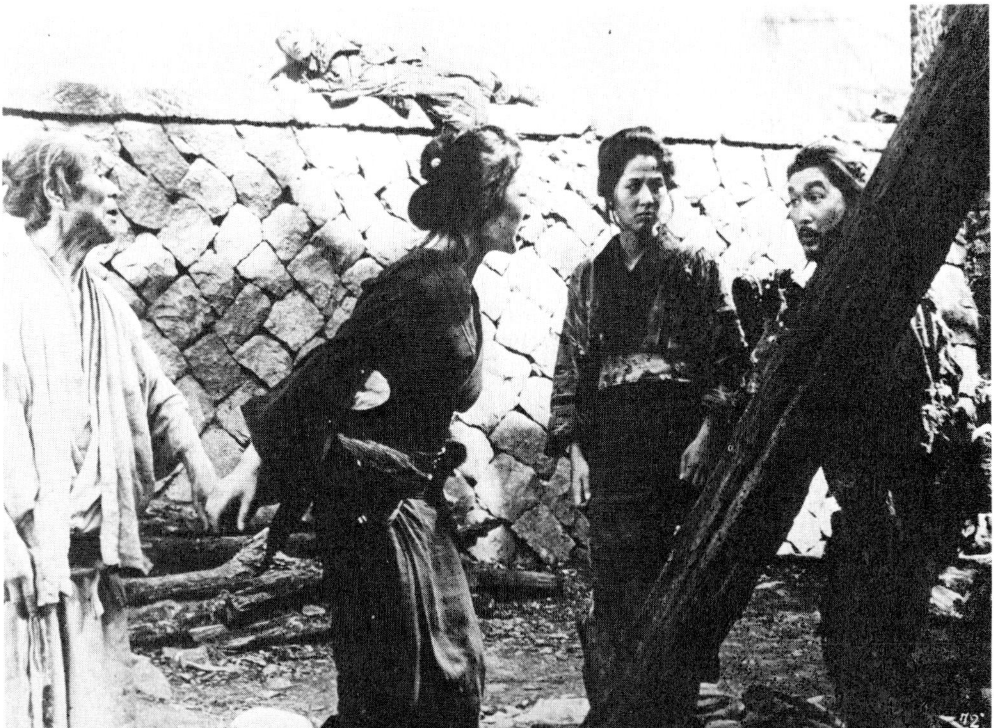

pragmatic dramaturgy, considered independently of any 'geometry'. Or rather, the geometry itself is 'spontaneous', nascent, incompletely rationalized, as it were.

*Cobweb Castle (Kumo-no-su jō*, 1957),[13] made earlier in the same fruitful year that produced *The Lower Depths*, is indisputably Kurosawa's finest achievement, largely because it carries furthest the rationalization process of his geometry.

As most readers know, this film is an adaptation of Shakespeare's *Macbeth*, structurally faithful to the point of respecting the play's division into acts; the spoken word is, however, sparingly used. Furthermore, in a way evocative of the two adaptations from the Russian, the film plays upon essential similarities between the European and Japanese 'middle ages'.

In connection with the early films, I have already referred to an opposition between extreme violence or pathos and moments of static, restrained tension which is, in fact, to be found in nearly all of Kurosawa's films. *Cobweb Castle* is entirely founded upon this principle. The film's overall plan involves two regularly alternating types of scene. Those of the first type are characterized by *violent agitation*, repeated rather than developed. They are, in one way or another, peripheral to that central zone of the classical diegesis which we call plot-line, and to its hardest core, 'character building', tending on the contrary to be theatrical signs for elided action. Examples are: the dashing messengers, whose agitation stands for an 'off-stage' battle; the headlong ride through the storm-swept forest, which signifies the invisible gathering of occult forces (Fig. 49); the confused gallopings which signify rather than depict the battle that is to follow the 'king's' murder; the portentous panic of Miki's horse, which *prefigures* the off-screen murder of his master; the ominous invasion of the throne-room by a flock of birds, presumably fleeing the advancing forest (Fig. 50). Contrasting with these are similarly protracted, tensely static, dramatic moments: the scene with the 'witch' following that first mad ride (Fig. 51); Asaji ('Lady Macbeth') waiting for her husband Washizu to return after murdering his lord (Fig. 52); the funeral procession endlessly advancing towards the castle gates, a scene in which time and space are dilated with blatant artificiality; and the long introduction to the ghost scene, as described below. The dance-like scene in which Asaji waits for the first murder to be accomplished also incorporates a trait otherwise reserved to the scenes of agitation – the evocation of an off-screen event – while as we shall see, the opposition between the two types is dialectically resolved in the final sequence.

Figs. 49, 50. Kurosawa Akira, *Cobweb Castle*

13. Shown in England and the United States as *Throne of Blood*.

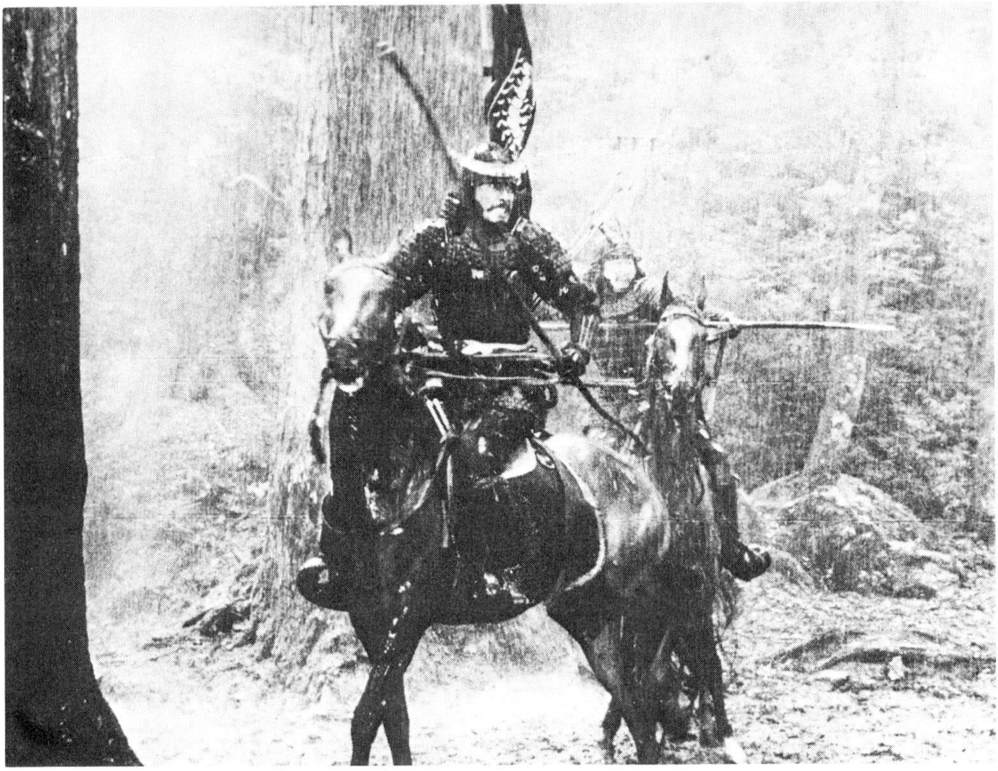

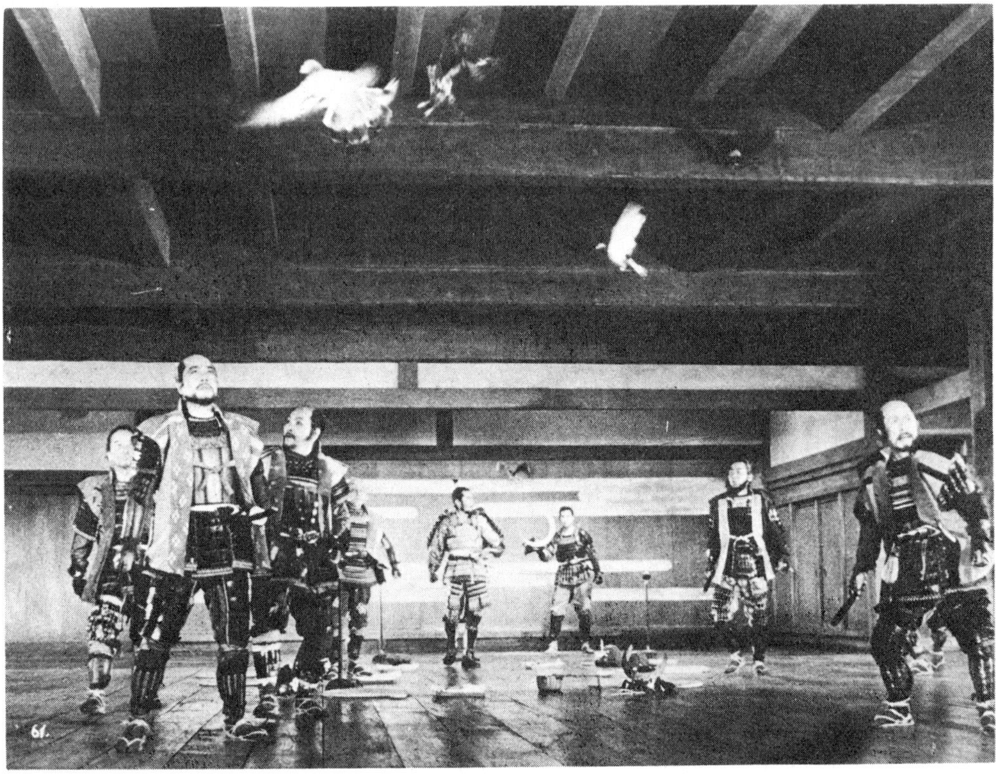
61.

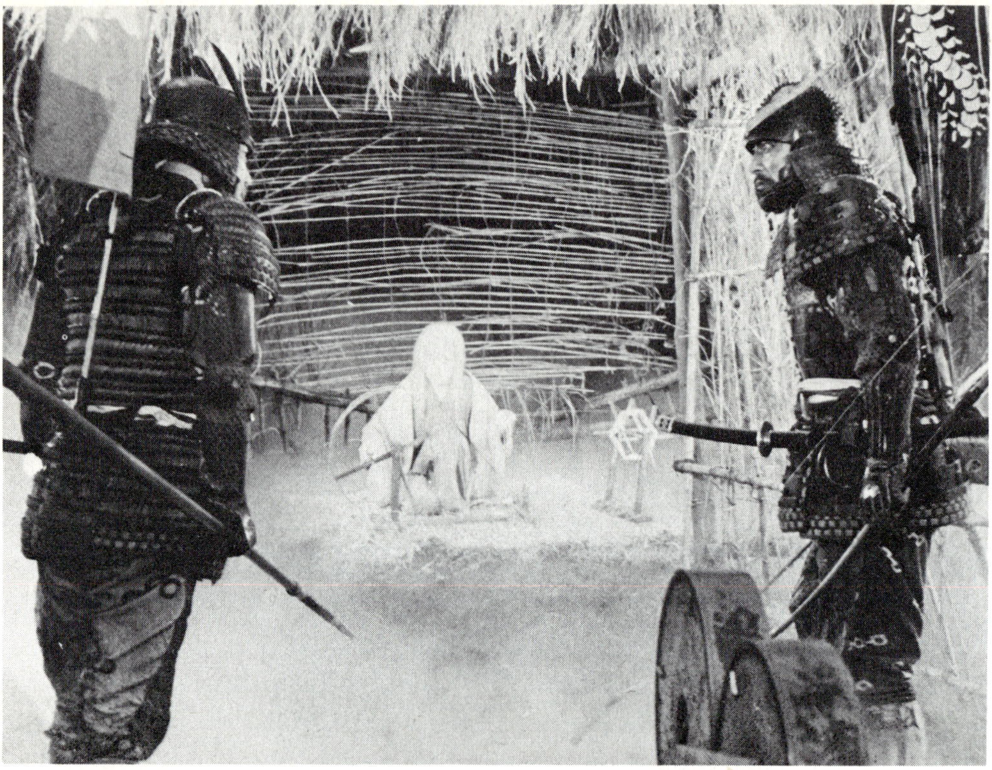

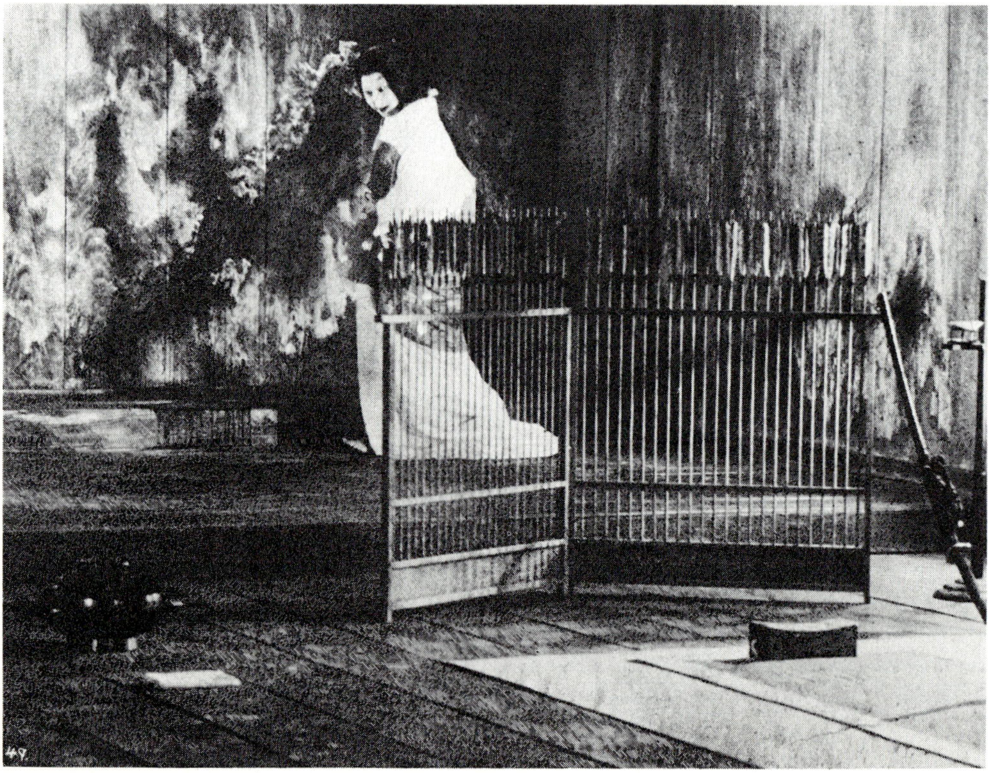

This dramatically 'full' stasis and this 'empty' agitation are also interrelated in a sequence early in the film which shows Washizu's and Miki's blind wanderings through the mist-shrouded forest after their encounter with the witch. Twelve times the horsemen advance towards the camera, turn and ride away, in twelve shots that are materially separate but identical, apparently, in the space they frame – grey, misty, almost entirely abstract. Not until the last shot, in fact, do we realize that this was supposed to have been a forest. This aspect of the scene is strongly reminiscent of the strategies of the oriental theatre in general, with its conventional representation of (for example) long journeys within the avowedly limited here-and-now of scenic space. Kurosawa, however, on the basis of what is, in fact, a coded figure ('durational montage',[14] the model for all of the scenes of de-centred agitation in the film) builds one of the most sustained variation structures in narrative cinema, combining in never-repeated order three or four well-defined stages chosen from the range provided by each and all of the principal parameters of the action: the distance from the camera at which the approaching horses pause, the duration of their turn and the radius of the arc described, their distance from the camera when the shot begins and ends. At times they ride into view out of the mist or disappear into it; at others, the shot begins when they are already in sight, or it ends before they have vanished. From the eighth to the eleventh shot, a shift occurs, the process grows increasingly complex, the riders reverse direction as they ride laterally to the invisibly panning camera, become separated as one rides out of the shot, then join up again, ride out together leaving an empty shot, re-enter unexpectedly in close-up, etc. (these four shots may in fact be regarded as a series of variations of the 'second order'). The last shot, which shows a landscape emerging from the rising mist, provides a final return to the original motif: the horsemen ride towards the camera as in the beginning, but at a perceptibly slower pace than the steady trot which has marked the rest of the sequence, then pull up in medium shot. 'At last we are out of that forest', says Washizu, speaking the first words of a sequence in which the only sounds have been the hooves and whinnying of the horses, and an unobtrusive, very simple, sustained line of woodwind music. The sequence is actually brought to its close by a thirteenth shot of the two men sitting near the edges of the frame, their battle pennants flying in the wind, calmly, amicably discussing the witch's prediction – but already separated, symbolically, by the castle, the seat of power which they will dispute, looming in the distance, squarely between them. This shot is also a striking instance of a

Figs. 51, 52. Kurosawa Akira, *Cobweb Castle*

14. As Christian Metz has dubbed it.

'geometrical' strategy which determines the imagery of most of the film: a rigorous *symmetry* of shot-composition associated at times with a temporal symmetry, in the organization of the set-up/editing relationship (*découpage*). This is exemplified by the remarkable banquet sequence.

It begins with a shot of an ageing courtier singing and dancing in the centre of a large dining-hall between two rows of courtiers sitting face to face along opposite walls. Washizu and Asaji, each seated on a low dais, preside from the far end. (The 'near' end of the hall will appear only towards the end of the sequence, with the entrance of the assassin, which will of course further singularize that dramatic moment.) The camera pans with the moving dancer through three well-defined and symmetrically framed stations: first, he is flanked in the background by two anonymous guests, then by the two empty mats still awaiting Mike ('Banquo') and his son, and finally by Asaji and Washizu. We cut to an absolutely centred, frontal, medium shot of Washizu. He looks to his left, and there is a close-up of the empty mats. We cut back to Washizu who looks away from the mats again, and the principle of symmetry is respected also in these repeated and opposite eye movements around the pivotal cutaway. The same eye movement is repeated a few shots later with Asaji (whose shot matches, in both senses, with an identically symmetrical shot of Washizu called forth by her glance at him, and followed by her turning back to face the camera). We cut back to the dancer in a shot identical to the symmetrical frame in which we last saw him (Washizu and Asaji in background): Washizu suddenly calls in anger for the performance to end, having detected in the words of the singer a parallel with his own history. The startled performer kneels, then scurries back to his seat on the left side of the hall, followed in a panning movement which is the symmetrical complement (or continuation) of the sequence's first shot. He takes his place, bowing to his lord. The next shot is perfectly symmetrical to this last frame; it shows the opposite row of guests – but with the two empty mats at the far end offering a disquieting flaw in the symmetry. After a repeat of the earlier three-shot figure (ABA), in which Washizu again looks at the empty mats, we come to the first apparition of the ghost, shown in a long, single shot, completely symmetrical in its *construction* rather than its framing. The first composition shows Washizu from the absent Miki's 'viewpoint', with the empty mat in the lower foreground. The camera tracks slowly towards Washizu, who now looks for the third time towards the empty mats (the camera) and jumps up in terror. The camera draws quickly back to the starting position (end of first period of symmetry); the whitened figure of Miki is sitting on the mat reserved for him. Terrorized, Washizu staggers away to the left, passing before Asaji, who rises and tries to reassure the guests ('He's always this way when he's been drinking!'). The camera pans with him until Miki is out of shot; then, as he calms down and returns to his seat, the camera, panning back, fails to find the ghost. Actually, however, as a supreme refinement, the ghost's presence or absence remains ambiguous for a moment, since the slightly higher angle of the camera on its return makes Miki's mat invisible, even when Washizu has reached his dais. Only when the warlord finally squats down again, does the camera tilt imperceptibly so that the frame is exactly as at the beginning, with the empty mat in the lower foreground – and the second period of symmetry is seen here to absorb the first. The following shots introduce a new, wider angle. The entire right-hand row of guests is seen, together with both Asaji and Washizu seated at the end. The medium shot of Washizu reappears, followed by a shot symmetrical to the penultimate one (the left-hand row in its entirety, again with Asaji and Washizu in the background). A servant rises at the near end of the row – and his movement, on the following cut, which brings back the correspondingly symmetrical shot seen previously, is perfectly matched with that of his opposite number as he rises to serve the right-hand row. This extravagant visual sleight of hand may be regarded as the central point of symmetry within the sequence, since it comes between the ghost's two apparitions. We now return to a series of shots which very nearly repeat the beginning of the sequence: Washizu looks at the two empty mats, close-up of Miki's, etc. This time, however, when Washizu reacts (in a fixed frame) to the second apparition, we see it in reverse angle to his terrified gaze. This is the first appearance of the classical form of the reverse angle in this scene (it is used only sparingly in the film as a whole). The next shot, as Washizu again leaves his dais and staggers across the hall with drawn sword, involves another long pan and tracking shot, similar to the previous one but extended, pivoting much further to the left for its final composition, showing the empty mat from an angle symmetrical with that of the earlier final composition and, like that one, tilting slightly downwards to include the mat as Washizu slashes at the empty air above it. Following Asaji's dismissal of the guests, the confrontation between the couple is filmed in two symmetrical reverse shots. The final image, in which Washizu murders the assassin who has returned with only the one head (Miki's son having escaped him), is a wide, perfectly symmetrical frame in which the two figures are like puppets in the centre of a stage, performing some

Fig. 53. Kurosawa Akira directing *Cobweb Castle*

15. For a more comprehensive examination of this notion of the 'roles' of the camera, see my remarks on Dreyer's *Vampyr* in Roud (ed.) *A Dictionary of the Cinema*. (forthcoming)

bloodless execution ritual. This is the first element of violence actually to appear on the screen: it is so distanced, however, that it hardly modifies the de-centering of violence which characterizes all but the last few moments of the film.

It is also interesting to note the part played by changes in the 'role' of the camera in the sequence just described. The camera, especially in the two long tracking shots, alternately sees the scene 'with' Washizu, 'with' the witnesses and even 'through Miki's eyes'. Most of these role changes, moreover, take place within the continuity of the shot, and are perceived 'belatedly'. We suddenly realize, for example, that we have been looking at the space occupied by Miki's ghost when we thought it was still off-camera; we realize, in other words, that the camera no longer sees the scene from Washizu's viewpoint but from that of the witnesses – and that this shift took place some seconds before. This lends significant ambiguity to the subsequent disappearance of the ghost from Washizu's subjective vision, which is signalled only by a gradual calming down of the hallucinated man.[15]

The entire film, as I have said, is structured by a dichotomous principle of tension and relaxation, though only here is it applied from shot to shot rather than from scene to scene. The resolution of this dichotomy, as I have suggested, is delivered in the final sequence, when, after the motionless mass of soldiers has listened in complete silence to Washizu's harangue, he suddenly finds himself pursued about the ramparts of his own castle by the unerring rain of whistling arrows shot by his own archers. This bravura passage is usually recognized by Western critics as such, but nothing more; it is seen as grotesque *and* gratuitous or brilliant *but* gratuitous. On the contrary, it is the very keystone of the film's formal structure. Here at last that tense, horizontal alternation between scenes of decentered frenzy and dramatic but static scenes is resolved into a vertical orgasm of on-screen violence. While the hieratic symmetry is swept away by this holocaust, it is reasserted in the epilogue, a near-repeat of the opening sequence: the foggy landscape, the chanting chorus, Washizu's tomb.

While in formal detail *Cobweb Castle* is undeniably a unique work, its general outline – long, rigidly controlled retention of or preparation for violence, ultimately culminating in a brief, paroxysmic outburst, is clearly Japanese. It finds an interesting expression during the 1960s and 1970s in a particular kind of 'gangster film' (*yakusa-eiga*) which deals with intricate conflicts of interest and ethics between rival gangs. The classical pattern of this genre, conformed to all but universally, consists of a long series of provocations greeted by displays of admirable restraint or by quickly stifled reactions which threaten throughout the film to erupt into carnage. Only in the very last reel does this actually happen, and we are invariably treated to a full-scale blood-bath (preceded, invariably as well, by a ritual 'march into battle' through a misty dawn (for example), to the martial melancholy of a squarely syncopated, semi-Westernized, lusty crooning on the sound-track).[16]

In his very next film, *Three Bad Men in a Hidden Fortress* (*Kakushi toride no san-akunin*, 1959),[17] Kurosawa was to illustrate a new aspect of the Japanese cinema, made possible by technological progress, which has helped to perpetuate one of the classical traits already defined and discussed.

The wide-screen processes developed from Henri Chrétien's anamorphic lens (Cinemascope *et al.*) were actually in general use the world over for only about a decade and a half. However, long after they had come to be regarded as an obstacle to the economically indispensable compatibility with the television frame[18] and been all but abandoned in the West, two of the world's major film industries blithely went on making 'scope films almost exclusively: those of Japan and Hong Kong. The Hong Kong approach

KUROSAWA AKIRA

16. All of the most popular sports in Japan today also conform to this pattern of contained violence followed by its 'cathartic' eruption. The ancient form of wrestling called *sumo* in its competitive form consists of long tournaments involving brief, explosive clashes of no more than a few seconds, each preceded by long minutes of ritual warm-up. The same pattern is found in baseball, introduced into Japan over one hundred years ago and which must now be regarded as the national sport. One could also cite the very popular bowling and golf.

17. Shown in the West as *The Hidden Fortress*.

18. In point of fact, Japanese television frequently shows these films using a scanner which transforms a profile two-shot into a reverse-field series with swish-pan articulations (*à la* Ito Daisuke!) or into a *tête à tête* between the handle of a sheathed sabre and the tip of a straw hat.

is almost always that of Hollywood, with the respect for centering, for diagonal rather than symmetrical balance, for the clarity of depth indices, etc. Even the most modest picture from Japan, on the other hand, often displays more or less systematically de-centered, centripetal compositions, with a predominance of geometrical foreground elements, frontal camera angles, etc., all very much in the tradition of the 'classical' period. The sharp contrast between the *essentially vertical* form of the human body and face (even the trapezoid formed by sitting cross-legged on the floor is vertical) and the wide-screen proportions are consistent with a traditionally contradictory approach to the representation of the human body. The willingness among *ukiyo-e* artists to let the edge of the paper truncate face or body in their portraits has already been stressed, and many observers have emphasized the way in which Japanese artists have always accentuated the natural tendency of the traditional costume to contradict the contours of the body.

An otherwise unremarkable example of the picaresque samurai parabole, *Three Bad Men in a Hidden Fortress*, together with Ichikawa's *Conflagration* made that same year, is possibly the first instance of a specifically Japanese use of the newly introduced wide-screen. The vast landscape shot in which a tiny horse and rider gallop across the lower right-hand corner involves a de-centering similar to that of the great painted screens of the Muromachi period. Throughout the film, Kurosawa's centripetal compositions emphasize, designate the shape and boundaries of the frame (see Fig. 54).

This film was the first of a series of four which added little to the crowning achievements of the 1950s. *Bad Guys Sleep Well* (*Warui yatsu hodo yoku nemuru*, 1960) was a moderately interesting return to the 'melodramatic' social realism of the 1940s. Its vehement, quasi-satirical, essentially moral indictment of the 'evil world of big business' anticipates one aspect of Oshima Nagisa's work. The film's strong visual style derives from the preceding decisive breakthroughs, and it is an underrated work, largely no doubt, as with *Record of a Living Thing*, for reasons related to the interests of the dominant classes in Japan, the film's ideological confusion notwithstanding. *Sanjuro of the Camellias* (*Tsubaki Sanjuro*, 1962)[19] was Kurosawa's response to the pressure of a demand for a 'sequel' to the popular *Yojimbō*. Its slight interest lies in an attempt to develop an *architectonic humour*, to produce actual editing or framing as *gag*. As for *Yojimbō* (1961), generally regarded as the high-point of Kurosawa's fourth manner, it is truly nothing more than a fusion of the latter-day *chambera* tradition with the

19. Distributed in the West as *Sanjuro*.

Hollywood Western, which gave birth to that Cinecittà hybrid, the spaghetti Western.

Kurosawa's last major work, at present writing, is *High and Low* (*Tengoku to jigoku*, 1963). In this film, perhaps more than in any previous one (save *Living* and *Cobweb Castle*), the dramatic geometry is triumphant. The first long section of the film takes place in a single room: the ultra-modern parlour of a shoe magnate whose chauffeur's son has been mistakenly kidnapped in place of his own. The kidnapping itself, and the more spectacular bits of action, such as the arrival of the squad of detectives disguised as delivery workers, take place *off-screen*. These procedures were for a while popular among sophisticated American directors, drawn to the unities of the classical Western theatre (*Rope, The Big Knife, The Connection*). In Kurosawa's work, it is directly related to the structural de-centering of *Living* and *Cobweb Castle*. The sequences during which the detectives wait with the magnate for telephone calls from the kidnapper, involve frequent permutations of position and composition through editing, with all the facilities offered by the wide screen. The quasi-theatrical unity is suddenly interrupted by a breath-taking, though similarly claustrophobic sequence in the speeding 'bullet train' from which the kidnapper has cunningly obliged the magnate to throw an attaché case full of money. After a return to the original *in camera* principle (this time the setting is a briefing room at police headquarters) the film seems to break away from the systematically restricted viewpoint. The kidnapper, a poor medical student, is shown in his pitiful daily existence. This revelation completely breaks down the traditional 'suspense' pattern

Fig. 54. Kurosawa Akira, *Three Bad Men in a Hidden Fortress*

Fig. 55. Kurosawa Akira, *High and Low*

which the first part of the film so laboriously established. Then, when a pile of refuse upon which the student has disposed of the attaché case is set afire, the red smoke rising into the smog is seen from the magnate's apartment in *sudden colour*. Two concertina-linked shots appear that intrude violently upon the otherwise black-and-white context. These trigger off the next shift in narrative/representational mode to an action-packed chase, with the police only a few steps behind the kidnapper, who does not hesitate to kill to cover his tracks, etc. Faithful to the ideology that had dominated Kurosawa's films since the very start, this one tells us that 'there is much misery among us but our police force is excellent' and that 'a chauffeur may earn less than a capitalist but class difference can succumb to good will and human solidarity.' As the rather conventional chase sequence develops, Kurosawa's geometry gradually softens. But for two-thirds of the film, he still demonstrates those earlier concerns, whose outlines were soon to become definitively blurred.

*Red Beard* (*Akahige*, 1965) is a visually handsome, curiously fragmented chronicle of the career of an important figure in the development of nineteenth-century Japanese clinical medicine. It has little to recommend it beyond a cathartic sensationalism typical of both Japanese and

American cinema during the 1960s and 1970s. *Dodeskaden* (1972),[20] Kurosawa's first colour film, was made after a period of tragic inactivity, caused by the relative unpopularity of so many of his films in Japan and by the notorious and apparently insurmountable reluctance of Western finance to invest in any Japanese director at all. (The way in which the direction of *Tora! Tora! Tora!* was taken away from Kurosawa typifies this objective racism.)[21] *Dodeskaden*, whose narrative loosely intertwines the eccentric, fantasy lives of the inhabitants of a shanty town, was an ambitious undertaking, and its mingling of conventionally realistic with highly unrealistic images is sympathetically Japanese and/or 'Brechtian'. Its theatricality of acting, sets and lighting is an interesting response to the experiments of the younger generation. Moreover, the influence of Oshima and his contemporaries seems evident in the extravagant accumulation of symbolic parable. The shanty town is clearly Japan herself, overrun with the excrement of unbridled capitalism. In the old tramp who builds Western-style dream-castles literally in the air and who foolishly lets his child die because of his delusions of scientific knowledge, Kurosawa seems to be denouncing the ultimate falseness, for the Japanese, of superficially acquired Western learning, in contrast with true native wisdom, incarnated by the sage old silversmith. Though ideologically conservative, this film was a sincere effort to move with the times artistically, made by a film-maker who had kept the Japanese cinema 'alive' single-handed for over a decade and who had planted the seeds for a veritable renaissance of the Japanese cinema in the middle and late 1960s. It is in this context that *Dodeskaden* must be viewed and its serious shortcomings understood.

It was Kurosawa who, more than anyone else, provided a foreign market and, consequently, a new economic and cultural dimension for the Japanese film industry. It would seem that its stiflingly repressive structures have ultimately broken the one true master which the post-war Japanese cinema has known.

KUROSAWA AKIRA

20. The word is primarily onomatopoeic, referring to the sound of the tramway as imitated by a mentally retarded boy. However, it is also said to have a religious significance.

21. A recent exception for Kurosawa was made by a great 'Western' nation, the Soviet Union. Applauded at the Moscow Festival of 1975, *Dersu Uzala* is lovely literature . . . but can scarcely be said to bear any of the hallmarks of Kurosawa's maturity.

And now?

Kurosawa, despite the essential singularity of his undertaking, was nonetheless a late avatar of a tradition whose roots, as we have seen, are fundamentally Japanese, and even more fundamentally, *non-Western*, whatever the fruitfulness of the encounter with Western aesthetics.

Was the Japanese film-art destined to go the way of the 'fine arts' in Japan, to join the cosmopolitan concert of international modernism, in which Tokyo aspires to compete with Darmstadt, Milan, Paris and New York?

Some feel that this has indeed been the chief characteristic of the 'young' cinema of the 1960s and early 1970s with Oshima, for example, cast in the role of a Far-Eastern Godard.

I find it difficult to accept this judgement. At bottom, however, I feel that the films of the 1960s – of whatever country – are still too close to us for any kind of serious historical perspective.

At the same time it is impossible for me to ignore this recent period, which now seems closed, in the history of the cinema of Japan, if only because it is just possible – and I believe that the pages which follow suggest this often enough – that we are dealing here with a renaissance of a truly Japanese tradition, drawing perhaps on aspects of Japanese history and culture largely untapped by the classical cinema of the 1930s, yet in some subtle ways not totally unrelated to it.

I should point out here that I have dealt only with independent directors of the 'fiction' and 'documentary' cinemas, to the exclusion of the avant-garde. There are several reasons for this choice, some objective, others quite subjective. The Japanese 'underground' film is still very much just that: in Japan itself, during my stays there, no fixed exhibition centres for such films were in operation and I was able to see only a very few, quite at random. A few others it has been possible to see in London and Paris, but a serious over-view would require, I suspect, at least as much field-work as has gone into the preparation of this book. Moreover, those films which I have seen have been so closely involved with the various Western models, whether it be the classical surrealist film of the French 1920s or the West Coast 1940s, or the so-called structuralist film of the East Coast 1960s, that they interest my present endeavour not at all. Moreover, I have grown strongly to suspect that the cosmopolitanism – albeit tinged often enough with an 'exotic' use of traditional materials – which seems to be the general rule in music and painting has indeed quite broadly informed this aspect of Japanese film-making. Are the results any 'better' (even by the standards of the Western avant-garde)? I frankly have no way of knowing.

But then, in a sense, this entire book has been intended as an indictment of Western (capitalist) cultural imperialism. Japan, of course, is now an imperialist nation in her own right; and it is not surprising that in order to accede to this status, traditional values have ultimately had to be distorted or repressed – traditional values which, in themselves, as I have tried to point out, are not necessarily 'bad' – it all depends on the use to which they are put. Needless to say, Japanese capitalism has preserved, in forms chosen by it, those which suit its requirements. However, in my view it is important for the future of Japanese society that there be kept alive concepts and attitudes which may be bound up with such features as the neo-feudal paternalism of the modern firm or the veritable apartheid inflicted on Japanese women, but which at the same time have truly progressive potentialities, assuming the transformation of production relationships.

I feel that the independent cinema of the 1960s and early 1970s pointed to the possibilities for this 'progressive conservatism'. This is why I have made considerable effort to deal with it, however prematurely, however inadequate the tools at my disposal.

# Part 6 Post-Scriptum

# 25. Oshima Nagisa

In 1963, Oshima Nagisa had already made six features, including *Night and Fog in Japan* and *The Catch*, had made his first break with the 'majors' and was fast becoming both the leader and theoretician of a new independent cinema. It was at this time that he wrote an important article the title of which might be translated as 'The situation of the post-war Japanese cinema with regard to the status of the subject.'[1] In it Oshima sets forth what amounts to a theory of the development of the Japanese cinema since the war, deduced from the nation's recent history.

Oshima was born in 1932, and was only fifteen, as he emphasizes, during the general strike of 1947. This was the high-point of class struggle during the Occupation period and it was soon followed by the forced retreat of the working class and its vanguard, the Communist Party, during the period of the Cold War, with the anti-communist purges, the Korean War, the Party's adventurist errors and its increasing isolation from the masses. For a man of Oshima's generation and university background it was normal that the high-point of his own youthful commitment to the struggle should have been that second great defeat for the progressive forces of Japan: the renewal of the Japano-American Security Pact in 1959, which consecrated the military and economic integration of Japan into the sphere of American imperialism. Oshima made his debut as a director at the time of that struggle, the largest mass movement in the history of the country. It is not therefore surprising that the man and his films should have been marked by the great hopes it aroused – and by the great bitterness that followed on its failure.

Chief among the political consequences of this failure was an acceleration of the necessary transformation of the JCP. Its base was widened, but it lost much of its petty bourgeois following. During the 1960s, a large ultra-leftist movement developed among Japanese youth and especially, of course, among students.

The development of the Japanese cinema after 1959 is

1. *Sengo Nihon eiga no jokyo to shutai*. My access to this text is through a French translation kindly supplied to me by the Shibata Organization, Tokyo. An Italian translation has been published in the *Quaderno Informativo*, no. 27 of the Mostro Internazionale del Nuovo Cinema, Pesaro, 1971, pp. 19–23.

intimately related with these political developments, and in 1963 Oshima's views on the history of class struggle and of cinema in Japan are directly informed by the ideology dominant in progressive but 'non-aligned' intellectual circles at that period. Oshima felt that what characterized the development of social and political conflict during the period that preceded the struggle against the Security Pact, in other words since the 1945 defeat, was the collective 'sense of victimization'. This he saw as the source of the 'negative', defensive nature of the great political and social protest movements of that period: struggle *against* dismissals, *against* witch-hunting, and above all *against* war and *against* the Bomb. The Japanese people had a sense of being the victims of feudalism and of the war, yet in Oshima's view this very 'sense of victimization' was in itself ultimately a residue of feudal thought, of feudal submission, of collective self-castration and the negation of the individual. For the generation which had known the rigours of late feudalism and the terrors of war only in the dim reaches of their childhood, this appeal to the 'sense of victimization' no longer had, according to Oshima, any mobilizing power; it was because the Communist Party had continued to rely upon it that the anti-Pact movement had been a failure. Oshima felt that the 'true state of mind' of the masses was glimpsed by the new radical groups (in particular the 'group-singing movement') who appealed to the people's 'desire to sing, to do something else. Here was the birth of a movement rooted in the *subjective will* of the people.' This subjectivity was still merely a 'pseudo'-subjectivity, a mere conviction that self-assertion is desirable; it could ultimately be co-opted by the age-old sense of victimization. And the ideal goal of those for whom 'the Marxist myth had been broken' was to inspire the masses to achieve and propagate a *true subjectivity* . . . apparently an essential condition for raising the class struggle to the revolutionary level.

Seen from this point of view, the miserabilist neo-realism of the 1940s and 1950s was merely the most 'socially conscious' expression of the 'sense of victimization'. Kinoshita's films, with their passive gaze on life as it passes, were the dominant version of the same theme. During the period which immediately preceded the renewal of the Pact, and which saw the rise of 'pseudo-subjectivism', the development of 'pseudo-subjectivistic' directors could be observed.[2] They were primarily concerned with bringing to the fore the aspirations of the individual but failed to see them in any but a position of sterile conflict with his or her surroundings, that is with society or nature. It was not until the appearance of Oshima himself and one or two others

---

2. Oshima cites Masumura Yasuzo, whose best-known film in the West is *Red Angel* (*Akaitenshi*, 1966), as the leader of this tendency.

that the aspiration to a true subjectivism, a true assertion of the individual as subject, could find expression in film, and its presence was to be defined in terms of certain basic criteria, set forth by Oshima: refusal to appeal to the collective consciousness of the audience; refusal to echo the established forms in any way; insistence upon establishing the subjective individuality of the author. To achieve these aims it was, in particular, essential to overthrow that postulate of traditional cinema

'which since the beginning of sound [?] had held that the picture exists to tell the story' and to 'create a cinematic method whereby picture and editing themselves would be the very essence of cinema.' And, of course, 'works so conceived must reject all the characteristics of the traditional methods of the Japanese cinema such as naturalism, melodrama, the man-and-his-environment pattern, recourse to the sense of victimization, a tendency to politicism, modernism [?] etc. . . . After which, there should be born a cinema deserving to be called an independent art-form.

This was probably the first coherent manifesto in favour of *an avant-garde movement in Japanese film*, partly grounded in transgression and in the opposition between 'lucid creator' and 'mass ideology'. These principles, which came to pre-eminence in the West during the late classical, the romantic and modernist periods, were gradually introduced into Japan with the practice of Western-style oil-painting, music and literature. In the West, they are deeply rooted in the 'rugged individualism' of bourgeois ideology.

Japanese history, however, is still at a stage in which the respect for the individual as such can indeed be seen as constituting an objectively progressive ideological aim. Economic and ideological individualism had, until very recently, developed in direct proportion with Japanese capitalism; by 1963, it had produced an ideology of 'the free individual' that had come to be a veritable class syndrome. Oshima articulates this rising romantic vision of the individual – and consequently of the artist – in contrast to the objectively materialist attitudes of traditional Japan.[3] Nevertheless, he was led to conceptualize, from his own political experience and that of his peer group, a dialectical relationship between mass consciousness and 'true' subjectivity. It is dialectical insofar as the 'truth' of this subjectivity stems from an awareness that the individual derives his status from the social context. The problematical nature of Oshima's work arises from the question: what is the relation between this *me* and the struggle *out there*?

This was a crucial period of transition, in which Japanese capitalism was entering a golden age; the country was enlisted in the spread of an American imperialism already

3. It is worth remarking that even today, Oshima's personality has considerably more impact on Japanese society than his films: for some years he was the daily 'guest star' on a popular, breakfast-time TV talk-show.

involved in the Vietnam aggression. This situation understandably produced, among those newly awakened to the reality of class struggle, a confusion comparable to that of so many artists and intellectuals in the capitalist West. In Japan, Marxism was fusing with the individualistic humanism of Rousseau and J. S. Mill as they had been introduced to Japan in the late nineteenth century and remained 'frozen' ever since, in keeping with a pattern we have already described. This partly accounts for the singularity of the important Japanese films of the 1960s. Oshima's article failed to understand that class-consciousness can assume only historically available forms; 'the sense of victimization' like the classical tendency to mistake the fantasies of the petty bourgeoisie for the aspirations of the 'masses' were reflections of those confused times. The remarkable insights contained in that article into cinematic (as opposed to political) problems were in fact the postulates of Oshima's film work, already in progress, which articulated an analytical and critical approach to the history of film language, not unrelated indeed to that of Godard.

Oshima is a prolific director. At present writing, he has made over twenty features, plus shorts and TV films, in seventeen years. While the intrinsic qualities of many of these films individually are not to be underestimated, his chief importance lies in the reflective quality of his work *as a whole*. Although the substance of his political thought is questionable, it is nevertheless powerfully operative in his reflection on film and its *political history*, i.e. as ideological production. For this reason it is, like Godard's, exemplary. Oshima is related to European film-makers such as Godard, Straub, Bene, Chytilova. Yet neither emulation nor 'importation' are really involved. Avant-garde modern painting, serial music and 'underground' film-making have tended in Japan to relinquish national identity for a cosmopolitan modernism. The independent 'commercial' cinema, a more *direct* product of the concrete economic and ideological situation, is also specifically Japanese in its mode of rejection of the dominant codes. As we have already seen, the 'idea that the picture was only there to tell the story' was historically foreign to the Japanese film.

During his early career at Shochiku, Oshima specialized in *seishun-eiga*, films dealing with the social and/or personal problems of 'youth', a genre very popular during the 1950s and 1960s. Oshima's 'subjectivity' is seldom apparent in those early films, but one does recall a long, meditative close-up of a boy munching on an apple in *A Cruel Tale of Youth* (*Seishun zankoku monogatari*, 1960), which offers a strange contrast with an otherwise heavily coded context. It was not until *Night and Fog in Japan* (*Nihon no yoru to kiri*,

1960) that Oshima's historical, critical and theoretical concerns became clear. Though still produced within the Shochiku structure, this film seems to have been made almost clandestinely. It was, moreover, withdrawn under political pressure from theatrical distribution after only a few days. The film has two narrative levels: a *present* which takes place shortly after the failure of the struggle against the Security Pact; a *past* which takes place in the early 1950s, at a time when the Communist student movement was suffering from the combined effect of the Cold War and the adventurist errors of the Party's leadership.[4] In the 'present' (actually situated a few months ahead of the film's date of production and meant to coincide with the date of release), we attend the marriage of a young man who has long been active in the Party and its student organization, with a girl involved with the 'new Left'. (The couple had met during a demonstration against the Pact.) This ceremony is to be the symbolic duelling-ground for two generations of the student Left. The groom is accused by the bride's friends of having been a 'Stalinist agent' in the student movement seven years earlier. These scenes take place in a strange, baroque summer-house and garden, and involve the introduction, in many different guises, of the *theatrical sign* (see below) which was to become central in the new Japanese cinema. The flashbacks illustrating the difficult days of the early 1950s are set in a student's residence hall. Their heavy, dusty academicism is intended to evoke the miserabilist cinema of the period in which the action is situated (and which, in the 1963 article, is associated with the erroneous ideological and political practices of the whole era).

The *elements of theatricality* introduced into the present-tense narrative are of great importance. They vary greatly – from the appearance and structure of the set itself, to the heavily archetypal image given to even the most 'positive' characters (an outlaw revolutionary appears melodramatically out of the fog in a macintosh). There is a systematic replacement of straight cuts by extravagant lateral pans from one character to another, as they stand spread out across the 'stage'; dramatic black-outs occur, with characters singled out of the pitch-darkness by spot-lights. This theatricality, together with the reference to Japanese film history, are the principal traits of Oshima's work over the next decade and a half. They are the source of his originality and the key to an understanding of his relationship both to his contemporaries and his predecessors, such as Kurosawa, Ozu and Mizoguchi.

In his next film, *The Catch* (*Shiiku*, 1961), produced independently of the major companies, Oshima delivers a

4. These included the conviction that the time was ripe for sabotage and guerrilla warfare.

POST-SCRIPTUM

scathing attack upon the stultification of traditional social structures, as exemplified in a small village, and upon the 'victimization' syndrome. At the same time, he espouses for this one film the anti-montage, anti-close-up tendencies of the classical Japanese cinema. Here he was, in a sense, coming to terms with one aspect of the academic *découpage* of the post-war era, and his pastiche of late Mizoguchi is very convincing. At the same time, it attests to a tacit awareness that the old ways could further the cause of the new. The film is set in a Japanese village during the last months of the Pacific War. The inhabitants capture a black American aviator and are told by the authorities that they must keep him 'until further notice'; having this additional mouth to feed aggravates the latent conflicts within the tiny community, already shaken by the prospect of defeat. The black is finally lynched by the villagers, who are unable to face their own social realities.

I am unfamiliar with Oshima's next three films, generally regarded as of secondary importance in his career.[5] However, *Floating Ghost in Broad Daylight* (*Hakuchu no tōrima*, 1967)[6] and *Tales of the Ninja* (*Ninja bugeicho*, 1967) are significant attempts to come to terms with certain aspects of the radical editing of Eisenstein's silent films. Each of these films, though of moderate length (c. 90 minutes), involves over 2,000 separate shots (by way of comparison, we may recall that *Potemkin* contains about 1,500). The complex narrative of *Floating Ghost in Broad Daylight*, involving frequent flashbacks, relates the failure of an experiment in rural communal living by a group of urban intellectuals, and its tragic aftermath. This film is Oshima's most extreme and literal application of the view, defined in the 1963 article, that editing and imagery have a latent specificity, beyond their function as 'narrative vehicle'. It is also a seminal instance of the 'Shōin complex' in the new Japanese cinema, a matter which requires some consideration, since it was to play a primordial role in the work of all the important directors of this period.

Yoshida Shōin was a celebrated reformist, fiery pamphleteer and agitator, who played a considerable part in the ideological and political preparation for the Meiji restoration. Two years before his execution by the *bakufu*, around 1858, Yoshida began to employ in his writings the twin metaphors of madness (*kyō*) and foolishness (*gu*). Precedent for this usage could be found as early as the Muromachi period (fourteenth and fifteenth centuries). The celebration of 'madness' in Kenkō's *Tsurezuregusa* (*Essays on Idleness*, written in the fourteenth century), or by the outrageous Zen monk Ikkyu,[7] had affirmed a new concept of personality willing to break with prece-

5. *Amakusa Shiro Takisada* (1962); *Here I am: Belette* (*Watashi wa Belette*, 1964); *Pleasure* (*Etsuraku*, 1965).

6. 'Floating ghost' (*tōrima*) is a term that has come to signify a man who rapes or molests women. The film has been shown privately in France under the more appropriate title of *L'Obsédé en plein jour*. While it has never been released in the West, there does exist an English subtitled version (under the title *Violence at Noon*) in the Pacific Film Archive, Berkeley, which has a large number of post-war Japanese films.

7. Ikkyu Oshō (1394–1481). The following is one celebrated example of his brand of eccentricity. 'When Shūko went to study the zen philosophy under him, Ikkyu made tea for him, but when he took the bowl and was going to drink it, knocked the bowl out of his hand with his iron Nyoi sceptre. This was too much for Shūko, who started up from his seat, whereupon Ikkyu shouted out "Drink it up!" Shūko then saw the point and, quite equal to the occasion, retorted "Willows are green and flowers are red." "Good," said Ikkyu, quite satisfied that the other understood. Which is, being interpreted, things must remain as they are, for the nature of phenomena cannot be changed any more than spilt tea can be drunk.' (Sadler, A. L., *Cha-no-yu*, p. 75.) Here indeed is a more remote but nonetheless significant origin of a modern attitude: the enigmatic enunciation of a materialist critique of transcendentalism inscribed within a critique of the sign.

dent to do justice to a reality which few were able to perceive. Madness was understood as the gift of those who see reality more deeply and sharply, and who must therefore behave in ways which most will interpret as eccentric. In the last years of the Tokugawa shogunate, men of high purpose – *shishi* – found no alternative than to represent themselves and their exploits as mad and foolish ... The madman must break through the stagnation of established procedure to pursue his own vision of reality.... Yoshida as *madman* was a critic who stood outside of society. As *fool*, he was completely engaged; every action of his was informed by sincerity, he was a man without a shred of self-interest. All in all, he shows us a new kind of personality intent on alerting Japan to what was happening ...[8]

In the late 1950s and the 1960s, Japanese society again enters a period of crisis intimately related with that of the capitalist world as a whole, embarked upon what may perhaps be its final delaying struggle against socialism. In Japan, however, the contradictions specific to capitalism at this stage are determined by another conflict, much sharper than in other highly developed capitalist countries: the conflict between a system of traditional social relations and mental attitudes which still, in many respects, can be experienced as even more constricting than in Yoshida's time, considering the lip-service paid the liberal ideal under modern capitalism. Small wonder, then, that over the past fifteen years Japan has produced the most eccentric cinema of revolt that the world has known.

*Floating Ghost in Broad Daylight* is a film in which Sato Kei, one of the principal members of Oshima's troupe, plays a psychopathic rapist/killer. It is characteristic of the new cinema to portray madness and/or innocence as a form of revolt, coupled with its formal manifestation as 'arty' or 'gratuitous' manipulation and organization of the signifier. 'Straightforward' narrative has rarely been subjected to a more *excessive découpage* than in this film. Almost no account is taken of orientational matching; eyeline, position and direction are disregarded more often than not, so that every shot-change rings out like a pistol-shot, so to speak, all the more so as Oshima delights in juxtaposing very different shot sizes.

In the lengthy final sequence, two women sit face to face in a railway carriage reflecting on the tragedy they have just lived through. The camera traces complicated patterns between the two women, panning from one to the other across the span of window between them. This *extravagant* presentation of a conversation piece that would 'normally' be the object of a reverse-field set-up, will become increasingly frequent among Oshima's generation. Reminiscent of

[8]. Harootunian, H. D. *Toward Restoration*, pp. 221, 223–4.

POST-SCRIPTUM

the Ito school and of *The Red Bat*, it is significant of the new school's 'scandalous profligacy' in the face of the economy of thrift so essential to the Western (bourgeois) mode of representation.

Oshima's next film, though generally regarded as a minor exercise and 'disowned' by him today, points up a further and important difference between Oshima's generation and the 'serious' directors who had begun their careers in the 1940s and whose relation to the world of popular culture was primarily one of condescension. *Sanjuro of the Camellias* and *Tokyo Olympiad* are, each in its own way, passing concessions to popular taste. The school epitomized by the films of Oshima sustains rich and complex relationships with contemporary popular culture. Several film-makers who work in a manner related to that of Oshima (Suzuki Seijun, in particular) function entirely within the genre codes of mass-audience cinema. One of his most important protégés, Wakamatsu Koji, made his reputation directing 'pornographic' films for the Eroduction circuit; and Oshima's own *Tales of the Ninja* in a filmic transposition of the artist's own drawings for a famous adult comic book (*manga*), a genre which has become immensely fashionable since the second half of the 1960s among both working people and radical bourgeois youth.[9]

9. Oshima is also a baseball fan, and the television film which he devoted to Japan's finest professional team, the Yomiuri Giants, is said to be a very careful and interesting piece of work.

These sophisticated strips sometimes convey political or pseudo-political parables. Their cathartic violence and frank sexuality appeal to the libertarian, nihilist tendencies in the 'new Left'. Film-makers, determined to find a 'cinematic specificity', were inevitably drawn to a national school of strip cartooning which, through a reactivation of certain aspects of traditional graphic styles, has exploited the cine-montage dimension of the medium. Oshima's film was an exercise in dynamizing still pictures through extremely rapid and prolific editing and an extravagant sound-effect track, while the swash-buckling tale of battles among and around the *ninja*, those mysterious government spies of the Tokugawa era, was given a highly theatrical dialogue form, played by off-screen voices.

Following this attempt to bring home to his class the 'foolish wisdom' of the popular art of his day, Oshima revived the 'mad' hero in *Double Suicide: Japanese Summer* (*Muri shinju: Nihon no natsu*, 1967). In a narrative reminiscent of the 'near-future' type of science fiction, a 'foreigner' – clearly an American – goes berserk with a rifle and symbolically threatens to destroy the foundations of Japanese society. The film has the slickly stark, black-and-white photography, the stylish, pragmatic, faintly 'expressionistic' efficiency of a Losey film, such as *The Damned*, with which it also shares the same sense of artificial urgency, the same 'hermetically sealed' setting. In keeping with the strong aversion for anything resembling self-repetition which seems to have informed most of Oshima's career[10], the other film made in 1967 is totally different. In *Treatise on Japanese Bawdy Songs* (*Nihon shunka-kō*) Oshima evokes a very real episode of recent history and one that was very close to him: the struggle over the Security Pact and the birth of the 'new student Left' in the 'group-singing movement' (*uta-goe undō*). In utter contrast to *Double Suicide*, this film is in smiling, syrupy colour, and the style of *découpage* seems as deliberately flat and academic as *Floating Ghost* was extravagant. On at least two occasions in his career, Oshima's eclectic investigations seem to have led him to contradict a central thesis of his 1963 article: that the picture and editing should not simply tell a story.

His very next film is, however, his strongest illustration of that assertion. In it, he combines some of the extravagance of *Floating Ghost* with the discipline of *The Catch* and a Kurosawa-like geometricalization of theatrical elements more radical than any that had appeared in his work since *Night and Fog in Japan*. With *The Hanging* (*Kosheiki*, 1968),[11] we have perhaps the first Japanese film which makes explicit the affinities between the national cinema's

Fig. 56. Oshima Nagisa, *Tales of the Ninja*

10. An overt rebellion against one of the main traits of the classical period.

11. Distributed in the West as *Death by Hanging*.

POST-SCRIPTUM

Figs. 57, 58. Oshima Nagisa, *The Hanging*

12. The incident was drawn from a real case; Koreans are the principal 'niggers' of Japan. This status goes back to the not very distant era when Korea was a colony of Japan.

chief historical tendencies and a Marxist concept of a *reflexively critical representation*, first given theoretical form by Brecht and now, in the West and in Japan, central to the issue of the relationship of the performing arts to the class struggle.

*The Hanging* brings to the fore the character of the *fool*, in the person of a young Korean, sentenced to death for rape.[12] The theme of rape, and of explosive male sadism in general, is disquietingly recurrent in the cinema of Oshima and his contemporaries, giving ambiguous voice to an age-old phallocratic tradition. The rapist here represents, or *assumes*, through a long psycho-drama of 'consciousness raising', which is the film's basic narrative movement, the condition and revolt of Japan's *lumpen* proletariat. 'R' is hung for his crime, but his body refuses to die. The prison officials revive him, and before attempting to execute him again, they find themselves compelled by the logic of a demented legalism (a narrative logic symbolic of the constraints and hypocrisies of liberal ideology and class guilt) to force 'R' to remember and confess his crime – indeed, to recognize his identity as 'R'. For after the failed hanging, 'R's mind is a blank slate upon which consciousness must be written all over again. Only when they have succeeded in doing so will they feel authorized to hang him. Obsessed by their obligation to the dream-logic of the 'law', the officials begin to *play*; they re-enact the boy's past, even 'returning to the scene of the crime', where the educational officer finds himself actually committing the crime himself. Back in the execution chamber, the body of the educational officer's victim, lying in a coffin, awakes to become . . . 'R's sister, and it is she who leads him, through symbolic intercourse, to the awareness that he is 'R', i.e. to class and ethnic consciousness. Now that he can measure the real balance of power, 'R' allows himself to be hung again: but when the trap has been sprung and the rope has jerked . . . the noose hangs empty.

Even this capsule summary should suggest one of the film's major aspects: a remarkable discrepancy in 'levels of reality'. And indeed, with reference to nearly every parameter, a cascade of shifts from coded realism to theatricality and back again becomes an essential structural principle.

The film begins with a protracted helicopter shot, zeroing gradually in on the penitentiary and then on the neat little bungalow which houses the execution chamber: the absence of people (see Fig. 57), the editing and off-screen narration of this opening, mark it first as 'neutral documentary' *on* capital punishment, then, after an imperceptible shift, as militant pseudo-documentary *against* capital

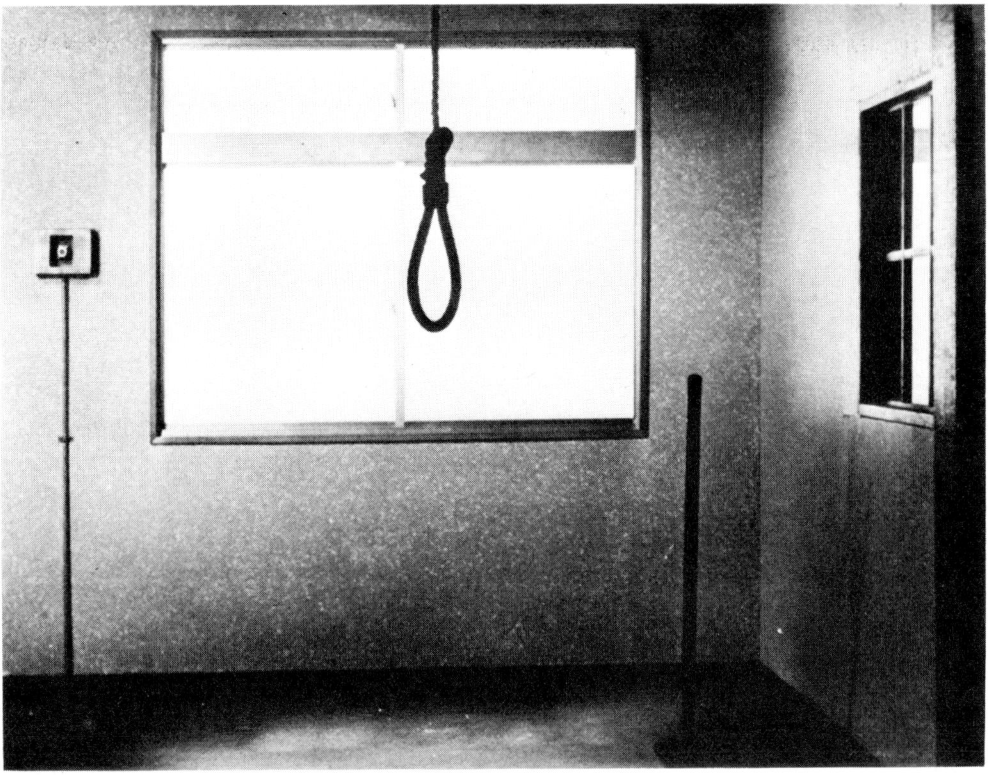

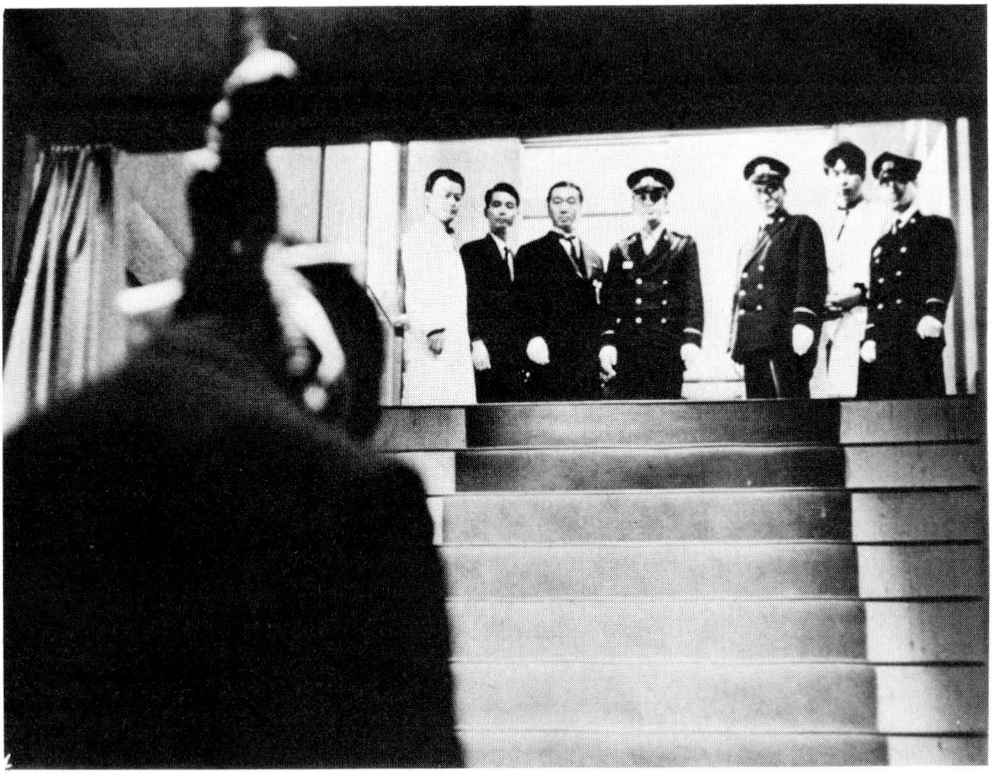

POST-SCRIPTUM

punishment. As characters and synch dialogue appear, and as the first hanging takes place, we find we have gradually moved into the ambiguously transparent world of 'documentary fiction'. Then suddenly, the first of a series of Brechtian title boards announces that ' "R"'s body refuses to die', and the film again shifts from the head-on discourse of humanist indictment (the death penalty as such is never at issue; again, it has been discarded as a false problem) to the mad logic of the moral parable, reminiscent of *Double Suicide*. The officers set about convincing 'R' of the reality of his sin against the State. They become more and more involved in the psycho-drama, acting out his crime amongst themselves (Fig. 59), acting out his 'poverty-stricken childhood', first without his help, then finally enlisting it. The film takes on an increasingly theatrical quality. A room in the death-house becomes a set, with newspapers covering the walls. Suddenly, however, a paroxysmic clash beween the signs of this developing theatricality on the one hand and the 'realistic' indices of location shooting occurs at the point when the whole company follow 'R' out of the death-house. For this 'reality' is at the same time a high point of unreality: outside the death-house is the very shanty-town where 'R' presumably once lived with his family. Emerging from among the shacks, all chase after 'R' in close formation across the city to the high school which has been the scene of 'R's crime. They find a girl, perhaps 'R's victim, on the roof, and the educational officer is so intent on getting 'R' to re-enact his crime that he *assumes* 'R's criminal desire and strangles the girl in his stead. The mode of theatricalization shifts once again as we suddenly find ourselves back in the death-house, where only the educational officer and 'R' are able to 'see' the very material body of the girl lying in her coffin. The sister suddenly appears in her place, for a long political dialogue in an incestuous mood with 'R'. Although this scene takes place in the very midst of the prison officials, it seems set on a stage apart. The ultimate in theatricalization occurs at the very end. While all the figures symbolic of authority gather in judgement before the national flag (Fig. 60), 'R', who has been hypocritically told that he is free to go, opens the door to the outside world and is met by a blinding light that drives him back to the gallows, where the dismayed officials will soon be confronted with the empty, swinging noose.

This distribution and amplification of the *theatrical sign*, which has been defined by Jindrich Honzl in an important study,[13] is an essential dimension of the modern Japanese cinema. Honzl felt that the theatre's specificity derives not from actors, sets or the theatrical text *per se*, but from the possibility of constant transferral of the function of one to

Figs. 59, 60. Oshima Nagisa, *The Hanging*

13. 'La mobilité du signe théâtral, in *Travail Théâtral*, No. 4, July/September 1971.

337

that of another (as when a text sets the scene against a blank backdrop, a property is treated as a character, an actor performs the role of a tree, etc.). The dominant cinema, on the whole, cannot tolerate the presence of the protean sign of theatricality, except in such 'safe' contexts as the musical comedy, where it is understood from the outset that we are *at the theatre*, where 'anything goes'. In the later films of Godard and Straub, in *Caligari* too, the presence of the theatrical sign is fundamentally perturbing. Although theatricality in Oshima's film does function according to the model provided by Honzl for the theatre *per se* (the role-playing, the newspaper-covered walls, the blinding light) he has shown in *The Hanging* (as Yoshida was to do in *Eros Plus Massacre*) that there is a mobility and extensibility of the theatrical sign which is specific to the medium of film. For is not the type of disjunction afforded in the theatre by the substitution of a man for a tree present also in the shift from prison to shanty-town . . . or in the supression from the track of all sound save dialogue in the prison interiors?

Closely associated with the structuring of these different levels of theatricality and 'reality', but in no way a direct or linear expression of it, is a movement in the mode of *découpage*. The film begins, as we have indicated, with the presentation of three successive, wholly coded modes, in which editing and shot design obey the laws of distinct genres: the 'objective' documentary, the militant propaganda film, and then, with the introduction of dialogue, the 'normal' fiction film. As the absurd, legalistic logic begins to take over and as the first signs of theatricality appear, there is the beginning of a more mechanical formalization: long, single-take sequences separated by abrupt ellipses. This series is followed by another in which each cut takes us systematically away from the centre of the action, and then, as the shot proceeds, a pan following some secondary action will lead us back to that centre. Ultimately, through a series of subtle variations on and combinations of these various modes, more or less 'arbitrary,' more or less 'natural', we move to the climactic sequence in which the camera pans continually and obtrusively from 'R' and his sister lying nude under the Japanese flag, to the haggard officials surrounding them, who are embroiling themselves ever deeper in their legal and patriotic casuistics.

*The Hanging* exemplifies the contradiction central to Oshima's work. It instantiates the encounter of the principle of Marxist analysis which views class struggle as the motor of history with the ideology of the individual or subject which is consubstantial with the bourgeois myth of self-fulfilment and whose libertarian version is the ideal of self-liberation. In Japan, these imported idea-forces are further determined by the traditional view of self-fulfilment as a kind of physical and mental discipline, so that political consciousness and self-fulfilment come only too easily to be seen as one. Madness also plays a role, since it has always been viewed in Japan as an especially appropriate form of individual revolt. Yet the eccentricity of the 'mad' director ultimately provides another link with a vital concern of the Western revolutionary artist. Inherited primarily from Brecht and Eisenstein – and/or from a reading of traditional Japanese art in the light of their teachings – is the concern of Oshima and his fellows in so many of their films that representation should acknowledge its production, that picture, sound, editing, should have their own specific articulation – a view expressly formulated by Oshima in his 1963 article.

*Diary of a Shinjuku Thief* (*Shinjuku dorobō nikki*, 1968) is the film by Oshima which has so often been referred to as an 'imitation' of Godard (as everyone knows, the Japanese are essentially imitators!). This judgement ignores Oshima's previous experimentation, for all the 'eccentricities' of this film represent merely their further development. It also ignores the intellectual and political climate prevailing among Japanese urban youth over the previous decade and the manner in which this climate contributed to the codification of *seishun-eiga*, many of whose themes are recognizable in Oshima's film. In *Diary of a Shinjuku Thief*, he carries the disjunctive, 'disparate' dimension of *The Hanging* to an extreme which remains unique in his work. However, the system of shifts and differentiations is far less rational than in the previous film. Gone entirely are the systematic patterns reminiscent of Kurosawa; the 'fool' seems to have taken control altogether, stringing scene after scene together in a spirit of pseudo-improvisation, mixing styles and materials, theatre with cinema, colour with black-and-white, documentary with fiction. At the diegetic level proper, both 'fool' and 'madman' are present: the first as a neurasthenic boy who calls himself 'Birdy Hilltop' and lives in a world of passive fantasy, the second as an aggressive girl (once the victim of a knife attack by a demented American child!) who plays store detective to Birdy's shoplifting. Their 'search for liberating satisfaction' is overseen by an elderly man playing his own role (the director of the famous Kinokunya bookstore in the entertainment quarter Shinjuku), an enlightened spokesman for the pre-war generation, who takes the couple to consult a weird sexologist. Their case is also examined by Oshima' usual troupe of actors, otherwise absent from the film, but used here to discuss their attitudes towards sex in an outrageous and hilarious sequence of *cinéma vérité*. The scene then shifts to the open-air performance of an actual troupe of 'underground' actors, and in the last sequence, an acting out of the psychoanalytic cure, the couple succeed at last in making love as the off-screen voice of the girl tells the story of the American boy, which clearly is the actress's personal experience, incorporated into the diegesis like the sexologist's routine. The exaggerated confusion and naïveté of the film's political statements, the characteristic attempt at an assimilation of the different student movements of 1968[14] are certainly manifestations of the 'fool', telling the world what is wrong with it, 'the mad fool who corrected loyalty and clarified the Way, who was unmoved by profit and merit' (Yoshida Shōin).

In the next film, however, madman and fool though present, are much more restrained and all the unities, so lightly dispensed with in *Diary of a Shinjuku Thief*, reappear with a new force: *Boy* (*Shōnen*, 1969) is a very deliberate return to a thoroughly encoded cinema of linear narrative, disrupted here and there by curious incidental strategies of distance, such as the bleeding of colour from the image or brief suspensions of the sound-track. Theatricality is present only at one remove, 'naturalized' into the diegesis itself, in the role-playing of the characters. A swindler has trained his wife and little boy to fake street accidents. These serve as pretext for a uniquely Japanese form of con-game, based on the acceptance that a cash settlement will right any wrong. Here the 'madman' seems much less mad, if only because the cause of his madness is clearer than the metaphysical nausea of the Shinjuku students: it is 'acquisitive society' and, ultimately, the contradictions of capitalism. Although *Boy* is dramatically very effective, Oshima seems to have abandoned momentarily the effort towards a specificity of editing and imagery. Whatever he may have thought in 1963, he now felt perhaps that such efforts prevented wider contact with Japanese audiences. For with few exceptions, such as *Floating Ghost in Broad Daylight*, Oshima's more ambitious films, like those of Yoshida, Wakamatsu and Matsumoto, were regarded as avant-garde films and shunned by all but a small élite.

*Secret Story of the Post-'Tokyo War' Period* (*Tokyo senso senyo hiwa*, 1970)[14] had an even more unified 'look' than the previous film. Shot in black-and-white, it had something of the chic elegance of *Floating Ghost* and made only passing tribute to the mixtures of 'real' and 'fictional' found in *Diary of a Shinjuku Thief*, in that an actual group of young, would-be political film-makers play their own collective role. In this film, Oshima delineates from a symp-

POST-SCRIPTUM

14. There are inter-title references to France. In the same spirit, newsreel footage of the attack on Shinjuku Police Station supplies an 'historical anchor' in the final sequences.

15. Seen in the West as *He Died After the War* (or *The Man Who Left His Will on Film*). The original title refers to the period of disillusionment which followed the street-fighting of 1968, grandiloquently dubbed by ultra-leftists the 'Tokyo War'.

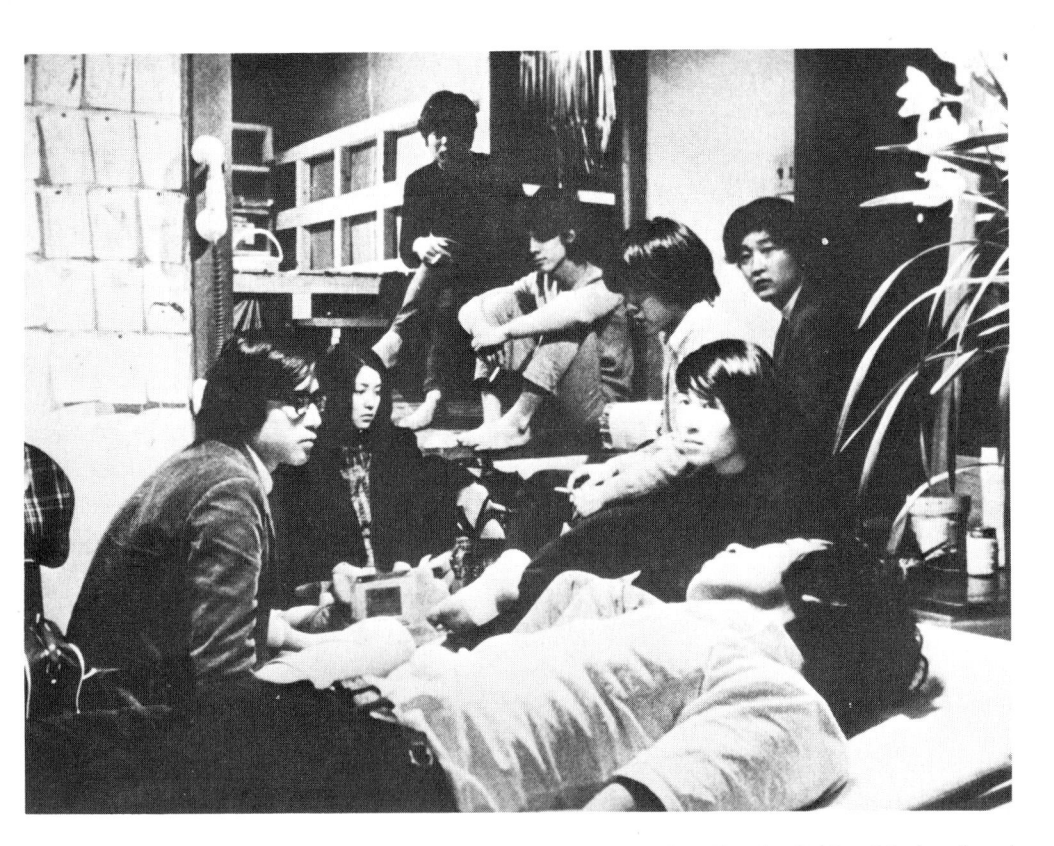

Fig. 61. Oshima Nagisa, *Secret Story of the Post-'Tokyo War' Period*

tomological point of view, the symbolic structure of his mad hero's folly, designating it as schizophrenia. The character talks of himself as of another, throughout the film pursues a 'traitor' who is himself. In this situation one may see a multitude of symbols – and this polysemia will grow increasingly rich in his later films; the contradictions within the radical movement, Japan's multiply divided self, and the dilemma of Oshima himself, unable to establish a dialectical relationship between his art and his politics. Moreover, this 'clinical' model determines the actual structure of the narrative: in the opening scene, the main character witnesses a suicide which will in fact be his own. As in the films of Robbe-Grillet, essentially mechanistic reductions of the textual complexities of his important novels, only one of the levels that determine the linearity of the dominant cinema is under attack here, the level of the signified: the Western mode of representation as we have analysed it remains intact, which could not be said of *The Hanging* or *Diary of a Shinjuku Thief*. Nevertheless, this underrated film is an ambitious attempt to develop a dialectical narrative form in that it does consider the mechanisms of the unconscious in relation to the contradictions of political film-making. It marks the appearance, within our metaphor of Oshima's development, of a single character

341

within whom fool and madman are separate and rivals. The boy 'innocently' pursues his 'mad' other self to the death. Moreover, the element of role-playing in the boy's long monologues about his enemy, and in his girl-friend's accommodating complicity, are a renewal of the theatrical mode.

*Ceremonies* (*Gishiki*, 1971) is the film by which Oshima became widely known in the West. In many respects this chronicle of a powerful bourgeois family from the end of the Pacific War to the present is close to *Boy*. It has that same dramatic power, achieved at the cost of an almost total 'transparency' of the signifier. However, the textual depth of the diegesis is possibly the richest which the film-maker has achieved. In *Ceremonies* the family stands, of course, for the present ruling class, the political or apolitical options of the sons for the contradictions of Oshima's generations, the child buried in Mongolia (by the Russians?) for the lost hope of the immediate post-war period, etc. Most of these symbols seem quite richly dialectical, such as the baseball theme which signifies both the pressure on the family structure of the new ideology (the son is kept away from his mother's bedside by a crucial game) and the continuity of that family (the son's father played baseball and the son cannot bear to part with his glove). Here, as in *Boy*, the themes of madness and theatricality are confined to diegetic representation, in a number of scenes of great virtuosity. These include the 'brideless' wedding, the jilted bridegroom's hysterical attempt to 'rape' his grandfather, the psycho-drama around the fascist son's coffin or the 'surrealist' baseball sequence at the very end. Fundamentally theatrical, too, is the endless succession of family ceremonies which determines the rhythm of the narrative, anchoring each of the successive flashbacks, and relentlessly underscoring the living-death of the bourgeois family system. For this is a stultifying, evil theatre, not the free theatre of the madman rolling on the floor, or the fool's theatre of 'democracy', baseball. It is the theatre of repressive fathers, a theatre of lies which can contain only one authentically liberating gesture; that of ritual suicide.

Oshima's next film was inspired by another decisive step in the resurrection of Japan's imperialist past: the end of the American occupation of Okinawa and the restitution to Japan of her century-old colony. *Little Summer Sister* (*Natsu no imoto*, 1972)[16] is a strange film: made on a particularly limited shoe-string budget[17] this film, more than any preceding one, suggests that Oshima actually felt the need to rid his cinema of any but the most neutral style, perhaps to achieve a 'white writing' of the kind Barthes ascribed to Maurice Blanchot, perhaps simply to reach a

16. Distributed in the West as *Dear Summer Sister*.

17. This does not necessarily explain the film's 'austerity'. The lavish *Ceremonies* cost less than half the normal Japanese budget for such a feature.

wider audience. However, the film develops a tedious, involved, often heavy-handedly flippant metaphor of portentous ambivalence. It concerns a very young adolescent who comes to Okinawa in search of her illegitimate brother and who, through a series of farcical errors and misunderstandings, reaches a form of self-awareness cum political consciousness which must remain enigmatic to all but those who adhere completely to Oshima's idiosyncratic ideology. The theatrical element is more of a stereotype than a formal or poetic dimension. There is a sequence of after-dinner singing which is but a pale echo of the wonderful song-fest in *Ceremonies* and, towards the end, a strange beach sequence, in which the symbolic characters, all dressed in white, 'like ghosts', confront the scabrous secrets of their past. In a way, it is an ambitious film, with a flatness, a 'transparency' that are not easy to achieve. Despite some slight 'auteurist' appreciation in Europe, the film has generally and correctly been regarded as a failure.

Subsequently, Oshima was unable to make a film for three years. Whether this was wholly due to the increasingly precarious conditions of independent film-making in Japan (and, in particular, to the disappearance of the one independent distributor, ATG) or whether it was also due to the need for a period of reflection, one can only guess. His latest film, however, *Corrida of Love* (*Ai no corrida*, 1976)[18] proves that Oshima is still the finest director of his generation. Financed by a French producer who gave him *carte blanche*, and profiting by the liberalization of censorship in many capitalist countries (except Japan!), he has made one of the first authentic masterpieces of 'hard-core' erotic cinema. The film marks several new departures in Oshima's work: the themes of rape and male virility are definitively subverted in this tale of a prostitute who so subjugates her macho lover (and employer) that he ultimately consents to be strangled and castrated by her during the rites of love. Moreover, the symbolic dimension is far less ciphered, one does not have to bear the constant weight of portentous, hidden meanings. The film's language and structure are quite simple but of an unsurpassable mastery. The on-screen diegesis consists almost solely of the lovers' sex-play, so that the narrative is extremely, often disconcertingly elliptical. The imagery is strongly connotative of late nineteenth-century prints in the *ukiyo-e* tradition, and confer upon the film a timeless quality; most of it could be set at any time between 1900 and 1940. It is not until the sudden appearance on the screen of soldiers marching off to war that history intrudes upon the closed 'empire of the senses'; and not until the very last shot do we realize that this paroxysmic instance of *amour fou* is drawn from the

18. Its French title, *L'Empire des sens*, attests to the film's debt to French culture, though it has far more to do with Georges Bataille's *Histoire de l'oeil* than to Barthes' essay on Japanese culture.

POST-SCRIPTUM

minutes of a celebrated trial that took place in 1936.

This is certainly Oshima's finest film since *The Hanging*. Yet somehow one feels that it sidesteps the issues raised in the work of the late 1960s. Over the last decade, Oshima, like so many politically conscious film artists, has clearly been torn between the wish to 'communicate' and the need to experiment. He seems – consequently, perhaps – to function within several separate ideological frameworks: that of traditional Japan, which obviously both fascinates and repels him; that of a Western (cosmopolitan) bourgeoisie, still problematic for the Japanese Left, and which is complicated by the libertarianism so virulent and ambivalent in Japan. And somewhere, in all of that, is Marxism. This is an extremely complicated task for one man. This remarkable artist's latest film shows a healthy awareness of the need to unify and simplify his undertaking if it is to continue to grow.

# 26. Independence: its Rewards and Penalties

Japanese capitalism, from the very start, tended to assume the monopolistic form, partly because it had 'caught the train at that station', partly because in Japan it was undeniably the most socially effective form: the reconstitution of the concentric *nexi* of feudalism satisfied a permanent need. The contemporary pattern, which began to develop quite early, offers social mobility to the individual of the middle, lower middle and even to some extent the working class on the basis of his performance in the sacrosanct college entrance exams. Through them he is given access to a university of high or low standing, to a job that is more or less desirable, in a firm that is more or less prestigious. Upon entering a firm, the individual knows almost to a day the stages of his or her promotion and how high she or he can expect to rise. Paternalism is the great weapon of Japanese capitalism, for it suits the national character as nowhere else. The working day is long, holidays very brief, but at least until the crisis of the mid-1970s, salaries have kept abreast of inflation and there are many social benefits. For the small shopkeeper, the small landowner, the lawyer who sets up his own practice, or the independent film-producer or director, on the other hand, the working day is even longer and more gruelling, holidays and benefits are non-existent and the earnings meagre.

As we have seen, the Japanese cinema was quick to follow the example of the first American trust, and the prolific national production (rarely less than 400 features a year) was traditionally divided among a now gradually dwindling number of 'major companies'. At present writing and for the past decade or so, these have been five in number: Nikkatsu, Shochiku, Toho, Daiei and Tohei.[1] In order to understand the extent to which the industry is dominated by these firms, one must realize that not only do they control distribution and exhibition, but that nearly all Japanese technicians, writers and directors are employed by them on a yearly basis. Most dramatic of all for free-lancers, all the best professional equipment – in fact most

1. The status of Daiei has become interestingly ambivalent. Since its bankruptcy in 1971, Daiei has been managed by a consortium including the left-wing technicians' union. To what extent this has actually influenced production policies, I am at present unable to ascertain.

equipment of any kind – is owned by these firms, who are not in the habit of renting it out, even supposing that the several productions always in progress could spare it, even for a brief period.

Making a film outside the established commercial system, but according to professional standards, is more difficult in Japan than in any other advanced industrial country. This, of course, explains why the precarious independent productions often have dialogue scenes shot with a 'wild' track and are frequently edited with a silent viewer, or with no viewer at all.

The system does offer 'small compensations'. Since technicians have, generally speaking, employment security, they can arrange, between company films, to work on independent productions – for even lower wages than usual.[2] Often too a 'personal' statement or two will pass unnoticed in a major company's yearly crop. But it must not be too personal; and one must not have any illusions as to the permanence of such a situation. A gifted young director, after two films for one of the majors, ran afoul of the hierarchy; for over ten years now he has been a fixture of Shinjuku bars, talking about films with those who are still making them.

Many of the noted 'independents' of Oshima's generation[3] began, as did Oshima himself, with a major company and subsequently turned independent, sometimes more than once, in hopes of finding greater ideological and artistic freedom. The inevitable price is severe material constraint. Others, like Hani Susumu and Teshigahara Hiroshi began heroically as independent directors, became attached to a major company (Shochiku in both these cases) and now appear to operate on a 'semi-independent' basis. As these two men were, together with Oshima and Yoshida, the two most important directors to appear in the late 1950s and early 1960s, a few words must be said about their work. Talented as their early films show them to have been, neither has been able to cope with the political and theoretical challenges raised by the films of their contemporaries and the events of the last decade.

Hani Susumu is, in any case, a figure apart. His best film is probably *She and He* (*Kanojo to kare*, 1963), a delicate, almost clinical study of a young woman whose stubborn, seemingly masochistic drive to do good in the face of adversity makes her a kind of 'Princess Mishkin' – and an early manifestation of the 'Shōin fool'. In this film, Hani's mastery of the pragmatically inventive *découpage,* abounding in subtle touches, is equal to that of Antonioni during that same period (*La Notte, L'Eclisse* would be fair comparisons). A factor that may be related to this 'mastery of the

---

2. Low wages are, of course, the key to the success of an industry which bases its profits on quantity rather than 'quality' or even differentiation. At the same time, the fact that in Japan, the cinema is not an élitist profession – a script-girl makes the wages of a typist, and directors and movie stars are seldom wealthy, even by Japanese standards – provides a thought-provoking contrast with the United States and Europe.

3. Independence did not begin with the Japanese 'new wave'. Kinugasa, as we saw, tried it in the 1920s and many of the most radical films of the 1940s and 1950s were, not surprisingly, independent productions as well.

codes', and one which sets Hani quite apart, is his propensity for shooting films abroad on themes of encounter between individual Japanese and other cultures. *The Song of Bwana Toshi* (*Bwana Toshi no uta*, 1965) recounts the amusing tribulations of a Japanese engineer sent to Africa to prepare for the establishment of a Japanese firm. Its editing is tight and elliptical, its irony gentle and wry. Of the artfully erotic films which he has made on and off in Japan, *The Inferno of the First Love* (*Hatsukoi jigoshi-heri*, 1968) is the most ambitious. Compared with Oshima's films made at the height of his 'baroque' period, it seems on the whole a rather facile manipulation of the surface characteristics of the political and aesthetic avant-garde of that time. It has none of the theoretical aspects that make all of Oshima's films at that period so important. The film does contain some brilliantly impressive passages such as an 'assault' on a little girl in a park, in which the use of the telephoto lens is artful. The main characters are definitely first cousins of the 'mad' young people in *Diary of a Shinjuku Thief* and Yoshida's *Eros Plus Massacre*. But Hani is merely echoing the preoccupations of the day, using them to concoct a style; he does not seem fundamentally committed to them, and his eclecticism has nothing to do with Oshima's constant concern to renew himself.

Teshigahara Hiroshi seems to have followed a less convoluted path. While his first film, *Pitfall* (*Otoshiana*, 1962) anticipated, in many ways, important developments of the late 1960s and early 1970s, he has since been severely hampered by a fascination with the baroque psychological symbolism of modern Japanese literature, and an increasingly desperate effort to render certain effects of literary style through cinema. *Pitfall* was an extremely interesting attempt to mingle elements of the traditional ghost-drama (*kwaidan-eiga*) – certainly one of the richest popular traditions in the Japanese film – with a portrayal of class struggle somewhat in the mood of early Pudovkin. It has evil agents of the bosses prowling about in impeccable white suits, or running in slow motion. The film's theatricality (a woman *who does not know she is dead* tries to pick a postcard off the floor and finds she cannot; for her, and for the camera, it is painted on the wood) and its shifts in tone and in levels of 'reality', point to important developments to come. Independently produced in precarious circumstances, the film had some small success abroad. On the strength of it, Teshigahara joined the Shochiku company to make *Woman of the Dunes* (*Suna no onna*, 1964), a sumptuous adaptation of Abe Kobo's symbolic fantasy. This film's aggressive aestheticism and sensuality aroused much Occidental enthusiasm over its 'metaphysical' beauties,

POST-SCRIPTUM

achieved by what was in fact no more than a technically masterful revitalization of the decorative style of the 1930s. The film's reception in the West typifies the ease with which presumably perspicacious Westerners accept from Japan that which would be unacceptable to them from the West. (The problem is an obvious one, but worth stressing once.) *The Face of Another* (*Tanin no kao*, 1966) and *The Torn Map* (*Moetsukita chizu*, 1968)[4] are even more extravagantly chic, increasingly abstruse explorations of psychological symbolism. The distancing procedures of *Pitfall* seem definitely a thing of the past.

The masterpiece of Yoshida Yoshishige is *Eros Plus Massacre* (*Eros purass gyakusatsu*, 1969). Few films in the Western cinema are as freely disjunctive and as *dialectical* in their approach to narrative space-time. The mythical space-time of Teshigahara, in contrast, simply tends to dissolve chronology along with the historical dimension as such. This film offers, moreover, a remarkable reading of the new theatricality, memorable embodiments of the archetypal 'madman', as well as an empirical but provocative use of strategies borrowed from traditional art, notably the principle of de-centred composition. These are allied with more directly Brechtian procedures, such as theatricalized interpolations, title boards, mixtures of historical fact and fiction, past and present, etc. The film's length precludes a full-scale analysis. It is a three-and-a-half-hour fantasmagoria around the life and death of a noted Japanese anarchist, Osugi Sakao, strangled by the police with his wife and child early in this century. Scenes of present-day Japan (a 'rebel' adolescent couple reminiscing about the martyrs in relation to their own personal and ideological problems) alternate with 're-enactments' of scenes from the anarchist's private life, involving, in particular, his complex relations with three different women. In addition, there are radically unrealistic scenes in which the brutal execution and other crucial events are *staged* and given intense lyrical developments (through editing, music, camera movement). The historical characters, moreover, move back and forth between the two periods; a woman in old-style dress takes the ultra-modern 'bullet train', gets off at modern Tokyo Station, but is picked up by an old-style rickshaw and eventually re-enters her own historical period again when the rickshaw takes her to Osugi's house. Even those sequences in which no hiatus is perceptible at the narrative level proper, shift suddenly from 'realism' to a perturbing abstraction, through the use of telephoto lens, focus pull, slow motion; or else there is a sudden compositional de-centering, as in the long walk beneath the cherry blossoms, in which Osugi and one of his women appear

4. In the West, *Man Without a Map*.

348

Fig. 62. Yoshida Yoshishige, *Eros Plus Massacre*

only as small heads bobbing on the lower edge of the black-and-white, wide-screen frame. The acting is critically used as well. A fine example is the climactic fantasy sequence showing three successive versions of the imagined death of the martyr at the hands of the three women gone suddenly berserk, toppling *shōji* after *shōji* in headlong flight through a cunning labyrinth of *découpage*. This sequence is the finest cinematic reflection I have seen on *histrionic death*; in it, the conventional representation of personal catastrophe is distanced and at the same time given a tragic dimension by the paroxysmically repetitious inscription of that stereotyped operation which Kinugasa has so aptly described as 'finding artistic circumstances in which to have people die.'

In subsequent films, Yoshida seemed to hesitate. He tended, at first, to further exaggerate the devices of *Eros*, in the misguided hope of expressing his complex political and moral preoccupations by some miracle of poetic equivalence. In *Heroic Purgatory* (*Rengoku eroica*, 1970) his attempt to build an *eccentric systemics* breaks down completely into narrowly limited exercises in the problems of 'a new grammar', such as the editing of radically de-centred wide-screen shots. But the perpetually roving form of *Eros* could not provide the basis for any grammar at all. Yoshida then seems to have decided that the dominant mode and codes were, after all, the most convenient way of conveying a sophisticated message. As early as 1962, in *Akitsu Spa* (*Akitsu onsen*), he had mastered a certain slick, post-war assimilation of Western style with a visual native veneer. In *Confessions Among Actresses* (*Kokuhakuteki joyu-ron*, 1971–2),[5] he develops a reflection on the 'mask' of the actor – the discrepancy between public and private life, with an implicit moral condemnation of the 'masks' that modern society makes us wear. Such a theme is as valid as any other, but it is a shame that Yoshida so felt the need to centre his film upon its literary expression, that he forgot completely the achievements of *Eros* and their brilliant response to Oshima's 1963 appeal for pictures and editing that would not simply tell the story.

His next film, and, of the films I know, the most recent, was *Martial Law* (*Kaigenrei*, 1973).[6] It indicates a new departure. Returning to black and white after the heavily coded colour of the previous film, he constructs an extremely elaborate visual pattern around the story of Kita Ikki, an ambiguous, national socialist theoretician who was charged with 'moral' responsibility in one of the more spectacular assassination plots of the pre-war Showa era, and executed in 1936. The heavily theatrical portrait of Kita is tinged with psychoanalytical hints as to the origins of his mystical and political obsessions and involves occasional, discreetly introduced fantasy images. These elements all constitute an original contribution to the reflection on distancing undertaken by Yoshida's generation. The film's cavalier assumption that the audience is thoroughly familiar with the historical facts, causes considerable problems for most Westerners. This, however, is closely related to the *Chūshingura* phenomenon, so common in Japanese cinema, and the active, historically informed response demanded by such a film is significantly rare in the cinema of the Western capitalist world. The radically disjunctive character of the *découpage* (shots almost never match directly and are never repeated) creates an added element of 'distance', but only up to a point. After a while, for want of any creative work on the codes of orientation, this disjunctiveness, and the systematic de-centering of the image, ultimately become decorative and the homogeneity of the diegetic process reasserts itself in full.

That the figure of Kita should now elicit mixed feelings among radical intellectuals in Japan[7] is a sign of a developing ideological crisis, exacerbated, in Japan, by the divisions of the Left. In many respects, this film is a complex provocation, an ideological catalyst.

Yoshida's tangential contact with Oshima may justify

---

5. Shown abroad as *Confessions, Theories, Actresses*.

6. Shown abroad as *Coup d'Etat*.

7. His final refusal to praise the emperor, in whose name his plotting against the government was undertaken, 'I am not in the habit of joking when I am about to die', generally elicits satisfied responses from the audience.

our regarding him as a disciple of a director who is six years his junior. However, Oshima's most important protégé is a director of almost his own age whom he eventually helped out of the relatively profitable 'gutter' of Eroduction[8] and into the independent ghetto. By that time, we might add, Wakamatsu Koji was no longer welcome in the sphere in which he had learned his trade and made his reputation. Wakamatsu was a country boy from Japan's still relatively under-developed northernmost island, Hokkaido. After arriving in Tokyo, he became entangled with the underworld for a couple of years. From there it was presumably an easy step into the production of what passes in Japan for pornographic films. However, it should be borne in mind that since the 1964 Olympic Games, mass erotica has been heavily censored, and while the Japanese films of the 1960s and 1970s are far more inventive and the actors more enthusiastic than their American or European counterparts, they are strictly 'soft-core'. On the other hand, sado-masochistic practices, always fairly widespread in the popular cinema of the Far East, are, on the whole, ignored by censors whose original directives were aimed at 'cleaning up Tokyo' according to what were judged to be foreign standards.[9] These standards continue to be applied quite mechanically whenever a naked girl or an erect penis comes along. It was in the 'free space' provided by the S-M market that Wakamatsu was able to give free rein to his talents and no doubt to his fantasies.

Since Wakamatsu has made over forty films, it goes without saying that seeing all or even many of them is not an easy task. The earliest film which I have screened, *The Embryo Hunts in Secret* (*Taiji ga mitsuryo suru toki*, 1966),[10] was also the first to be shown in Europe. The fact that it was selected for the same Knokke-le-Zoute Festival which revealed Michael Snow's *Wavelength* is an indication of this film's eccentricity in both the West and Japan. A man locks a girl in an empty apartment and tortures her for days on end, until she finally escapes and kills him. This ultra-slender plot is drawn out with all the tortuous ingenuity of the fantasizing mind. However, there are no concessions to the slick imagery of commercial erotica. The film is shot in a raw, black-and-white 'crime magazine' style, in which the only glimmers of comforting sophistication – of 'aesthetic distance' – are the periodic long-shots from outside an open doorway. These briefly remove us from the horrific centre of the diegesis, bracketing the torture scenes which are the film's only narrative substance. However, even such elementary structural concerns as this are incidental to Wakamatsu's work at this period. For he was, and in a sense has remained, a *primitive*: he had

INDEPENDENCE: ITS REWARDS AND PENALTIES

8. The Eroduction circuit is an 'independent' distribution system supplied by specialized 'independent' companies who have been cashing in on the strategy of 'sexual liberation' applied by the ruling classes of most capitalist countries.

9. One is reminded of the bans on mixed bathing so as not to shock early Meiji visitors from the West.

10. Shown in the West as *Embryo*.

POST-SCRIPTUM

learned the rudiments of 'film grammar' and still relied on them completely. A film like *Yuke yuke nidome no shojo* (roughly translated as *Go, Go, You Who Are a Virgin for the Second Time*, 1969), a soul-searching roof-top dialogue between a girl with a special proclivity for being gang-raped and a boy who turns out to have the corpse of a person he has murdered in his room, is typical of this primitivism. As the film builds to paroxysm after paroxysm, an imbalance seems to grow between the slickness of editing and camera-work (the crime magazine photography of *Embryo* is far behind), the conventions of the narrative proper, on the one hand, and the deliriously transgressive substance of the diegesis on the other. This imbalance, this tension, is heightened by the constant, nagging yet fascinating presence of what, for want of a closer ideological analysis, I shall call a pseudo-existentialist discourse. Although still working for the Eroduction circuit, Wakamatsu had by now 'taken off' completely; henceforth his films would not only be box-office failures but would have the greatest difficulty being shown at all. He was, nevertheless, able to go on working within the sex circuit for several years. This was probably due to the financial success of his earlier films, and perhaps to the curious 'freedom' enjoyed in Japan (as to some extent in the United States) by the producers of really rock-bottom mass cinema, a consideration to which we shall return.

The tensions accumulating in *Yuke yuke* could only be solved by a shift in frame of reference, and this is what happened, in that very same year, in Wakamatsu's most important and most beautiful film known to me, *Violated Women in White* (*Okasareta byakui*, 1969).[11] The film was inspired by the notorious massacre of the 'Chicago nurses' and is said to have been shot within a week of that horrendous event. Actual, recent events have often provided the raw material for Wakamatsu's fantasies, as they now did for Adachi Masao, his new script-writer, who was to influence the new direction of his work. For Wakamatsu's and Adachi's reading of the demented American's crime is emphatically and specifically informed by the rather mechanical association of unbridled sexual fulfilment with revolutionary politics, an association which characterizes not only much independent film-work, but also the ideology of certain ultra-Leftist groups in Japan.[12]

Politically, we are dealing with a typical petty bourgeois illusion. The person or crimes of a young homicidal psychopath are totally unacceptable as images of political revolution, let alone as mobilizing symbols, except, of course, for a narrow fringe of the petty bourgeoisie, whose revolt lacks class perspective. On the artistic plane, how-

11. Shown in the West as *Violated Angels*.

12. After this film, Adachi scripted the extravagant *Sexjack* (1970), inspired by the 'Red Army Faction's' hijacking of an airliner to Korea. The film took place 'off-stage' of the event, so to speak, and in fact ridiculed a fantasy 'Red Army cell' of students, given to group sex and empty rhetoric, sheltered by a prudish proletarian who is the 'real revolutionary', blowing up bridges at night, etc. It is the group's chagrined reaction to their discovery of this that leads to their hijacking the plane. However critical this film might appear of petty bourgeois 'revolutionism', Wakamatsu and Adachi were known to have connections with the irresponsible terrorists whose involvement with adventurist Palestine groups made consternating headlines, and the former produced a perfunctory propaganda document shot by the latter in a PFLP training camp.

ever, it is interesting to observe the convergency between the ideology subtending and *fruitfully nourishing* this film, and certain literary speculations within a Marxist framework that have been carried out in Europe.

We must not forget that De Sade's work is fiction, that the 'crimes' committed within it are 'written' crimes, and that it will depend upon the reader's freedom, his capacity to 'generalize' his reading, whether these crimes appear as fantasies or as methods for decoding. Incest is a taboo, an order demanding to be 'read' as much as any order (in so far as society experiences it as the crime of crimes, it demands a 'reading' *more* than any other).[13]

I will not pretend to have all the keys to the decoding implicitly proposed by *Violated Women in White*. I will simply suggest some of the more obvious directions. The first images of the diegesis proper – I will deal shortly with the important epilogue and prologue – show a young man firing his pistol into the sea, a patent image of incest.[14] This theme is the thrust of the entire diegesis proper, which ends with a return to the womb. After thus spending his displaced sexual energy, the boy enters the nurses' secluded dormitory and proceeds to 'write in blood' a text which, while it has all the relevant characteristics of the fantasy, solicits our capacities to generalize, *produces* these fantasies as methods of decoding.

Numerous distancing techniques are used for this purpose. At the level of the diegesis proper, Wakamatsu displaces and extends one of the essential figures of the pornographic film, durational reiteration: when the nurses, having found the young man wandering about their isolated dormitory, lead him almost forcefully inside to watch two of their number making lesbian love, this scene is drawn out with the endless repetition of the voyeuristic fantasy. Then, when the growing sexual tension overflows and the boy draws his pistol, jerks open the *shōji* and riddles the two women with bullets, the shock and hysteria of the other nurses produces an even longer period of throbbing stasis; for long minutes, there is scarcely a movement, scarcely a sound but the muted sobbing and whimpering of the terrified nurses. The cathartic force and beauty of the film is produced by the repetition of this orgasmic structure to the exclusion of any other. The ritual of repeated gesture, sudden explosion, and long, panting subsidence shapes the entire film; it extends even to the one long speech, the head nurse's quasi-monologue to the killer, which is similarly agitated and repetitive.

The sparing and startling insertions of colour which suddenly theatricalize the violence serve to designate these

INDEPENDENCE: ITS REWARDS AND PENALTIES

13. Pleynet, Marcellin, 'Sade lisible' in *Theorie d'Ensemble*.

14. And though one might expect that this Freudian theme would be dependent upon the linguistic over-determination provided by the Greco-Christian cultures that sprang up around *mare nostrum*, it is interesting to observe that the Chinese character used in Japanese to signify *the sea* contains within it a recognizable variant of the character for *mother*.

crimes as fiction, exposing all that ominous black blood for what it really is: red paint.[15] This grating distancing effect is particularly remarkable at the climax of the scene in which the killer has been flaying alive one of the nurses off-screen, to the accompaniment of endlessly repeated, blood curdling screams. This is followed by a long, sinister silence. When the whimpering head nurse is invited by the killer to come and see a 'real angel' (in red, that is, not in white) the sudden intrusion of colour totally theatricalizes her horrified reaction; it shows us, as black and white could not, that the flesh is clearly intact and swabbed with red paint. Similarly, in the penultimate shot in the diegesis proper, when the naked killer abandons his gun and lays his head on the surviving, *youngest* nurse's belly amidst the 'bloody' corpses, the sudden shift to colour again causes the sequence to lose both its literal ('horrible') *and* fantasy ('exciting') dimensions. (These two scenes are illustrated in Figs. 63 and 64, but for want of colour plates the demonstration is unfortunately weakened.)

Finally, the main body of the film as just described is bracketed by two essentially extra-diegetic sequences meant to ground the hero's psychosis in social reality, to designate it as emblematic of social and political repression and revolt. The aesthetic consequence of this strategy is to challenge in advance all the manifest significations of the diegesis proper through a prologue consisting of still images borrowed from the daily repertoire of commercial erotica. Later, the diegesis is suspended and in a sense negated by the epilogue. The coloured tracking shots around the two 'lovers' are followed by a black-and-white action shot of the police surrounding the home, then a freeze-frame close-up of a vicious-looking policeman with upraised club. The epilogue which follows consists of a montage of stills illustrating student rebellion and police repression.

The sexual alienation which produces an individual 'revolt' such as the one which inspired this film is indeed linked to the economic, political and ideological alienation of capitalist society – though certainly not in any simple terms of cause and effects such as is suggested here. Totally unacceptable, however, is the ultra-Leftist ideology which holds that the true vanguard of revolution are those who have perceived, albeit 'biologically', such recondite correlations. *Violated Women in White*, on the other hand, like most of the masterworks of the Japanese cinema of that period, proves that when such erroneous concepts are *put to work* by gifted artists, they can be extraordinarily productive. Such are the contradictions of artistic practice in all cultures.

Figs. 63, 64. Wakamatsu Koji, *Violated Women in White*

15. Question: 'Why is there so much blood in your films, Mr Godard?' Answer: 'It isn't blood, it's red paint.'

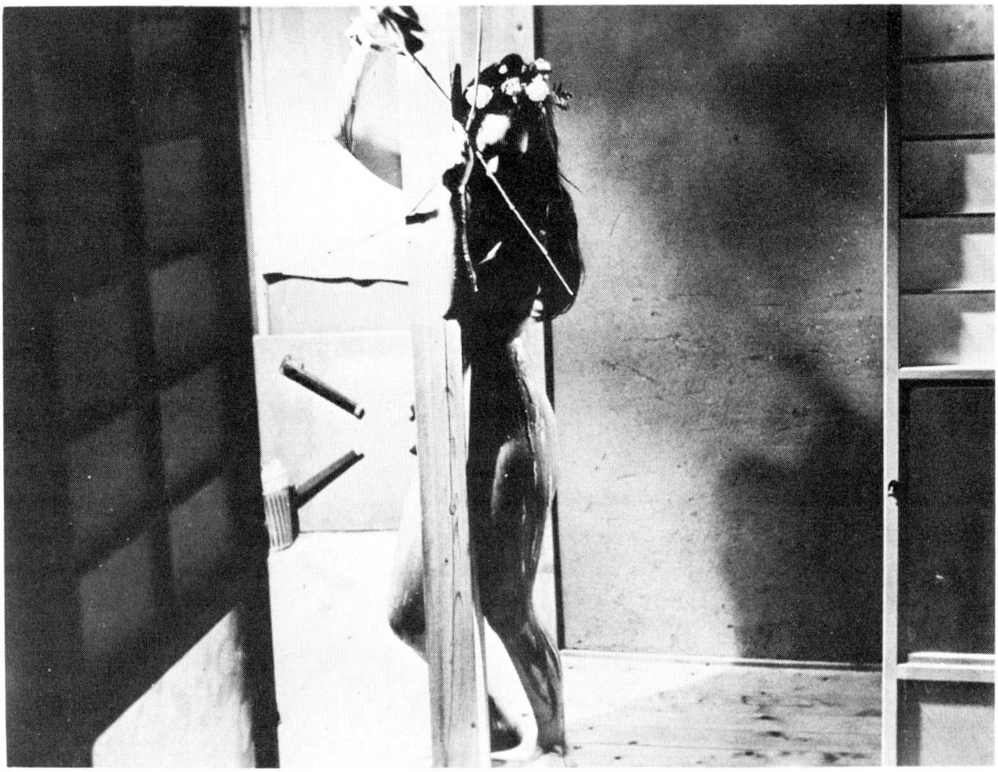

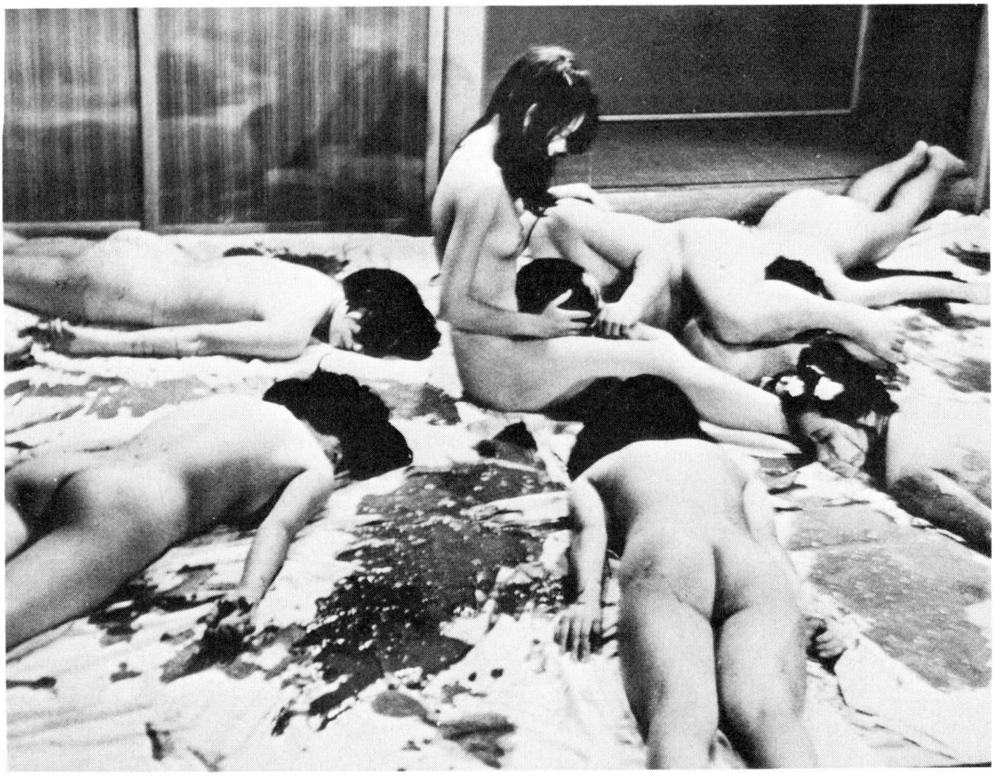

POST-SCRIPTUM

Matsumoto Toshio is not a primitive, but an avowed disciple of Brecht, and it is he, I feel, who has brought maximum clarification to the productive confrontation between Japanese culture and Western materialist theories of representation. He began by making 'experimental' shorts[16] and commissioned documentaries, all unfamiliar to me. His first feature-length film, *Funeral of Roses* (*Bara no soretsu*, 1969), which takes transvestism as its theme for reflection, introduces frequent, staged returns to the level of production. It involves one set of diegetic disruptions which certainly sticks in the mind: at the point when the hero(ine) has just brought the film's Oedipal parallel to its logical climax by gouging out his/her eyes, there is a cut to a TV-type, frontal shot of a professorial gentleman whom we have never seen before and who rhetorically challenges the audience's involvement: 'That shocked you, didn't it ... etc.' We subsequently return to the principal diegesis and the blinded and bleeding boy in (Western) 'drag' staggers out into the street, followed by a hand-held camera that observes the spontaneous reactions of *real* passers-by to this unaccustomed spectacle – of which the camera filming is clearly a part.

This resolutely dialectical approach to film-making is masterfully developed in Matsumoto's second feature, *Pandemonium* (*Shura*, 1971),[17] based upon a recent *shingeki* version of a seldom performed *kabuki* text. We recognize in its irony an affinity with that dimension of Elizabethan tragedy (and nineteenth-century French melodrama) which Camus distilled into his play *Le Malentendu*. A samurai, incognito, has succeeded in amassing a large sum of money badly needed in order to participate in the vendetta of 'the forty-seven rōnin', for his family's 'liege' was Asano, Lord of Ako. The action of the film is, in fact, laid 'in the wings' of the *Chūshingura* saga; by adopting both the popular theatrical heritage and a traditional narrative, Matsumoto also indicates their inter-textuality. The samurai, who goes by the name of Gengo, falls prey to an apparently unscrupulous couple, who swindle him out of his treasure. He sets out to wreak bloody vengeance on them and there ensues a holocaust of Elizabethan proportions. However, it soon becomes apparent – to the audience, but not, until the very last scene, to Gengo – that the couple are in fact servants of his own uncle, and that their only purpose is to obtain that same sum of money for 'the young master', whom they have never met. The entire film is organized around this misunderstanding and the manifold implications of uncertainty that develop out of it. Moreover, the fact that the spectator is given the key to the 'enigma' almost from the very start provides a distanc-

16. Apparently he has continued to do so, an exceptional and significant instance.

17. Distributed in the United States as *The Demon*.

356

ing framework within which the other strategies are developed.

The opening sequence shows Gengo being pursued through a village at night by the disembodied lanterns of a squad of police runners. The scene's somewhat eccentric editing involves several overlap matches, but it is only retrospectively that these quirks are seen to have been (inevitably on first viewing) *unread signals* to the effect that this sequence was not part of the film's primary level of reality. In an ambivalent close-up, which at first appears to match directly with the end of the flight scene (Gengo's discovery of mutilated bodies in an empty house), an (already) open-eyed Gengo gives a start: 'Oh, a dream!' Next, in a series of almost perfectly coded scenes, the initial situation is set forth. Against the pleading of his faithful old retainer, Gengo lets the brother of a prostitute who has caught his fancy lure him to the brothel where she is allegedly to be sold to a rich, repulsive merchant whom she loathes. This long period of exposition is almost completely straightforward. The long slow pans that unexpectedly articulate one reverse-field sequence, producing long, 'optically motionless' passages of black on the screen, border on ambiguity only – for at the first viewing they come too early in the film to be read for what they are, the acknowledgement of another fundamental 'anomaly': it is always *night* in this film, and in fact much of the architecture is simply slabs of darkness.[18] Gengo and the brother go to the brothel and observe surreptitiously, through a finger-hole in the *shōji*, the scene in which a merchant does, indeed, seem to be buying the girl. The actors first appear side by side, facing the camera in a theatrical disposition (Fig. 65 shows this arrangement in part), not unlike that of the *kabuki* or doll theatre stages. Just as the transaction is about to be concluded, the hero bursts into the room and after a quick exchange of defiant declarations, flings the amount necessary for the girl's redemption at the feet of the brothel owner. (It is, of course, the exact sum required for participation in the vendetta.) His faithful retainer now appears and pleads with his master not to be foolish.

It is at this point that a huge amplification of the overlap matches in the dream-prologue undermines permanently the unity of the diegesis, creating henceforth a constant threat of ambivalence and uncertainty. We cut *again* to Gengo and the girl's brother peering into the room. Once again the hero bursts in upon the scene, but this time the confrontation follows altogether different paths. The samurai disdains the girl, gladly abandoning her to the merchant and prepares to leave in a righteous huff. The girl cuts her throat and falls bleeding to the *tatami*. The samurai

INDEPENDENCE: ITS REWARDS AND PENALTIES

18. On one level, 'night' can be read as the darkness of the space around the proscenium of the Western stage.

wrests the blade from her hand *before* she can cut her throat and her dramatic gesture has the desired effect: Gengo flings the money at the feet of the brothel-keeper and ... exactly as before, the faithful retainer makes his entrance.

One can assume that after this pair of radical disjunctions, one inside the other, the spectator is disconcerted. This precarious situation is sustained throughout; although such disruptions are relatively infrequent, their effect is to create a permanent threat to the linearity and unity of the diegesis. Coded fantasy signals may or may not indicate a departure from the film's primary level of reality. Against abstract blackness, Gengo rends the air with his sword – and in reverse field splits the heads of his tormentors. A longer shot, situating Gengo alone in his room, immediately designates these reverse fields as fantasy. Soon afterwards, he steals into the house where the guilty couple lie asleep; in extreme slow motion, accompanied by stylized sound-effects, he slaughters them. In retrospect, this ambiguous slow-motion[19] seems confirmed as a fantasy signal when the actual couple start up in bed ... But they have been awakened by the very 'real' slaughter of another couple in another room. The scene had been 'actual' after all, Gengo had simply mistaken the victims.

Conversely, the spectator can be induced into taking for prime reality representations which, in another context, would be clearly perceived as fantasy, simply by making the shift from 'reality' to 'fantasy' so gradual as to be imperceptible. Thus, the shot of the couple coughing blood and dying in agony after the samurai has presented them with a jug of poisoned *sake*, however grotesque, is introduced in such a way that no solution of continuity is perceived; the scene is, however, immediately belied by the next shot in which the couple decide not to drink their terrifying guest's *sake* just now, as it is cold, and there is a warm flask on the brazier. Later, when another character unwittingly does drink the *sake*, his death is even more suddenly and extravagantly grand-guignolesque than the earlier fantasy, but it is soon clear that it must be regarded as part of the 'real' diegesis. Jean Ricardou has remarked, in writing of Borges, 'in fiction, the real and the virtual have the same status, since both are established and governed by the laws of writing.'[20] Matsumoto's film is one of the most masterful demonstrations of this theorem to be encountered in cinema. It is, moreover, one of the most important and beautiful films made in Japan since Kurosawa's prime, the others being *Death by Hanging*, *Eros Plus Massacre*, *Violated Women in White* and *People of the Second Fortress*. The particular value of all these films lies in the clarity and directness of their suggestion that an authentically

Figs. 65, 66. Matsumoto Toshio, *Pandemonium*

19. In the traditional popular cinema and in such modern genres as *yakusa eiga*, the slow-motion effect is somewhat differently and, in a sense, somewhat *less* coded than it is in the West, often serving simply to slow down the flashing movements of this or that martial art so that they may be seen, 'analyzed' by the naked eye. Of course, the modern proximity of Western connotations (lyrical, oneiric) create, often enough, similar passing ambiguities in such films, but I doubt that in such a context they have ever been part of a systematic investigation of precisely these phenomena, as in *Shura*, where they take on a very different tone.

20. Ricardou, Jean, 'Realités variables, realités variantes' in *Problèmes du Nouveau Roman,* Paris, Editions du Seuil, H 1966, pp. 23–43.

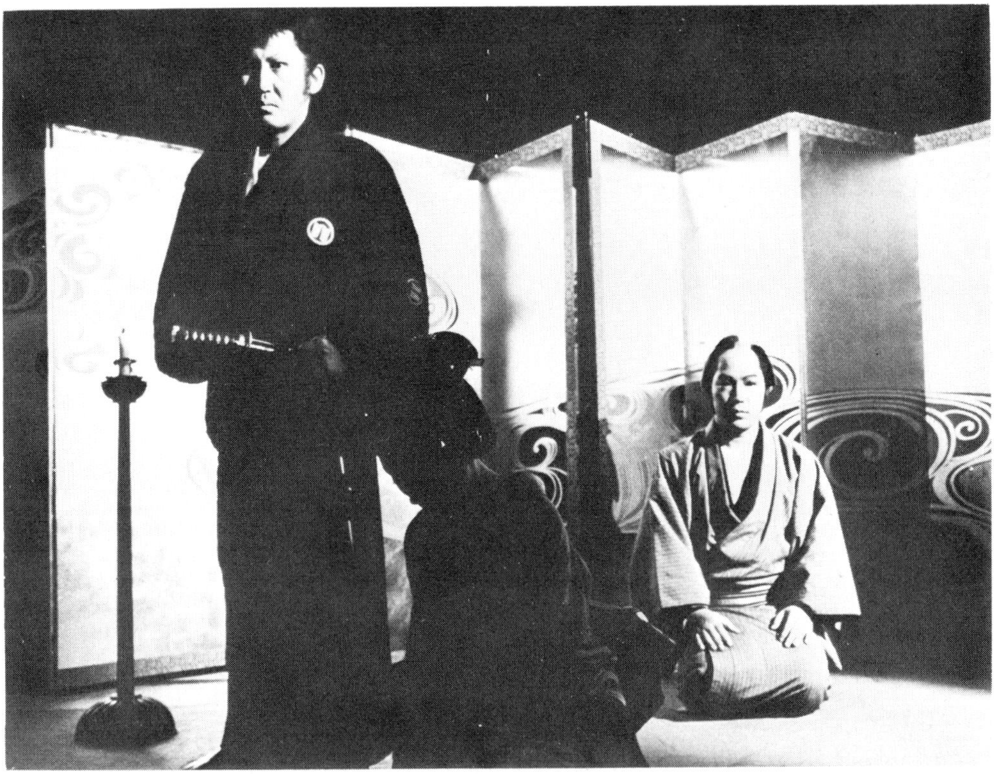

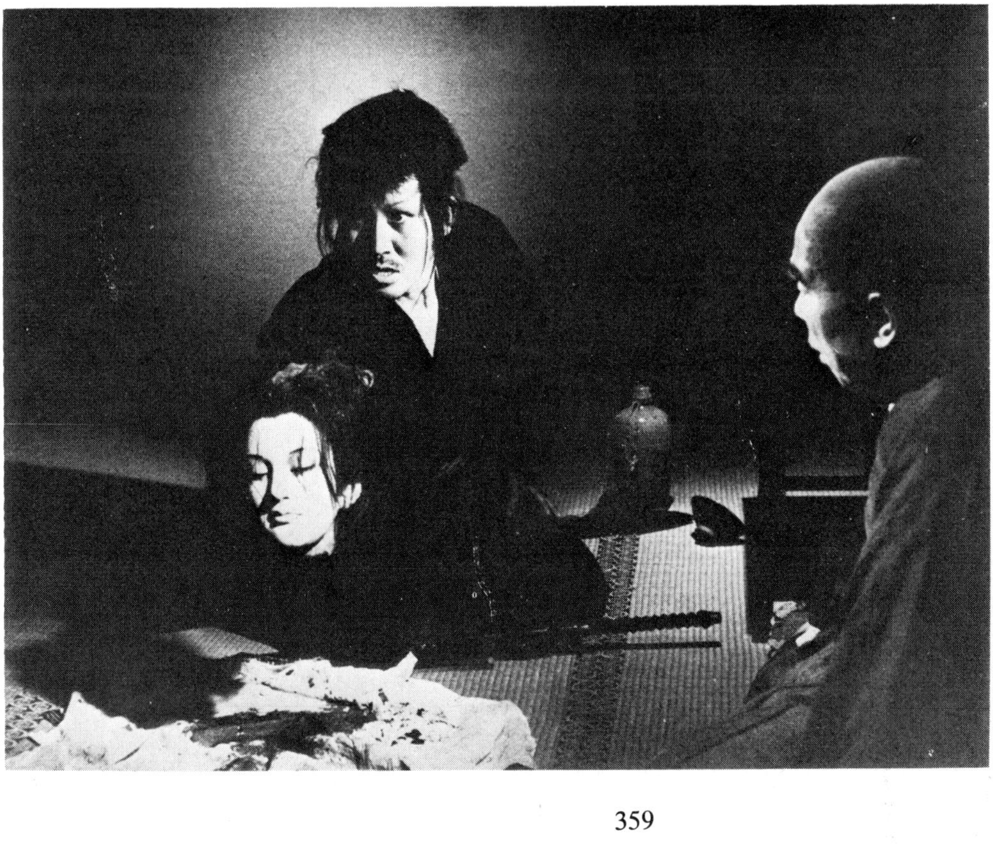

modern, revolutionary cinema in Japan must involve a conjunction of traditional artistic practice with elements of a materialist theory of art, dialectical and historical in nature, as it is developing in the West.

The difficulties of independent film-making in Japan are such that it is not surprising to find less activity there than elsewhere in the field of independent 'radical' documentary. Two really monumental undertakings, one of them still in progress, are nevertheless worth describing. Although similar in some respects, they are of different ideological inspiration and of unequal importance, from the specifically cultural, artistic point of view.

Ogawa Shinsuke and his tiny crew of friends have for nearly eight years (1967–74) devoted all their energies to one long 'work in progress', dealing with, or rather *implicated in,* the struggle of a few hundred farmers, supported by radical students, against their final eviction from Sanriziku. This is a farming district near Tokyo where the government have been building the new Narita airport, destined to relieve congested Haneda. Another suitable airport, nearer to Tokyo, and which has the advantage of already existing, is in the hands of the American armed forces, for it must not be forgotten that under the terms of the Security Pact, Japan is the 'aircraft-carrier' of American imperialism. The connecting thread of all these films – there are five altogether, with a total running time of some 15 hours – is the farmers' growing political consciousness. Understandably enough, their resistance to expropriation was at first neither political nor even economic, for they were fairly prosperous farmers and the rates paid for expropriation were high. It stemmed rather from the perennial attachment to the land on the part of those who have worked it for centuries but who have owned if for only a few decades. However hopeless, and in many respects politically naïve their struggle, the farmers learned through it, and through their contacts with the boys and girls from the *Zengakuren* student organization, to locate the responsibilities for what was happening to them . . . and to their country. For this fight is part of the life-and-death struggle being waged by the people of Japan and their mass organizations against State Monopoly Capitalism to preserve their natural environment, unquestionably the most directly threatened in the world.

Now, it is interesting that as the struggle progressed, and the film-makers began organizing their footage into a first, and then a second very long film, they also took part, in other ways, in the action. This double practice led them to modify their whole approach. Their first film, *Summer in*

*Sanriziku* (*Sanriziku no natsu*, 1967)[21] is a rather indigestible assemblage, well over two hours long, with an overemphasis on the spectacular student battles with the police. Its form is quite eclectic; it attempted to include a maximum of direct political discourse (discussions among the peasants about politics and tactics) and at the same time to convey the duration and intensity of the actual skirmishes with the police.

Four years later, Ogawa and his team produced the third and best-known film in the series. It is also the most important one, since it attempts, like Godard and *Slon* in France, Kramer and Newsreel in the United States, and the filmmakers working under Santiago Alvarez in the Cuban CIAC, to find 'new ways of filming to go with new ideas about the world.' *People of the Second Fortress* (*Daini toride no hitobito*, 1971)[22] deals with a much briefer period, only a few days or so, at a crucial stage in the resistance; the farmers had built a series of underground tunnels as a last retreat, but were still defending an above-ground area by means of barricades and bamboo staves, and by chaining themselves to the trees that were to be bulldozed. Ogawa's and his cameramen's work had now come to *fit* the rhythms and patterns of the farmers' speech and behaviour. The ten-minute takes in which peasant women set about determining the best way to chain themselves to trees, or in which a farmer repetitiously explains the ventilation arrangements and other problems in digging the underground fortresses, display a remarkable *material* understanding of the concrete modes of behaviour and discourse specific to those who work the land. The film's truly graphic sensitivity to cultural 'otherness' has few precedents. It is not too much to say that the camera (or rather more precisely the editing) of the French master Jean Rouch is 'condescending' by comparison.

Tsuchimoto Noriate is a well-known maker of television documentaries and author of an independent film on the radical student movement, *Pre-history of Partisans* (*Partisan jenchi*, 1970). His producer is Takagi Ryutaro. Their series on the Minamata tragedy is already very long, as well: three films totalling over ten hours, and a fourth is now (1976) nearing completion. Minamata is the name of a fishing village in Kyushu in which the deadly effects of waste waters rich in ethylate mercury, discharged by a huge chemical combine, first came to light. Mercury poisoning – the Minamata disease – has been responsible for dozens of deaths in that part of Japan. Because of it, hundreds of children have been born with terrible physical handicaps. The campaign to stop the polluting and to obtain adequate compensation for the victims has been a major national

21. Shown occasionally in the West as *Summer at Narita*.

22. Distributed in the West as *Peasants of the Second Fortress*.

issue. The film which revealed this tragedy to the world, *Minamata: The Victims and Their World* (*Minamata: kanjo-san to sono sokai*, 1970), is a long, impressively rigorous exposition of the facts, together with deeply moving portraits of the afflicted families and their complex social problems. The film is fundamentally reformist, in that the victims themselves, with whom and *for whom* the film was made (the Victims' Association is co-producer) are primarily motivated by their 'consciousness of being victimized,' as Oshima might say.

The second film in the series, *Minamata Revolt* (*Minamata ikki*, 1973), is a lengthy documentation of the confrontations over compensation between the Victims' Association and the Company, and displays a higher level of consciousness on the part of the victims' spokesmen. Somewhat as in Ogawa's later film, the structure of specifically filmic discourse is stronger (long takes, refusal to edit the redundant discourse of the country people, sparing use of flash-documents, etc.). I have not seen the five-hour film which Takagi and Tsuchimoto have devoted to the purely medical aspects of the situation. In it, a specifically political enterprise is extended to another – but, to these Marxists, an allied domain – that of scientific and medical research. The medical film is intended for specialists, whereas the other two were distributed through the same channels as the films of Ogawa.

Ogawa's enterprise is no doubt the more theoretically and aesthetically important, while Tsuchimoto's films are no doubt more relevant to the actualities of class struggle in Japan. Both are good examples of an attack on the notion of films as separate entities, and both are significant exceptions to the distribution monopoly held by the major companies. Each, in its own small way, is trying to give the floor to the 'madmen', the 'fools', and the masses.

The margin of manoeuvre for the film-maker with 'independent' ambitions in Japan is tiny, when compared with other capitalist countries. Consequently, a great many directors, spurred on by the examples of Oshima, Yoshida and others, have chosen, for a variety of personal motives, to 'subvert' the popular genres from within the framework of the major companies, particularly Nikkatsu and Toei, which may be very loosely compared with American firms such as Republic Pictures or American International. Suzuki Seijun is a typically prolific example of this type of director. His *The Tokyo Drifter* (*Tokyo nagaremono*, 1966) is very popular today among students and film buffs, in somewhat the way Aldrich's *Kiss Me Deadly* was popular in France during the 1950s. It is something of a pioneer film. Into this tritely complicated tale of gang rivalry, which tells how a disabused young hero 'tries to go straight', Suzuki introduced, in moderate doses, the theatrical stylizations of *Night and Fog in Japan*. In this context, these produced a quite indescribable effect of 'distancing', now frequently encountered in the gangster films, sex films, delinquent high-school girl films and other genres which play in the flea-houses of Asakusa, Ueno or Shinjuku. 'Outrageous' political or social messages, generally of a libertarian or ultra-Leftist cast, are just as frequent.

These widely distributed films represent no more than a desperate dialogue for initiates between young middle-class city-dwellers, who see the films in first-run, or in all-night 'film society programmes', and film directors who show awareness of a growing crisis within Japanese capitalism but are unable to address the masses more directly. They demonstrate, in the ultimate absurdity of their well-meaning contortions and vociferations, the efficacy of the capitalist monopoly of the audio-visual media as a vital part of a power structure that will not relinquish them without a struggle.

Only a radical change in the balance of political power in Japan can modify the increasingly bleak alternative which has faced the film-maker over the past several decades: either humiliating subservience to the law of profit, with only an illusory latitude of expression for all but a very, very few, or else the frustrating isolation and material privations of the independent ghetto. It is a sad situation for a cinema with such a prestigious past.

# List of Works Consulted

*Titles marked with an asterisk are of major interest.*

Adair, John *see* Worth, Sol.
Anderson, Joseph L. and Richie, Donald, *The Japanese Film: Art and Industry*, New York, Grove Press, 1960.
*Barthes, Roland, *L'Empire des Signes*, Geneva, Editions Skira, 1970.
Beasley, W. G., *The Modern History of Japan*, New York, Praeger, 1963; London, Weidenfeld, 1963.
Benedict, Ruth, *The Chrysanthemum and the Sword, Patterns of Japanese Culture*, London, Routledge, 1967; Tokyo, Rutland, Charles E. Tuttle, 1972.
Bowie, Henry P., *On the Laws of Japanese Painting*, New York, Dover Publications, 1952.
Brecht, Bertolt, *Brecht on Theatre: the Development of an Aesthetic* (trans. and notes by J. Willett). London, Methuen, 1964; New York, Hill and Wang, 1964.
*Brower, R. H. and Miner, E., *Japanese Court Poetry*, Stanford University Press, 1961; London, Cresset Press, 1962.
Burch, Noël, *Marcel L'Herbier*, Paris, Seghers, 1973.
– *Theory of Film Practice* (trans. by Helen Lane), London, Secker Martin & Warburg, 1973, New York, Praeger, 1973.
Chatain, Jean and Sauvage, Francis, *Clés pour le Japon*, Paris, Editions Sociales, 1974.
Chikamatsu Monzaemon *see* Keene, Donald,
Derrida, Jacques, *De la Grammatologie*, Paris, Editions de Minuit, 1967.
– *L'Ecriture et la différence*, Paris, Editions du Seuil, 1967.
– *Speech and Phenomena, and Other Essays on Husserl's Theory of Signs* (trans. and introduction by David B. Allison), Chicago, Northwestern University Press, 1973.
*Doi Takeo, *The Anatomy of Dependence* (trans. by John Bester), Tokyo, New York, San Francisco, Kodansha International, 1973.
*Drexler, Arthur, *The Architecture of Japan*, New York Museum of Modern Art (Reprint edition, 1966, published for Museum by Arno Press).
Dubois, J., Giacomo, M., Grespin, L., Marcellesi, Chr., Marcellesi J.-B. and Mevel, J.-P., *Dictionnaire de Linguistique*, Paris, Larousse, 1973.
Eisenstein, S. M., *Notes of a Film Director*, London, Laurence & Wishart, 1959; New York, Dover, 1970.
– *see also* Nizhny, V.
*Engel, Heinrich, *The Japanese House: A Tradition for Contemporary Architecture*, Rutland, Tokyo, Tuttle, 1964.
*Ernst, Earle, *The Kabuki Theatre*, New York, Grove Press, 1956.
Granet, Marcel, *La Civilisation chinoise, la vie publique et la vie privé*, Paris, Albin Michel, 1969.
Hall, Edward T., *The Hidden Dimension*, New York, Doubleday, 1966; London, Bodley Head, 1969.
– 'A system for the notation of proxemic behaviour' in *The American Anthropologist*, No. 65, 1963, pp. 1003–26.
Harootunian, H.D., *Towards Restoration, the Growth of Political Consciousness in Tokugawa Japan*, Berkeley, University of California Press, 1970.
Hillier, J., *The Japanese Print, a New Approach*, Rutland, Tokyo, Tuttle, 1960; London, G. Bell, 1960.
Honzl, Jindrich, 'La Mobilité du signe théâtral' in *Travail Théâtral* (Paris) No. 2.
Ihara Saikaku *see* Sargent, G. W.
*Japan Film Yearbook*, Tokyo, 1937 and 1938.

Kato Hidetoshi, (ed. & trans.), *Japanese Popular Culture: Studies in mass communication and cultural change made at the Institute of Science and Thought, Japan*, Rutland, Tokyo, Tuttle, 1959.

Kato Shuichi, *Form, Style, Tradition: Reflections on Japanese Art and Society* (trans. by John Bester), Berkeley, University of California Press, 1971.

Kawai Kazuo, *Japan's American Interlude*, Chicago, University of Chicago Press, 1960.

Keene, Donald, *Bunraku, the Art of the Japanese Puppet Theatre*, Tokyo and Palo Alto, Kodansha International, 1973.

– *Japanese Literature*, London, Murray, 1953; New York, Grove Press, 1955.

– *Major Plays of Chikamatsu* (trans. by Donald Keene), New York and London, Columbia University Press, 1961.

– *Nō, the Classical Theatre of Japan*, Tokyo and Palo Alto, Kodansha International, 1973.

Lee, Sherman E., *A History of Far Eastern Art*, Englewood Cliffs, N.J., Prentice-Hall, and New York, Harry N. Abrams, Inc., 1964; London, Thames and Hudson, 1964.

Leyda, Jay, *Dianying: An Account of Film and the Film Audience in China*, Cambridge, Mass., MIT Press, 1972.

Marx, Karl, *Capital* (trans. from third German edition by Samuel Moore and Edward Aveling), New York, International Publishers, 1967; London, 1887, reprinted 1938.

Metz, Christian, *Film Language, a Semiotics of the Cinema* (trans. by Michael Taylor), New York, Oxford University Press, 1974.

Michelson, Annette, 'Screen/Surface: the politics of illusionism' in *Artforum*, September 1972.

Miner, E. *see* Brower, R.H.

*Morris, Ivan, *The World of the Shining Prince: Court Life in Ancient Japan*, London, Oxford University Press, 1964; Harmondsworth, Penguin Books, 1969.

*Nakamura Hajime, *Ways of Thinking of Eastern Peoples: India, China, Tibet, Japan* (ed. by Philip P. Wiener), Honolulu, East-West Center Press, 1969.

Needham, Joseph, *Science and Civilization in China* (Vol. 1: *Introductory Orientations*), Cambridge University Press, 1956.

Nizhny, Vladimir, *Lessons with Eisenstein* (trans. and ed. by Ivor Montagu and Jay Leyda), London, Allen and Unwin, 1962; New York, Hill and Wang, 1962.

*Norman, E. Herbert, *Japan's Emergence as a Modern State, Political and Economic Problems of the Meiji Period*, IPR Inquiry Series, International Secretariat, Institute of Pacific Relations, Publication Office, New York City, 1940.

Oshima Nagisa, 'Situazione e sogetto del cinema giapponese dal doppa guerra' in *Quaderno informativo*, No. 27, Mostro Internazionale del Nuovo Cinema, Pesaro 11–18 Settembre, 1971, pp. 19–23.

Panofsky, Erwin, *L'Oeuvre d'art et ses significations*, Paris, Gallimard, 1969.

Pezeu-Massabuau, J., *Géographie du Japon*, Paris, Presses Universitaires de France, 1968.

Picon, Gaëton, *L'Usage de la lecture*, Vol. 2, Paris, Mercure de France, 1961.

Pyle, Kenneth B., *The New Generation in Meiji Japan, problems of cultural identity*, 1885–1895, Stanford University Press, 1969.

Richie, Donald *see* Anderson, Joseph L.

Sadler, A.L., *Cha-no-yu, the Japanese Tea Ceremony*, Rutland, Tokyo, Tuttle, 1962.

*Sansom, George, *A History of Japan* (Vol. I, to 1334; Vol. II, 1334 to 1615; Vol. III, 1615 to 1867), Stanford University Press, 1969.

– *An Historical Grammar of Japanese*, Oxford University Press, 1928.

*– *The Western World and Japan, a study in the interaction of European and Asiatic cultures*, New York, 1950; London, Cresset Press, 1950.

*Sargent, G.W., *The Japanese Family Storehouse or The Millionaire's Gospel Modernized* (trans. from the Japanese [of Ihara Saikaku] with introduction and commentary by G. W. Sargent), Cambridge University Press, 1969.

Sauvage, Francis *see* Chatain, Jean.

Sieffert, René, *La Tradition secrète du Nō suivi d'une journée de Nō* (trans. and commentary by René Sieffert), Paris, Gallimard, 1960.

Takahashi Kohachiro, 'La Restauration Meiji au Japon et la révolution française' in *Recherches Internationales à la lumière du Marxisme*, No. 62, 1er trimestre, 1970 (Paris).

*Tel Quel: Théorie d'Ensemble*, Paris, Editions du Seuil, 1968.

*Ueda Makoto, *Literary and Art Theories in Japan*, Cleveland, Western Reserve University Press, 1967.

Whitehouse, Wilfrid and Yahagisawa Eizo (trans.), *Ochikubo Monogatari or The Tale of the Lady Ochikubo, A Tenth-century Japanese novel*, Tokyo, The Hokuseido Press, 1965.

Willett, John, *see* Brecht, Bertolt.
Wittfogel, Karl August, *Oriental Despotism: A Comparative Study of Total Power*, New Haven, Yale University Press, 1957.
Worth, Sol and Adair, John, *Through Navajo Eyes; an exploration in film Communication and Anthropology*, Bloomington, Indiana University Press, 1972.
Yahagisawa Eizo *see* Whitehouse, Wilfrid.
Zeami *see* Sieffert, René.

# Appendix 1

**Check-lists of films of Mizoguchi, Ozu, Kurosawa and Oshima**

The English titles given in parentheses are those under which films have been shown in the West.

**Mizochuchi Kenji (1898–1956)**

1922 *Ai ni yomigaeru* The Day When Love Returns
1923 *Kokyō* Birth-Place
*Seishun no yumeji* Dreams of Youth
*Jōen no chimata* Street of Burning Passion
*Haizan no uta wa kanashi* Sad is the Song of the Vanquished
*813* [based on an Arsène Lupin story by M. Leblanc]
*Kiri no minato* Misty Harbour
*Haikyo no naka* Amongst the Castle's Ruins
*Yoru* Night
*Chi to rei* Blood and Soul
1924 *Tōge no uta* Song of the Mountain Pass
*Kanshiki hakushi* The Sad Idiot
*Akatsuki no shi* Death at Dawn
*Itō junsa no shi* Death of Policeman Itō
*Gendai no joō* Queen of Modern Times
*Josei wa tsuyoshi* The Gentle Sex Are Strong
*Jinkyo* The World of Man
*Shichimenchō no yukue* The Missing Turkey
*Samidare zoshi* A Tale of Early Summer Rain
*Kanraku no onna* Pleasure Girl
*Musen fusen* No Money, No War
1925 *Kyokyubadan no joō* Queen of the Circus Troop
*Gakuso o idete* After Years of Study
*Daichi wa hohoemu* The Smile of the Earth
*Shirayuri wa nageku* Lament of the White Lily
*Gaijo no suketchi* Street Sketch
*Ningen* Humanity
*Furusato no uta* Song of the Home Country
*Akai yūhi ni terasarete* The Red Glow of Sunset
1926 *Nogi taisho to Kuma-san* General Nogi and Mr Kuma

       *Dōka ō* The King of Copper Coins
       *Kami ningyo haru no sasayaki* The Spring Murmur of a Paper Doll
       *Shin onoga tsumi* My Sin, Continued
       *Kyoren no onna shishō* Passion of a Woman Teacher
       *Kaikoku danji* Sons of the Sea Country
       *Kane* Money
1927 *Ko on* Obligation to the Emperor
       *Jihi shincho* The Bird of Mercy
1928 *Hito no issho* The Life of a Man [in three parts]
       *Musume kawaiya* What a Lovely Girl!
1929 *Nihon-bashi* Japan Bridge
       *Asahi wa kagayaku* The Rising Sun Shines
       *Tokyo koshin kyoku* Tokyo March
       *Tokai kokyogaku* The Symphony of a City
1930 *Furusato* Home Country [first sound film]
       *Tojin Okichi* Okichi, the Foreigner's Mistress
1931 *Shikamo karera wa yuku* And Yet They Proceed
1932 *Toki no ujigami* The Patron Deity of Time
       *Mam-Mō kenkoku no reimei* The Dawn of the Foundation of Manchukuo and Mongolia
1933 *Taki no shiraito* 'White Threads of the Waterfall'
       *Gion matsuri* Gion Festival
       *Jimpuren* The Jimpu Group
1934 *Aizo toge* Mountain Pass of Love and Hate
       *Orizuru O-Sen* O-Sen of the Paper Cranes
1935 *Maria no O-Yuki* O-Yuki, Alias Maria
       *Gubijinsō* Poppies
1936 *Naniwa erejī* The Elegy of Naniwa
       *Gion no shimai (kyodai)* Sisters of Gion
1937 *Aienkyō* The Gorge Between Love and Hate
1938 *Roei no uta* Camp Song
       *Ā furusato* O Homeland!
1939 *Zangiku monogatari* Tale of Late Chrysanthemums
1940 *Naniwa onna* Woman of Naniwa
1941 *Geido ichidai otoko* The Life of an Artist
1941–2 *Genroku chūshingura* A Tale of Loyal Retainers of the Genroku Era
1944 *Danjuro sandai* Three Generations of Danjuro
1945 *Hisshō ka* Song of Faith in Victory [co-directors: Makino Masahiro, Shimizu Hiroshi, Tasaka Tomotaka]
       *Meitō Bijomaru* Bijomaru, the Famous Sword
1946 *Josei no shori* Woman's Victory
       *Utamaro o meguro gonin no onna* Five Women Around Utamaro
1947 *Joyu Sumako no koi* The Love of Actress Sumako
1948 *Yoru no onnatachi* Women of the Night
1949 *Waga koi wa moeru* Our(My) Love Burns
1950 *Yuki fujin ezu* Portrait of Mrs Yuki
1951 *Oyusama* Miss Oyu
       *Musashino Fujin* The Lady of Musashino
1952 *Saikaku ichidai onna* The Life of a Woman, by Saikaku (The Life of Oharu)
1953 *Ugetsu monogatari* Stories of the Moon After Rain
1954 *Sanshō dayū* Sanshō the Bailiff
       *Uwasa no onna* The Woman They Talk About
       *Chikamatsu monogatari* A Story by Chikamatsu
1955 *Yokihi* Princess Yang
       *Shin Heike monogatari* New Tales of the Heike (Taira) Clan
1956 *Akasen shitai* Red Light District (Street of Shame)

## Ozu Yasujiro (1903–1963)

- 1927 *Zange no yaibo* Sword of Penitence
- 1928 *Wakōdo no yume* Dreams of Youth
  - *Nyōbō funshitsu* Wife Lost
  - *Kabocha* Pumpkin
  - *Hikkoshi fūfu* A Couple Moving House
  - *Nikutaibi* Body Beautiful
- 1929 *Takara no yama* Treasure Mountain
  - *Wakaki hi* Days of Youth
  - *Wasei kenka tomodachi* Fighting Friends
  - *Daigaku wa deta keredo* I Graduated, But . . .
- 1930 *Kashain seikatsu* Life of an Office-Worker
  - *Tokkan kozō* A Straightforward Apprentice
  - *Kekkon-gaku nyūmon* Introduction to the Wedding Ceremony
  - *Hogaraka ni susume* Be Cheerful
  - *Rakudai wa shita keredo* I Flunked, But . . .
  - *Sono yo no tsuma* That Night's Wife
  - *Ero-shin no onryō* The Revengeful Spirit of Eros
  - *Ashi ni sawatta kōun* Luck Touched My Legs
  - *Ojyōsan* Young Miss
  - *Shukujyō to hige* The Lady and the Beard
- 1931 *Bijin aishū* Beauty's Sorrows
  - *Tōkyō no gasshō* Chorus of Tokyo
- 1932 *Haru wa gofujin kara* Spring Comes from the Ladies
  - *Umarete wa mita keredo* I Was Born, But . . .
  - *Seishun no yume ima izuko* Where Are the Dreams of Youth?
  - *Mata au hi made* Until the Day We Meet Again
- 1933 *Tōkyō no onna* Woman(en) of Tokyo
  - *Hijōsen no onna* War-Emergency Women
  - *Dekigokoro* Passing Fancy
- 1934 *Haha o kowazu ya* A Mother Ought to be Loved
  - *Ukigusa monogatari* A Story of Floating Weeds
- 1935 *Hako-iri musume* The Sheltered Girl
  - *Tōkyō no yado* An Inn in Tokyo
- 1936 *Daigaku yoitoko* College is a Nice Place
  - *Hitori musuko* Only Son [first sound film]
  - *Shukujyo wa nani wasureta ka* What Did the Lady Forget?
- 1941 *Todake no kyōdai* Toda Brother and Sister
- 1942 *Chichi ariki* There Was a Father
- 1948 *Nagaya shinshi roku* Record of a Tenement Gentleman
  - *Kaze no naka no mendori* A Hen in the Wind
- 1949 *Banshun* Late Spring
- 1950 *Munakata shimai* The Munakata Sisters
- 1951 *Bakushū* or *Mugi-aki* Autumn Barley-Time (Early Summer)
- 1952 *Ochazuke no aji* The Flavour of Green-Tea-with-Rice
- 1953 *Tōkyō monogatari* Tokyo Story
- 1956 *Sōshun* Early Spring
- 1957 *Tōkyō boshoku* Tokyo Twilight
- 1958 *Higan-bana* Equinox Flowers
- 1959 *Ohayō* Good morning!
  - *Ukigusa* Floating Weeds
- 1960 *Aki biyori* A Fine Day in Autumn (Late Autumn)
- 1961 *Kobayakawa no aki* Autumn in the Kobatakawa Family (Early Autumn)
- 1962 *Samma no aji* The Taste of Mackerel Pike (An Autumn Afternoon)

### Kurosawa Akira (1910– )

- 1940 *Uma* The Horse
- 1943 *Sugata Sanshiro*
- 1944 *Ichiban utsukushiku* The Most Beautiful
- 1945 *Zoku Sugata Sanshiro* Sequel to Sugata Sanshiro
- 1945 *Tora no o o fumu otokotachi* They Who Tread on the Tiger's Tail
- 1946 *Asu o tsukuru hitobito* The People Who Make Tomorrow
  *Waga seishun ni kuinashi* No Regrets for Our Youth
- 1947 *Subarashiki nichiyōbi* Wonderful Sunday
- 1948 *Yoidore tenshi* Drunken Angel
- 1949 *Shizukanaru ketto* The Quiet Duel
- 1949 *Nora inu* Stray Dog
- 1950 *Shubun* Scandal
  *Rashōmon* [i.e. The Rashō Gate]
- 1951 *Hakuchi* The Idiot
- 1952 *Ikiru* Living
- 1954 *Shichinin no samurai* Seven Samurai
- 1955 *Ikimono no kiroku* Record of a Living Thing
- 1957 *Kumo-no-su jō* Cobweb Castle (Throne of Blood)
- 1957 *Donzoko* The Lower Depths
- 1958 *Kakushi no toride no san-akunin* Three Bad Men in a Hidden Fortress (The Hidden Fortress)
- 1960 *Warui yatsu yoku nemuru* Bad Guys Sleep Well
- 1961 *Yojimbō*
- 1962 *Tsubaki Sanjuro* Sanjuro of the Camellias (Sanjuro)
- 1963 *Tengoku to jigoku* High and Low [Literally, Heaven and Hell]
- 1965 *Akahige* Red Beard
- 1969 *Dodeskaden*


### Oshima Nagisa (1932– )
This list is exclusive of shorts and TV films.

- 1959 *Ai to kibō no machi* Town of Love and Hope
- 1960 *Seishun zankoku monogatari* A Cruel Tale of Youth
  *Taiyō no hakeba* The Sun's Graveyard
  *Nihon no yoru to kiri* Night and Fog in Japan
- 1961 *Shiiku* The Catch
- 1962 *Amakusa Shiro Tokisada*
- 1964 *Watashi wa Bellette* Here I am: Bellette
- 1965 *Etsuraku* Pleasure
- 1966 *Ninja bugeicho* Tales of the Ninja
- 1967 *Hakuchu no tōrima* 'Floating Ghost' in Broad Daylight [i.e. rapist]
  *Muri shinju: Nihon no natsu* Double Suicide: Japanese Summer
  *Nihon shunka-kō* Treatise on Japanese Bawdy Songs
- 1968 *Koshikei* Death by Hanging
  *Shinjuku dorobō nikki* Diary of a Shinjuku Thief
- 1969 *Shōnen* Boy
- 1970 *Tokyo senso senyo hiwa* Secret Story of the post-'Tokyo War' Period
  *Gishiki* Ceremonies
- 1972 *Natsu no imoto* Little Summer Sister
- 1975/6 *Ai no corrida* Corrida of Love or *l'Empire des sens*

# Appendix 2

**Archive holdings in Japan: Japanese films produced before 1946**

It may be considered that most films produced since the war still exist in Japan, though are perhaps not readily accessible. The absence of any given film from these lists, even though it may at present be regarded as lost, does not mean that such is the case. As confirmation of what was said on this matter in the Preface, since my last visit to Japan (Autumn, 1973) the Film Centre has been able to add to its collection at least thirty-two re-discovered films – indicated below by †. Nor are these, of course, the only films I have been unable to view. Films studied for this book are marked *.

**Film Centre of the National Museum of Modern Art, Tokyo**

| | | | |
|---|---|---|---|
| 1921 | Rojō no reikon* | Souls on the Road | Osanai Kaoru and Murata Minoru |
| 1921 | Kantsubaki* | Winter Camellia(s) | Inoue Masao |
| 1921 | Goketsu jirai-ya* | Heroic Thunder-boy | Makino Shozō |
| 1928 | Jūjiro* | Crossways | Kinugasa Teinosuke |
| 1929 | Fue no siratama† | Eternal Love | Shimizu Hiroshi |
| 1929 | Wakaki hi* | Days of Youth | Ozu Yasujiro |
| 1930 | Kaigara Ippei (part one only)* | | Kiyose Eijiro |
| 1930 | Shingun* | The March | Ushiwara Kiyohiko |
| 1930 | Wakamono yo naze nakuka† | Why Do You Cry, Young People | Ushiwara Kiyohiko |
| 1930 | Hogaraka ni ayume† | Walk Cheerfully | Ozu Yasujiro |
| 1930 | Rakudai wa shita keredo† | I Flunked, But . . . | Ozu Yasujiro |
| 1930 | Sono yo no tsuma* | That Night's Wife | Ozu Yasujiro |
| 1931 | Shukujō to hige* | The Lady and the Beard | Ozu Yasujiro |
| 1931 | Koshiben Ganbare† | Worker Ganbare | Naruse Mikio |
| 1931 | Madamu to nyobō* | The Neighbour's Wife and Mine | Gosho Heinosuke |
| 1931 | Beni kōmori* | The Red Bat | Tanaka Tsuruhiko |
| 1931 | Tokyo no gasshō | Tokyo Chorus | Ozu Yasujiro |
| 1932 | Umarete wa mita keredo* | I Was Born, But . . . | Ozu Yasujiro |
| 1932 | Jōriku daiippo† | First Steps Ashore | Shimazu Yasujiro |
| 1932 | Mito Kōmon | Mito Kōmon | Tsuji Yoshiro |
| 1933 | Seishun no yume izuko† | Where Are the Dreams of Youth | Ozu Yasujiro |
| 1933 | Izu no odoriko* | The Dancing Girl of Izu | Gosho Heinosuke |
| 1933 | Hanayome no negoto† | The Bride Talks in Her Sleep | Gosho Heinosuke |
| 1933 | Aibu† | Caresses | Goshu Heinosuke |
| 1933 | Hijosen no onna† | Women on the Firing Line | Ozu Yasujiro |
| 1933 | Dai Chūshingura† | Tale of Loyal Retainers | Kinugasa Teinosuke |
| 1933 | Daigaku no waka-danna† | The Boss's Son at College | Shimizu Hiroshi |

| Year | Japanese Title | English Title | Director |
|---|---|---|---|
| 1933 | Tōkyō no onna* | Woman(en) of Tokyo | Ozu Yasujiro |
| 1933 | Kimi to wakarete* | After Our Separation | Naruse Mikio |
| 1933 | Yogoto no yume* | Nightly Dreams | Naruse Mikio |
| 1933 | Dekigokoro* | Passing Fancy | Ozu Yasujiro |
| 1933 | Keisatsukan* | Police | Uchida Tomu |
| 1934 | Fukeizu† | A Woman's Family-Tree | Nomura Y. |
| 1934 | Tonari no Yae-chan* | Our Neighbour Miss Yae | Shimazu Yasujiro |
| 1934 | Ukigusa monogatari* | A Story of Floating Weeds | Ozu Yasujiro |
| 1934 | Haha o kowazuya* | A Mother Ought to Be Loved | Ozu Yasujiro |
| 1934 | Karisome no kuchibeni | Trifling Lipstick | Suzuki Jukichi |
| 1934 | Hanamuko no negoto† | The Groom Talks in His Sleep | Gosho Heinosuke |
| 1934 | Orizuru O-Sen* | O-Sen of the Paper Cranes | Mizoguchi Kenji |
| 1934 | Muteki | Foghorns | Murata Minoru |
| 1935 | Jinsei gekijo† | Theatre of Life | Uchida Tomu |
| 1935 | O-Koto to Sasuke | O-Koto and Sasuke | Shimazu Yasujiro |
| 1935 | Hyaku-man-ryō no tsubo* | The Pot Worth a Million Ryō | Yamanaka Sadao |
| 1935 | Tsuma yo bara no yo ni* | Wife, Be Like a Rose | Naruse Mikio |
| 1935 | Jinsei no onimotsu* | The Burden of Life | Gosho Heinosuke |
| 1935 | Shoshū rei | Orders to Call Out the Men | Watanabe Kuniyo |
| 1935 | Tōkyō no yado* | An Inn in Tokyo | Ozu Yasujiro |
| 1935 | Maria no O-Yuki† | Maria, Alias O-Yuki | Mizoguchi Kenji |
| 1935 | Gubijinso† | Poppies | Mizoguchi Kenji |
| 1935 | Enoken no Kondo Isamu* | Enoken plays Kondo Isamu | Yamamoto Kajiro |
| 1936 | Inojino kamuri† | The Crown of Life | Uchida Tomu |
| 1936 | Tochuken Kumoemon* | Tochuken Kumoemon | Naruse Mikio |
| 1936 | Naniwa Eregy* | The Elegy of Naniwa | Mizoguchi Kenji |
| 1936 | Gion no shimai (kyodai) | Sisters of Gion | Mizoguchi Kenji |
| 1936 | Arigatōsan† | Thank You Very Much | Shimizu Hiroshi |
| 1936 | Akanishi Kakita* | Akanishi Kakita | Itami Mansaku |
| 1936 | Ani imoto* | Elder Brother, Younger Sister | Kimura Sotoji |
| 1936 | Hitori musuko* | Only Son | Ozu Yasijiro |
| 1936 | Byakui no kajin [one reel only] | Beautiful Women in White | Abe Yutaka |
| 1936 | Taii no musume | The Captain's Daughter | Nobuchi Akira |
| 1936 | Oboroyo no onna† | Woman of the Mist | Gosho Heinosuke |
| 1937 | Sengoku buntōden | Tale of Thieves in Wartime | Tagisawa Eisuke |
| 1937 | Hanakago no uta† | The Song of the Flower-basket | Gosho Heinosuke |
| 1937 | Ninjō kamifusen* | Humanity/Paper Balloons | Yamanaka Sadao |
| 1937 | Kaze no naka no kodomo* | Children in the Wind | Shimizu Hiroshi |
| 1937 | Wakai hito | Young People | Toyoda Shiro |
| 1937 | Asakusa no hi | Lights of Asakusa | Shimazu Yasujiro |
| 1937 | Shingun no uta | Marching Song | Sasaki Yasuchi |
| 1937 | Soma no kinsan | Mr Kin of Soma | Inaba Kaji |
| 1937 | Hanabi no machi† | Expectation of Fireworks | Ishida Tamizo |
| 1937 | Kaiki Edogawa Ranzan | The Mysterious Edogawa Ranzan | Shimamura Kenji |
| 1937 | Yoru no hato† | Dove of Night | Ishida Tamizo |
| 1937 | Hokushi no sora o tsuku | Aim For the Sky Over 'Hokushi' [Japanese name for a Chinese town] | Watanabe Kunio |
| 1937 | Hanagata senshu* | A Star Athlete | Shimizu Hiroshi |
| 1937 | Hitohada kannon* | The Helping Hand of the Goddess of Mercy | Kinugasa Teinosuke |
| 1937 | Joi Kinoyu, sensei | Miss Kinuyo, Doctor | Nomura Hiromasa |
| 1937 | Yoru no hato† | Night Dove | Ishida Tamizo |
| 1938 | Abe ichizoku* | The Abe Clan | Kumagaya Hisatora |
| 1938 | Robō no ishi* | The Stone on the Road | Tazaka Tomotaka |
| 1938 | Taiyō no ko | Child(ren) of the Sun | Abe Yutaka |
| 1938 | Denen kokyōgaku* | The Pastoral Symphony | Yamamoto Satsu |

| Year | Japanese Title | English Title | Director |
|---|---|---|---|
| 1938 | Tojuro no koi | The Love of Tojuro | Yamamoto Kajiro |
| 1938 | Hana chirinu* | Fallen Blossoms | Ishida Tamizo |
| 1938 | Tsuzurikata kyoshitsu* | Composition Class | Yamamoto Kajiro |
| 1938 | Tsuruhachi Tsurujiro* | Tsuruhachi and Tsurujiro | Naruse Mikio |
| 1938 | Uguisu* | The Bush Warbler | Toyoda Shiro |
| 1938 | Ouma no tsuji | Duel at Ouma | Takizawa Hidesuke |
| 1938 | Nihonjin | Japanese People [incomplete] | Shimazu Tasujiro |
| 1938 | Aisō hitōroku | A Tragic Story of Love and Hate | Tonoyama Bompei |
| 1938 | Yakko Ginpei | Gpnpei, Servant | Osone Tatsuo |
| 1938 | Ginetsu | The Heat of the Earth | Takizawa Hidesuke |
| 1938 | Gonin no sekkohei* | Five Scouts | Tasaka Tomotaka |
| 1938 | Ajia no musume | Girl of Asia | Tanaka Shigeo |
| | | | Numaha Isao |
| 1938 | Yukinojō henge† | The Ghost of Yukinojō | Kinugasa Teinosuke |
| 1938 | Anma to onna† | The Masseuse | Shimizu Hiroshi |
| 1938 | Tōyōheiwa no michi | The Way to Peace in the Orient | Suzuki Juichin |
| 1938 | Haha to ko† | Mother and Child | Shibuya Mioru |
| 1938–9 | Aisenkatsura | Aisenkatsura | Nomura Kosho |
| 1939 | Tsuchi* | Earth | Uchida Tomu |
| 1939 | Tsuchi to heitai* | Earth and Soldiers | Tasaka Tomotaka |
| 1939 | Danryū* | Warm Current | Yoshimura Kimisaburo |
| 1939 | Kokoro no taiyō | The Sun of the Heart | Fukuda Shuzo |
| 1939 | Enoken no ganbari senjutusu* | Enoken's Persistent Tactics | Nakagawa Nobuo |
| 1939 | Oshidori uta gassen | A Friendly Singing Contest | Makino Masahiro |
| 1939 | Hataraku ikka* | The Whole Family Works | Naruse Mikio |
| 1939 | Hatagoya sōdō | Disturbance at the Inn | Mori Issei |
| 1939 | Byakuran no uta | The Song of the White Orchid | Watanabe Kunio |
| 1939 | Kodomo no shiki | Four Seasons of Children | Shimizu Hiroshi |
| 1939 | Shanghai rikusentai* | Shanghai Report | Tomagaya Hisatura |
| 1939 | Shinpen Tangezasen* | The New Tangezasen | Nakagawa Nobuo |
| 1939 | Tsukiyo karasu* | Crow in the Moonlight | Inouye Kintaro |
| 1939 | Zangiku monogatari* | Tale of Late Chrysanthemums | Mizoguchi Kenji |
| 1939 | Ani to sono imoto | The Elder Brother and His Younger Sister | Shimazu Yasujiro |
| 1939 | Atarashiki kazoku | The New Family | Shibuya Minoru |
| 1939 | Kuramatengu Edonikki | The Edo Diary of Kuramatengu | Matsuda Sadaji |
| 1939 | Ju-man-ryō hibun | Secret Story of 100 000 ryō | Arai Ryohei |
| 1939 | Mukashi no uta* | Old Songs | Ishida Tamizo |
| 1939 | Chiheisen | The Horizon | Yoshimura Misao |
| | | | Shirai Shintaro |
| 1940 | Hebihimesama* | The Snake-Princess | Kinugasa Teinosuke |
| 1940 | Kojima no haru | Spring Comes to a Little Island | Toyoda Shiro |
| 1940 | Nobuko | Nobuko | Shimizu Hiroshi |
| 1940 | Shina no yoru | Night in China | Fushimi Osama |
| 1940 | Moyuru ozora | The Great Burning Sky | Abe Yutaka |
| 1940 | Akatsuki ni inoru | Prayers at Dawn | Sasaki Yasushi |
| 1940 | Bijo Zakura | A Girl Named Zakura | Osone Tatsuo |
| 1940 | Butai sugata | Figures on the Stage | Nomura Hiromasa |
| 1940 | Gonza to Sukeju | Gonza and Sukeju | Furuno Eisaku |
| 1940 | Nihonmatsu shōnen tai | 'Two Pine trees' Boys Unit | Akiyama Kosaku |
| 1940 | Utsukushiki rinjin | Beautiful Neighbours | Oba Hideo |
| 1940 | Ane no shussei | Elder Sister at the Front | Kondo Katsuhiko |
| 1940 | Arashi ni saku hana | Flowers Blooming in the Storm | Hagiwara Ryo |
| 1940 | Yajikita kaidan dōchu | The Mysterious Journey from Yajikita | Furuno Eisaku |
| 1940 | Rakka no mai | Dance of Falling Blossoms | Nishihara Takashi |
| 1940 | Fuyukihakase no kazoku | Dr Fuyaki's Family | |
| 1940 | Nessa no chikai | Oath of Enthusiasm | Watanabe Kunio |

| Year | Japanese Title | English Title | Director |
|---|---|---|---|
| 1940 | Kinuyo no hatsukoi | Kinuyo's First Love | Nomura Hiromasa |
| 1940 | Kofuku na kazoku | A Happy Family | Hara Kenkichi |
| 1940 | Nishizumi senshachōden* | The Story of Tank-Commander Nishizumi | Yoshimura Kimisaburo |
| 1940 | Miyamoto Mushashi | Miyamoto Mushashi | Inagaki Hiroshi |
| 1940 | Yoku-do banri | Thousands of Miles of Good Soil | Kurata Bunjin |
| 1940 | Bokuseki† | Trees and Stones | Gosho Heinosuke |
| 1940 | Keijo† | Seoul | Shimizu Hiroshi |
| 1940 | Keshoyuki† | Keshoyuki | Ishida Tamizo |
| 1941 | Todake no kyodai* | Toda Brother and Sister | Ozu Yasujiro |
| 1941 | Uma* | The Horse | Yamamoto Kajiro |
| 1941 | Genroku chūshingura* | A Tale of Loyal Retainers in the Genroku Era [Part 1] | Mizoguchi Kenji |
| 1941 | Jirō monogatari | The Story of Jirō | Shima Koji |
| 1941 | Kawanakajima kaisen | The Battle for Kawanakajima | Kinugasa Teinosuke |
| 1941 | Shidō monogatari | A Story of Guidance | Tomagaya Hisatura |
| 1941 | Tōgyo | Fighting Fish | Shimazu Yasujiro |
| 1941 | Waga ai no ki | The Story of Our Love | Toyoda Shiro |
| 1941 | Hideko no shasho-san | Miss Hideko, Bus Conductor | Naruse Mikio |
| 1941 | Hachijū-hachinenme no taiyō | The Sun of the 88th Year | Takizawa Hideyuki |
| 1941 | Onna no yado | Women's Lodgings | Inuzuka Minoru |
| 1941 | Magokoro no uta | The Song of a True Heart | Hijikawa Iseo |
| 1941 | Shanghai no tsuki | Shanghai Moon | Naruse Mikio |
| 1941 | Sakura no kuni | Cherry-tree Country | Shibuya Minoru |
| 1941 | Satsuma no misshi | The Satsuma Envoy | Suganuma Kanji |
| 1941 | Mikaeri no to† | Tower of Orphans | Shimizu Hiroshi |
| 1941 | Donguri to shiinomi† | Acorns | Shimizu Hiroshi |
| 1941 | Kanzashi | Hair-pins | Shimizu Hiroshi |
| 1941 | Utajo oboegaki† | Memories of a Female Singer | Shimizu Hiroshi |
| 1942 | Aru onna | One Woman | Shibuya Minoru |
| 1942 | Genroku chūshingura* | A Tale of Loyal Retainers in the Genroku Era [Part 2] | Mizoguchi Kenji |
| 1942 | Hawai Maree oki kaisen* | The War at Sea off Hawaii and Malaya | Yamamoto Kajiro |
| 1942 | Yama sando | The Way to the Mountain | Shima Koji |
| 1942 | Aikoku no hana | The Blossoms of Patriotism | Sasaki Keisuke |
| 1942 | Musashibo Benkei | Musashibo Benkei | Watanabe Kunio |
| 1942 | Minami no kaze | South Wind | Yoshimura Kimisaburo |
| 1943 | Chichi ariki* | There Was a Father | Ozu Yasujiro |
| 1943 | Sugata Sanshiro* | Sugata Sanshiro | Kurosawa Akira |
| 1943 | Hana saku minato* | The Blossoming Port | Kinoshita Keisuke |
| 1943 | Muhô-Matsu no isshô | The Life of Matsu the Untamed | Inagaki Hiroshi |
| 1943 | Ahen sensō | Opium War | Makino Masahiro |
| 1943 | Kessen no ōzora e | Towards the Decisive Battle in the Sky | Watanabe Kunio |
| 1943 | Bōro no kesshitai | Suicide Troops of the Watch-tower | Imai Tadashi |
| 1943 | Ie ni sannan nijo ari | Three Men, Two Women in a House | Mizuko Harumi |
| 1943 | Kamen no butō | Masked Ball | Sasaki Keisuke |
| 1943 | Sayon no kane | The Bell of Sayon | Shimizu Hiroshi |
| 1943 | Aiki minami no tobu | Flying South in His Plane | Sasaki Keisuke |
| 1943 | Meijin Chōji bori | Master Sculptor Chōji | Higiwara Ryo |
| 1943 | Ai no sekai | The World of Love | Aoyagi Nobue |
| 1943 | Heiroku yume monogatari | Heiroku's Dream Story | Aoyagi Nobue |
| 1943 | Kaigun* | Navy | Tasaka Tomotaka |
| 1943 | Hoppō ni kane ga naru | Bells Ring in the North | Osone Tatsuo |
| 1943 | Jingisukan | Genghis Khan | Matsuda Sadaji / Ushihara Kiyohiko |
| 1943 | Jūkei kara kita otoko | The Man Who Came From a Great Joy | Yamamoto Hiroyuki |
| 1943 | Waga ya no kaze | The Wind Around Our House | Tanaka Shigeo |

| | | |
|---|---|---|
| 1943 *Kekkon meirei* | Wedding By Command | Numaha Isao |
| 1943 *Asagiri gunka*† | War-Song for a Misty Dawn | Ishida Tamizo |
| 1944 *Ichiban utsukushiku*\* | The Most Beautiful | Kurosawa Akira |
| 1944 *Kimikoso tsugi no arawashida* | You'll Be the Next Wild Eagle | Sasaki Keisuke |
| 1944 *Yasen gungakutai* | Military Combat Band | Makino Masahiro |
| 1944 *Tanoshiki kana jinsei* | What a Beautiful Life | Naruse Mikio |
| 1944 *Gojū no tō* | Fifty Pagodas | Gosho Heinosuke |
| 1944 *Sanjaku Sagohei* | Sanjaku Sagohei | Ishida Ryozo |
| 1944 *Yottsu no kekkon* | Four Weddings | Aoyagi Nobuo |
| 1944 *Gekiryū* | Swift Current | Ieki Niyoji |
| 1944 *Kakute kamikaze wa fuku* | Thus the Heavenly Wind [*kamikaze*] Will Blow | Marune Santaro |
| 1944 *Kokusai mitsuyu dan* | International Smugglers' Ring | Ito Daisuke |
| 1944 *Monpe-san* | The Woman in Peasant Trousers | Tanaka ? |
| 1944 *Oyako Zakura* | Zakura Father and Son | Koishi Eichi |
| 1944 *Miyamoto Musashi*† | Miyamoto Musashi | Mizoguchi Kenji |
| 1945 *Toro no o o fumu otokotachi*\* | They Who Tread on the Tiger's Tail | Kurosawa Akira |
| 1945 *Otomo no iru kichi* | The Girl at the Military Base | Sasaki Keisuke |
| 1945 *Izu no musume-tachi*† | The Girls of Izu | Gosho Heinosuke |

**Japan Film Library Council, Tokyo**

As of October 1973: the films given are most but not all of the titles not included in the Film Centre catalogue. The JFLC is a private organization which channels most of the foreign cultural relations of the Japanese industry, and also works in close contact with the Film Centre.

| | | |
|---|---|---|
| 1908 *Taiko-kin junanme*\* | Chronicle of Taiko [excerpt] | Unknown director |
| 1908 *Sendai-Hagi*\* | Sendai-Hagi | Unknown director |
| 1917 *Ninin Shizuka*\* | Two People Named Shizuka | Ogachi Tadashi |
| 1920 *Shibukawa Bangoro*\* | Shibukawa Bangoro | Unknown director |
| 1926 *Kurutta ippeiji*\* | Page of Madness | Kinugasa Teinosuke |
| 1927 *Son-no joi-i*\* | Honour the Emperor, Expel the Barbarians | Ikeda Tomiyasu |
| 1928 *Horo Zanmai* | Vagaband Gambler | Inagaki Hiroshi |
| 1928 *Jitsuroku chūshingura*\* | The True Story of the Loyal Retainers | Makino Shōzo |
| 1929 *Kutsukake Tokigiro* | Kutsukake Tokigiro | Nezu Aru |
| 1933 *Taki no shiraito*\* | 'White Threads of the Waterfall' | Mizoguchi Kenji |

**Kyoto Film Library**

The titles given are those found, as of October 1973, in neither of the above archives. All, however, came in fact, from Matsuda Shunji's remarkable private (rental) archive in Tokyo, which contains several treasures like the early Makino *Chūshingura* as well as clips from hundreds of other early films, but whose catalogue I cannot, for practical reasons, reproduce here.

| | | |
|---|---|---|
| 1922 *Ninin Shizuka*\* | Two People Named Shizuka | Obora Gengo |
| 1924 *Kunisada Chuji*\* | Kunisada Chuji | Makino Shōzo |
| 1927 *Sunae jubaku*\* | The Curse of the Sand-Picture | Kanemori Banshō |
| 1928 *Benten kozō*\* | Benten Apprentice [excerpt] | Kinugasa Teinosuke |
| 1928 *Toribeyama shinju*\* | Double Suicide on Mt Toribe | Fuyushima Taizo |
| 1929 *Habu no minato*\* | Habu Harbour | Nezu Arata |
| 1931 *Mabuta no haha*\* | The Mother He Never Knew [literally, 'The Mother of His Eyelid'] | Inagaki Hiroshi |
| 1932 *Hototogisu Namiko* | Namiko, the 'Coocoo' | Tanaka Eizu |

# Publishers' Acknowledgements

For granting permission to reproduce copyright material the publishers are grateful to the following:

Cambridge University Press for Joseph Needham, *Science and Civilization in China*, and Ihara Saikaku, *The Japanese Family Storehouse*; Case Western Reserve University Press for Makoto Ueda, *Literary and Art Theories in Japan*; W. Dawson and Sons Ltd for G. B. Sansom, *A History of Japan*; Dover Publications for Henry P. Bowie, *On the Laws of Japanese Painting*, and S. M. Eisenstein, *Notes of a Film Director*; Johns Hopkins University Press for Jacques Derrida, *De la Grammatologie*; Alfred A. Knopf Inc. and Michael Gordon for G. B. Sansom, *The Western World and Japan*; Lawrence and Wishart Ltd for S. M. Eisenstein, *Notes of a Film Director*; Oxford University Press and Alfred A. Knopf Inc. for Ivan Morris, *The World of the Shining Prince*; Random House Inc. and Tavistock Publications Ltd for Michel Foucault, *The Order of Things*; Routledge and Kegan Paul Ltd and Houghton Mifflin Company for Ruth Benedict, *The Chrysanthemum and the Sword*; Routledge and Kegan Paul Ltd and Wilfrid J. Whitehouse for *Ochikubo Monogatari*; Secker and Warburg Ltd and Oxford University Press, New York, for Earle Ernst, *The Kabuki Theatre*; Éditions du Seuil for Marcellin Pleynet, *Sade lisible*; Éditions d'Art Albert Skira for Roland Barthes, *L'Empire des signes*; Stamford University Press for R. H. Brower and E. Miner, *Japanese Court Poetry*, and G. B. Sansom, *A History of Japan*; University of Chicago Press for Kawai Kazuo, *Japan's American Interlude*; Charles E. Tuttle Co. Inc. for Heinrich Engel, *The Japanese House*; University Press of Hawaii for Nakamura Hajime, *Ways of Thinking of Eastern Peoples*; Weidenfeld (Publishers) Ltd and Holt, Rinehart and Winston for W. G. Beasley, *The Modern History of Japan*; Yale University Press for Karl A. Wittfogel, *Oriental Despotism*.

# Index of Films

Actor's Revenge, An (Yukinojō henge) (Ichikawa), 288, 289–90
Actress, The (Joyu) (Kinugasa), 139, 282
Adauchi senshu (The Champion of Revenge) (Uchida), 153
After Our Separation (Kimi to wakarete) (Naruse), 186–7, 188
Ai no corrida (Corrida Of Love) (Oshima), 343–4
Ai no machi (Town of Love) (Tasaka), 161
Akaitenshi (Red Angel) (Masumura), 362n2
Akahige (Red Beard) (Kurosawa), 320–1
Akanashi Kakita (Itami), 192n8
Akasen chitai (Red Light District/Street of Shame) (Mizoguchi), 276
Akitsu onsen (Akitsu Spa) (Yoshida), 350
Akitsu Spa (Akitsu onsen) (Yoshida), 350
Alone on the Pacific (Taiheiyō hotoribotchi) (Ichikawa), 288, 289
Anges du Péché, Les (Bresson), 194
Argent, L' (L'Herbier), 128, 147
Arsenal (Dovzhenko), 147, 283
Assassinat du Duc de Guise, L' (Le Bargy and Calmettes), 76
Asu o tsukuru hitobito (Those Who Make Tomorrow) (Kurosawa), 294
Autumn in the Kobayakawa Family (Kobayakawa-ke no aki) (Ozu), 278
Avenging Ghost of Yukinojō, The (Yukinojō henge) (Ichikawa), 288, 289–90

Bad Guys Sleep Well (Warui yatsu hodo yoku nemuru) (Kurosawa), 318
Bara no soretsu (Funeral of Roses) (Matsumoto), 356
Battleship Potemkin, The (Eisenstein), 115, 126n4, 145, 213n5, 291, 293, 299n5, 301n8, 330
Be Cheerful (Hogaraka ni susume) (Ozu), 154n1
Beni kōmori (The Red Bat) (Tanaka), 111–115, 116, 132, 151, 332
Benten, Apprentice (Benten kozō) (Kinugasa), 126
Benten kozō (Benten, Apprentice) (Kinugasa), 126
Biruma no tategoto (The Burmese Harp) (Ichikawa), 287–8
Birth of a Nation (Griffith), 104

Blaue Engel, Der (Sternberg), 147, 291
Blood and Soul (Chi to rei) (Mizoguchi), 217
Boy (Shōnen) (Oshima), 340, 342
Brasier Ardent, Le (Mosjoukine), 133
Burden of Life, The (Jinsei no onimotsu) (Gosho), 258–60
Burmese Harp, The (Biruma no tategoto) (Ichikawa), 287–8
Bush Warbler, The (Uguisu) (Toyoda), 257
Bwana Toshi no uta (The Song of Bwana Toshi) (Hani), 347
By the Blue Sea (Barnett), 258n7

Cabinet of Dr Caligari, The (Wiene), 117–18, 126n4, 138–9, 145, 217, 338
Catch, The (Shiiku) (Oshima), 325, 329–30, 333
Ceremonies (Gishiki) (Oshima), 342
Champion of Revenge, The (Adauchi senshu) (Uchida), 153
Chelsea Girls, The (Warhol), 64
Chess Master, The (Oshō) (Ito), 275, 282, 286
Chi to rei (Blood and Soul) (Mizoguchi), 217
Chichi ariki (There was a Father) (Ozu), 173, 174, 175, 179–83, 185, 278
Chien Andalou, Un (Buñuel), 147
Chienne, La (Renoir), 147
Chikamatsu Monogatari (A Story by Chikamatsu) (Mizoguchi), 246, 276
Children in the Wind (Kaze no naka no kodomo) (Shimizu), 256
Children of the Atom Bomb (Genbaku no ko) (Shindo), 283, 290
Children of the Bee-hive (Hachi no su no kodomotachi) (Shimizu), 256
Children of the Great Buddha (Daibutsu-sama no kodomotachi) (Shimizu), 255
Chorus of Tokyo, The (Tōkyō no gasshō) (Ozu), 153, 155–7
Chronicle of Taiko (Taiko junanmi), 81n21, 86
Chūshingura (A Tale of Loyal Retainers/'The Forty-Seven Ronin') (Makino), 81–2, 84–5
Chūshingura (Kinugasa), 237

378

*Citizen Kane* (Welles), 297
*Cobweb Castle (Kumo-no-su jō)* (Kurosawa), 297, 299, 306n9, 308, 310–17, 319
*Confessions Among Actresses/Confessions, Theories, Actresses (Kokuhakuteki joyu-ron)* (Yoshida), 350
*Conflagration (Enjo)* (Ichikawa), 288–9, 318
*Contactos* (Viota), 161
*Corner in Wheat, A* (Griffith), 83n26
*Corrida of Love (Ai no corrida)* (Oshima), 343–4
*Coup d'Etat (Kaigenrei)* (Yoshida), 350
*Crab-Canning Ship, The (Kanikosen)* (Yamamura), 282–3
*Cronaca di un amore* (Antonioni), 175, 216, 225
*Crossways (Jūjiro)* (Kinugasa), 81n17, 126n4, 136–8, 138n11
*Crowd, The* (Vidor), 154
*Crows in Moonlight (Tsukiyo karasu)* (Inoue), 257
*Cruel Tale of Youth, A (Seishun zankoku monogotari)* (Oshima), 328

*Daibutsu-sama no kodomotachi (Children of the Great Buddha)* (Shimizu), 255
*Daigaku wa deta keredo (I Graduated, But . . . )* (Ozu), 154n1
*Daini toride no hitobito (People of the Second Fortress/Peasants of the Second Fortress)* (Ogawa et al.), 358, 361
*Damned, The* (Losey), 333
*Dancing Girl of Izu, The (Izu no odoriko)* (Gosho), 121
*Darkness at Noon (Mahiru no ankoku)* (Imai), 283
*Dawn (Reimai)* (Osanai), 146
*Dawn of the Foundation of Manchukuo and Mongolia, The (Ma-mō kenkoku no reimei)* (Mizoguchi), 144, 243
*Days of Youth (Wakaki hi)* (Ozu), 154
*Dear Summer Sister (Natsu no imoto)* (Oshima), 342–3
*Death by Hanging (Kosheiki)* (Oshima), 301n8, 333–9, 341, 358
*Death of a Salesman* (Benedek), 130, 130n8
*Dekigokoro (Passing Fancy)* (Ozu), 155–6, 157–8, 180n21
*Demon, The (Shura)* (Matsumoto), 356–8
*Denen kokyōgaku (The Pastoral Symphony)* (Yamamoto), 299n6
*Dersu Uzala* (Kurosawa), 321n21
*Diary of a Shinjuku Thief (Shinjuku dorobō nikki)* (Oshima), 339, 340, 341, 347
*Docks of New York, The* (Sternberg), 188
*Dr Mabuse der Spieler* (Lang), 97, 136, 156, 194
*Dodeskaden* (Kurosawa), 321
*Donzoko (The Lower Depths)* (Kurosawa), 200, 283, 296, 304, 308–10
*Double Suicide: Japanese Summer (Muri shinju: Nihon no natsu)* (Oshima), 333, 336
*Double Suicide on Mt Toribe (Toribeyama shinju)* (Fuyushima), 121

*Drunken Angel (Yoidore tenshi)* (Kurosawa), 294, 295, 296, 297

*Early Autumn (Kobayakawa-ke no aki)* (Ozu), 278
*Earth* (Dovzhenko), 128, 136, 147
*Earth (Tsuchi)* (Uchida), 260, 291
*Earth and Soldiers (Tsuchi to heitai)* (Tasaka), 264, 266–8
*Eclisse, L'* (Antonioni), 161, 346
*Elegy of Naniwa, The (Naniwa erejī)* (Mizoguchi), 223, 224
*Embryo Hunts in Secret, The (Taiji ga mitsuryo suru toki)* (Wakamatsu), 351–2
*Enjo (Conflagration)* (Ichikawa), 288–9, 318
*Entotsu no mieru basho (Where Chimneys Are Seen)* (Gosho), 286–7
*Entrée d'un train en gare* (Lumière), 58, 65–6
*Eros Plus Massacre (Eros purass gyakusatsu)* (Yoshida), 338, 347, 348–50, 358
*Eros purass gyakusatsu (Eros Plus Massacre)* (Yoshida), 338, 347, 348–50, 358
*Etsuraku (Pleasure)* (Oshima), 330n5

*Face of Another, The (Tanin no kao)* (Teshigahara), 348
*Fallen Blossoms (Hana chirinu)* (Ishida), 15, 202–14, 216, 287
*Family Meeting (Kazoku kaigi)* (Shimazu), 258
*Farrébique* (Rouquier), 260, 291
*Ferme des sept péchés, La* (Devaivre), 297
*Fires on the Plain (Nobi)* (Ichikawa), 288
*Five Scouts (Gonin no sekkohei)* (Tasaka), 161, 264–5
*Five Women Around Utamaro (Utamaro o meguro gonin no onna)* (Mizoguchi), 228, 243, 275, 276
*Floating Clouds (Ukigumo)* (Naruse), 277
*Floating Ghost in Broad Daylight (Hakuchu no tōrima)* (Oshima), 330–2, 333, 340
*Floating Weeds (Ukigusa)* (Ozu), 277n9
*Foolish Wives* (Stroheim), 97, 107n13
*Fred Ott's Sneeze* (Dickson), 108
*Fröken Julie* (Sjöberg), 130
*Funeral of Roses (Bara no soretsu)* (Matsumoto), 356

*Gate of Hell, The (Jigoku-mon)* (Kinugasa), 139, 282
*Gattopardo, Il* (Visconti), 244
*Genbaku no ko (Children of the Atom Bomb)* (Shindo), 283, 290
*General Line, The* (Eisenstein), 116, 136, 147
*Genroku chūshingura (A Tale of Loyal Retainers in the Genroku Era)* (Mizoguchi), 17, 219, 221, 228, 234, 236–43, 276
*Gertrud* (Dreyer), 109, 117, 225n14
*Ghost of Yukinojō, The (Yukinojō henge)* (Kinugasa), 139n13, 289, 289n19
*Gion no shimai/kyodai (Sisters of Gion)* (Mizoguchi), 151, 219, 224, 225–30, 234, 246
*Girl They're Talking About, The (Uwasa no musume)* (Naruse), 188n2

*shiki (Ceremonies)* (Oshima), 342
*Glace à trois faces* (Epstein), 147
*Go, go, You Who Are a Virgin for the Second Time (Yuke yuke hidome no shojo)* (Wakamatsu), 352
*Gonin no sekkohei (Five Scouts)* (Tasaka), 161, 264–6
*Good Morning (Ohayō)* (Ozu), 277n9, 278
*Great Consoler, The* (Kuleshov), 147
*Great Train Robbery, The* (Porter), 64
*Gubijinsō (Poppies)* (Mizoguchi), 223–4

*Hachi no su no kodomotachi (Children of the Bee-Hive)* (Shimizu), 256
*Haha o kowazu ya (A Mother Ought to be Loved)* (Ozu), 166, 185
*Hakuchi (The Idiot)* (Kurosawa), 201, 299–301, 306, 308
*Hakuchu no tōrima (Floating Ghost in Broad Daylight)* (Oshima), 330–2, 333, 340
*Hana chirinu (Fallen Blossoms)* (Ishida), 15, 202–14, 216, 287
*Hanagata senshu (A Star Athlete)* (Shimizu), 249–55, 256
*Hanging, The (Kosheiki)* (Oshima), 301n8, 333–9, 341, 358
*Hara-kiri (Seppuku)* (Kobayashi), 282
*Hataraku ikka (The Whole Family Works)* (Naruse), 191, 260
*Hatsukoi jigoshi-heri (The Inferno of the First Love)* (Hani), 347
*Hawai-Marei oki kaisen (War at Sea off Hawaii and Malaya)* (Yamamoto), 264n4
*He Died After the War (Tōkyō senso senyo hiwa)* (Oshima), 340–2
*Heart, The (Kokoro)* (Ichikawa), 288
*Heroic Purgatory (Rengoku eroica)* (Yoshida), 349
*Hidden Fortress, The (Kakushi toride no san-akunin)* (Kurosawa), 308n12, 317–18
*High and Low (Tengoku to jigoku)* (Kurosawa), 297, 304, 319–20
*Hissho ka (Song of Faith in Victory)* (Mizoguchi), 243
*Hitori musuko (Only Son)* (Ozu), 166, 173, 174, 175–9, 180n21, 184, 185, 277, 293
*Hogaraka ni susume (Be Cheerful)* (Ozu), 154n1
*Homme du large, L'* (L'Herbier), 78, 120n7
*Horse, The (Uma)* (Kurosawa and Yamamoto), 291–2
*Hototogisu Namiko (Namiko, the 'Cuckoo')* (Tanaka), 257
*Human Condition, The (Ningen no joken)* (Kobayashi), 283–4, 286, 299
*Humanity, Paper Balloons (Ninjō kamifusen)* (Yamanaka), 195–7
*Hyaku-man ryō no tsubo (The Pot Worth a Million Ryō)* (Yamanaka), 192–5

*I Flunked, But... (Rakudai wa shita keredo)* (Ozu), 154n1
*I Graduated, But... (Daigaku wa deta keredo)* (Ozu), 154n1
*I Live in Fear (Ikimono no kiroku)* (Kurosawa), 306–8, 318
*I Was Born, But... (Umarete wa mita keredo)* (Ozu), 153, 155–6, 157
*Ichiban utsukushiku (The Most Beautiful)* (Kurosawa), 292–3, 297
*Idiot, The (Hakuchi)* (Kurosawa), 201, 299–301, 306, 308
*If I had a Million* (Lubitsch), 184
*Ikimono no kiroku (Record of a Living Thing/I Live in Fear)* (Kurosawa), 306–8, 318
*Ikuru (Living)* (Kurosawa), 296, 297, 299, 301–6, 308, 319
*Inferno of the First Love, The (Hatsukoi jigoshi-heri)*, (Hani), 347
*Inn in Tōkyō, An (Tōkyō no yado)* (Ozu), 15, 153, 157, 166, 167, 172, 180n21, 185, 188, 262
*Intolerance* (Griffith), 22, 93, 100–101, 102, 104
*Izu no odoriko (The Dancing Girl of Izu)* (Gosho), 121

*Japanese Tragedy, The (Nihon no higeki)* (Kinoshita), 283, 285, 290
*Jigoku-mon (The Gate of Hell)* (Kinugasa), 139, 282
*Jinsei no onimotsu (The Burden of Life)* (Gosho), 258–60
*Jirai-ya (Thunder Boy)* (Makino), 85n30
*Jitsuroku Chūshingura (The True Story of Loyal Retainers)* (Makino), 85n30, 108, 115–16, 119, 120
*Joyu (The Actress)* (Kinugasa), 139, 282
*Joyu Sumako no koi (The Love of Actress Sumako)* (Mizoguchi), 221, 243–4
*Jūjiro (Crossways)* (Kinugasa), 81n17, 126n4, 136–8, 138n11

*Kagi (The Key)* (Ichikawa), 288, 289
*Kaigenrei (Martial Law/Coup d'Etat)* (Yoshida), 350
*Kakushi toride no san-akunin (Three Bad Men in a Hidden Fortress/The Hidden Fortress)* (Kurosawa), 308n12, 317–18
*Kameradschaft* (Pabst), 147
*Kanikosen (The Crab-Canning Ship)* (Yamamura), 282–3
*Kanojo to kare (She and He)* (Hani), 346
*Kantsubaki (Winter Camellia(s))* (Inoue), 106–8
*Kaze no naka no kodomo (Children in the Wind)* (Shimizu), 256
*Kazoku kaigi (Family Meeting)* (Shimazu), 258
*Keisatsukan (Police)* (Uchida), 153
*Key, The (Kagi)* (Ichikawa), 288, 289
*Kimi to wakarete (After Our Separation)* (Naruse), 186–7, 188
*Kobayakawa-ke no aki (Autumn in the Kobayakawa Family/Early Autumn)* (Ozu), 278
*Kokoro (The Heart)* (Ichikawa), 288
*Kokuhakuteki (Confessions Among*

380

Actresses/Confessions, Theories, Actresses) (Yoshida), 350
Kokushi musō (The Unrivalled Hero) (Itami), 153
Kome (Rice) (Imai), 283
Kosheiki (The Hanging/Death by Hanging) (Oshima), 301n8, 333–9, 341, 358
Kuhle Wampe (Brecht), 147
Kumo-no-su jō (Cobweb Castle/Throne of Blood) (Kurosawa), 297, 299, 306n9, 308, 310–17, 319
Kurutta ippeiji (Page of Madness) (Kinugasa), 105, 126n4, 127–39, 206
Kwaidan (Kobayashi), 282

Lady and the Beard, The (Shukijyō to hige) (Ozu), 154
Lady in the Lake, The (Montgomery), 225
Letzte Mann, Der (Murnau), 79, 128, 155
Life of a Woman, by Saikaku, The (Saikaku no ichidai onna) (Mizoguchi), 244–5, 276
Life of an American Fireman, The (Porter), 64, 64n7
Life of Oharu, The (Saikaku no ichidai onna) (Mizoguchi), 244–5, 276
Little Summer Sister (Natsu no imoto) (Oshima), 342–3
Living (Ikuru) (Kurosawa), 296, 297, 299, 301–6, 308, 319
Love of Actress Sumako, The (Joyu Sumako no koi) (Mizoguchi), 221, 243–4
Lower Depths, The (Donzoko) (Kurosawa), 200, 283, 296, 304, 308–10

M (Lang), 104, 147, 291, 301
Mabuta no haha (The Mother He Never Knew) (Inagaki), 120–1
Madamu to nyobō (The Neighbour's Wife and Mine) (Gosho), 146, 260
Magnificent Seven, The (Sturges), 297n4
Mahiru no ankoku (Shadows in Sunlight/Darkness at Noon) (Imai), 283
Ma-mō kenkoku no seimei (The Dawn of the Foundation of Manchukuo and Mongolia) (Mizoguchi), 144, 243
Man with a Movie Camera, The (Vertov), 22, 128, 136, 147, 278
Man Without a Map (Moetsukita chizu) (Teshigahara), 348
March of Tokyo, The (Tōkyō koshin kyoku) (Mizoguchi), 153, 217
Maria no O-Yuki (O-Yuki, Alias Maria) (Mizoguchi), 224
Martial Law (Kaigenrei) (Yoshida), 350
Matatabi (The Wanderers) (Ichikawa), 290
Matsukashiki fue ya taiko (Those Dear Old Flutes and Drums) (Kinoshita), 286
May Day (Iwasaki), 152n3
Méditérranée (Pollet), 205
Ménilmontant (Kirsanoff), 79, 128, 155
Metropolis (Lang), 136
Minamata ikki (Minamata Revolt) (Tsuchimoto), 362

Minamata: kanjo-san to sono sokai (Minamata: The Victims and Their World) (Tsuchimoto), 362
Minamata Revolt (Minamata ikki) (Tsuchimoto), 362
Minamata: The Victims and Their World (Minamata: kanjo-san to sono sokai) (Tsuchimoto), 362
Moetsukita chizu (The Torn Map/Man Without a Map) (Teshigahara), 348
Mort de Marat, La (Lumière), 75–6
Most Beautiful, The (Ichiban utsukushiku) (Kurosawa), 292–3, 297
Mother (Okasan) (Naruse), 259, 277
Mother, The (Pudovkin), 130
Mother He Never Knew, The (Mabuta no haha) (Inagaki), 120–21
Mother Ought to be Loved, A (Haha o kowazu ya) (Ozu), 166, 185
Mr Pu (Pu-san) (Ichikawa), 287
Muri shinju: Nihon no natsu (Double Suicide: Japanese Summer) (Oshima), 333, 336

Nagaya shinshi roku (Record of a Tenement Gentleman) (Ozu), 278
Naked City, The (Dassin), 295
Namiko, the 'Cuckoo' (Hototogisu Namiko) (Tanaka), 257
Nana (Renoir), 97
Naniwa ereji (The Elegy of Naniwa) (Mizoguchi), 223, 224
Naniwa onna (Woman of Naniwa) (Mizoguchi), 243
Napoléon (Gance), 147
Natsu no imoto (Little Summer Sister/Dear Summer Sister) (Oshima), 342–3
Neighbour's Wife and Mine, The (Madamu to nyobō) (Gosho), 146, 260
New Tangesazan, The (Shinpen Tangesazen – Sogan no maki) (Nakawaga), 257–8
New Tales of the Taira Clan (Shin Heike monogotari) (Mizoguchi), 276
Next of Kin (Dickinson), 264
Night and Fog in Japan (Nihon no yoru to kiri) (Oshima), 325, 333, 363
Nightly Dreams (Yogoto no yuma) (Naruse), 186–8, 191
Nihon no higeki (The Japanese Tragedy) (Kinoshita), 283, 285, 290
Nihon no yoru to kiri (Night and Fog in Japan) (Oshima), 325, 333, 363
Nihon shunka-kō (Treatise on Japanese Bawdy Songs) (Oshima), 333
Nijushi no hitomi (Twenty-Four Eyes) (Kinoshita), 285–6
Ningen no joken (The Human Condition) (Kobayashi), 283–4, 286, 299
Ninin Shizuka (Two People Named Shizuka) (Oboro), 78n10
Ninja bugeicho (Tales of the Ninja) (Oshima), 330, 332–3
Ninjō kamifusen (Humanity, Paper Balloons) (Yamanaka), 195–7

381

Nishizumi senshahachō-den (The Story of Tank-Commander Nishizumi) (Yoshimura), 264n4
No Regrets for our Youth (Waga seishun ni kuinashi) (Kurosawa), 294, 295
Nobi (Fires on the Plain) (Ichikawa), 288
Nogiku no gotuku kimi narika (She Was Like a Wild Chrysanthemum) (Kinoshita), 286
Nora inu (Stray Dog) (Kurosawa), 294, 295, 296, 297
Notte, La (Antonioni), 289, 346–7
Nuit du Carrefour, La (Renoir), 147

October (Eisenstein), 22, 104, 115n11, 147
Ohayō (Good Morning) (Ozu), 277n9, 278
Okasan (Mother) (Naruse), 259, 277
Okasareta byakui (Violated Women in White/Violated Angels) (Wakamatsu), 352–4, 358
Old Songs (Mukashi no uta) (Ishida), 214–16
One Wonderful Sunday (Subarashiki nichiyōbi) (Kurosawa), 294, 295, 297
Only Son (Hitori musuko) (Ozu), 166, 173, 174, 175–9, 180n21, 184, 185, 277, 293
Or des mers, L' (Epstein), 147
Orizuru O-Sen (O-Sen of the Paper Cranes) (Mizoguchi), 105, 218–23, 224, 230n15
Osaka natsu no jin (The Summer Battle of Osaka) (Kinugasa), 139
O-Sen of the Paper Cranes (Orizuru O-Sen) (Mizoguchi), 105, 218–23, 224, 230n15
Oshō (The Chess Master) (Ito), 275, 282, 286
Otoshiana (Pitfall) (Teshigahara), 347
Our Neighbour Miss Yae (Tonari no Yae-chan) (Simazu), 258
Outrage, The (Ritt), 297
O-Yuki, Alias Maria (Maria no O-Yuki) (Mizoguchi), 224

Page of Madness (Kurutta ippeiji) (Kinugasa), 105, 126n4, 127–39, 206
Pandemonium (Shura) (Matsumoto), 356–8
Partisan jenchi (Pre-history of Partisans) (Tsuchimoto), 361
Passing Fancy (Dekigokoro) (Ozu), 155–6, 157–8, 180n21
Passion de Jeanne d'Arc, La (Dreyer), 104, 147, 291
Pastorae Symphony, The (Denen kokyōgaku) (Yamamoto), 299n6
Peasants of the Second Fortress/People of the Second Fortress (Daini toride no hitobito) (Ogawa et al), 358, 361
Pickup on South Street (Fuller), 246
Pitfall (Otoshiana) (Teshigahara), 347
Pleasure (Etsuraku) (Oshima), 330n5
Police (Keisatsukan) (Uchida), 153
Poppies (Gubijinsō) (Mizoguchi), 223–4
Pot Worth a Million Ryō, The (Hyaku-man ryō no tsubo) (Yamanaka), 192–5
Pre-history of Partisans (Partisan jenchi) (Tsuchimoto), 361
Pu-san (Mr Pu) (Ichikawa), 287

Queen Kelly (Stroheim), 145
Quiet Duel, The (Shizukanara ketto) (Kurosawa), 294–5, 296

Rakudai wa shita keredo (I Flunked, But . . . ) (Ozu), 154n1
Rashōmon (Kurosawa), 282, 296–8, 299, 306n9
Record of a Living Thing (Ikimono no kiroku) (Kurosawa), 306–8, 318
Record of a Tenement Gentleman (Nagaya shinshi roku) (Ozu), 278
Red Angel (Akaitenshi) (Masumura), 326n2
Red Bat, The (Beni kōmori) (Tanaka), 111–15, 116, 132, 151, 332
Red Beard (Akahige) (Kurosawa), 320–1
Red Light District (Akasen chitai) (Mizoguchi), 276
Reimai (Dawn) (Osanai), 146
Rengoku eroica (Heroic Purgatory) (Yoshida), 349
Rescued from an Eagle's Nest (Porter), 85
Rice (Kome) (Imai), 283
Rojō no reikon (Souls on the Road) (Murata and Osanai), 100–107, 107n15, 146
Rope (Hitchcock), 225, 319
Roue, La (Gance), 126n4

Saikaku no ichidai onna (The Life of a Woman, by Saikaku/The Life of Oharu) (Mizoguchi), 244–5, 276
Sang d'un poète, Le (Cocteau), 147
Sanjuro of the Camellias/Sanjuro (Tsubaki Sanjuro) (Kurosawa), 308n12, 318, 332
Sanriziku no natsu (Summer in Sanriziku/Summer at Narita) (Ogawa et al), 360–1
Sansho daiyū (Sansho the Bailiff) (Mizoguchi), 246
Scandal (Shubun) (Kurosawa), 294
Shichinin no samurai (The Seven Samurai) (Kurosawa), 306n9
Secret Story of the Post-'Tokyo War' Period (Tōkyō senso senyo hiwa) (Oshima), 340–2
Seishun zankoku (A Cruel Tale of Youth) (Oshima), 328
Seppuku (Hara-kiri) (Kobayashi), 282
Seven Samurai, The (Shichinin no samurai) (Kurosawa), 306n9
Sexjack (Wakamatsu), 352n12
Shadows in Sunlight (Mahiru no ankoku) (Imai), 283
Shakujyō wa nani o wasureta ka (What Did the Lady Forget?) (Ozu), 179, 180
Shanghai Report (Shanghai rikusentai) (Tomagaya), 264n4
Shanghai rikusentai (Shanghai Report) (Tomagaya), 264n4
She and He (Kanojo to kare) (Hani), 346
She Was Like a Wild Chrysanthemum (Nogiku no gotoku kimi narika) (Kinoshita), 286
Shiiku (The Catch) (Oshima), 325, 329–30, 333
Shin Heike monogatari (New Tales of the Taira Clan) (Mizoguchi), 276

*Shinjuku dorobō nikki (Diary of a Shinjuku Thief)* (Oshima), 339, 340, 341, 347
*Shinku chitai (Vacuum Zone)* (Yamamoto), 283
*Shinpen Tangesazen – Sogan no maki (The New Tangesazen)* (Nakagawa), 257-8
*Shirasagi (The White Heron)* (Kinugasa), 282
*Shōnen (Boy)* (Oshima), 340, 342
*Shizukanara ketto (The Quiet Duel)* (Kurosawa), 294-5, 296
*Shubun (Scandal)* (Kurosawa), 294
*Shukijyō to hige (The Lady and the Beard)* (Ozu), 154
*Shura (Pandemonium/The Demon)* (Matsumoto), 356-8
*Signora senza camelia, La* (Antonioni), 216
*Simple histoire, Une* (Hanoun), 301n8
*Sisters of Gion (Gion no shimai/kyodai)* (Mizoguchi), 151, 219, 224, 225-30, 234, 246
*So no go hachi no su kodomotachi* (Shimizu), 256
*Song of Bwana Toshi, The (Bwana Toshi no uta)* (Hani), 347
*Song of Faith in Victory (Hissho ka)* (Mizoguchi), 243
*Sono yo no tsuma (That Night's Wife)* (Ozu), 153, 154-6, 158, 162-3, 185
*Souls on the Road (Rojō no reikon)* (Murata and Osanai), 100-107, 107n15, 146
*Spione* (Lang), 128, 147, 154
*Star Athlete, A (Hanagata senshu)* (Shimizu), 249-55, 256
*Story by Chikamatsu, A (Chikamatsu monogatari)* (Mizoguchi), 246, 276
*Story of Floating Weeds, A (Ukigusa monogatari)* (Ozu), 157-8, 166, 166n16, 170, 172, 174, 185, 229, 260, 277
*Story of Tank-Commander Nishizumin, The (Nishizumi senshahachō-den)* (Yoshimura), 264n4
*Stray Dog (Nora inu)* (Kurosawa), 294, 295, 296, 297
*Street of Shame (Akasen chitai)* (Mizoguchi), 276
*Strike* (Eisenstein), 22, 104, 104n5, 278
*Subarashiki nichiyōbi (One Wonderful Sunday)* (Kurosawa), 294, 295, 297
*Sugata Sanshiro* (Kurosawa), 292
*Summer at Narita (Sanriziku no natsu)* (Ogawa et al), 360-1
*Summer Battle of Osaka, The (Osaka natsu no jin)* (Kinugasa), 139
*Summer in Sanriziku (Sanriziku no natsu)* (Ogawa et al), 360-1
*Suna no onna (Woman of the Dunes)* (Teshigahara), 347-8
*Sunless Street, The (Taiyo no nai machi)* (Yamamoto), 283
*Sword of Penitence (Zange no yaiba)* (Ozu), 154

*Taiheyō hotoribotchi (Alone on the Pacific)* (Ichikawa), 288, 289
*Taiji ga mitsuryo suru toki (The Embryo Hunts in Secret)* (Wakamatsu), 351-2

*Taiko junanmi (Chronicle of Taiko)*, 81n21, 86
*Taiyo no nai machi (The Sunless Street)* (Yamamoto), 283
*Taki no shiraito (White Threads of the Waterfall)* (Mizoguchi), 217-18, 221, 230n15
*Tale of Late Chrysanthemums (Zangiku Monogatari)* (Mizoguchi), 17, 84n, 27, 151, 219, 224, 225, 228, 230-6, 244, 245, 276
*Tale of Loyal Retainers in the Genroku Era, A (Genroku chūshingura)* (Mizoguchi), 17, 219, 221, 228, 234, 236-43, 276
*Tales of the Ninja (Ninja bugeicho)* (Oshima), 330, 332-3
*Tanin no kao (The Face of Another)* (Teshigahara), 348
*Tengoku to jigoku (High and Low)* (Kurosawa), 297, 304, 319-20
*Testament von Doktor Mabuse, Das* (Lang), 147, 291
*That Night's Wife (Sono yo no tsuma)* (Ozu), 153, 154-6, 158, 162-3, 185
*There was a Father (Chichi ariki)* (Ozu), 173, 174, 175, 179-83, 185, 278
*They Live By Night* (Ray), 194
*They Who Tread on the Tiger's Tail (Tora no o o fumu otokotachi)* (Kurosawa), 293
*Those Dear Old Flutes and Drums (Matsukashiki fue ya taiko)* (Kinoshita), 286
*Those Who Make Tomorrow (Asu o tsukuru hitobito)* (Kurosawa), 294
*Three Bad Men in a Hidden Fortress (Kakushi toride no san-akunin)* (Kurosawa), 308n2, 317-18
*Throne of Blood (Kumo-no-su jō)* (Kurosawa), 297, 299, 306n9, 308, 310-17, 319
*Thunder Boy (Jirai-ya)* (Makino), 85n30
*Tōchūken Kumoenen* (Naruse), 191
*Toda Brother and Sister (Todake no kyōdai)* (Ozu), 169-70, 173, 174, 179-80, 185
*Todake no kyōdai (Toda Brother and Sister)* (Ozu), 169-70, 173, 174, 179-80, 185
*Tokyo Drifter, The (Tōkyō nagaremono)* (Suzuki), 362-3
*Tōkyō koshin kyoku (The March of Tokyo/Tokyo March)* (Mizoguchi), 153, 217
*Tōkyō nagaremono (The Tokyo Drifter)* (Suzuki), 362-3;
*Tōkyō no gasshō (The Chorus of Tokyo)* (Ozu), 155-7
*Tōkyō no onna (Woman (Women) of Tokyo)* (Ozu), 158-60, 162-72, 173, 176, 184, 185
*Tōkyō no yado (An Inn in Tokyo)* (Ozu), 15, 153, 157, 166, 167, 172, 180n21, 185, 188, 262
*Tokyo Olympiad (Tōkyō Olympic)* (Ichikawa), 290, 332
*Tōkyō senso senyo hiwa (Secret Story of the Post-'Tokyo War' Period/He Died After the War)* (Oshima), 340-2
*Tonari no Yae-chan (Our Neighbour Miss Yae)* (Shimazu), 258

383

*Tora no o o fumu otokotachi (They Who Tread on the Tiger's Tail)* (Kurosawa), 293
*Tora! Tora! Tora!* (Fleischer), 321
*Toribeyama shinju (Double Suicide on Mt Toribe)* (Fuyushima), 121
*Torn Map, The (Moetsukita chizu)* (Teshigahara), 348
*Town of Love (Ai no machi)* (Tasaka), 161
*Treatise on Japanese Bawdy Songs (Nihon shunka-kō)* (Oshima), 333
*Trouble in Paradise* (Lubitsch), 79–80
*True Story of Loyal Retainers, The (Jitsuroku chūshingura)* (Makino), 85n30, 108, 115–16, 119, 120
*Tsubaki Sanjuro (Sanjuro of the Camellias/Sanjuro)* (Kurosawa), 308n12, 318, 332
*Tsuchi (Earth)* (Uchida), 260, 291
*Tsuchi to heitai (Earth and Soldiers)* (Tasaka), 264, 266–8
*Tsukyokarasu (Crows in Moonlight)* (Inoue), 257
*Tsuma yo bara no yo ni (Wife, Be Like a Rose)* (Naruse), 188–91
*Tsuruhachi Tsurujiro (Tsuruhachi and Tsurujiro)* (Naruse), 191
*Twenty-Four Eyes (Nijushi no hitomi)* (Kinoshita), 285–6
*Two People Named Shizuka (Ninin Shizuka)* (Oboro), 78n10

*Ueberfall* (Metzner), 79, 128
*Uguisu (The Bush Warbler)* (Toyoda), 257
*Ukigumo (Floating Clouds)* (Naruse), 277
*Ukigusa (Floating Weeds)* (Ozu), 277n9
*Ukigusa monogatari (A Story of Floating Weeds)* (Ozu), 157–8, 166, 166n16, 170, 172, 174, 185, 229, 260, 277
*Uma (The Horse)* (Kurosawa and Yamamoto), 291–2
*Umarete wa mita keredo (I Was Born, But . . .)* (Ozu), 153, 155–6, 157
*Unrivalled Hero, The (Kokushi musō)* (Itami), 153
*Utamaro o meguro gonin no onna (Five Women Around Utamaro)* (Mizoguchi), 228, 243, 275, 276
*Uwasa no musume (The Girl They're Talking About)* (Naruse), 188n2

*Vacances de Monsieur Hulot, Les* (Tati), 225
*Vacuum Zone (Shinku chitai)* (Yamamoto), 283
*Vampyr* (Dreyer), 115, 145, 147, 223n8, 316n15
*Variety* (Dupont), 194
*Violated Women in White/Violated Angels (Okasareta byakui)* (Wakamatsu), 352–4, 358

*Waga seishun ni kuinashi (No Regrets for Our Youth)* (Kurosawa), 294, 295
*Wakaki hi (Days of Youth)* (Ozu), 154
*Wanderers, The (Matatabi)* (Ichikawa), 290
*War at Sea off Hawaii and Malaya, The (Hawai-Marei oki kaisen)* (Yamamoto), 264n4
*Warui yatsu hodo yoku nemuru (Bad Guys Sleep Well)* (Kurosawa), 318
*Wavelength* (Snow), 19, 351
*Westfront 1918* (Pabst), 147, 264
*What Did the Lady Forget? (Shakujyō wa nani o wasureta ka)* (Ozu), 179, 180
*Where Chimneys Are Seen (Entotsu no mieru basho)* (Gosho), 286–7
*White Heron, The (Shirasagi)* (Kinugasa), 282
*White Threads of the Waterfall (Taki no shiraito)* (Mizoguchi), 217–18, 221, 230n15
*Whole Family Works, The (Hataraku ikka)* (Naruse), 191, 260
*Wife, Be Like a Rose (Tsuma yo bara no yo ni)* (Naruse), 188–91
*Wind, The* (Sjöström), 128, 129–30
*Winter Camellia(s) (Kantsubaki)* (Inoue), 106–8
*Woman in Question, The* (Asquith), 297
*Woman of Naniwa (Naniwa onna)* (Mizoguchi), 243
*Woman of the Dunes (Suna no onna)* (Teshigahara), 347–8
*Woman (Women) Of Yokyo (Tokyo no onna)* (Ozu), 158–60, 162–72, 173, 176, 184, 185
*Women of the Night (Yoru no onnotachi)* (Mizoguchi), 276

*Yogoto no yuma (Nightly Dreams)* (Naruse), 186–8, 191
*Yoidore tenshi (Drunken Angel)* (Kurosawa), 294, 295, 296, 297
*Yojimbō* (Kurosawa), 297n4, 318–19
*Yoru no onnotachi (Women of the Night)* (Mizoguchi), 276
*Yuke yuke nidome no shojo (Go, Go, You Who Are a Virgin for the Second Time)* (Wakamatsu), 352
*Yukinojō henge (The Avenging Ghost of Yukinojō/An Actor's Revenge)* (Ichikawa), 288, 289–90
*Yukinojō henge (The Ghost of Yukinojō)* (Kinugasa), 139n13, 289, 289n19

*Zange no yaiba (Sword of Penitence)* (Ozu), 154
*Zangiku Monogatari (Tale of Late Chrysanthemums)* (Mizoguchi), 17, 84n27, 151, 219, 224, 225, 228, 230–6, 244, 245, 276
*Zoku Sugata Sanshiro (Sequel to Sugata Sanshiro)* (Kurosawa), 292n1

# Index of Names

Adachi Masao, 352, 352n12
Adair, John, 161n10
Akutagawa Ryunosuke, 297
Anderson, Joseph L., 11, 58n1; and Richie, Donald: *The Japanese Film, see under* Richie, Donald
Antonioni, Michelangelo, 161, 175n19, 216, 289, 346–7
Ariwara Harihira, 49–50
Asquith, Anthony, 297

Babel, Isaac, 268
Bando Tsumasuboro, 282
Barker, Will C., 64, 93
Barnett, Boris, 147, 258n7
Barthes, Roland, 13–14, 16, 26, 30, 72–3, 77–8, 99, 107–8, 161n12, 172n18, 342, 343n17
Bazin, André 225n13
Beasley, W. G., 28n4, 30n10, 141–2
Bene, Carmelo, 328
Benedeck, Lazslo, 130
Benedict, Ruth, 263, 264
Bismarck, Prince Otto von, 29n9
Blanchot, Maurice, 342
Blasetti, Alessandro, 143
Bowie, Henry P., 194
Brecht, Bertolt, 11, 17, 19, 70n6, 73, 126, 147, 290, 308, 321, 334, 339, 356
Bresson, Robert, 152, 183, 194
Brower, Robert H. and Miner, Earl, 46–8, 160n7
Buñuel, Luis, 147

Callenbach, Ernest, 180n21
Camerini, Mario, 143
Camus, Albert, 356
Chikamatsu Monzaemon, 12–13, 69, 72n9, 258, 260
Clair, René, 192
Cocteau, Jean, 147

Dassin, Jules, 295
de Maupassant, Guy, 224
De Mille, Cecil B., 64, 93, 113
de Sade, Comte D. A. F., 353
Demeny, Georges, 62n3
Derrida, Jacques, 37–40, 40n12

Devaivre, Jean, 297
Dickens, Charles, 113, 219n5, 249n5
Dickinson, Thorold, 264
Dickson, W. K. L., 61, 62, 108
Dostoevsky, Feodor, 299–301
Dovzhenko, Alexander, 125, 128, 132, 147
Drexler, Arthur, 119
Dreyer, Carl, 104, 109, 115, 117, 123, 145, 147, 158n4, 223n8, 225n14, 291, 316n15
Dulac, Germaine, 145
Dupont, E. A., 194

Edison, Thomas Alva, 58, 61–3, 66, 145
Eisenstein, Sergei M., 11, 52, 80, 104n5, 115, 116, 126, 147, 213n5, 225, 278, 291, 293, 299, 299n5, 339
Engel, Heinrich, 198–200
Engels, Friedrich, 281
Epstein, Jean, 115, 124, 145, 147
Ernst, Earle, 25–6, 32, 59–60, 68n4, 70n6, 83, 85n29, 124, 274n7

Fellini, Federico, 19
Feuillade, Louis, 57–8, 76, 81
Feydeau, Georges, 68
Florey, Robert, 139
Freud, Sigmund, 111n5
Fuller, Samuel, 246
Futagawa Montabe, 83, 119
Fuyushima Taizo, 121

Gammon, Frank R., 61, 62
Gance, Abel, 115, 124, 145, 147
Godard, Jean-Luc, 19, 66, 109, 117, 158n4, 328, 338, 339, 354n15, 361
Gorki, Maxim, 101, 308
Gosho Heinosuke, 121, 146, 148, 152, 186–7, 258–60
Granet, Marcel, 12
Griffith, D. W., 20, 22, 62n3, 63–7 *passim*, 76, 80, 81, 83n26, 94, 97, 102, 104, 114, 156, 204, 226

Hamamura Yoshiyama, 159
Hani Susumi, 143n4, 346–7
Hanoun, Marcel, 301n8

385

Hayakawa Sessue, 93
Hayazaka Fumio, 246
Hiroshige Andō, 91–2, 274
Hitchcock, Alfred, 225
Hitomaro Kakinomoto, 44–7, 247
Hokusai Katsushika, 91, 258, 274
Hönzl, Jindrich, 336–8

Ibsen, Henrik, 68
Ichikawa Kon, 202, 287–90, 318
Ihara Saikaku, 53, 72, 247–9, 251, 258
Ikkyu Oshō, 330, 330$n$7
Imai Tadashi, 152$n$2, 283
Imamura Taihei, 279–81
Inagaki Hiroshi, 105$n$9, 120–21, 192–8
Ince, Thomas, 64, 93
Inoue Kintaro, 148, 257
Inoue Masao, 106
Ishida Tamizo, 15–16, 17, 143, 198, 200, 202–16, 287
Itami Mansaku, 153, 192$n$8, 260$n$8
Ito Daisuke, 110–11, 114, 115, 116, 132, 275, 282, 297, 332
Iwamoto Kenji, 80, 83$n$24, 98$n$8
Iwasaki Akira, 105$n$8, 152$n$3, 153, 230–1
Izumi Kyōka, 218

Kafka, Franz, 59
Karasawa Hiromitsu, 110
Kato Shuichi, 33–4
Katumoto Seiitiro, 148–9
Kawabata Yasunari, 126$n$5, 127–8
Kawai Kazuo, 271–2
Kawakami Otojirō, 59–60
Keene, Donald, 72$n$9, 96$n$6
Kinoshita Keisuke, 283, 285–6, 326
Ki no Tsurayaki, 12
Kinugasa Teinosuke, 16$n$10, 81$n$17, 105, 119, 126–39, 237, 282, 291, 329, 349
Kirsanoff, Dimitri, 79, 115, 130
Kishida Kunio, 145–6
Kita Ikki, 350
Kobayashi Masaki, 282, 283–4, 299
Kōrin Ogata, 33, 148
Kotani, Henry, 94
Kren, Kurt, 63, 205
Kristeva, Julia, 12
Kubelka, Peter, 63
Kuleshov, Lev, 147
Kurosawa Akira, 16$n$10, 120, 200, 201, 206, 255, 262, 282, 283, 286, 290, 291–321, 358

Lang, Fritz, 104, 145, 147, 156, 194, 206, 214, 291, 299, 301
Laughton, Charles, 184
Leni, Paul, 129, 155
Leyda, Jay, 26–7
L'Herbier, Marcel, 78, 115, 124, 128, 145, 147, 191
Losey, Joseph, 333

Lubitsch, Ernst, 79–80, 129, 155, 184
Lumière, Auguste, 61–3, 64, 65–6, 75–6
Lumière, Louis, 58, 61–3, 64, 65–6, 75–6

McLuhan, Marshall, 261
Makino Shozo, 57, 81–2, 82$n$23, 83, 84–5, 85$n$30, 108, 115–16, 119, 120
Marey, Jules-Etienne, 61, 62$n$3
Marx, Karl, 28
Masumura Yasuzo, 326$n$2
Matsuda Shunji, 15, 111
Matsumoto Toshio, 340, 356–60
Matsunosuke, see Onoue
Mayer, Carl, 124
Méliès, Georges, 61, 62, 76
Metz, Christian, 64$n$5, 104$n$5, 313$n$14
Michelson, Annette, 225
Mifune Toshiro, 282, 294–5, 295$n$2, 296, 306
Mill, J. S., 32, 328
Miner, Earl see Brower Robert H. and Miner, Earl
Mishima Yukio, 237$n$21, 288
Mizoguchi Kenji, 15, 16$n$10, 16–17, 66, 83, 84$n$27, 105, 119, 123, 143–4, 144$n$6, 146–7, 148, 151, 152, 153, 173, 185, 193, 198, 200, 214$n$6, 217–46, 255, 258, 259, 262, 275–6, 278, 289, 329, 330
Mizutani Yaeko, 107
Morimoto Kaoru, 202
Morita Kanya, 59
Morris, Ivan, 42$n$1, 43$n$2, 51–2
Mosjoukine, Ivan, 115, 133
Murasaki Shikibu, 43
Murata Minoru, 100–101, 105, 146
Murnau, F. W., 123, 129, 155
Muybridge, Eadweard, 61

Nakagawa Nobuo, 257–8
Nakamura Hajime, 12, 12$n$3, 91, 263
Naruse Mikio, 66, 143, 146, 160, 161, 186–92, 259, 260, 275–7
Natsume Soseki, 288
Needham, Joseph, 12, 40

Oboro Gengo, 78$n$10
Ogawa Shinsuke, 360–1, 362
Onoue Matsunosuke, 57, 84
Ophuls, Max, 184, 225
Osanai Kaoru, 100–101, 105, 145–6
Oshima Nagisa, 284, 301$n$8, 318, 321, 322, 325–44, 346, 347, 350, 351
Ozu Yasujiro, 15, 16$n$10, 16–17, 66, 83, 109, 118, 123, 143–4, 146–7, 148, 151, 152, 153, 154–85, 187, 188, 190–1, 194, 198, 200–01, 214, 229, 246, 255, 258, 259, 260, 261, 262, 275–6, 277–81, 293, 298, 329

Pabst, Georg Wilhelm, 147
Panofsky, Erwin, 273
Picon, Gaëtan, 124, 127
Pollet, Jean-Daniel, 205

Porter, William S., 64–5, 66, 85
Pudovkin, Vsevolod, 115, 129, 130, 347

Raff, Norman, 61, 62
Ray, Man, 124
Ray, Nicholas, 194
Renoir, Jean, 147, 192–3
Ricardou, Jean, 358
Richie, Donald, 80*n*15, 83*n*24, 192*n*7; and Anderson, Joseph: *The Japanese Film*, 11, 57*n*1, 66*n*9, 67*n*2, 77*n*4, 79*n*12, 80*n*15, 81, 81*n*18–20, 96*n*4, 106, 107*n*15, 153, 188*n*2, 224*n*10, 307
Richter, Hans, 124
Ritt, Martin, 297
Robbe-Grillet, Alain, 249, 301
Robida, Michel, 59*n*2
Robison, Arthur, 124
Rouch, Jean, 361
Rouquier, Georges, 291
Rousseau, Jean-Jacques, 32, 38, 39, 328
Ryu Chishu, 180

Sadoul, Georges, 63, 307–8
Saikaku, *see* Ihara
Sakamoto Takeshi, 157, 167
Sansom, G. B., 29–30, 35, 40–1, 59*n*2, 273
Sargent, G. W., 248, 251
Sato Kei, 331
Sato Tadao, 80*n*16, 84*n*28, 111, 158*n*3, 159, 160, 173, 174, 180*n*20, 183
Saussure, Ferdinand, 18, 39–40, 40*n*12
Schrader, Paul, 161*n*12
Shakespeare, William 31*n*12, 148, 310
Shaw, George Bernard, 68
Shiba Kōkan, 273–4
Shimazu Yasujiro, 148, 152, 258, 259
Shimizu, Hiroshi, 17, 66, 123, 143, 148, 152, 160, 161, 193, 247–56, 258
Shimura Takashi, 295*n*5
Shindo Kaneto, 283
Sieffert, René, 13
Sjöberg, Alf, 129
Sjöström, Victor, 123, 129–30
Smiles, Samuel, 59*n*2
Snow, Michael, 19, 109, 117, 351
Sollers, Philippe, 12
Sōtatsu, Nonomura, 33, 148
Spencer, Herbert, 32
Sternberg, Joseph von, 147, 188, 225, 291
Straub, Jean-Marie, 328, 338
Stroheim, Erich von, 145
Suzuki Seijun, 332, 362–3

Takagi Ryutaro, 361–2
Takahachi Kohachiro, 30
Tanaka Eizo, 257
Tanaka Junichiro, 11, 80*n*15
Tanaka Tsuruhiko, 111–15, 132, 151
Tanizaki Junichiro, 289
Tasaka Tomotaka, 161, 264–8
Tati, Jacques, 249
Tatlin, Vladimir, 125
Tchekov, Anton, 202, 203
Teshigahara Hiroshi, 346, 347–8
Tessier, Max, 11
Toki Zemmaro, 13
Tokugawa Ieyasu, 25
Tokutomi Sohō, 32
Tomagaya Hisatura, 264*n*4
Toyoda Shiro, 148, 257
Tsuchimoto Noriate, 361–2

Uchida Kisao, 150
Uchida Tomu, 153, 153*n*5, 260, 291
Ueda Makoto, 13*n*4, 52, 98*n*9, 183–4

Verne, Jules, 59*n*2
Vertov, Dziga, 123, 125, 128, 132, 147, 278
Vigo, Jean, 124*n*2, 147
Viota, Paulino, 161
Visconti, Luchino, 225, 244
Volkoff, Alexandre, 115
Vos, Frits, 49–50

Wakamatsu Koji, 332, 340, 351–4
Warhol, Andy, 63, 66, 109, 117
Welles, Orson, 225, 289, 297
Wiene, Robert, 124
Wittfogel, K. A., 28–9
Worth, Sol, 161*n*10
Wyler, William, 225, 244, 276

Yamada Isuzu, 218, 226
Yamamoto Kajiro, 262, 264*n*4, 291
Yamamoto Satsuo, 152*n*2, 283, 299*n*6
Yamanaka Sadao, 143, 186, 192–7, 260*n*8, 263
Yamamura So, 282–3
Yoshida Shōin, 330–31, 340
Yoshida Tieo, 77*n*4, 96*n*5, 111*n*3
Yoshida Yoshishige, 201, 288, 338, 346, 347, 348–51
Yoshimoto Nijō, 52
Yoshimura Kimisaburo, 264*n*4

Zeami, Motokiyo, 12, 126*n*6, 148